EARTHDIVERS

VOLUME ONE: KILL COLUMBUS

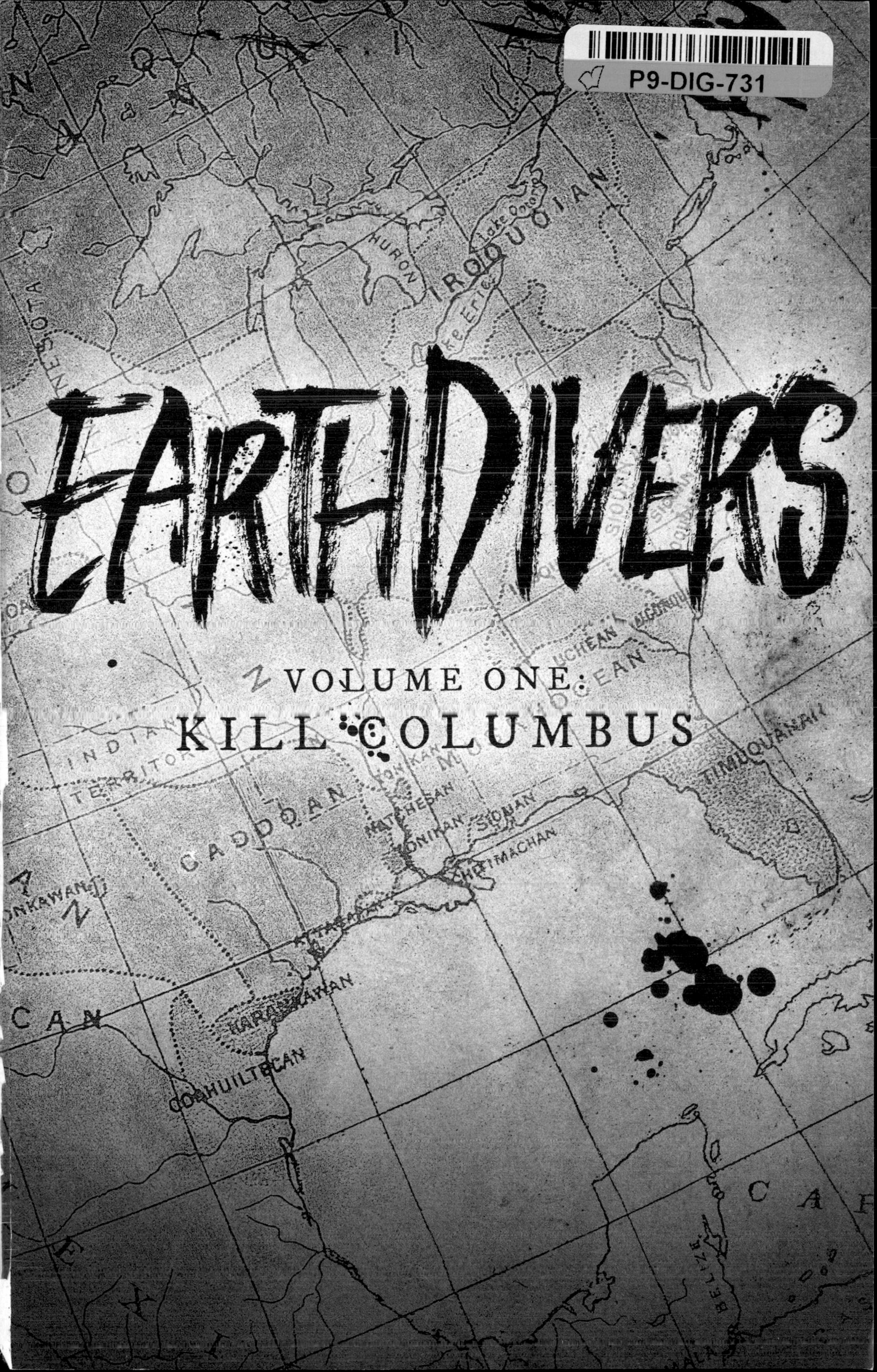
HURON
Lake Ontario
Lake Erie
IROQUOIAN
INDIAN
TERRITORY
CADDOAN
NATCHESAN
TONIKAN
SIOUAN
CHITIMACHAN
TIMUCUANAN
KARANKAWAN
COAHUILTECAN
BELIZE

Writer

Stephen Graham Jones

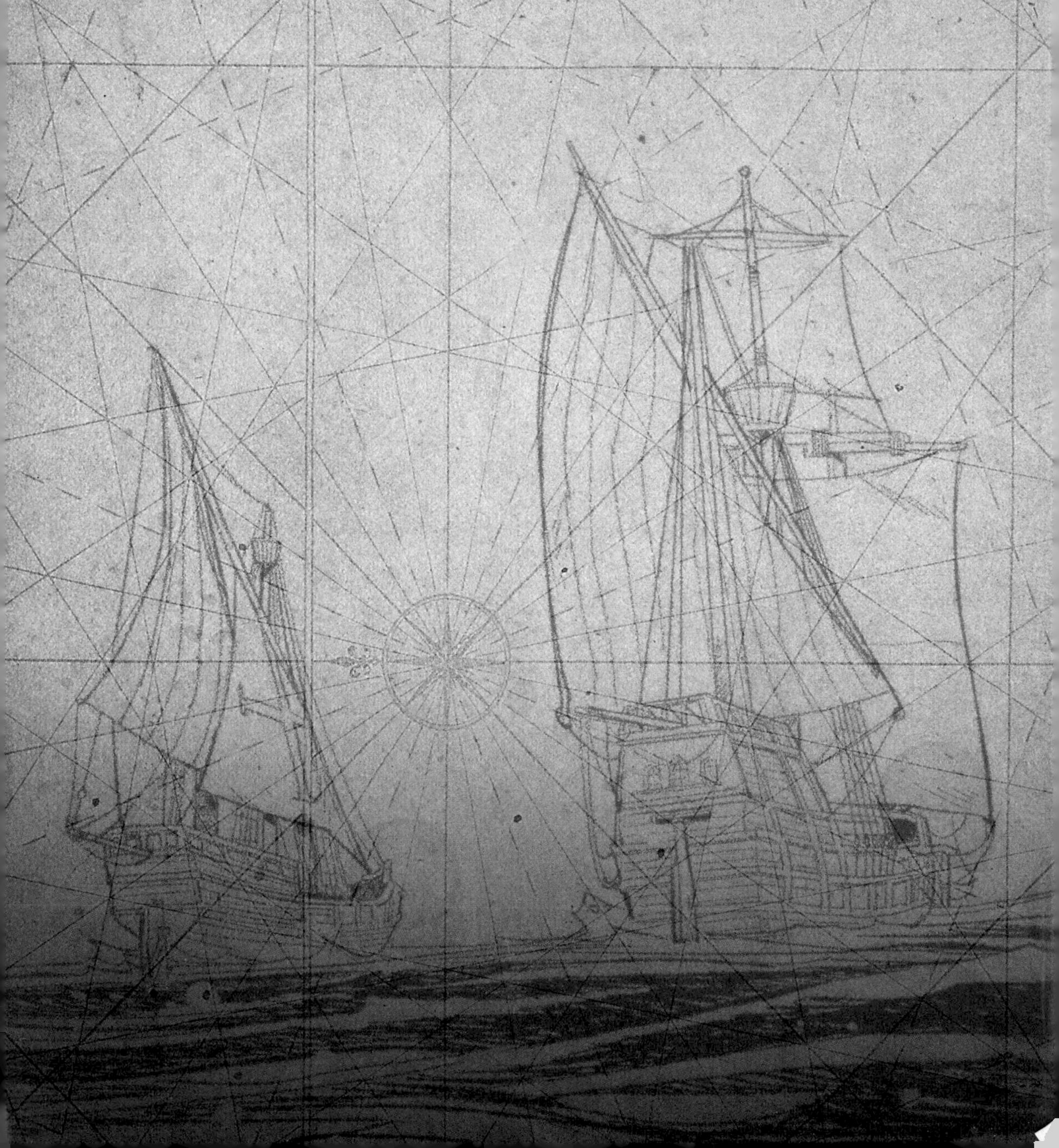

Artist
Davide Gianfelice

Colorist
Joana Lafuente

Letterer
Steve Wands

Cover Artist
Rafael Albuquerque

EARTHDIVERS *created by*
Stephen Graham Jones and Davide Gianfelice

IDW
ORIGINAL

@IDWpublishing
IDWpublishing.com

MAGGIE HOWELL
EDITOR
ORIGINAL SERIES, COLLECTED EDITION

JAKE WILLIAMS
ASSISTANT EDITOR
ORIGINAL SERIES, COLLECTED EDITION

NATHAN WIDICK
DESIGN & PRODUCTION

979-8-88724-045-9   26 25 24 23   1 2 3 4

Originally published as EARTHDIVERS #1-6.

Davidi Jonas, CEO
Amber Huerta, COO
Mark Doyle, Co-Publisher
Tara McCrillis, Co-Publisher
Jamie S. Rich, Editor-In-Chief
Scott Dunbier, VP Special Projects
Sean Brice, Sr. Director Sales & Marketing
Lauren LePera, Sr. Managing Editor
Shauna Monteforte, Sr. Director of Manufacturing Operations
Jamie Miller, Director Publishing Operations
Greg Foreman, Director DTC Sales & Operations
Nathan Widick, Director of Design
Neil Uyetake, Sr. Art Director, Design & Production

Ted Adams and Robbie Robbins, IDW Founders
For international rights, contact licensing@idwpublishing.com

Earthdivers: Origins

AN INTRODUCTION BY STEPHEN GRAHAM JONES

Before *Earthdivers*, I'd done two or three indie comics and scripted some others just for fun, but...did I really have what it took to do this? All I really had was the "kill Columbus" part, I mean, and I'm hardly the first Indian in America to think of *that*. Every Native kid who's ever sat in the back of their elementary school classroom and been forced to listen to what a hero and legend this dude not only was but apparently is still supposed to be, they've probably considered this.

What if, right?

It's what stories are made from.

Back then, though, the title I had for this was "Age of Discovery," which fit for a 1492 story. Trick was, though, it turned out IDW was also going to let me hit some other time periods, really mess things up. Meaning "Age of Discovery" no longer fit, but we also couldn't publish this without a title. So, I was casting around, trying to see which was the best of the bad alternates I kept coming up with, when, finally, I decided to talk to the smart person I live with: my wife, Nancy.

She was getting ready to go somewhere so I propped myself up on the bathroom counter while she messed with her hair (which already looked great) and I told her about this story, these people I'd dreamed up. Putting her earrings on now—which is to say, without even having to look over to me—she said, "It sounds like you want this to be a new world, with a different origin story. Are there any origin stories with cool titles?"

The summer before this, I'd skated through an academic conference here in Boulder and listened to a professor give a talk about earthdivers stories. It was a fascinating, compelling talk, and ever since then I'd had "earthdivers" lodged in my head, just rattling around. And that's how this title, and this whole book, happened.

Well, I make it sound easy. But Mark Doyle talked me through how to handle the exposition. Maggie Howell keeps my time-travel shenanigans straight. Davide Gianfelice does such amazing art that I'm able to erase more and more words—and somehow Steve Wands doesn't fly across the country and stab me for all those last-minute lettering changes. And the way Joana Lafuente colors this world, these *worlds*, such that we know where we are at all times and never get lost . . .

Building this title with all of them has been and continues to be the highest honor. I'm so lucky to be working with this team to kill Columbus.

There's a cave out in the desert, y'all.

There's a thousand kids sitting in the back of a history classroom.

And there are three small ships, bobbing out in the ocean.

For now.

Stephen Graham Jones
March 23, 2023
Boulder, CO

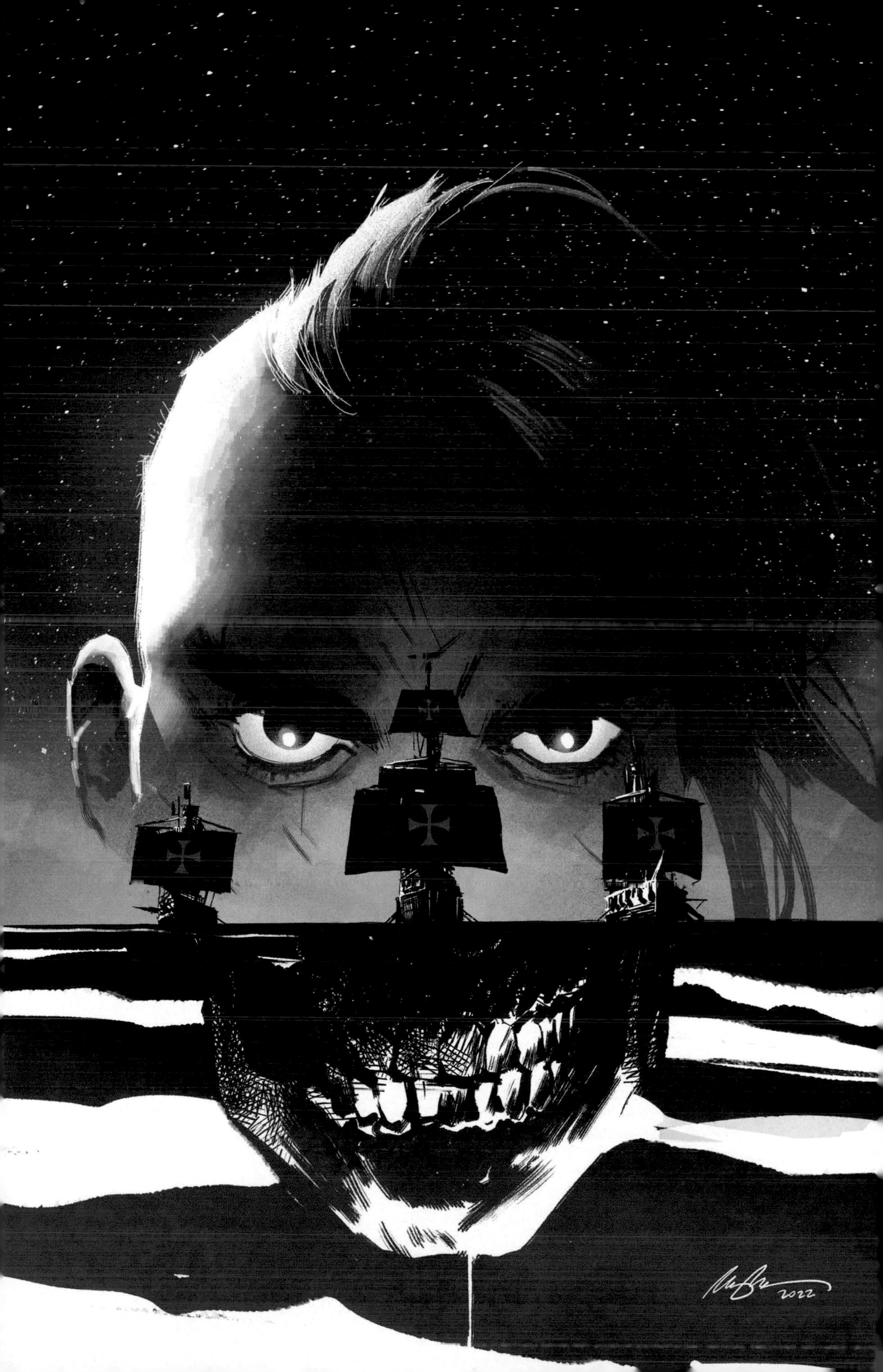
2022

CHAPTER ONE:

Here There Be Monsters

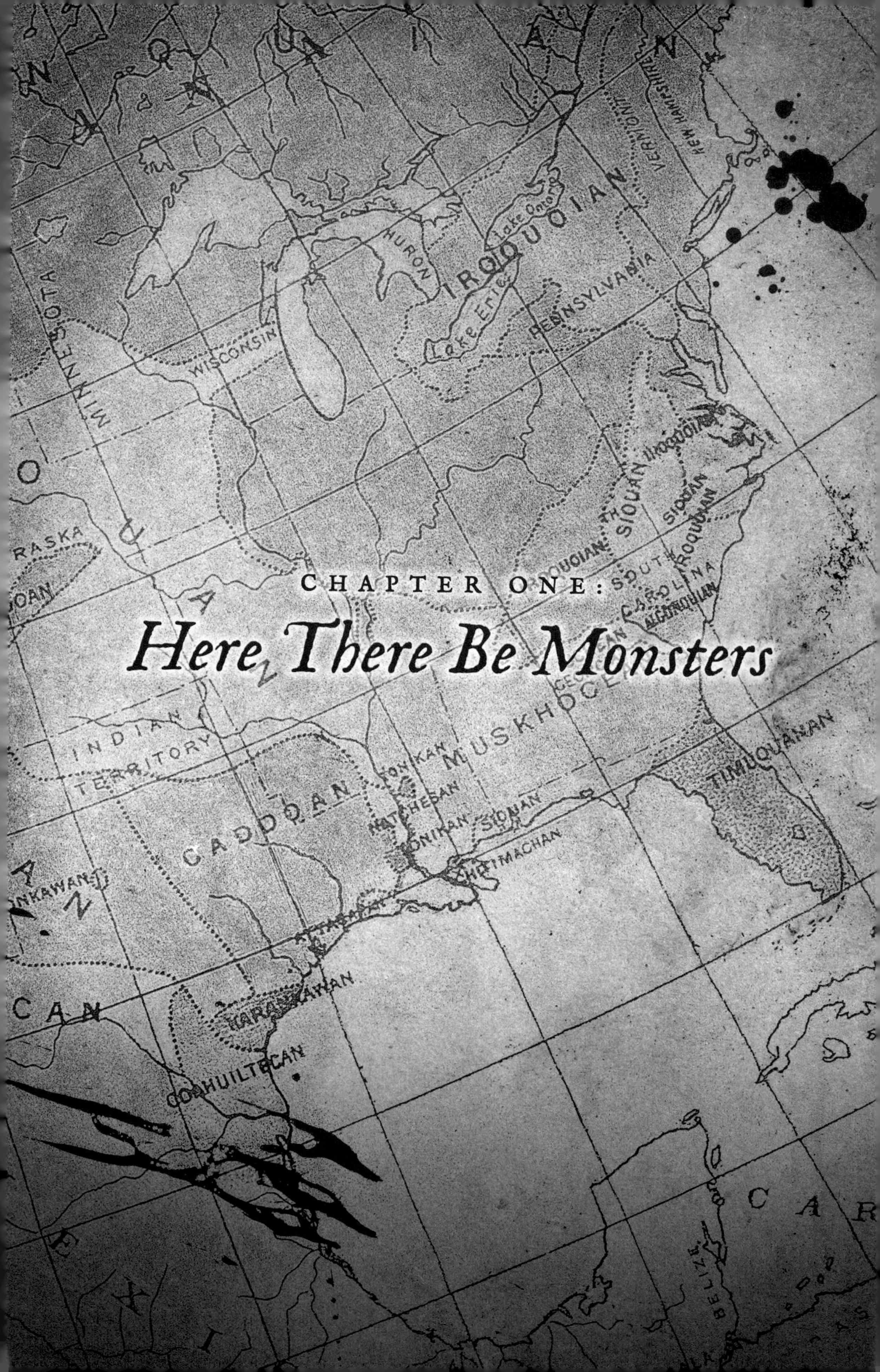

WISCONSIN
MINNESOTA
HURON
Lake Erie
PENNSYLVANIA
VERMONT
NEW HAMPSHIRE
IROQUOIAN
SIOUAN
SOUTH
CAROLINA
MUSKHOGEE
INDIAN
TERRITORY
CADDOAN
NATCHESAN
CHITIMACHAN
TIMUQUANAN
KARANKAWAN
COAHUILTECAN
BELIZE

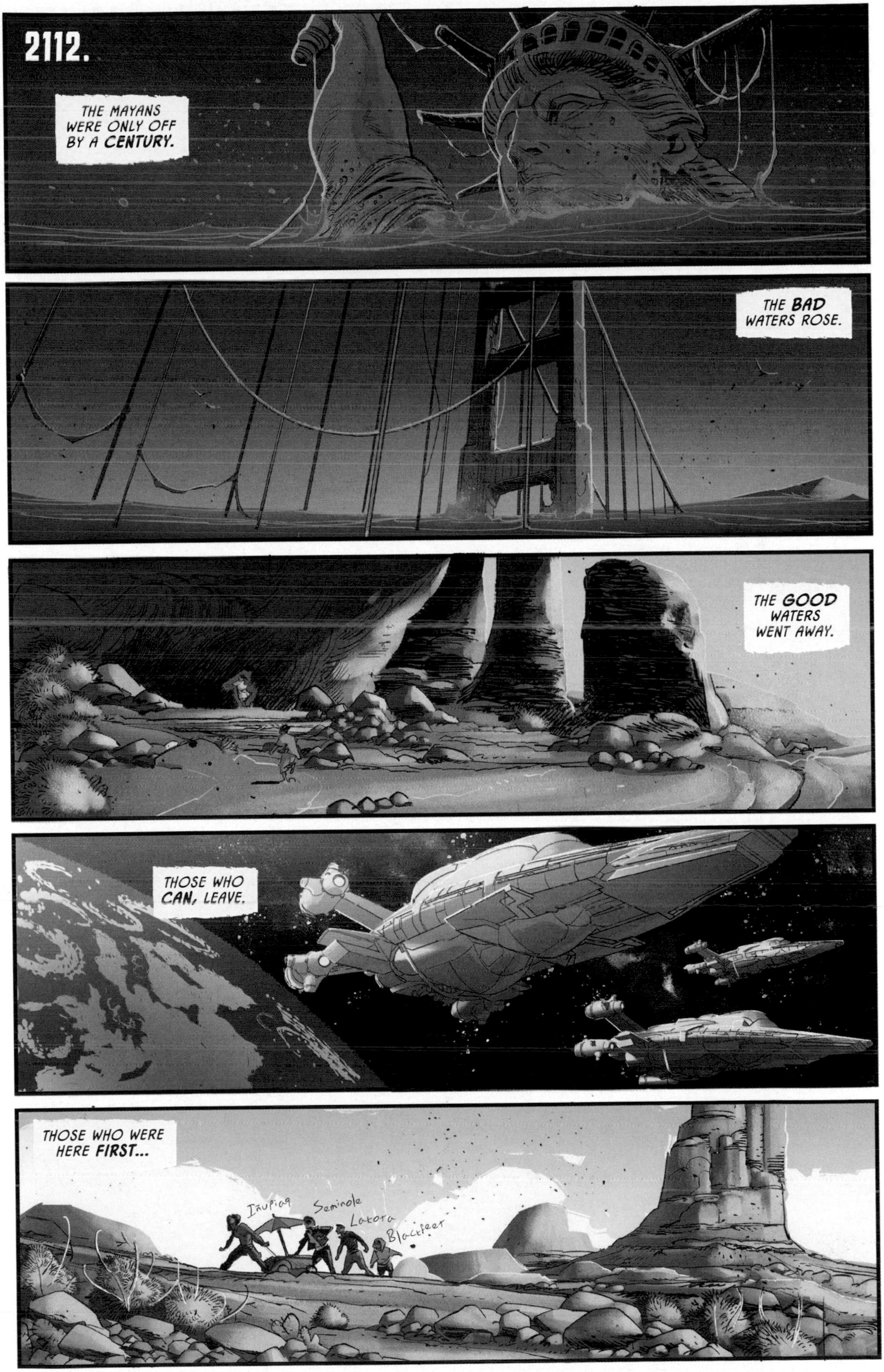
2112.
THE MAYANS WERE ONLY OFF BY A CENTURY.
THE BAD WATERS ROSE.
THE GOOD WATERS WENT AWAY.
THOSE WHO CAN, LEAVE.
THOSE WHO WERE HERE FIRST...
Iñupiaq
Seminole
Lakota
Blackfeet

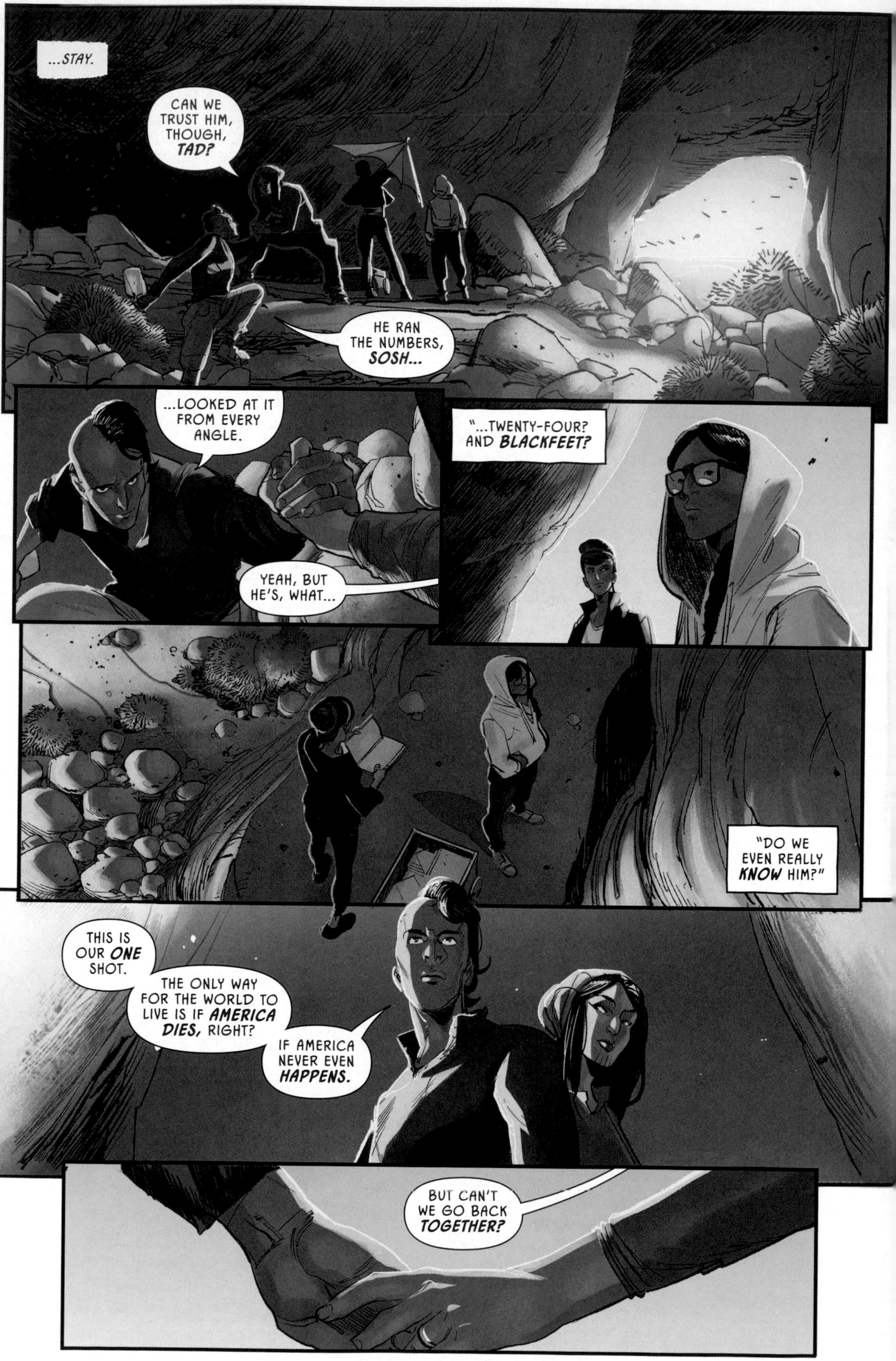

...STAY.
CAN WE TRUST HIM, THOUGH, TAD?
HE RAN THE NUMBERS, SOSH...
...LOOKED AT IT FROM EVERY ANGLE.
YEAH, BUT HE'S, WHAT...
"...TWENTY-FOUR? AND BLACKFEET?
"DO WE EVEN REALLY KNOW HIM?"
THIS IS OUR ONE SHOT.
THE ONLY WAY FOR THE WORLD TO LIVE IS IF AMERICA DIES, RIGHT?
IF AMERICA NEVER EVEN HAPPENS.
BUT CAN'T WE GO BACK TOGETHER?

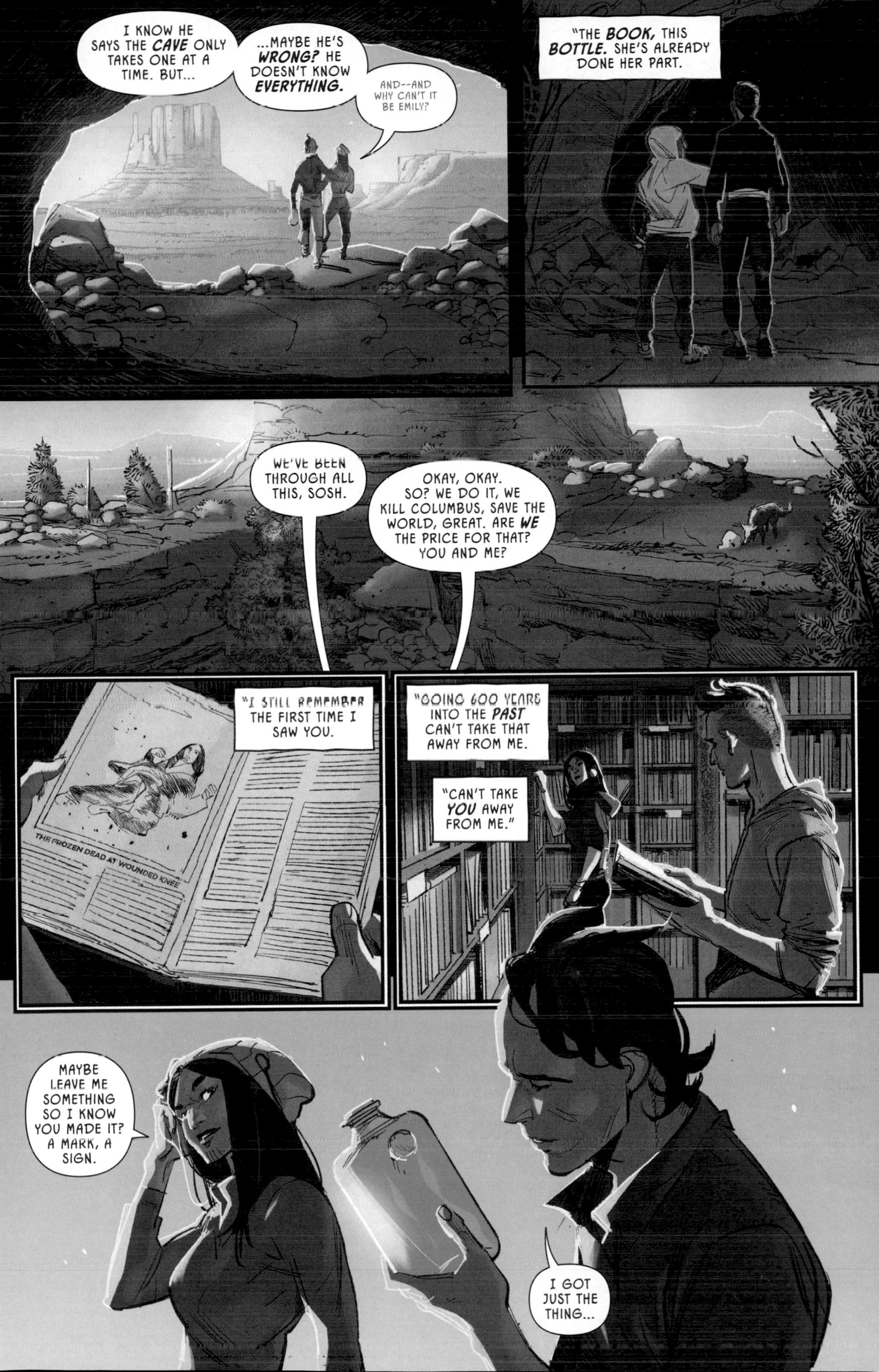
I KNOW HE SAYS THE CAVE ONLY TAKES ONE AT A TIME. BUT...
...MAYBE HE'S WRONG? HE DOESN'T KNOW EVERYTHING.
AND--AND WHY CAN'T IT BE EMILY?
"THE BOOK, THIS BOTTLE. SHE'S ALREADY DONE HER PART.
WE'VE BEEN THROUGH ALL THIS, SOSH.
OKAY, OKAY. SO? WE DO IT, WE KILL COLUMBUS, SAVE THE WORLD, GREAT. ARE WE THE PRICE FOR THAT? YOU AND ME?
"I STILL REMEMBER THE FIRST TIME I SAW YOU.
THE FROZEN DEAD AT WOUNDED KNEE
"GOING 600 YEARS INTO THE PAST CAN'T TAKE THAT AWAY FROM ME.
"CAN'T TAKE YOU AWAY FROM ME."
MAYBE LEAVE ME SOMETHING SO I KNOW YOU MADE IT? A MARK, A SIGN.
I GOT JUST THE THING...

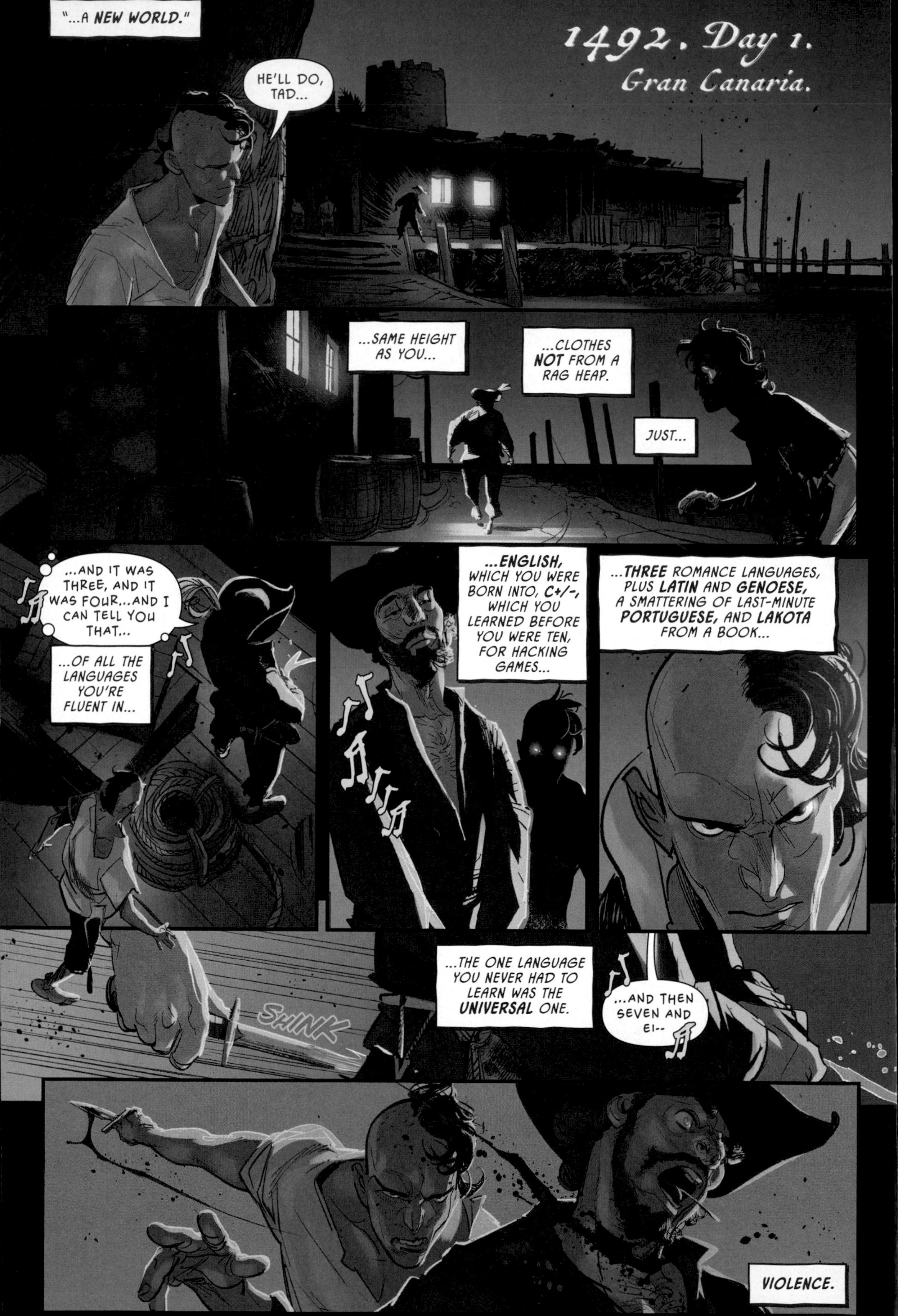
"...A NEW WORLD."
1492. Day 1.
Gran Canaria.
HE'LL DO, TAD...
...SAME HEIGHT AS YOU...
...CLOTHES NOT FROM A RAG HEAP.
JUST...
...AND IT WAS THREE, AND IT WAS FOUR...AND I CAN TELL YOU THAT...
...OF ALL THE LANGUAGES YOU'RE FLUENT IN...
...ENGLISH, WHICH YOU WERE BORN INTO, C+/-, WHICH YOU LEARNED BEFORE YOU WERE TEN, FOR HACKING GAMES...
...THREE ROMANCE LANGUAGES, PLUS LATIN AND GENOESE, A SMATTERING OF LAST-MINUTE PORTUGUESE, AND LAKOTA FROM A BOOK...
SHINK
...THE ONE LANGUAGE YOU NEVER HAD TO LEARN WAS THE UNIVERSAL ONE.
...AND THEN SEVEN AND EI--
VIOLENCE.

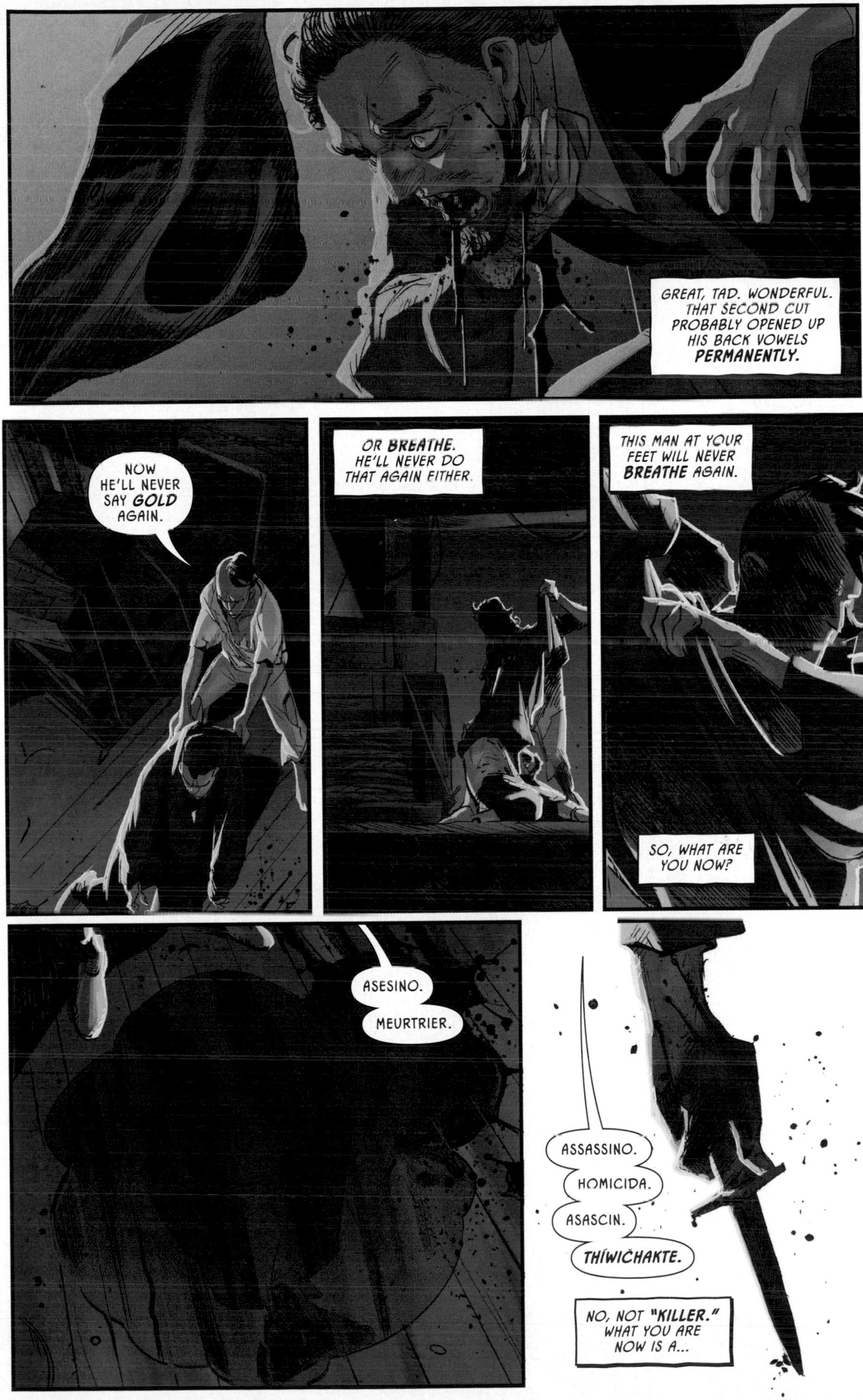
GREAT, TAD. WONDERFUL. THAT SECOND CUT PROBABLY OPENED UP HIS BACK VOWELS **PERMANENTLY.**
NOW HE'LL NEVER SAY **GOLD** AGAIN.
OR **BREATHE.** HE'LL NEVER DO THAT AGAIN EITHER.
THIS MAN AT YOUR FEET WILL NEVER **BREATHE** AGAIN.
SO, WHAT ARE YOU NOW?
ASESINO.
MEURTRIER.
ASSASSINO.
HOMICIDA.
ASASCIN.
THÍWIČHAKTE.
NO, NOT **"KILLER."** WHAT YOU ARE NOW IS A...

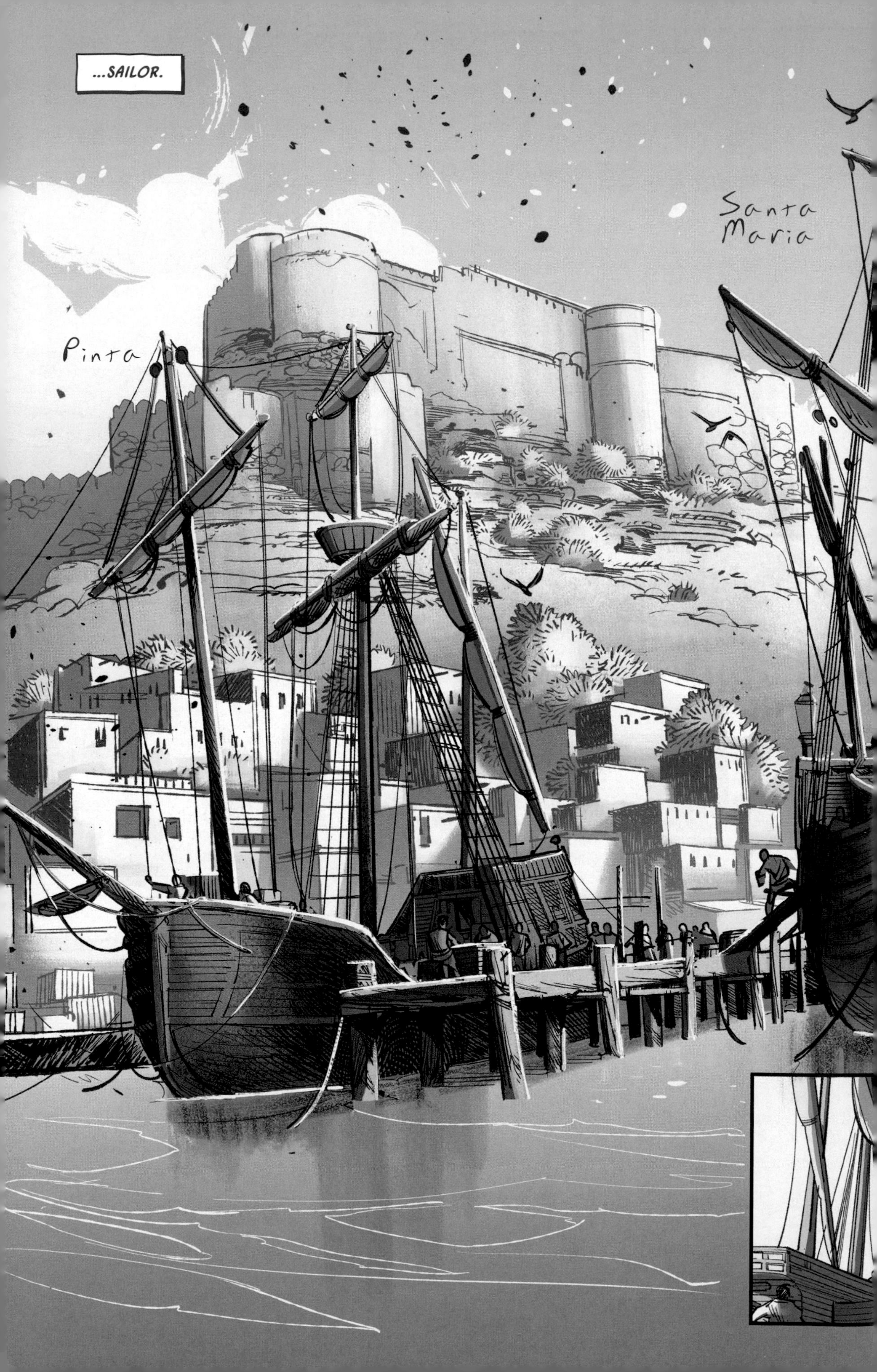
...SAILOR.
Santa Maria
Pinta

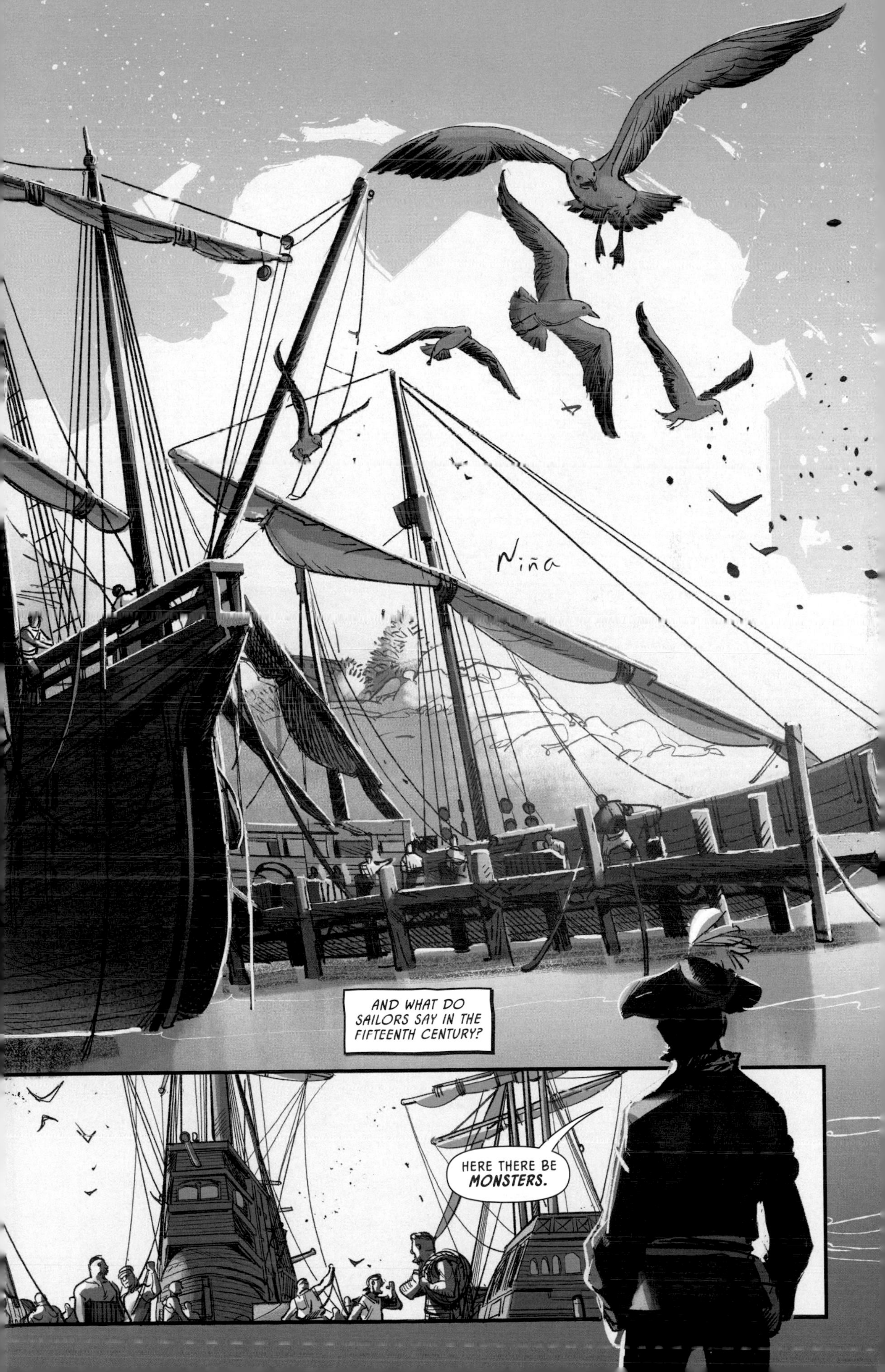
Niña
AND WHAT DO SAILORS SAY IN THE FIFTEENTH CENTURY?
HERE THERE BE MONSTERS.

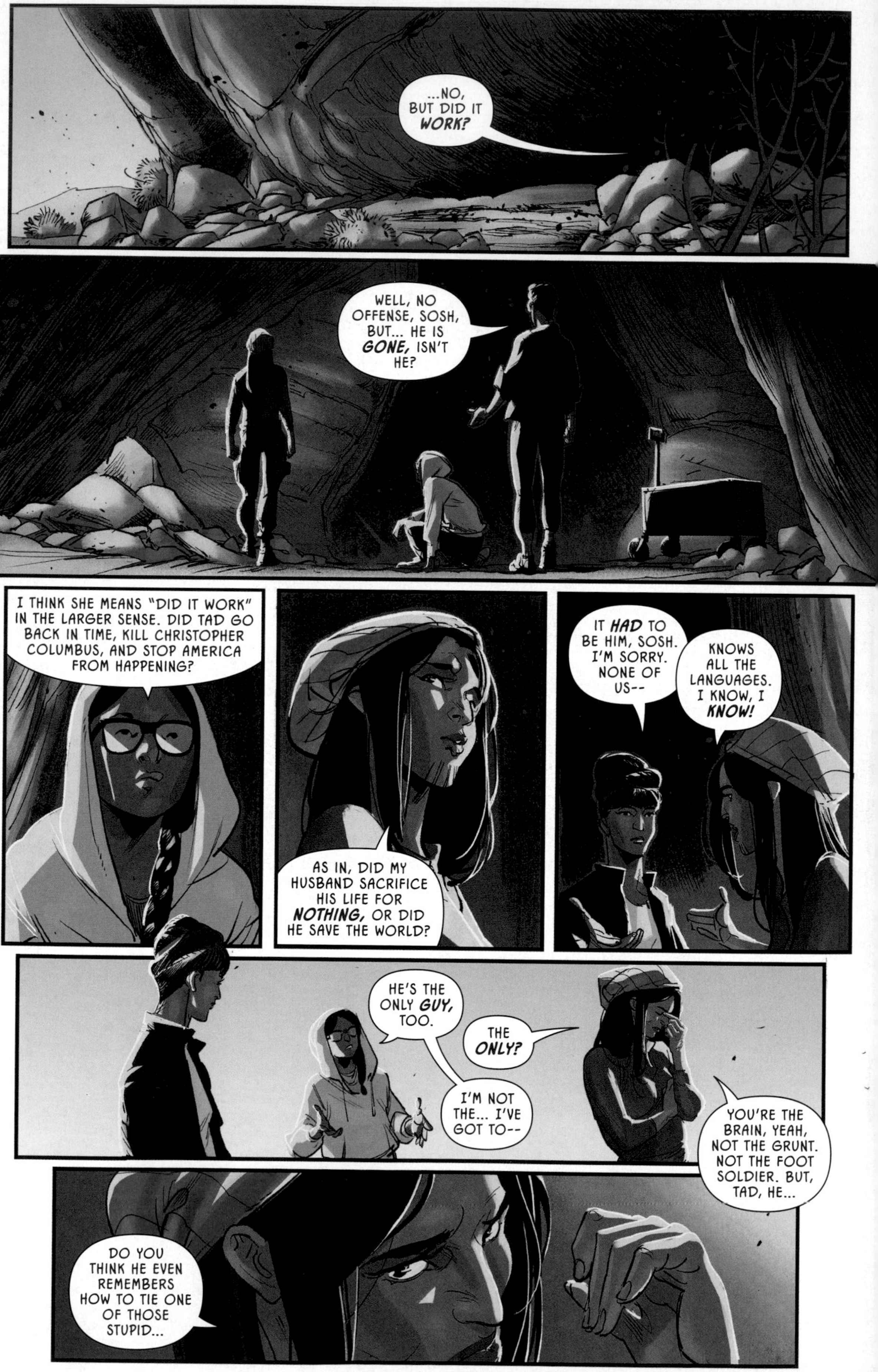
...NO, BUT DID IT *WORK?*
WELL, NO OFFENSE, SOSH, BUT... HE IS *GONE,* ISN'T HE?
I THINK SHE MEANS "DID IT WORK" IN THE LARGER SENSE. DID TAD GO BACK IN TIME, KILL CHRISTOPHER COLUMBUS, AND STOP AMERICA FROM HAPPENING?
AS IN, DID MY HUSBAND SACRIFICE HIS LIFE FOR *NOTHING,* OR DID HE SAVE THE WORLD?
IT *HAD* TO BE HIM, SOSH. I'M SORRY. NONE OF US--
KNOWS ALL THE LANGUAGES. I KNOW, I *KNOW!*
HE'S THE ONLY *GUY,* TOO.
THE *ONLY?*
I'M NOT THE... I'VE GOT TO--
YOU'RE THE BRAIN, YEAH, NOT THE GRUNT. NOT THE FOOT SOLDIER. BUT, TAD, HE...
DO YOU THINK HE EVEN REMEMBERS HOW TO TIE ONE OF THOSE STUPID...

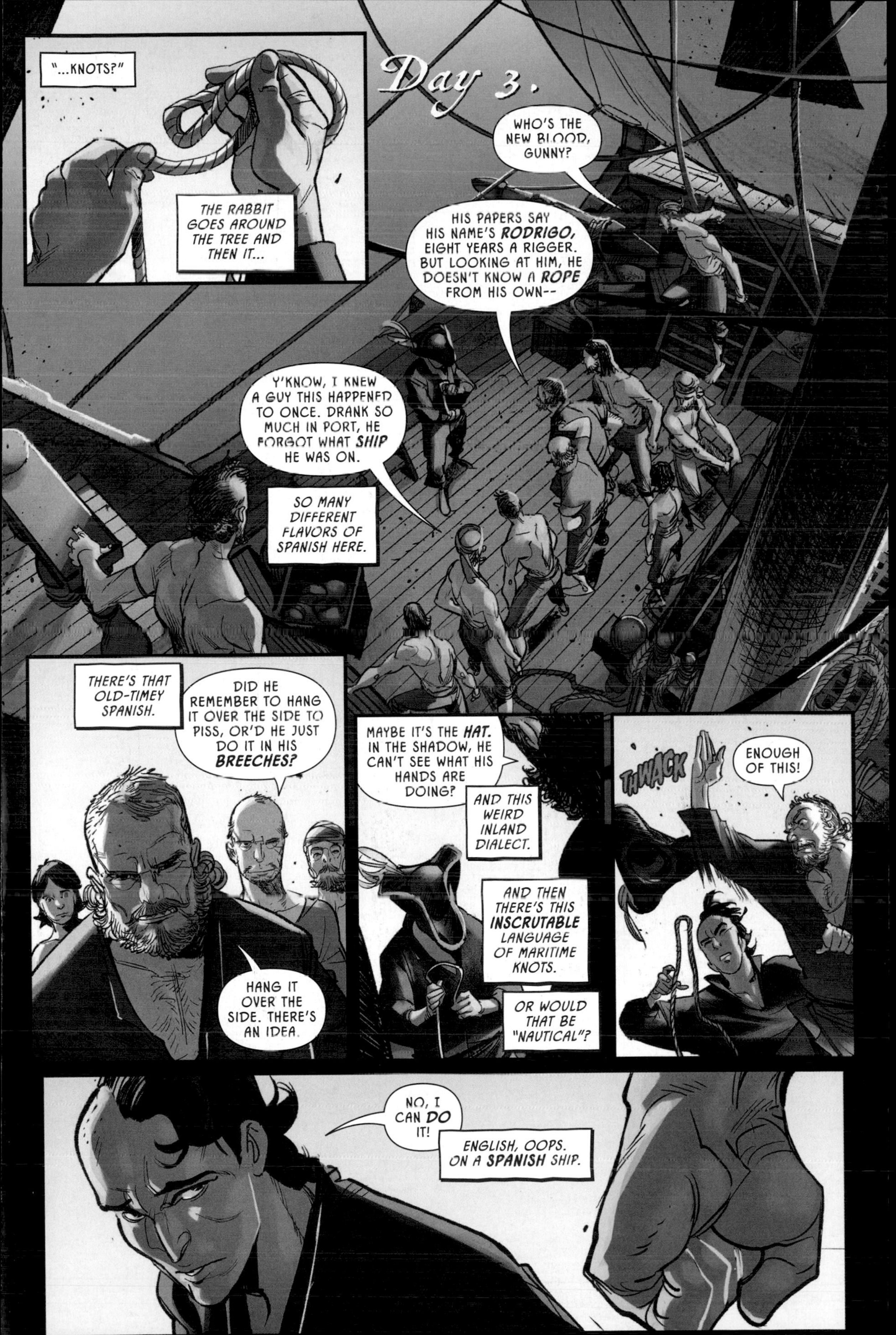
"...KNOTS?"
THE RABBIT GOES AROUND THE TREE AND THEN IT...
Day 3.
WHO'S THE NEW BLOOD, GUNNY?
HIS PAPERS SAY HIS NAME'S RODRIGO, EIGHT YEARS A RIGGER. BUT LOOKING AT HIM, HE DOESN'T KNOW A ROPE FROM HIS OWN--
Y'KNOW, I KNEW A GUY THIS HAPPENED TO ONCE. DRANK SO MUCH IN PORT, HE FORGOT WHAT SHIP HE WAS ON.
SO MANY DIFFERENT FLAVORS OF SPANISH HERE.
THERE'S THAT OLD-TIMEY SPANISH.
DID HE REMEMBER TO HANG IT OVER THE SIDE TO PISS, OR'D HE JUST DO IT IN HIS BREECHES?
HANG IT OVER THE SIDE. THERE'S AN IDEA.
MAYBE IT'S THE HAT. IN THE SHADOW, HE CAN'T SEE WHAT HIS HANDS ARE DOING?
AND THIS WEIRD INLAND DIALECT.
AND THEN THERE'S THIS INSCRUTABLE LANGUAGE OF MARITIME KNOTS.
OR WOULD THAT BE "NAUTICAL"?
THWACK
ENOUGH OF THIS!
NO, I CAN DO IT!
ENGLISH, OOPS. ON A SPANISH SHIP.

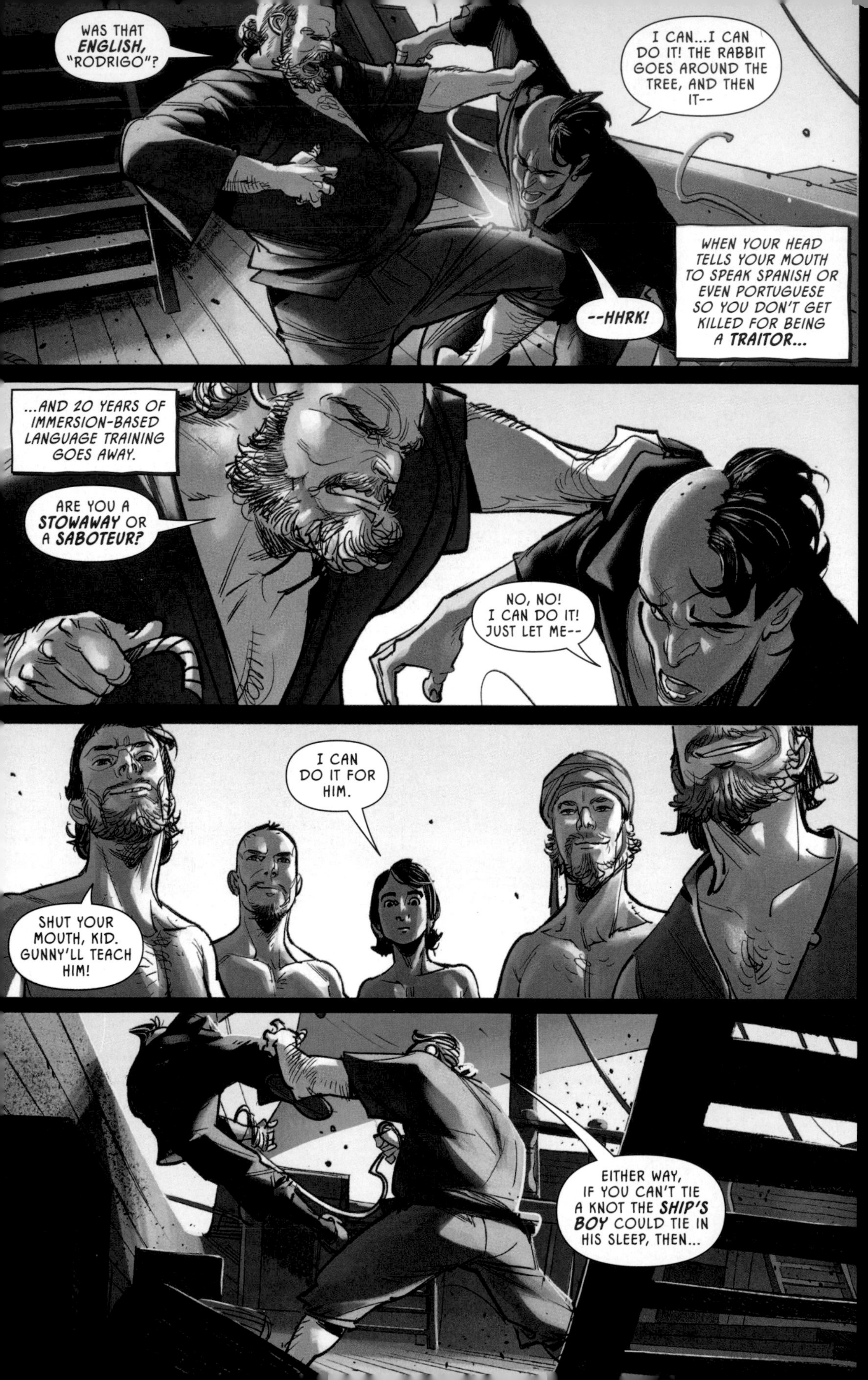

WAS THAT ENGLISH, "RODRIGO"?
I CAN...I CAN DO IT! THE RABBIT GOES AROUND THE TREE, AND THEN IT--
--HHRK!
WHEN YOUR HEAD TELLS YOUR MOUTH TO SPEAK SPANISH OR EVEN PORTUGUESE SO YOU DON'T GET KILLED FOR BEING A TRAITOR...
...AND 20 YEARS OF IMMERSION-BASED LANGUAGE TRAINING GOES AWAY.
ARE YOU A STOWAWAY OR A SABOTEUR?
NO, NO! I CAN DO IT! JUST LET ME--
I CAN DO IT FOR HIM.
SHUT YOUR MOUTH, KID. GUNNY'LL TEACH HIM!
EITHER WAY, IF YOU CAN'T TIE A KNOT THE SHIP'S BOY COULD TIE IN HIS SLEEP, THEN...

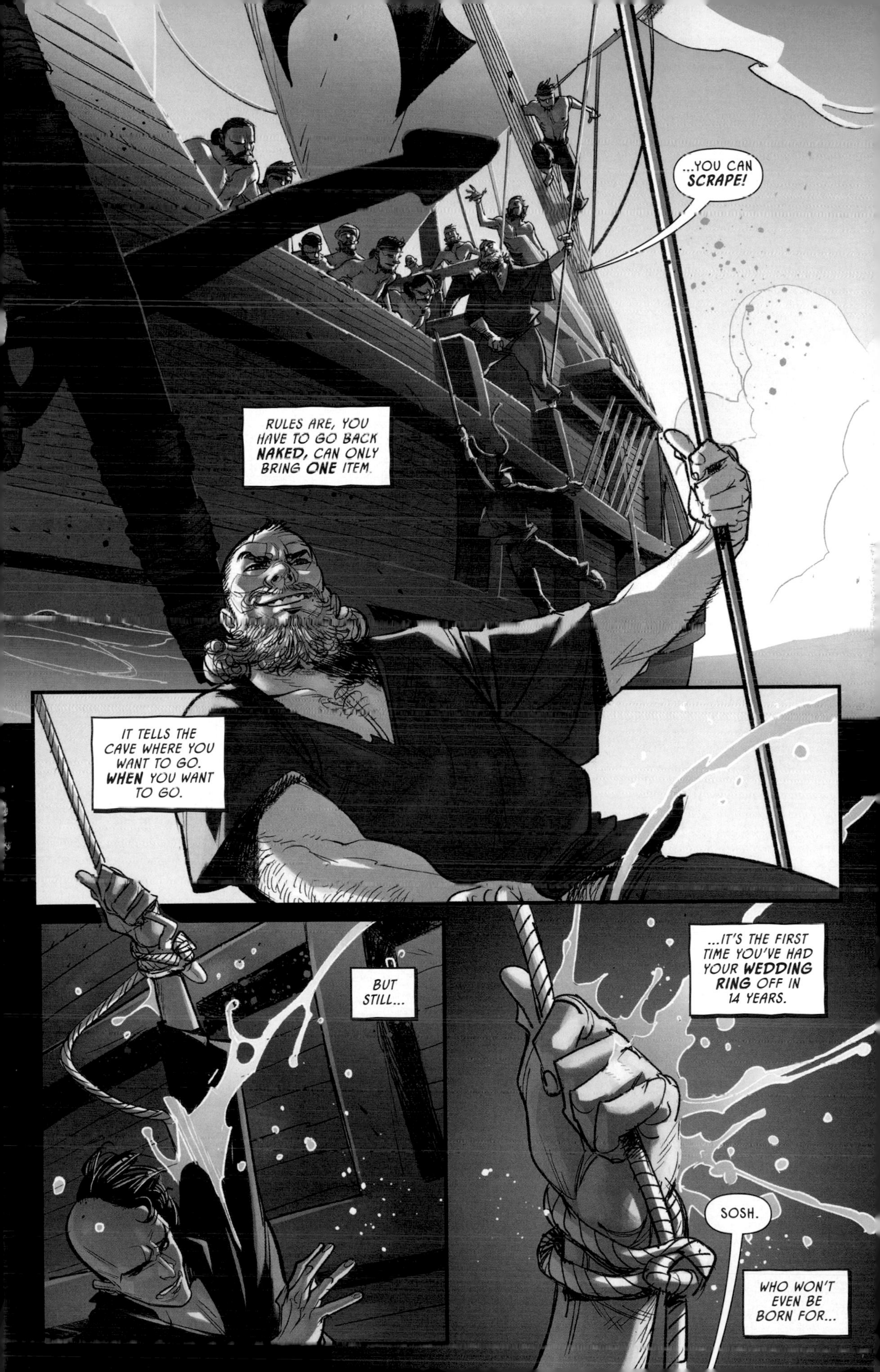
...YOU CAN SCRAPE!
RULES ARE, YOU HAVE TO GO BACK NAKED, CAN ONLY BRING ONE ITEM.
IT TELLS THE CAVE WHERE YOU WANT TO GO. WHEN YOU WANT TO GO.
BUT STILL...
...IT'S THE FIRST TIME YOU'VE HAD YOUR WEDDING RING OFF IN 14 YEARS.
SOSH.
WHO WON'T EVEN BE BORN FOR...

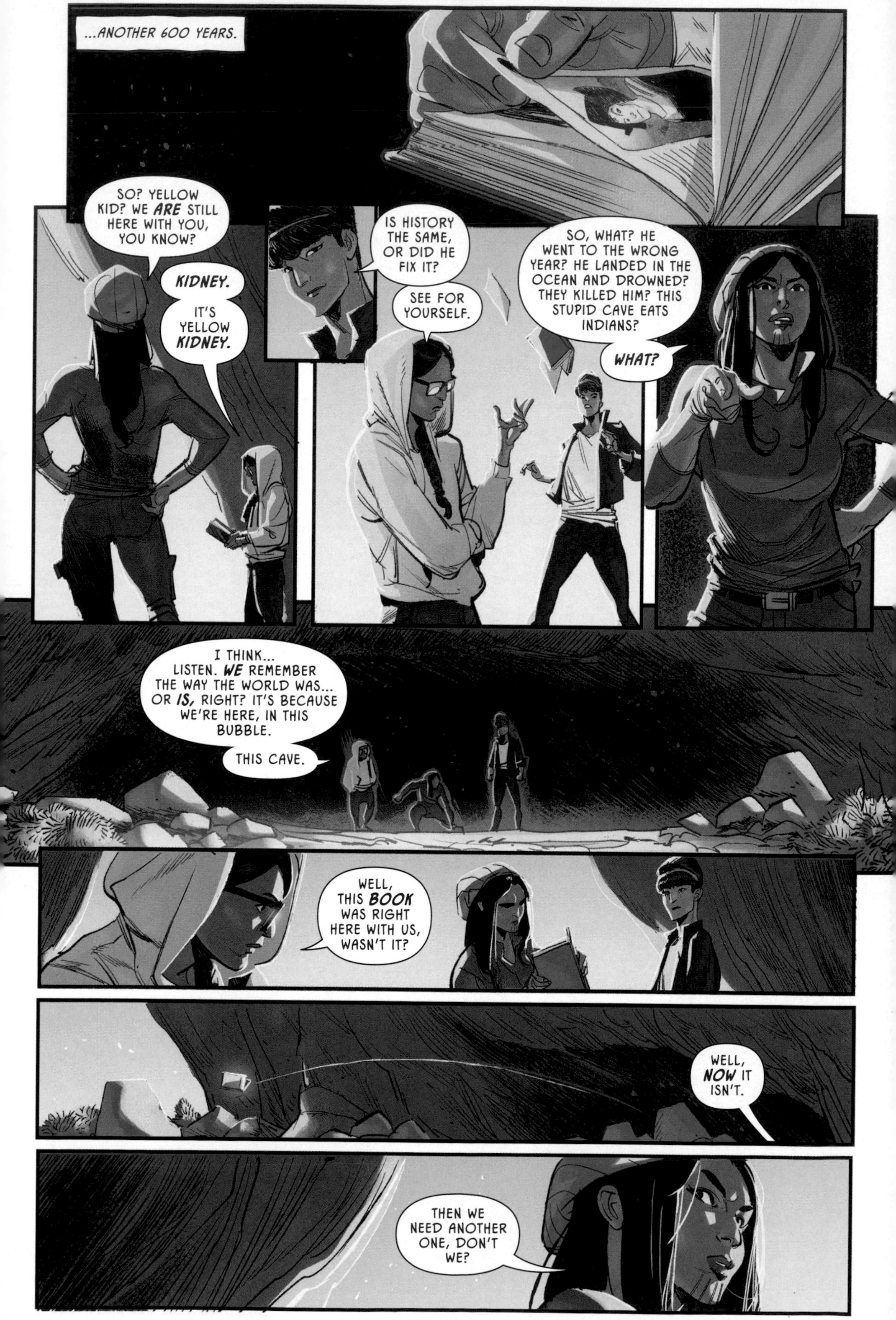
...ANOTHER 600 YEARS.
SO? YELLOW KID? WE ARE STILL HERE WITH YOU, YOU KNOW?
KIDNEY.
IT'S YELLOW KIDNEY.
IS HISTORY THE SAME, OR DID HE FIX IT?
SEE FOR YOURSELF.
SO, WHAT? HE WENT TO THE WRONG YEAR? HE LANDED IN THE OCEAN AND DROWNED? THEY KILLED HIM? THIS STUPID CAVE EATS INDIANS?
WHAT?
I THINK... LISTEN. WE REMEMBER THE WAY THE WORLD WAS... OR IS, RIGHT? IT'S BECAUSE WE'RE HERE, IN THIS BUBBLE.
THIS CAVE.
WELL, THIS BOOK WAS RIGHT HERE WITH US, WASN'T IT?
WELL, NOW IT ISN'T.
THEN WE NEED ANOTHER ONE, DON'T WE?

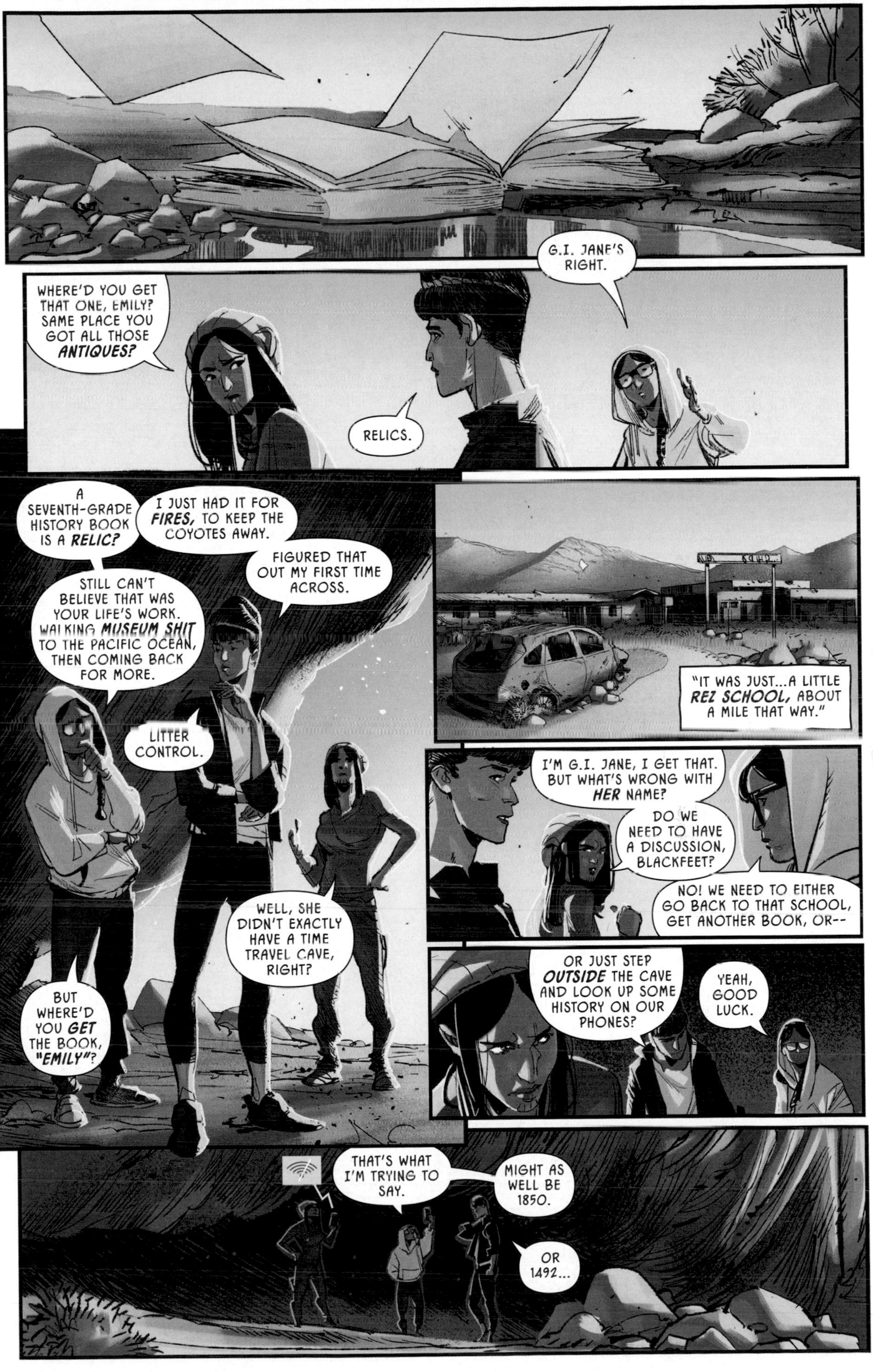

G.I. JANE'S RIGHT.
WHERE'D YOU GET THAT ONE, EMILY? SAME PLACE YOU GOT ALL THOSE ANTIQUES?
RELICS.
A SEVENTH-GRADE HISTORY BOOK IS A RELIC?
I JUST HAD IT FOR FIRES, TO KEEP THE COYOTES AWAY.
FIGURED THAT OUT MY FIRST TIME ACROSS.
STILL CAN'T BELIEVE THAT WAS YOUR LIFE'S WORK. WALKING MUSEUM SHIT TO THE PACIFIC OCEAN, THEN COMING BACK FOR MORE.
LITTER CONTROL.
WELL, SHE DIDN'T EXACTLY HAVE A TIME TRAVEL CAVE, RIGHT?
BUT WHERE'D YOU GET THE BOOK, "EMILY"?
"IT WAS JUST...A LITTLE REZ SCHOOL, ABOUT A MILE THAT WAY."
I'M G.I. JANE, I GET THAT. BUT WHAT'S WRONG WITH HER NAME?
DO WE NEED TO HAVE A DISCUSSION, BLACKFEET?
NO! WE NEED TO EITHER GO BACK TO THAT SCHOOL, GET ANOTHER BOOK, OR--
OR JUST STEP OUTSIDE THE CAVE AND LOOK UP SOME HISTORY ON OUR PHONES?
YEAH, GOOD LUCK.
THAT'S WHAT I'M TRYING TO SAY.
MIGHT AS WELL BE 1850.
OR 1492...

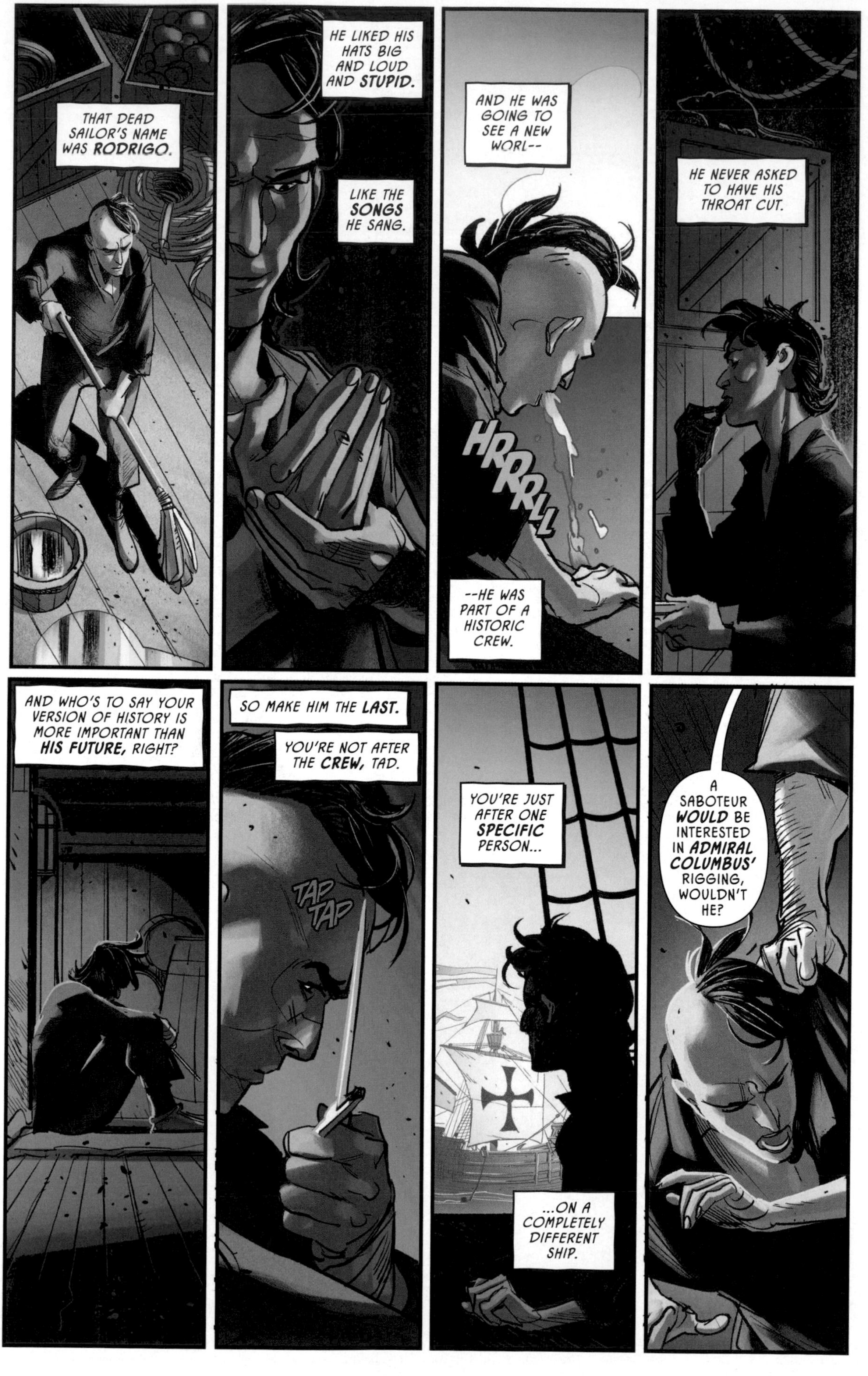
THAT DEAD SAILOR'S NAME WAS RODRIGO.
HE LIKED HIS HATS BIG AND LOUD AND STUPID.
LIKE THE SONGS HE SANG.
AND HE WAS GOING TO SEE A NEW WORL--
HRRRLL
--HE WAS PART OF A HISTORIC CREW.
HE NEVER ASKED TO HAVE HIS THROAT CUT.
AND WHO'S TO SAY YOUR VERSION OF HISTORY IS MORE IMPORTANT THAN HIS FUTURE, RIGHT?
SO MAKE HIM THE LAST.
YOU'RE NOT AFTER THE CREW, TAD.
TAP TAP
YOU'RE JUST AFTER ONE SPECIFIC PERSON...
...ON A COMPLETELY DIFFERENT SHIP.
A SABOTEUR WOULD BE INTERESTED IN ADMIRAL COLUMBUS' RIGGING, WOULDN'T HE?

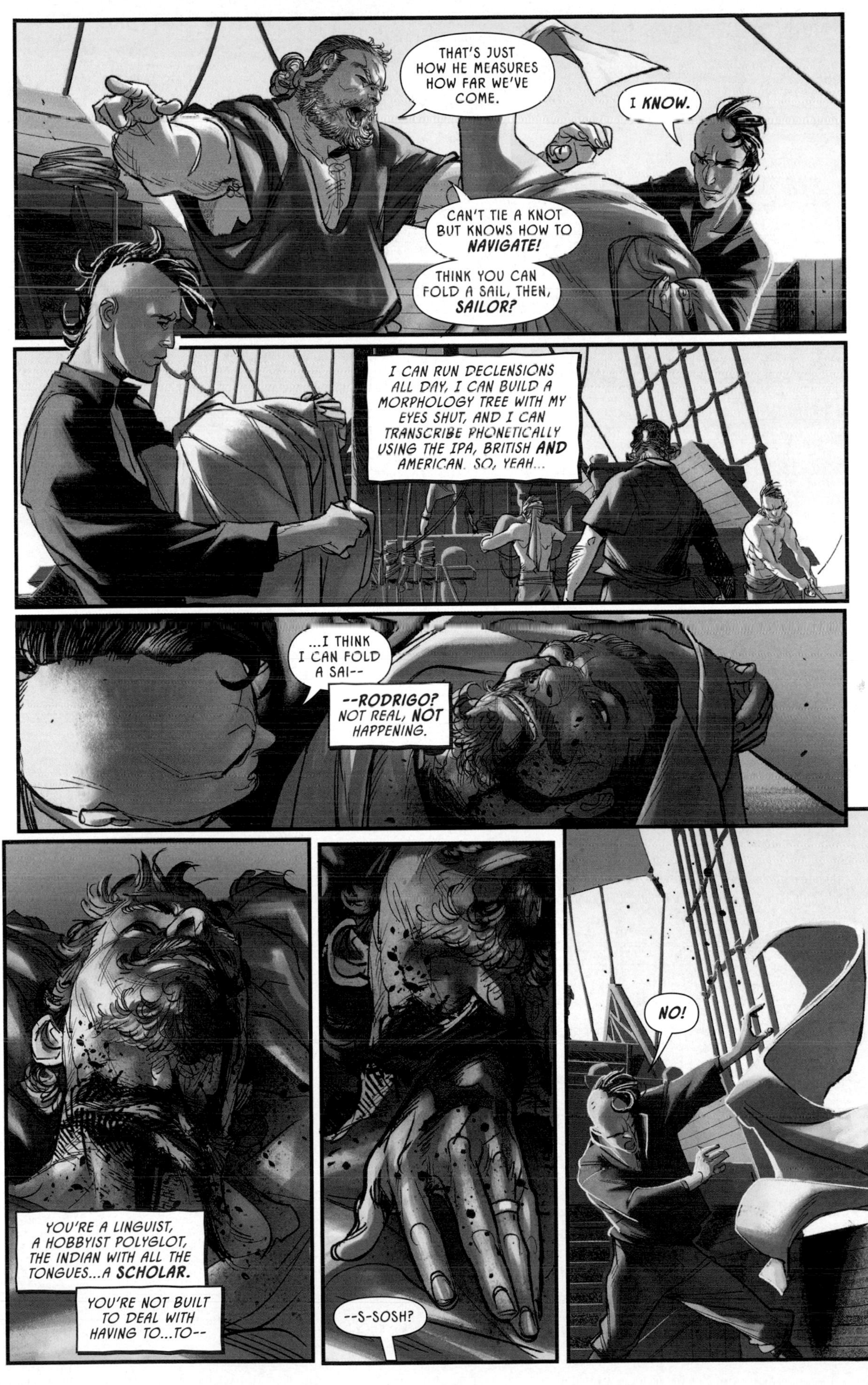
THAT'S JUST HOW HE MEASURES HOW FAR WE'VE COME.
I KNOW.
CAN'T TIE A KNOT BUT KNOWS HOW TO NAVIGATE!
THINK YOU CAN FOLD A SAIL, THEN, SAILOR?
I CAN RUN DECLENSIONS ALL DAY, I CAN BUILD A MORPHOLOGY TREE WITH MY EYES SHUT, AND I CAN TRANSCRIBE PHONETICALLY USING THE IPA, BRITISH AND AMERICAN. SO, YEAH...
...I THINK I CAN FOLD A SAI--
--RODRIGO? NOT REAL, NOT HAPPENING.
YOU'RE A LINGUIST, A HOBBYIST POLYGLOT, THE INDIAN WITH ALL THE TONGUES...A SCHOLAR.
YOU'RE NOT BUILT TO DEAL WITH HAVING TO...TO--
--S-SOSH?
NO!

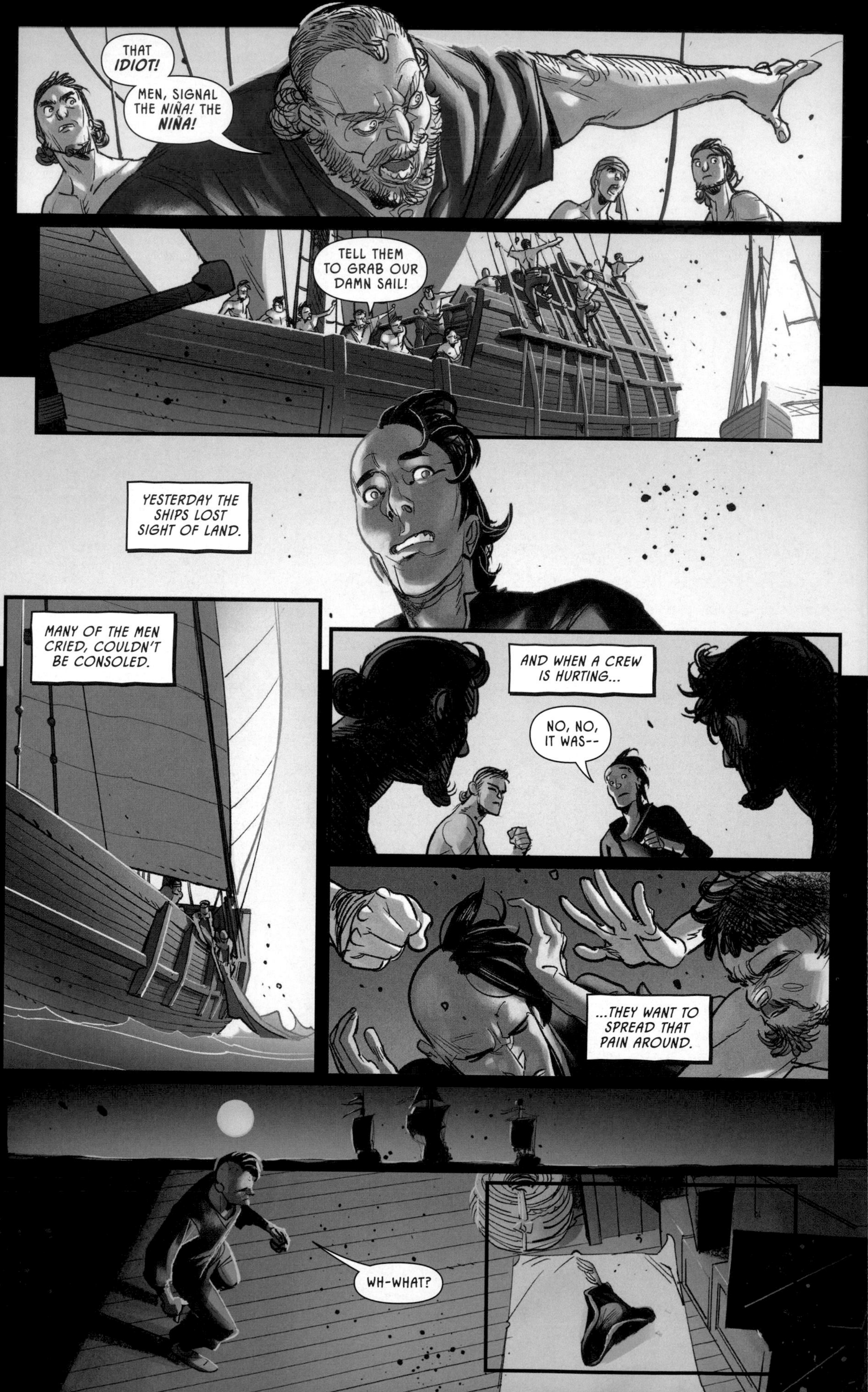
THAT *IDIOT!*
MEN, SIGNAL THE *NIÑA!* THE ***NIÑA!***
TELL THEM TO GRAB OUR DAMN SAIL!
YESTERDAY THE SHIPS LOST SIGHT OF LAND.
MANY OF THE MEN CRIED, COULDN'T BE CONSOLED.
AND WHEN A CREW IS HURTING...
NO, NO, IT WAS--
...THEY WANT TO SPREAD THAT PAIN AROUND.
WH-WHAT?

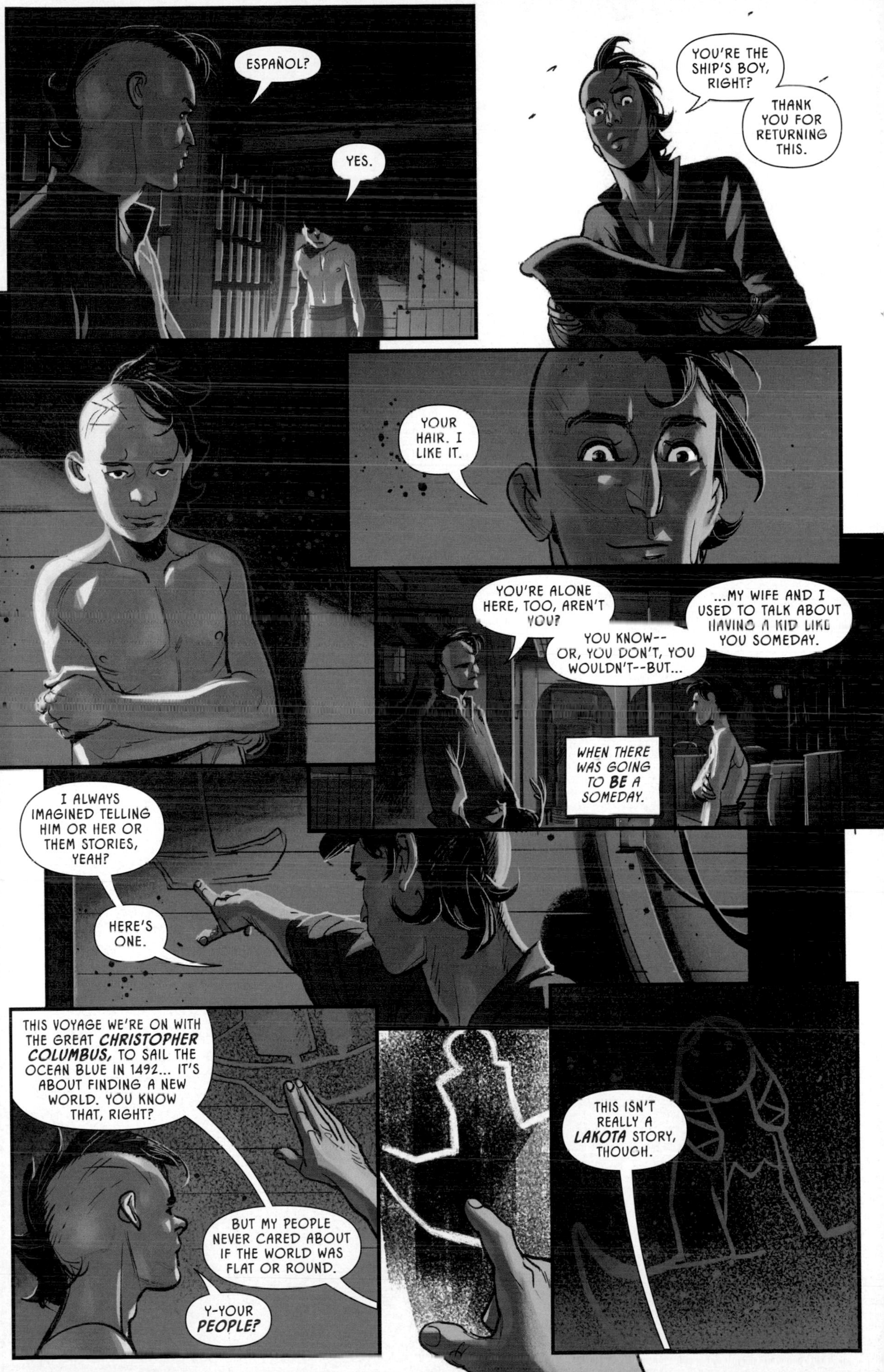
ESPAÑOL?
YES.
YOU'RE THE SHIP'S BOY, RIGHT?
THANK YOU FOR RETURNING THIS.
YOUR HAIR. I LIKE IT.
YOU'RE ALONE HERE, TOO, AREN'T YOU?
YOU KNOW-- OR, YOU DON'T, YOU WOULDN'T--BUT...
...MY WIFE AND I USED TO TALK ABOUT HAVING A KID LIKE YOU SOMEDAY.
WHEN THERE WAS GOING TO BE A SOMEDAY.
I ALWAYS IMAGINED TELLING HIM OR HER OR THEM STORIES, YEAH?
HERE'S ONE.
THIS VOYAGE WE'RE ON WITH THE GREAT CHRISTOPHER COLUMBUS, TO SAIL THE OCEAN BLUE IN 1492... IT'S ABOUT FINDING A NEW WORLD. YOU KNOW THAT, RIGHT?
BUT MY PEOPLE NEVER CARED ABOUT IF THE WORLD WAS FLAT OR ROUND.
Y-YOUR PEOPLE?
THIS ISN'T REALLY A LAKOTA STORY, THOUGH.

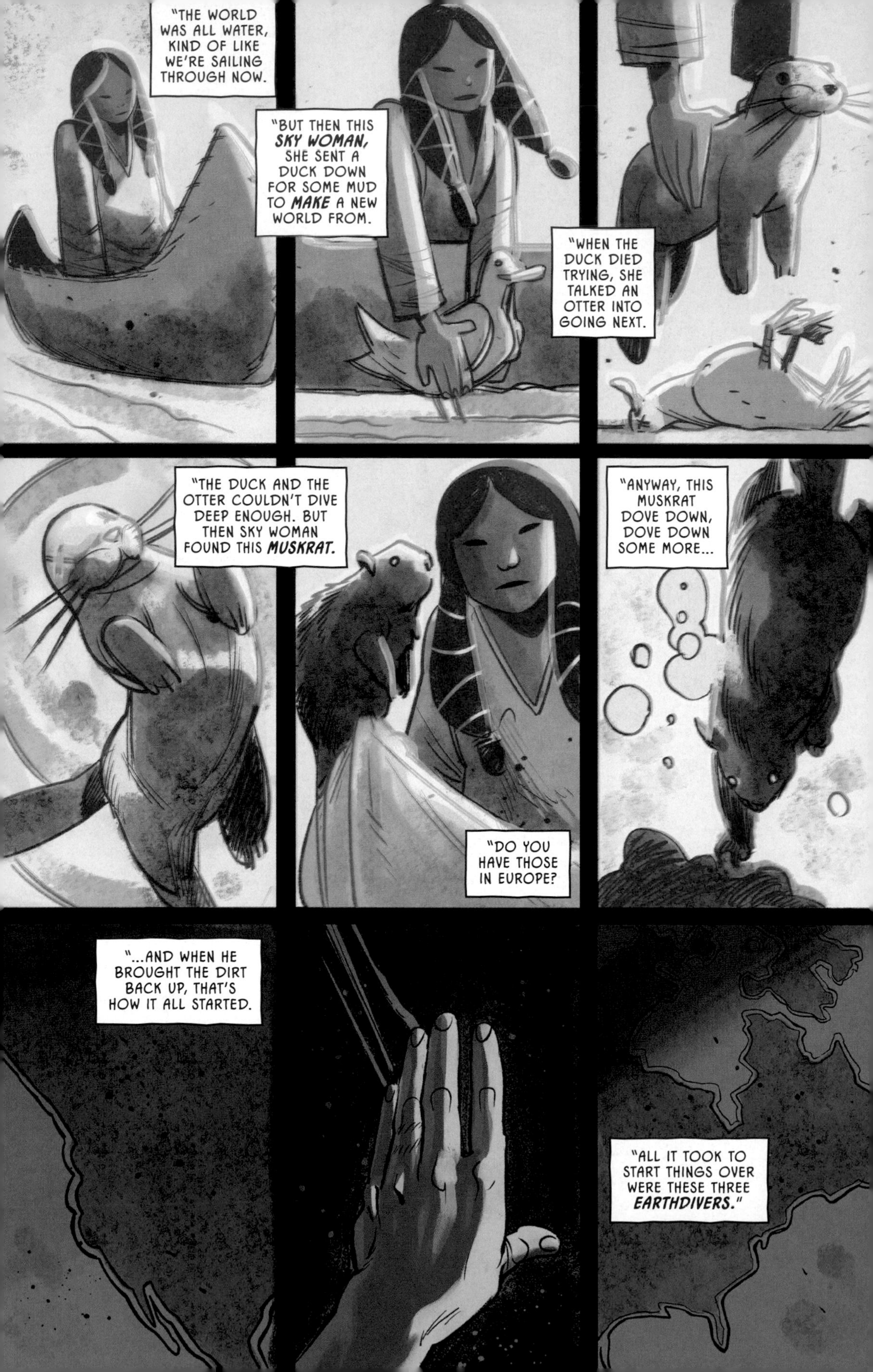
"THE WORLD WAS ALL WATER, KIND OF LIKE WE'RE SAILING THROUGH NOW.
"BUT THEN THIS SKY WOMAN, SHE SENT A DUCK DOWN FOR SOME MUD TO MAKE A NEW WORLD FROM.
"WHEN THE DUCK DIED TRYING, SHE TALKED AN OTTER INTO GOING NEXT.
"THE DUCK AND THE OTTER COULDN'T DIVE DEEP ENOUGH. BUT THEN SKY WOMAN FOUND THIS MUSKRAT.
"DO YOU HAVE THOSE IN EUROPE?
"ANYWAY, THIS MUSKRAT DOVE DOWN, DOVE DOWN SOME MORE...
"...AND WHEN HE BROUGHT THE DIRT BACK UP, THAT'S HOW IT ALL STARTED.
"ALL IT TOOK TO START THINGS OVER WERE THESE THREE EARTHDIVERS."

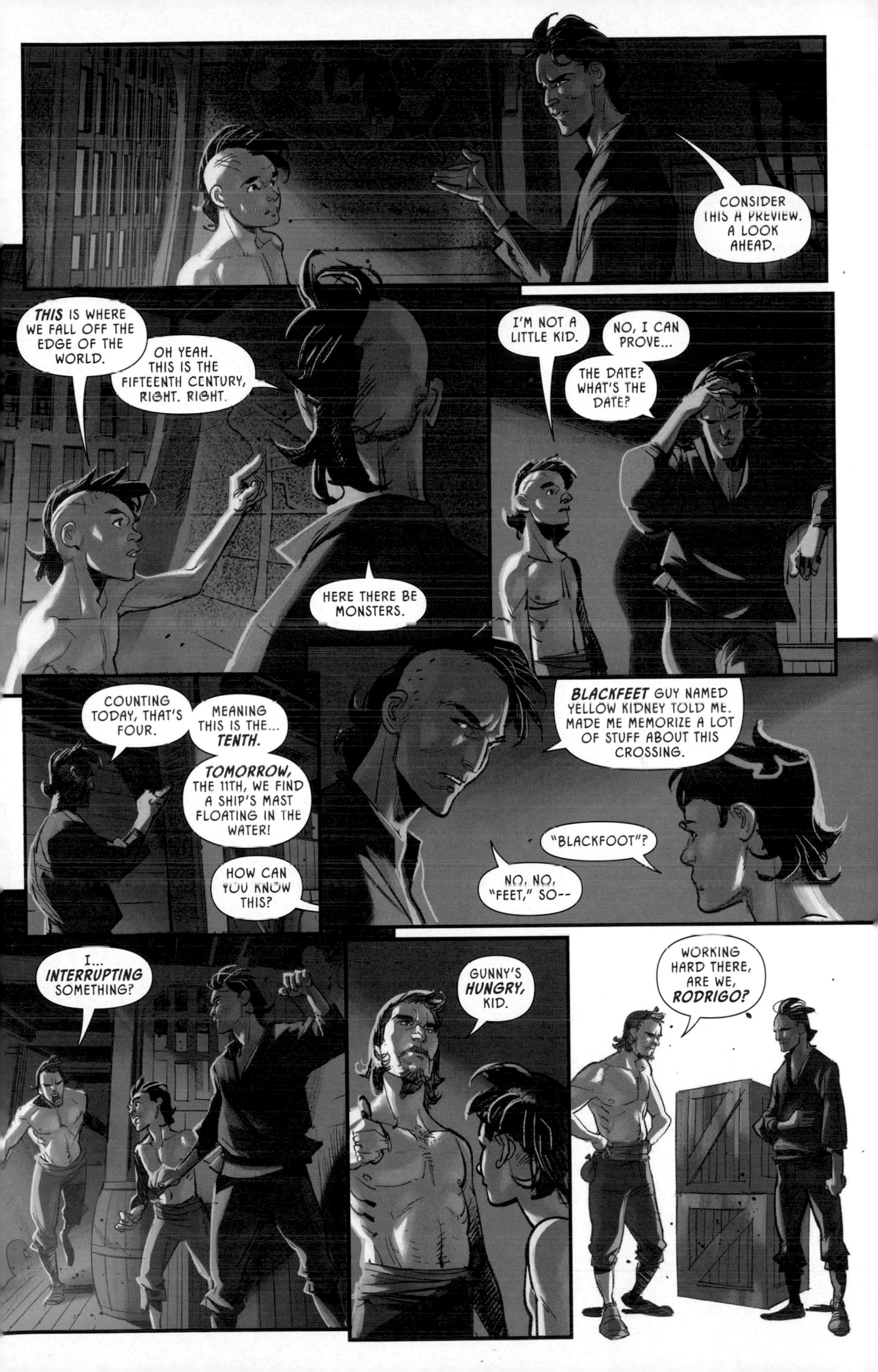
CONSIDER THIS A PREVIEW. A LOOK AHEAD.
THIS IS WHERE WE FALL OFF THE EDGE OF THE WORLD.
OH YEAH. THIS IS THE FIFTEENTH CENTURY, RIGHT. RIGHT.
HERE THERE BE MONSTERS.
I'M NOT A LITTLE KID.
NO, I CAN PROVE...
THE DATE? WHAT'S THE DATE?
COUNTING TODAY, THAT'S FOUR.
MEANING THIS IS THE... TENTH.
TOMORROW, THE 11TH, WE FIND A SHIP'S MAST FLOATING IN THE WATER!
HOW CAN YOU KNOW THIS?
BLACKFEET GUY NAMED YELLOW KIDNEY TOLD ME. MADE ME MEMORIZE A LOT OF STUFF ABOUT THIS CROSSING.
"BLACKFOOT"?
NO, NO, "FEET," SO--
I... INTERRUPTING SOMETHING?
GUNNY'S HUNGRY, KID.
WORKING HARD THERE, ARE WE, RODRIGO?

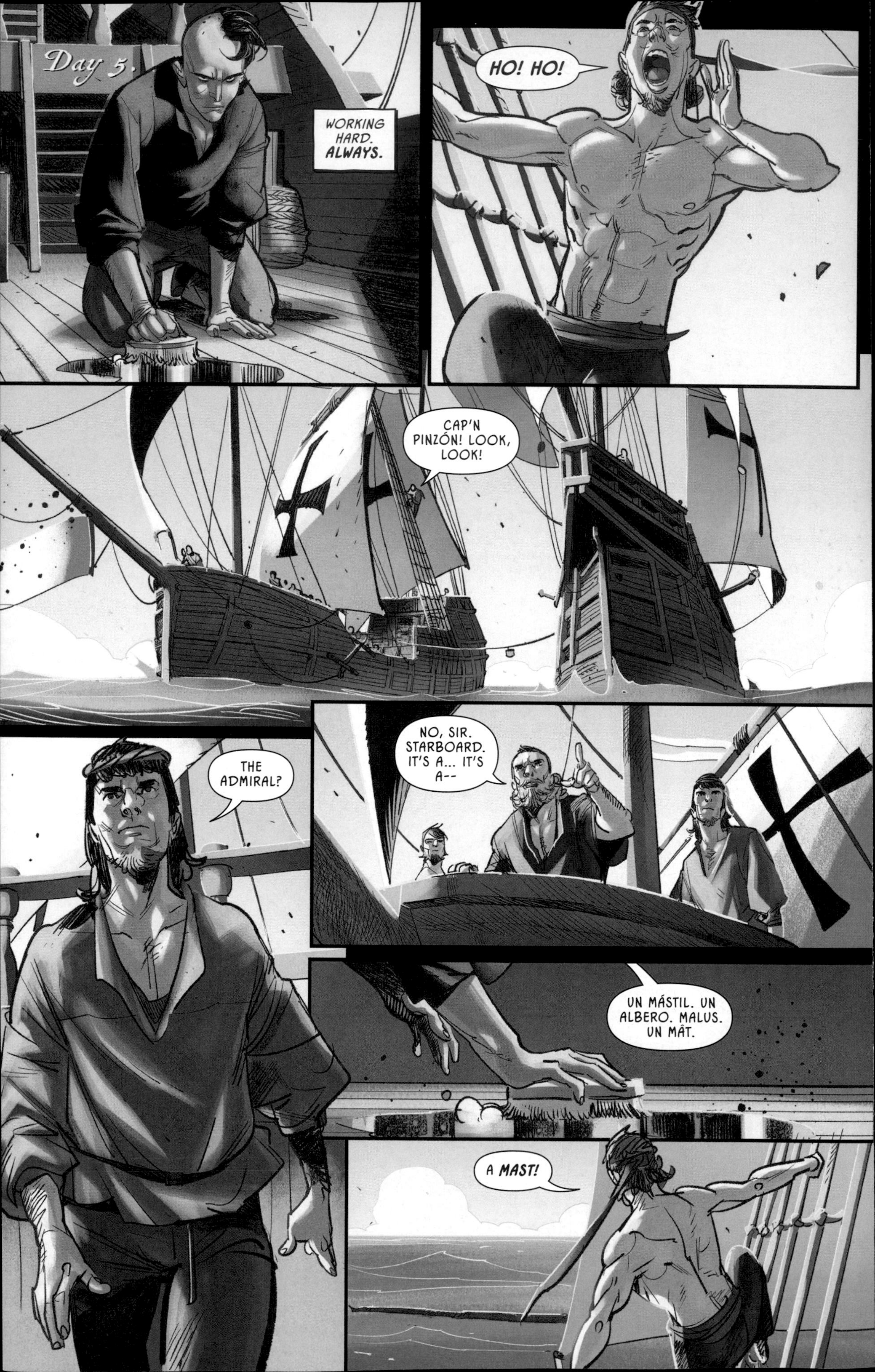
Day 5.
WORKING HARD. ALWAYS.
HO! HO!
CAP'N PINZÓN! LOOK, LOOK!
THE ADMIRAL?
NO, SIR. STARBOARD. IT'S A... IT'S A--
UN MÁSTIL. UN ALBERO. MALUS. UN MÂT.
A MAST!

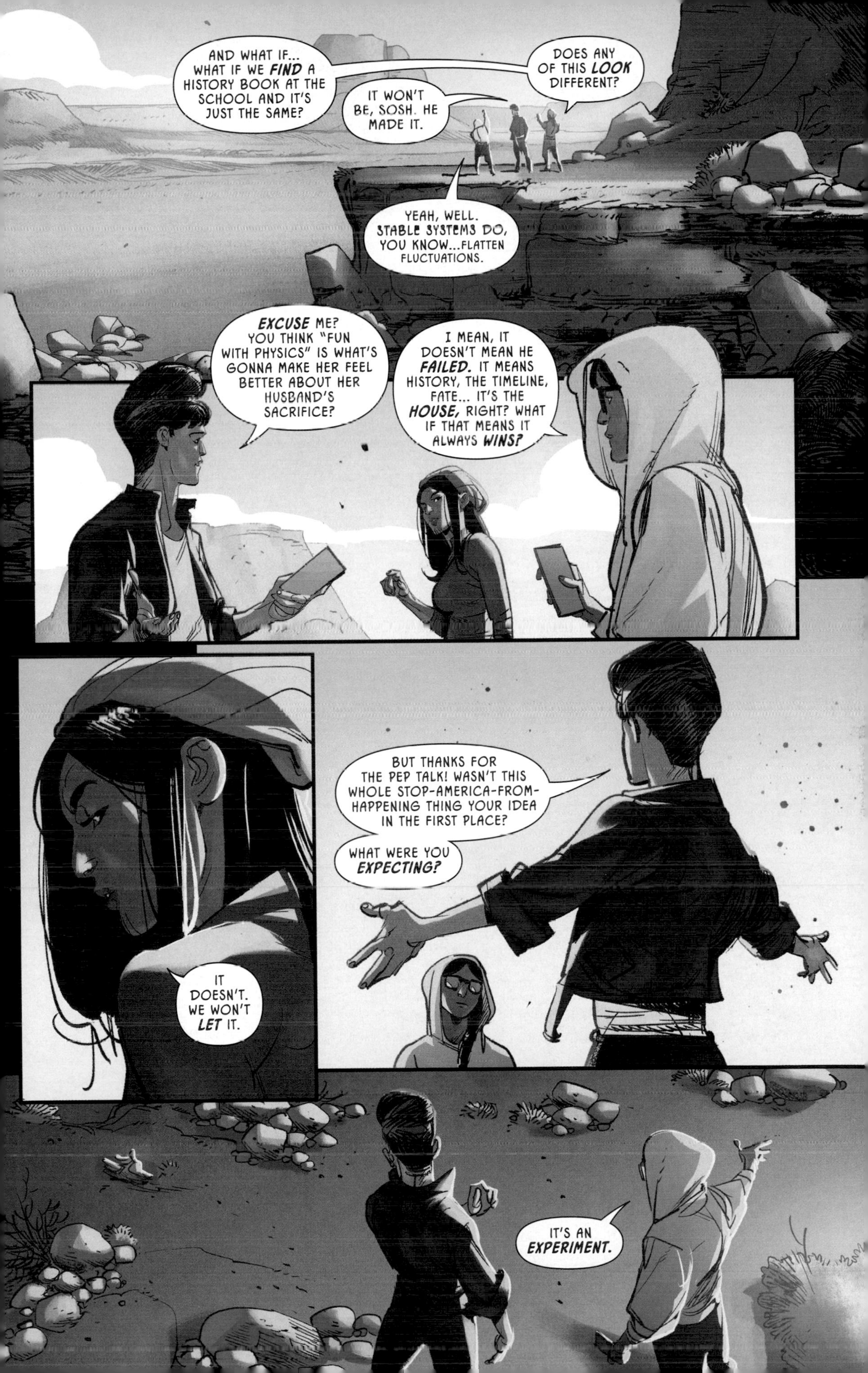
AND WHAT IF... WHAT IF WE FIND A HISTORY BOOK AT THE SCHOOL AND IT'S JUST THE SAME?
DOES ANY OF THIS LOOK DIFFERENT?
IT WON'T BE, SOSH. HE MADE IT.
YEAH, WELL. STABLE SYSTEMS DO, YOU KNOW...FLATTEN FLUCTUATIONS.
EXCUSE ME? YOU THINK "FUN WITH PHYSICS" IS WHAT'S GONNA MAKE HER FEEL BETTER ABOUT HER HUSBAND'S SACRIFICE?
I MEAN, IT DOESN'T MEAN HE FAILED. IT MEANS HISTORY, THE TIMELINE, FATE... IT'S THE HOUSE, RIGHT? WHAT IF THAT MEANS IT ALWAYS WINS?
BUT THANKS FOR THE PEP TALK! WASN'T THIS WHOLE STOP-AMERICA-FROM-HAPPENING THING YOUR IDEA IN THE FIRST PLACE?
WHAT WERE YOU EXPECTING?
IT DOESN'T. WE WON'T LET IT.
IT'S AN EXPERIMENT.

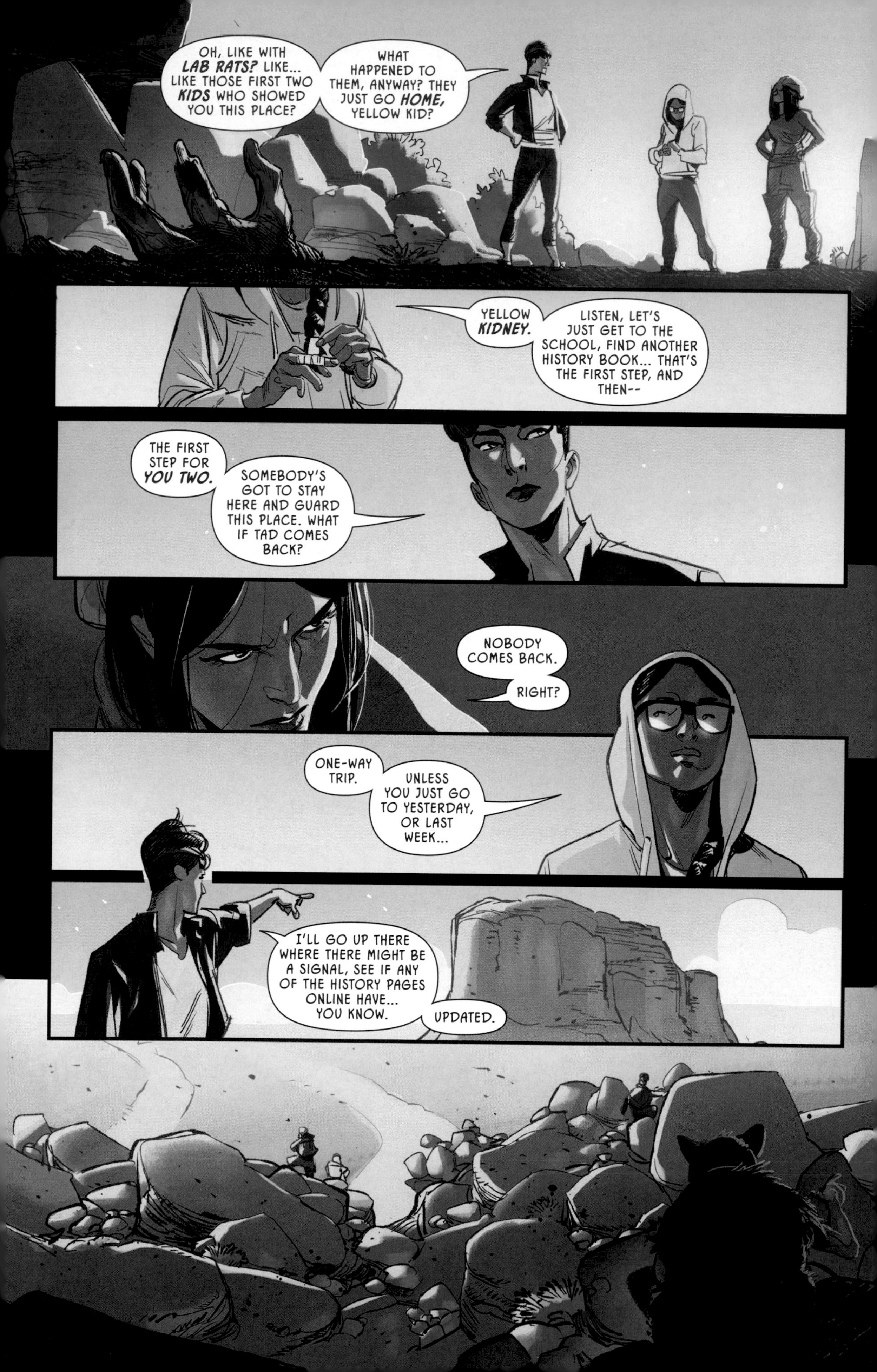
OH, LIKE WITH *LAB RATS?* LIKE... LIKE THOSE FIRST TWO *KIDS* WHO SHOWED YOU THIS PLACE?
WHAT HAPPENED TO THEM, ANYWAY? THEY JUST GO *HOME,* YELLOW KID?
YELLOW *KIDNEY.*
LISTEN, LET'S JUST GET TO THE SCHOOL, FIND ANOTHER HISTORY BOOK... THAT'S THE FIRST STEP, AND THEN--
THE FIRST STEP FOR *YOU TWO.*
SOMEBODY'S GOT TO STAY HERE AND GUARD THIS PLACE. WHAT IF TAD COMES BACK?
NOBODY COMES BACK.
RIGHT?
ONE-WAY TRIP.
UNLESS YOU JUST GO TO YESTERDAY, OR LAST WEEK...
I'LL GO UP THERE WHERE THERE MIGHT BE A SIGNAL, SEE IF ANY OF THE HISTORY PAGES ONLINE HAVE... YOU KNOW.
UPDATED.

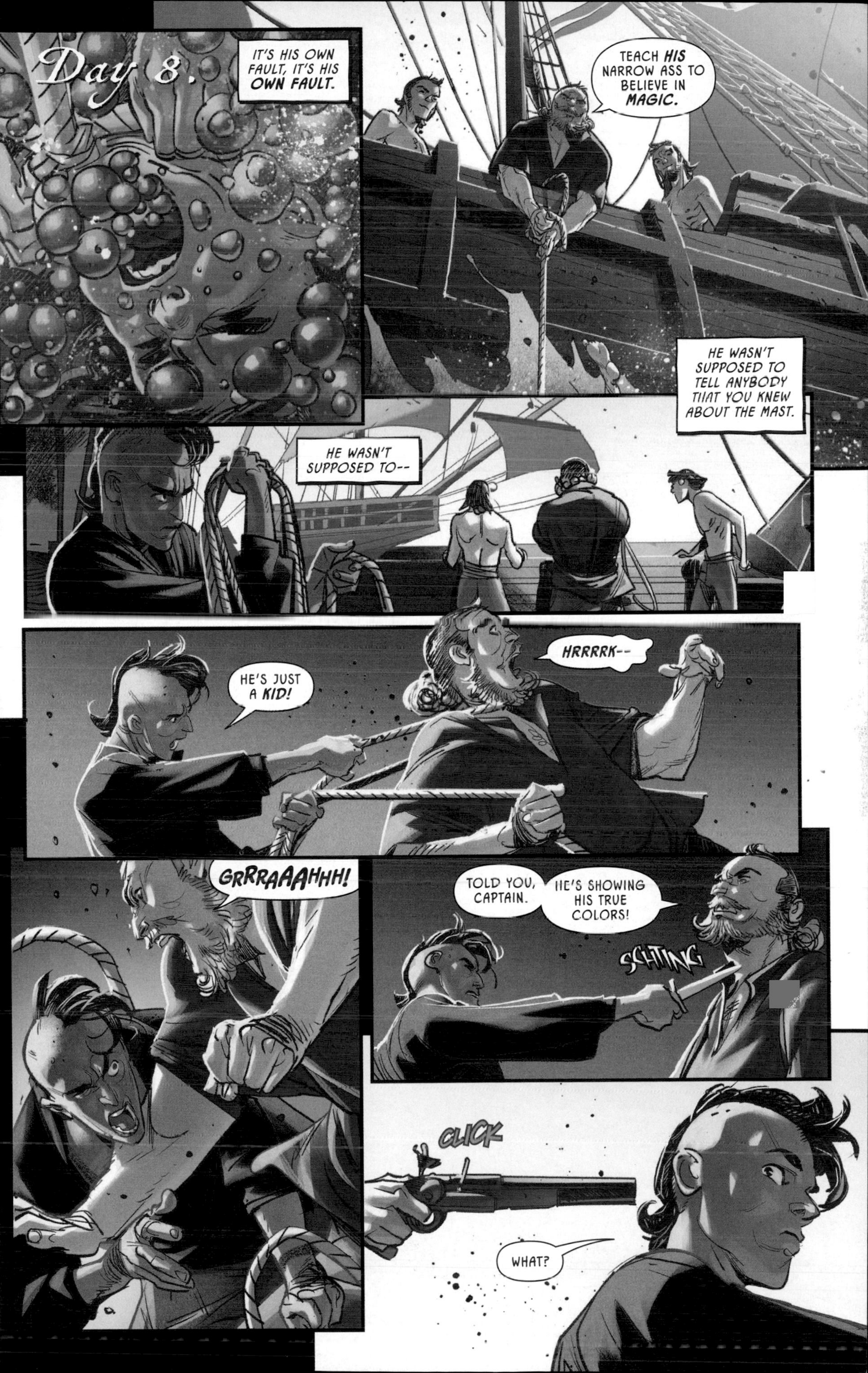
Day 8.
IT'S HIS OWN FAULT, IT'S HIS OWN FAULT.
TEACH HIS NARROW ASS TO BELIEVE IN MAGIC.
HE WASN'T SUPPOSED TO TELL ANYBODY THAT YOU KNEW ABOUT THE MAST.
HE WASN'T SUPPOSED TO--
HE'S JUST A KID!
HRRRRK--
GRRRAAAHHH!
TOLD YOU, CAPTAIN.
HE'S SHOWING HIS TRUE COLORS!
SCHING
CLICK
WHAT?

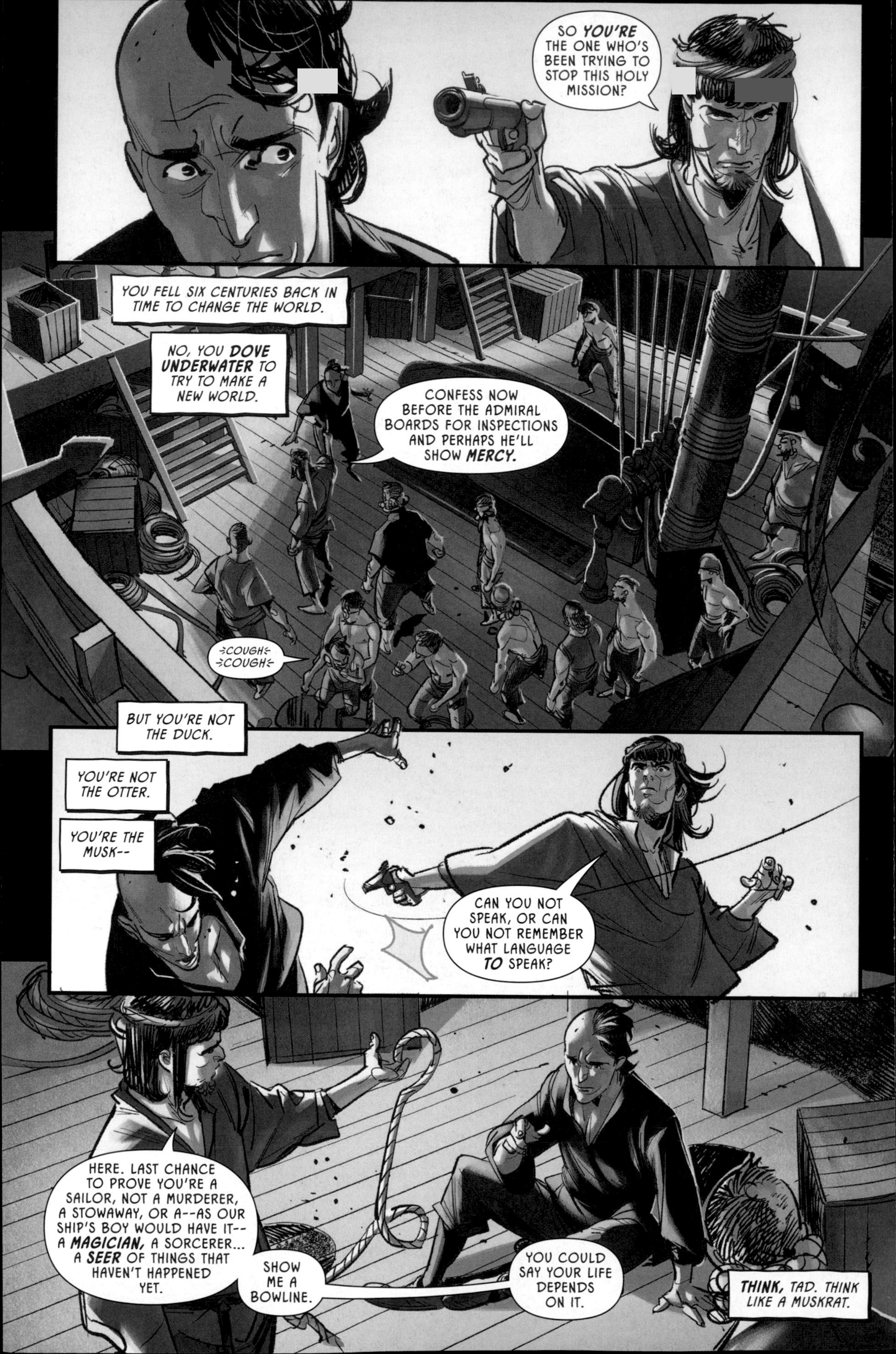
SO YOU'RE THE ONE WHO'S BEEN TRYING TO STOP THIS HOLY MISSION?
YOU FELL SIX CENTURIES BACK IN TIME TO CHANGE THE WORLD.
NO, YOU DOVE UNDERWATER TO TRY TO MAKE A NEW WORLD.
CONFESS NOW BEFORE THE ADMIRAL BOARDS FOR INSPECTIONS AND PERHAPS HE'LL SHOW MERCY.
COUGH COUGH
BUT YOU'RE NOT THE DUCK.
YOU'RE NOT THE OTTER.
YOU'RE THE MUSK--
CAN YOU NOT SPEAK, OR CAN YOU NOT REMEMBER WHAT LANGUAGE TO SPEAK?
HERE. LAST CHANCE TO PROVE YOU'RE A SAILOR, NOT A MURDERER, A STOWAWAY, OR A--AS OUR SHIP'S BOY WOULD HAVE IT--A MAGICIAN, A SORCERER... A SEER OF THINGS THAT HAVEN'T HAPPENED YET.
SHOW ME A BOWLINE.
YOU COULD SAY YOUR LIFE DEPENDS ON IT.
THINK, TAD. THINK LIKE A MUSKRAT.

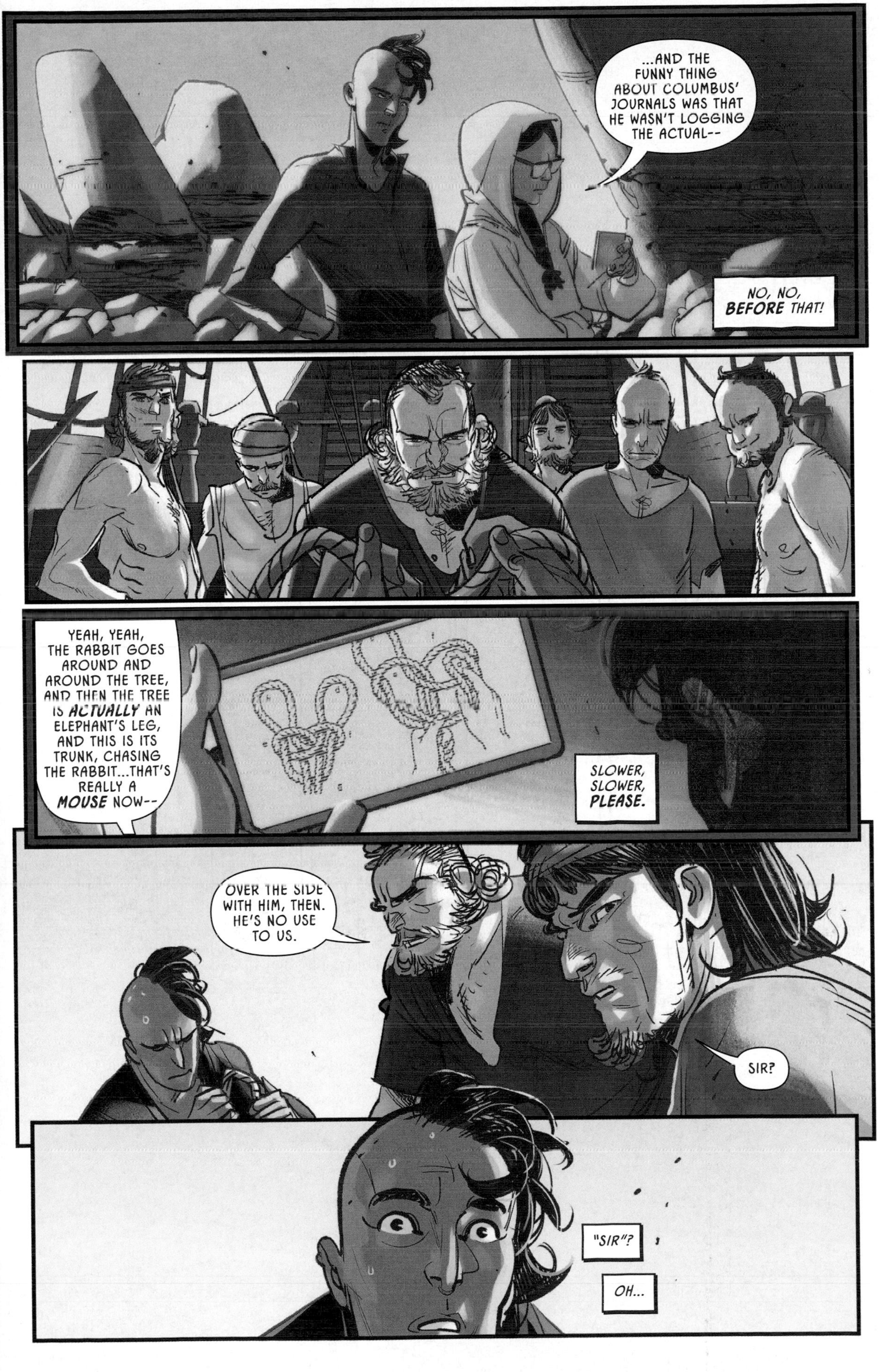
...AND THE FUNNY THING ABOUT COLUMBUS' JOURNALS WAS THAT HE WASN'T LOGGING THE ACTUAL--
NO, NO, BEFORE THAT!
YEAH, YEAH, THE RABBIT GOES AROUND AND AROUND THE TREE, AND THEN THE TREE IS ACTUALLY AN ELEPHANT'S LEG, AND THIS IS ITS TRUNK, CHASING THE RABBIT...THAT'S REALLY A MOUSE NOW--
SLOWER, SLOWER, PLEASE.
OVER THE SIDE WITH HIM, THEN. HE'S NO USE TO US.
SIR?
"SIR"?
OH...

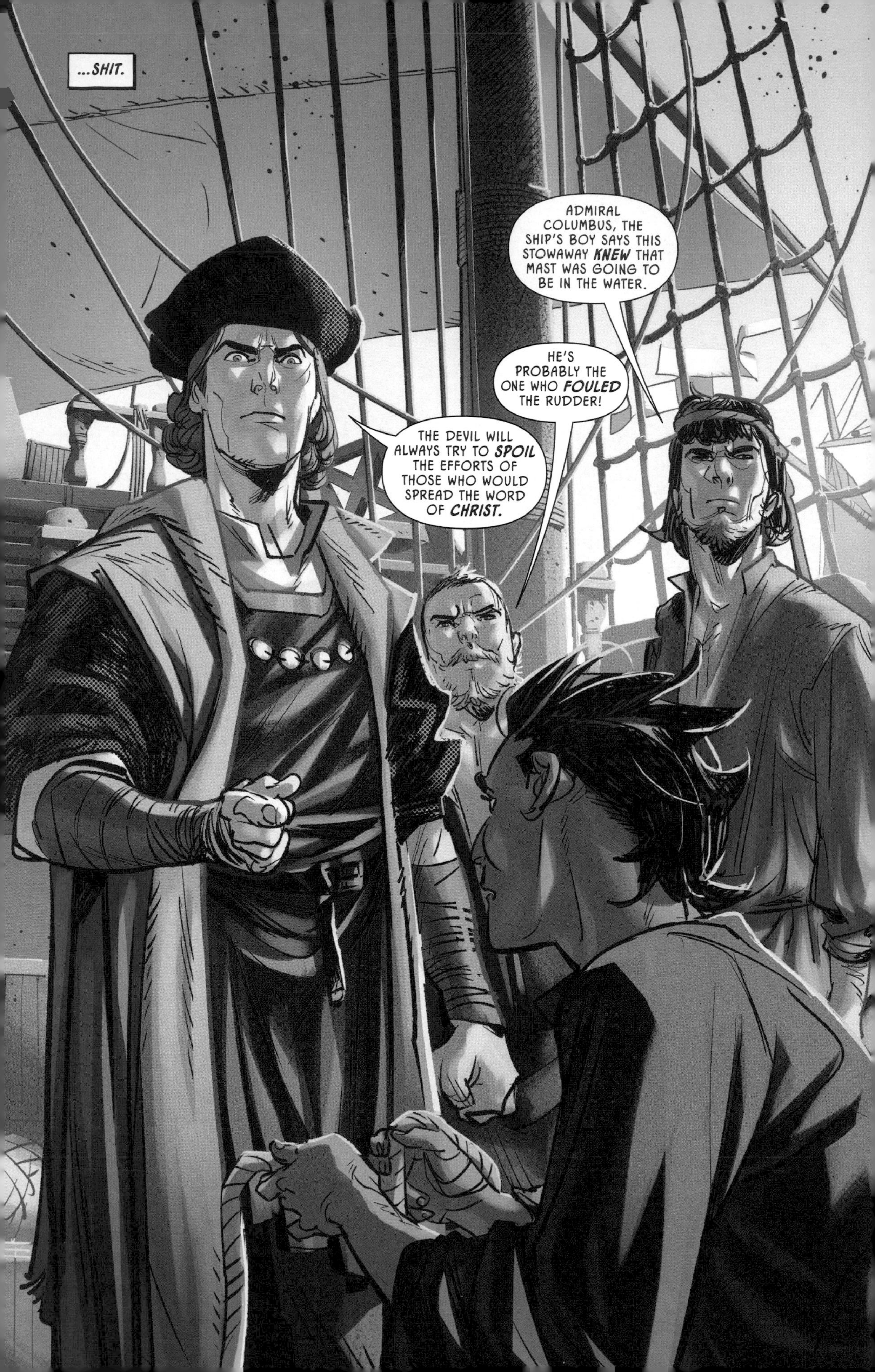
...SHIT.
ADMIRAL COLUMBUS, THE SHIP'S BOY SAYS THIS STOWAWAY KNEW THAT MAST WAS GOING TO BE IN THE WATER.
HE'S PROBABLY THE ONE WHO FOULED THE RUDDER!
THE DEVIL WILL ALWAYS TRY TO SPOIL THE EFFORTS OF THOSE WHO WOULD SPREAD THE WORD OF CHRIST.

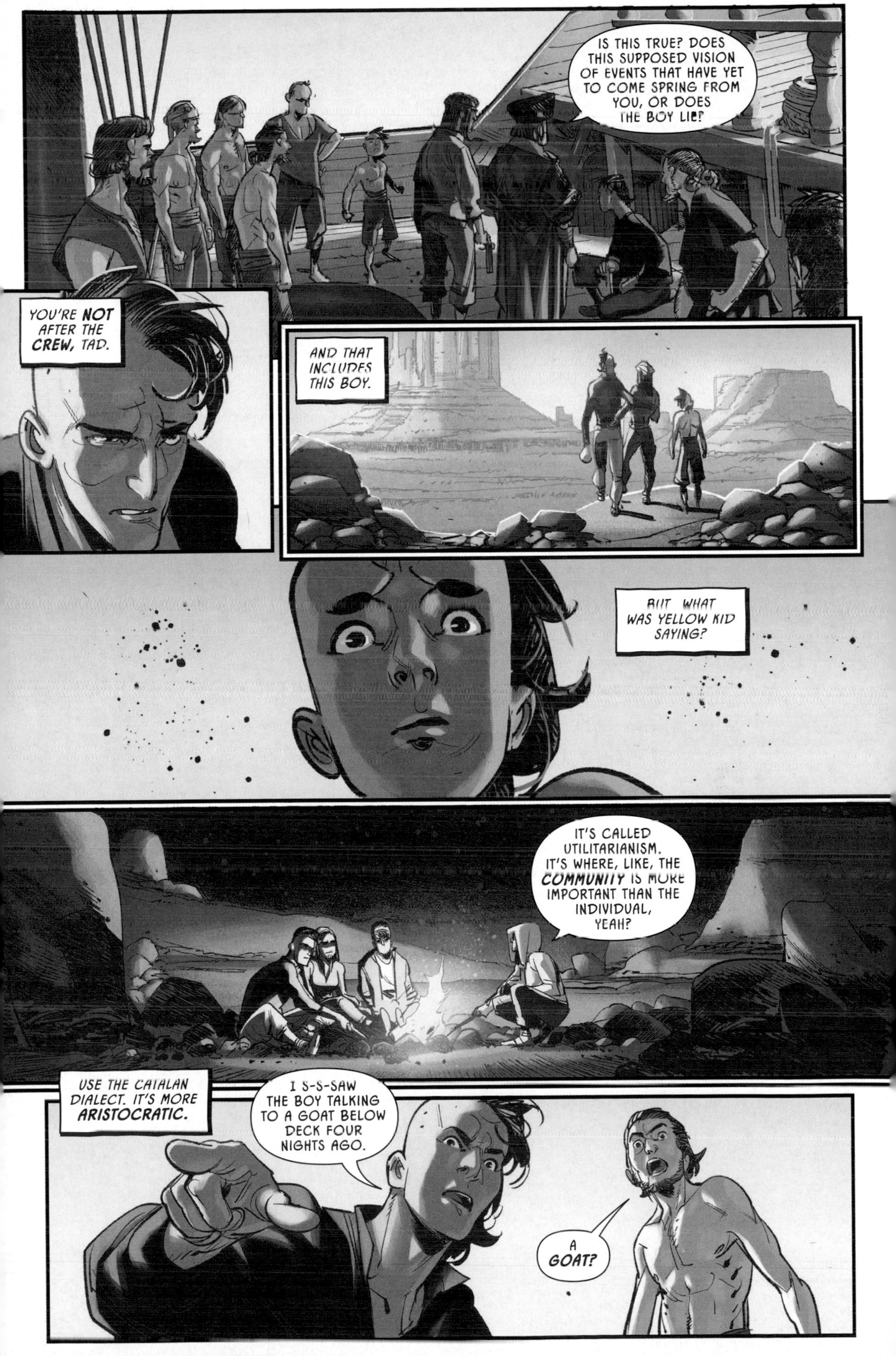
IS THIS TRUE? DOES THIS SUPPOSED VISION OF EVENTS THAT HAVE YET TO COME SPRING FROM YOU, OR DOES THE BOY LIE?
YOU'RE **NOT** AFTER THE **CREW,** TAD.
AND THAT INCLUDES THIS BOY.
BUT WHAT WAS YELLOW KID SAYING?
IT'S CALLED UTILITARIANISM. IT'S WHERE, LIKE, THE **COMMUNITY** IS MORE IMPORTANT THAN THE INDIVIDUAL, YEAH?
USE THE CATALAN DIALECT. IT'S MORE **ARISTOCRATIC.**
I S-S-SAW THE BOY TALKING TO A GOAT BELOW DECK FOUR NIGHTS AGO.
A **GOAT?**

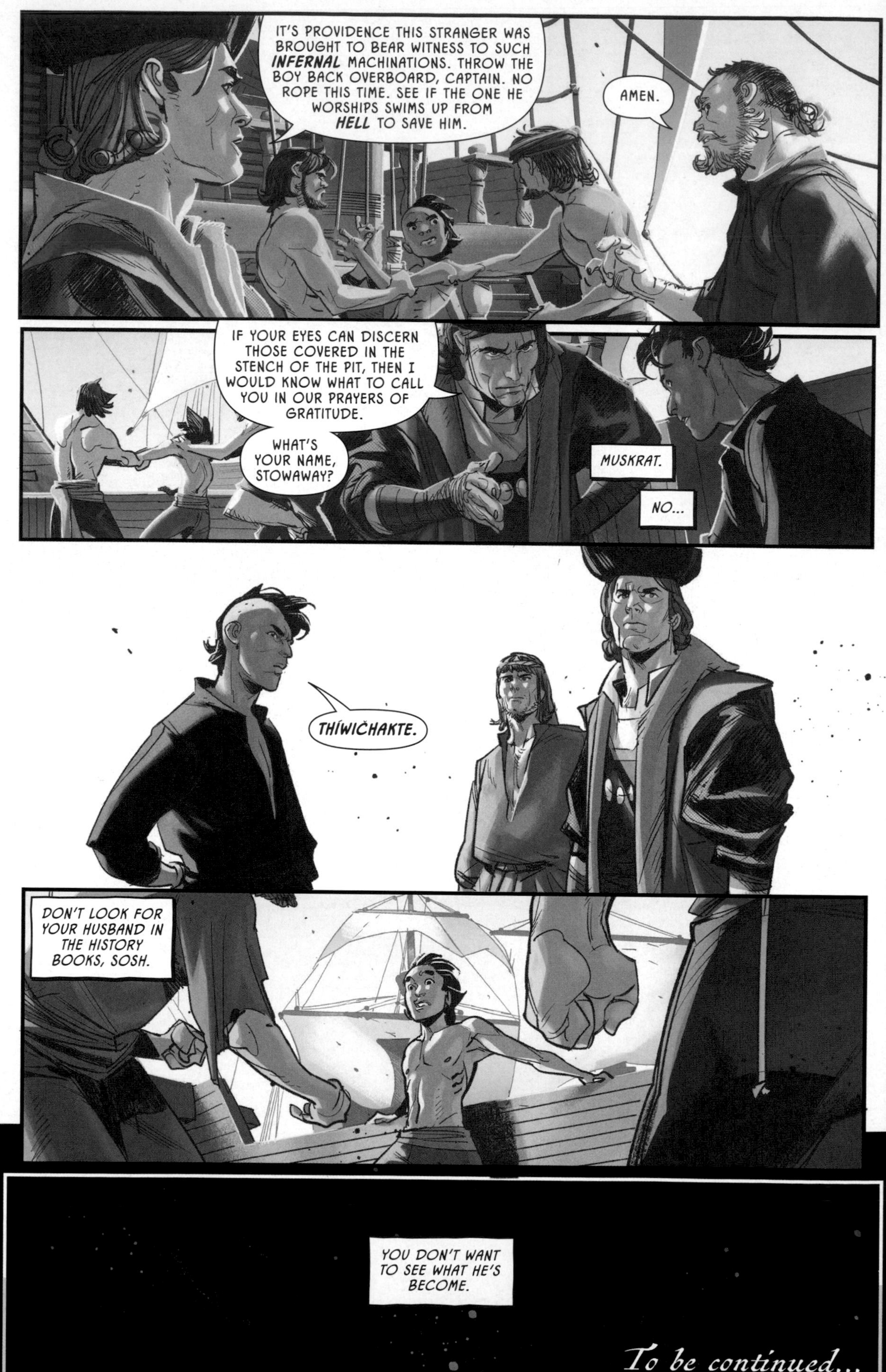
IT'S PROVIDENCE THIS STRANGER WAS BROUGHT TO BEAR WITNESS TO SUCH INFERNAL MACHINATIONS. THROW THE BOY BACK OVERBOARD, CAPTAIN. NO ROPE THIS TIME. SEE IF THE ONE HE WORSHIPS SWIMS UP FROM HELL TO SAVE HIM.
AMEN.
IF YOUR EYES CAN DISCERN THOSE COVERED IN THE STENCH OF THE PIT, THEN I WOULD KNOW WHAT TO CALL YOU IN OUR PRAYERS OF GRATITUDE.
WHAT'S YOUR NAME, STOWAWAY?
MUSKRAT.
NO...
THÍWIČHAKTE.
DON'T LOOK FOR YOUR HUSBAND IN THE HISTORY BOOKS, SOSH.
YOU DON'T WANT TO SEE WHAT HE'S BECOME.
To be continued...

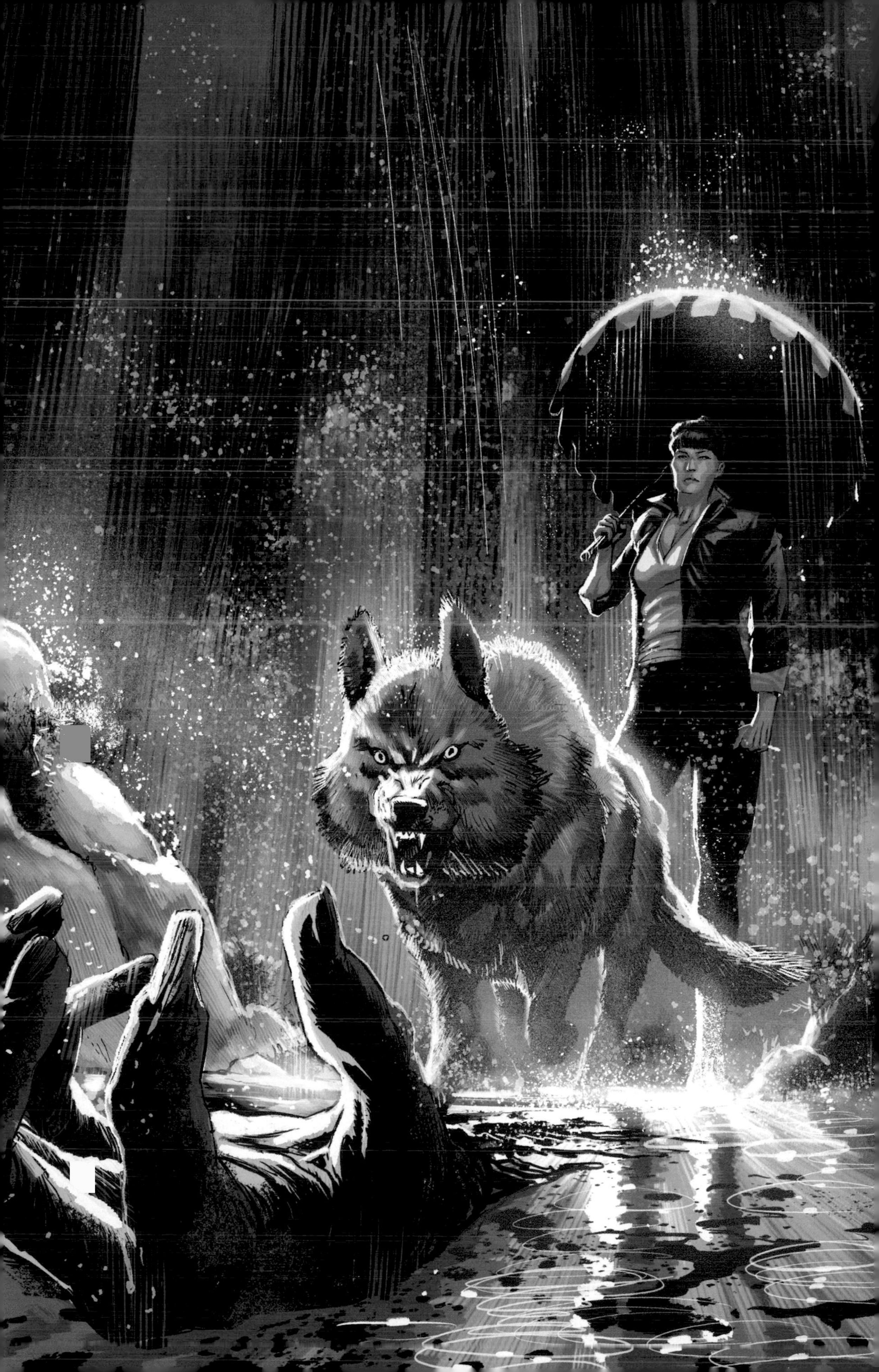

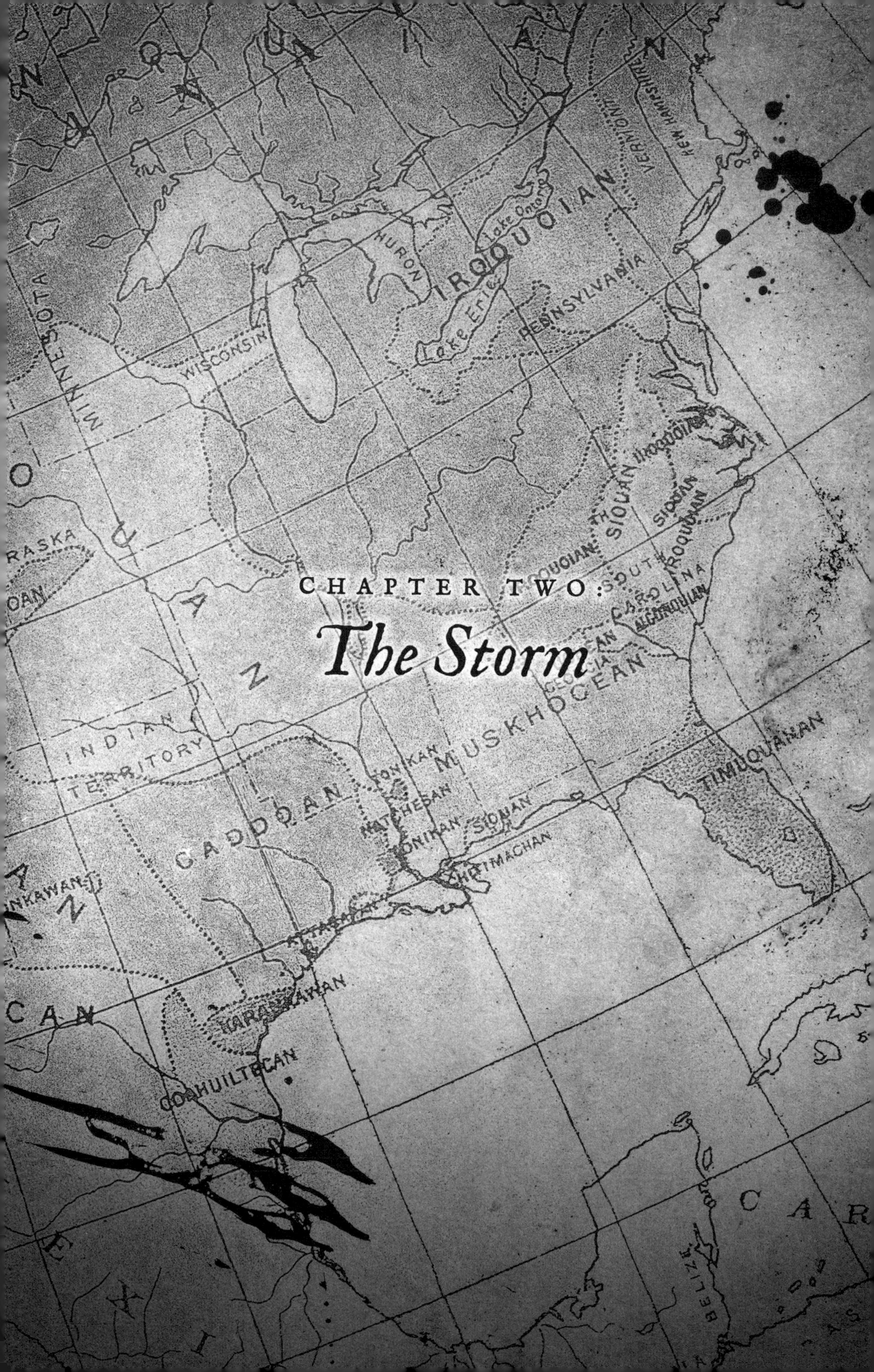
WISCONSIN
MINNESOTA
HURON
Lake Ontario
Lake Erie
IROQUOIAN
PENNSYLVANIA
VERMONT
NEW HAMPSHIRE
SIOUAN
IROQUOIAN
SOUTH CAROLINA
ALGONQUIAN
GEORGIA
MUSKHOGEAN
TIMUQUANAN
INDIAN TERRITORY
TONIKAN
NATCHESAN
CADDOAN
SIOUAN
CHITIMACHAN
KARANKAWAN
COAHUILTECAN
BELIZE

CHAPTER TWO:

The Storm

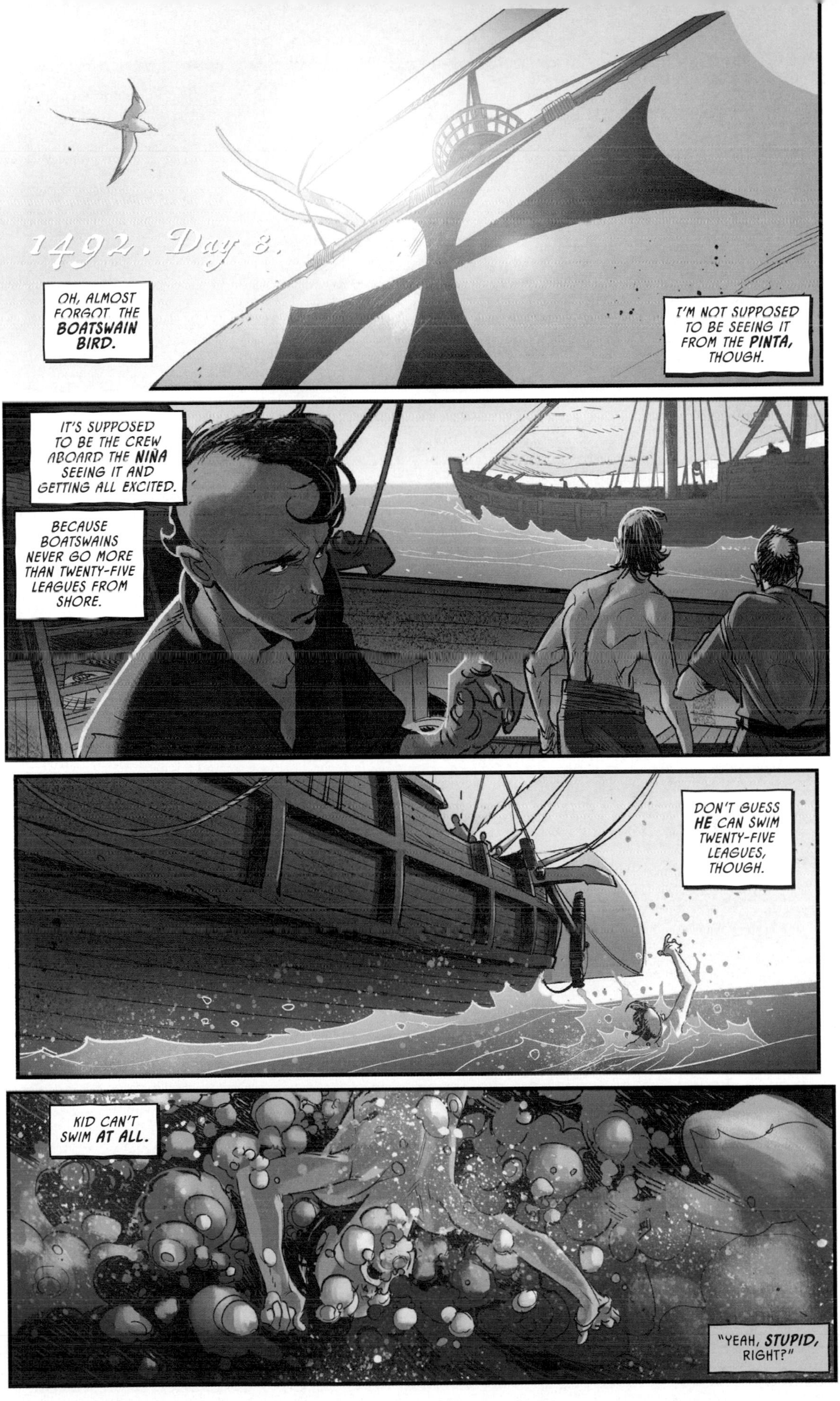

1492. Day 8.
OH, ALMOST FORGOT. THE BOATSWAIN BIRD.
I'M NOT SUPPOSED TO BE SEEING IT FROM THE PINTA, THOUGH.
IT'S SUPPOSED TO BE THE CREW ABOARD THE NIÑA SEEING IT AND GETTING ALL EXCITED.
BECAUSE BOATSWAINS NEVER GO MORE THAN TWENTY-FIVE LEAGUES FROM SHORE.
DON'T GUESS HE CAN SWIM TWENTY-FIVE LEAGUES, THOUGH.
KID CAN'T SWIM AT ALL.
"YEAH, STUPID, RIGHT?"

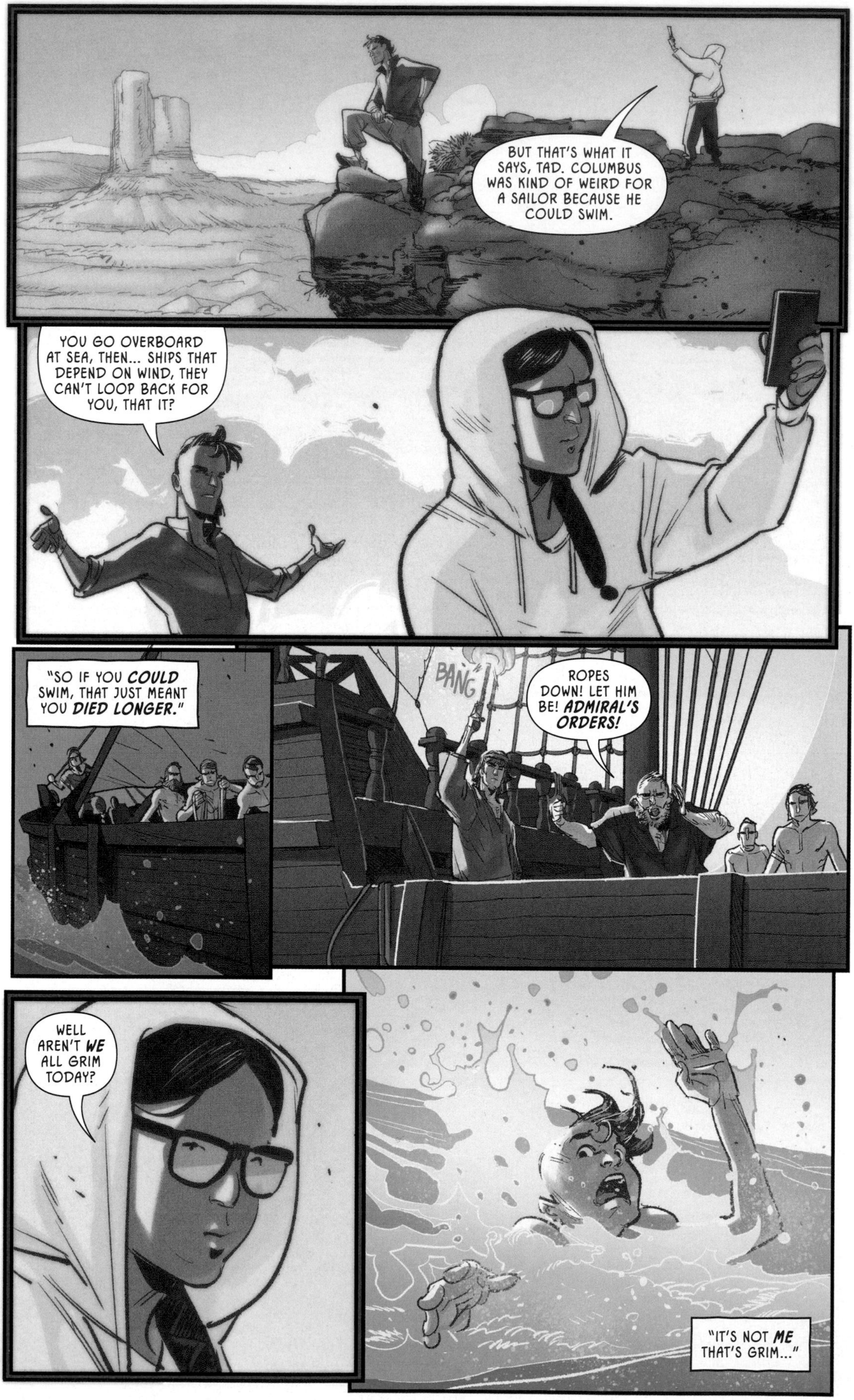
BUT THAT'S WHAT IT SAYS, TAD. COLUMBUS WAS KIND OF WEIRD FOR A SAILOR BECAUSE HE COULD SWIM.
YOU GO OVERBOARD AT SEA, THEN... SHIPS THAT DEPEND ON WIND, THEY CAN'T LOOP BACK FOR YOU, THAT IT?
"SO IF YOU **COULD** SWIM, THAT JUST MEANT YOU **DIED LONGER.**"
BANG
ROPES DOWN! LET HIM BE! **ADMIRAL'S ORDERS!**
WELL AREN'T **WE** ALL GRIM TODAY?
"IT'S NOT **ME** THAT'S GRIM..."

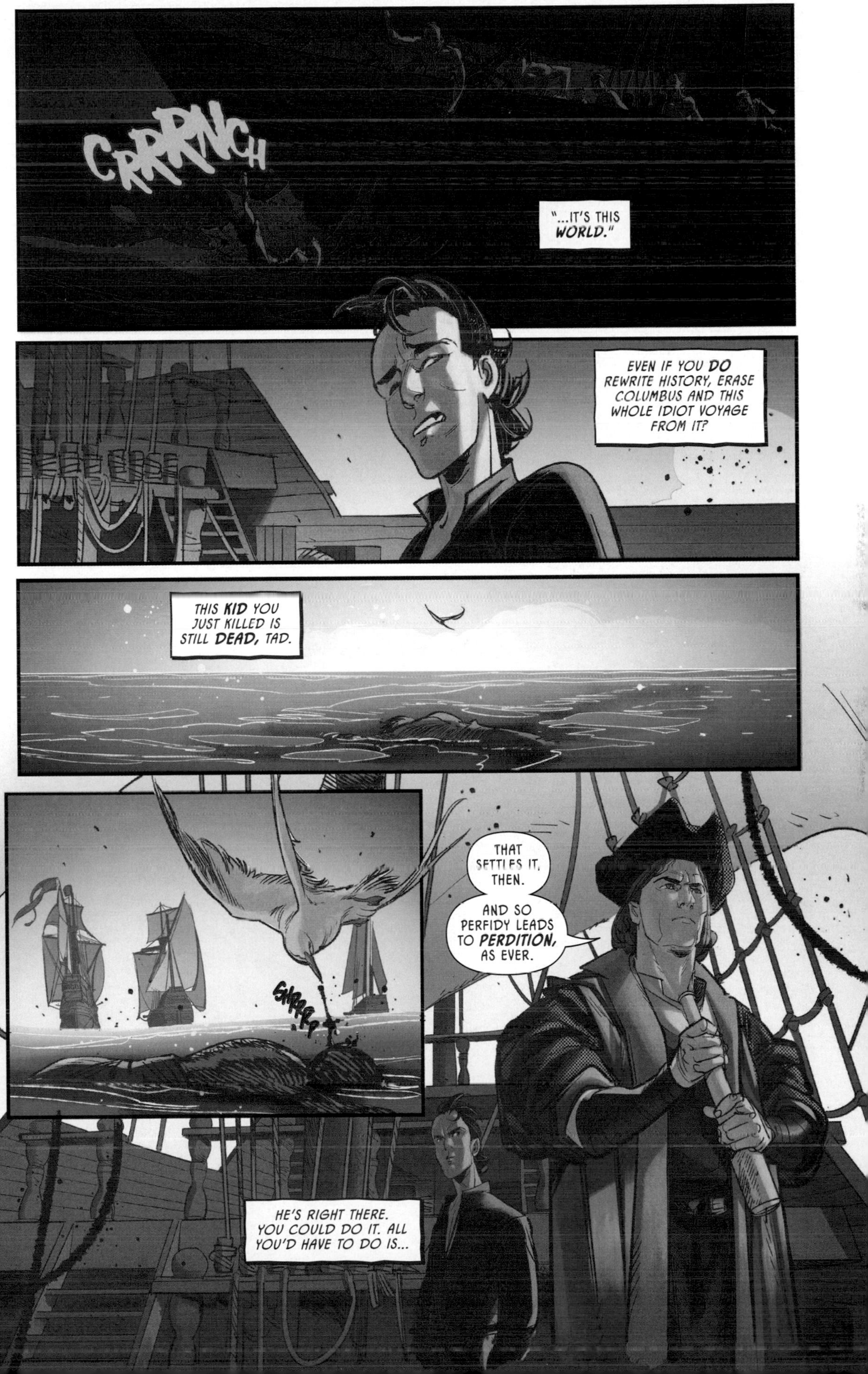

CRRRNCH
"...IT'S THIS WORLD."
EVEN IF YOU DO REWRITE HISTORY, ERASE COLUMBUS AND THIS WHOLE IDIOT VOYAGE FROM IT?
THIS KID YOU JUST KILLED IS STILL DEAD, TAD.
SHRRRP
THAT SETTLES IT, THEN.
AND SO PERFIDY LEADS TO PERDITION, AS EVER.
HE'S RIGHT THERE. YOU COULD DO IT. ALL YOU'D HAVE TO DO IS...

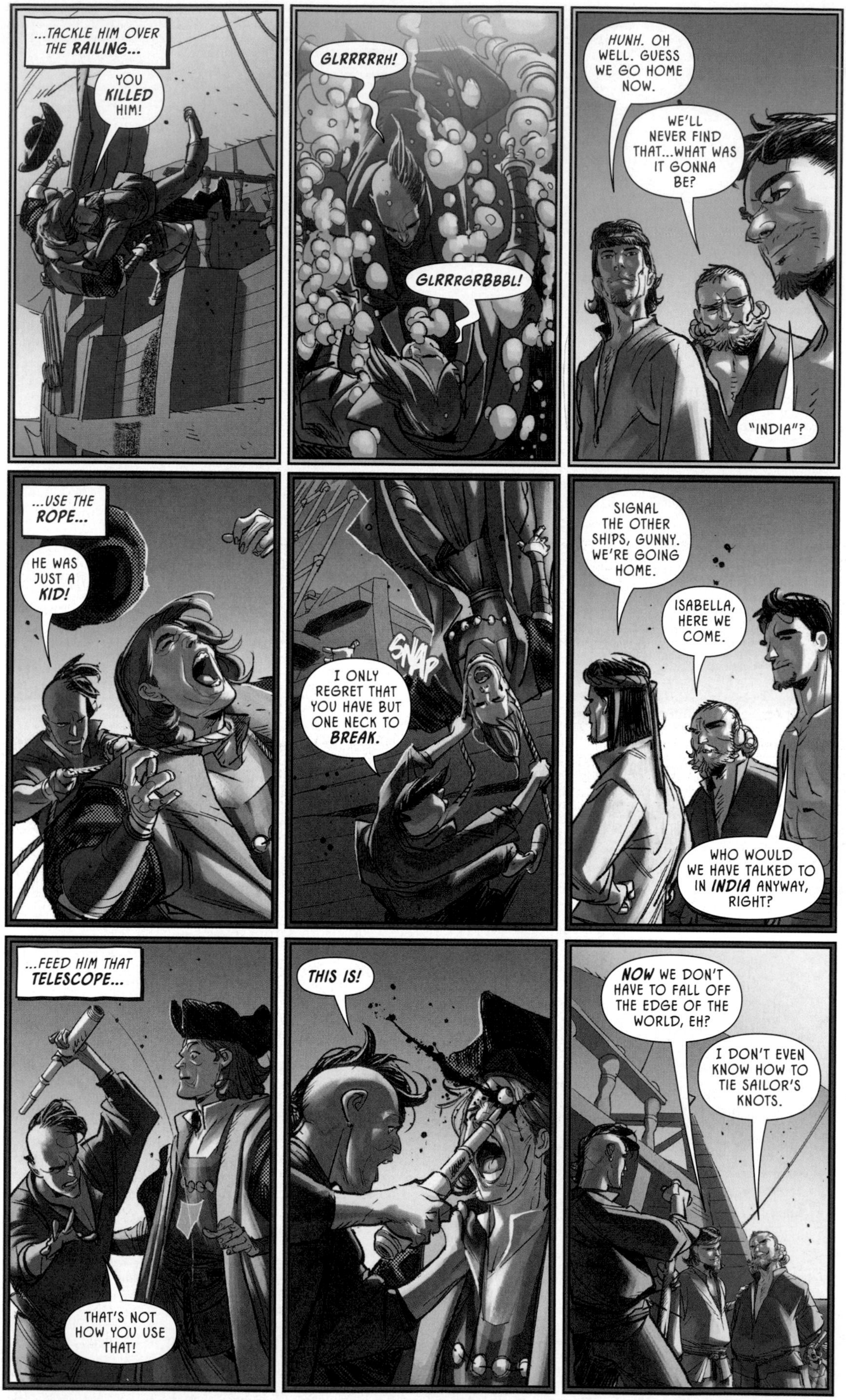
...TACKLE HIM OVER THE RAILING...
YOU KILLED HIM!
GLRRRRRH!
GLRRRGRBBBL!
HUNH. OH WELL. GUESS WE GO HOME NOW.
WE'LL NEVER FIND THAT...WHAT WAS IT GONNA BE?
"INDIA"?
...USE THE ROPE...
HE WAS JUST A KID!
SNAP
I ONLY REGRET THAT YOU HAVE BUT ONE NECK TO BREAK.
SIGNAL THE OTHER SHIPS, GUNNY. WE'RE GOING HOME.
ISABELLA, HERE WE COME.
WHO WOULD WE HAVE TALKED TO IN INDIA ANYWAY, RIGHT?
...FEED HIM THAT TELESCOPE...
THAT'S NOT HOW YOU USE THAT!
THIS IS!
NOW WE DON'T HAVE TO FALL OFF THE EDGE OF THE WORLD, EH?
I DON'T EVEN KNOW HOW TO TIE SAILOR'S KNOTS.

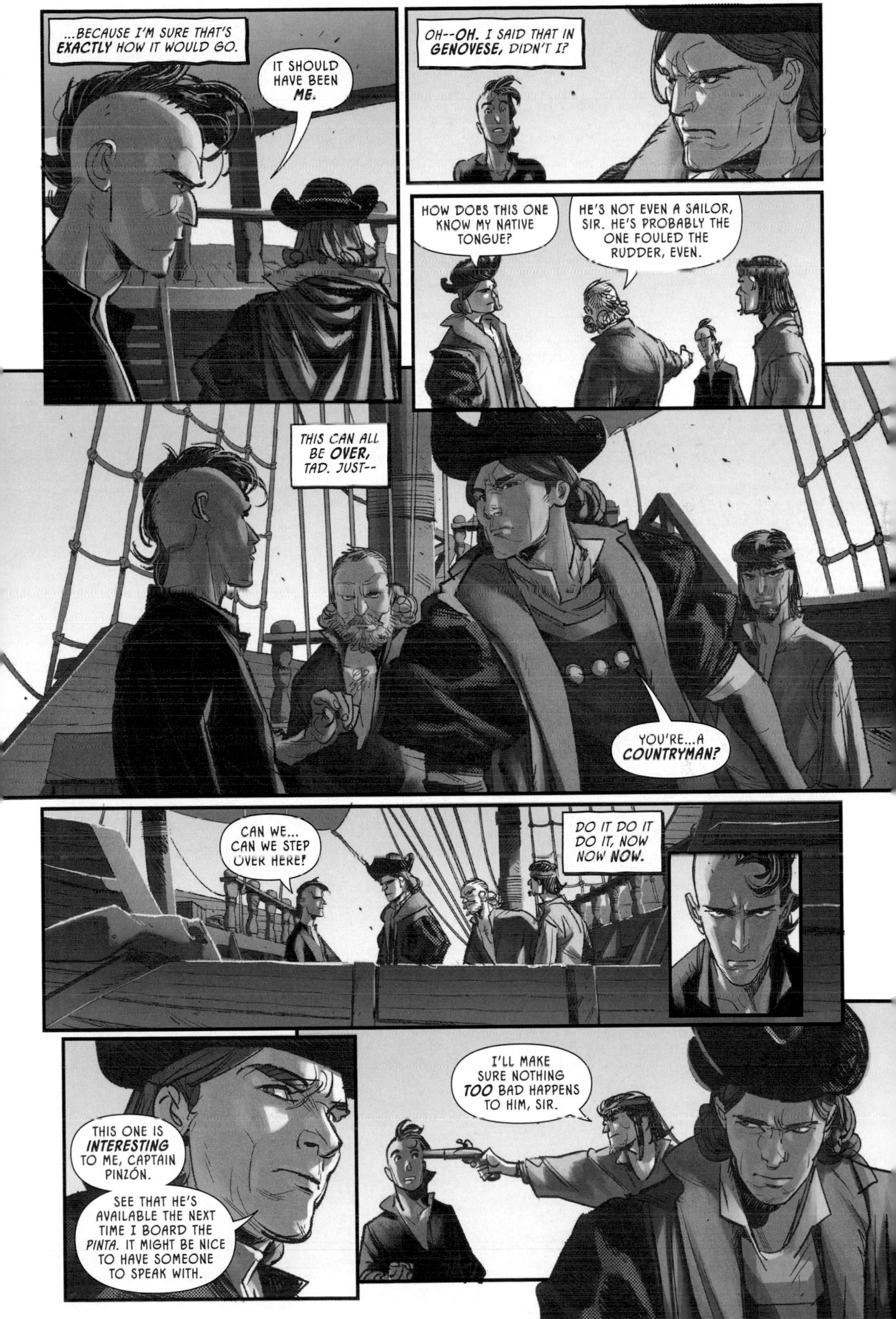

...BECAUSE I'M SURE THAT'S **EXACTLY** HOW IT WOULD GO.
IT SHOULD HAVE BEEN **ME.**
OH--**OH.** I SAID THAT IN **GENOVESE,** DIDN'T I?
HOW DOES THIS ONE KNOW MY NATIVE TONGUE?
HE'S NOT EVEN A SAILOR, SIR. HE'S PROBABLY THE ONE FOULED THE RUDDER, EVEN.
THIS CAN ALL BE **OVER,** TAD. JUST--
YOU'RE...A **COUNTRYMAN?**
CAN WE... CAN WE STEP OVER HERE?
DO IT DO IT DO IT, NOW NOW **NOW.**
THIS ONE IS **INTERESTING** TO ME, CAPTAIN PINZÓN.
SEE THAT HE'S AVAILABLE THE NEXT TIME I BOARD THE *PINTA.* IT MIGHT BE NICE TO HAVE SOMEONE TO SPEAK WITH.
I'LL MAKE SURE NOTHING **TOO** BAD HAPPENS TO HIM, SIR.

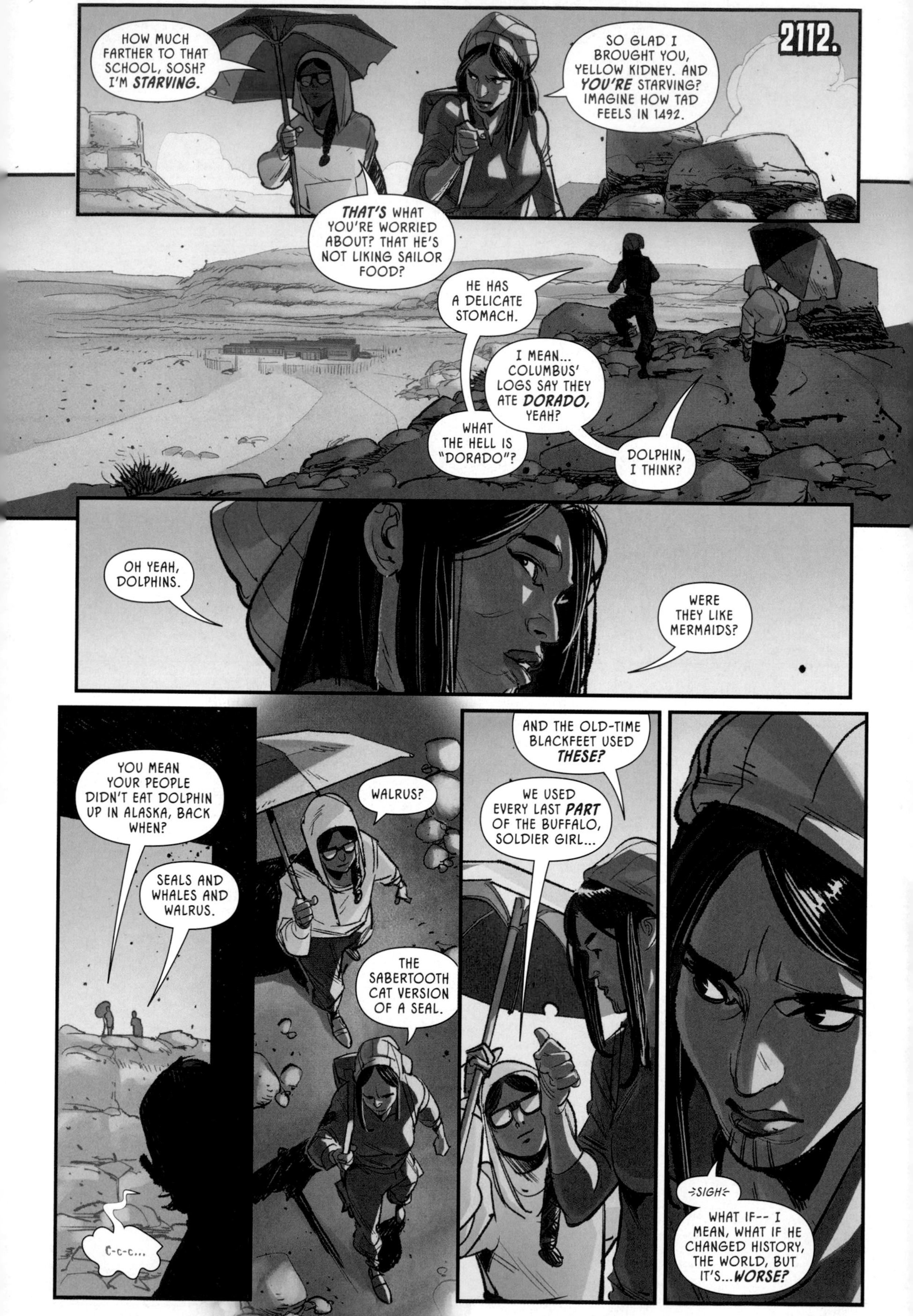

2112.
HOW MUCH FARTHER TO THAT SCHOOL, SOSH? I'M STARVING.
SO GLAD I BROUGHT YOU, YELLOW KIDNEY. AND YOU'RE STARVING? IMAGINE HOW TAD FEELS IN 1492.
THAT'S WHAT YOU'RE WORRIED ABOUT? THAT HE'S NOT LIKING SAILOR FOOD?
HE HAS A DELICATE STOMACH.
I MEAN... COLUMBUS' LOGS SAY THEY ATE DORADO, YEAH?
WHAT THE HELL IS "DORADO"?
DOLPHIN, I THINK?
OH YEAH, DOLPHINS.
WERE THEY LIKE MERMAIDS?
YOU MEAN YOUR PEOPLE DIDN'T EAT DOLPHIN UP IN ALASKA, BACK WHEN?
SEALS AND WHALES AND WALRUS.
C-C-C...
WALRUS?
THE SABERTOOTH CAT VERSION OF A SEAL.
AND THE OLD-TIME BLACKFEET USED THESE?
WE USED EVERY LAST PART OF THE BUFFALO, SOLDIER GIRL...
SIGH
WHAT IF-- I MEAN, WHAT IF HE CHANGED HISTORY, THE WORLD, BUT IT'S...WORSE?

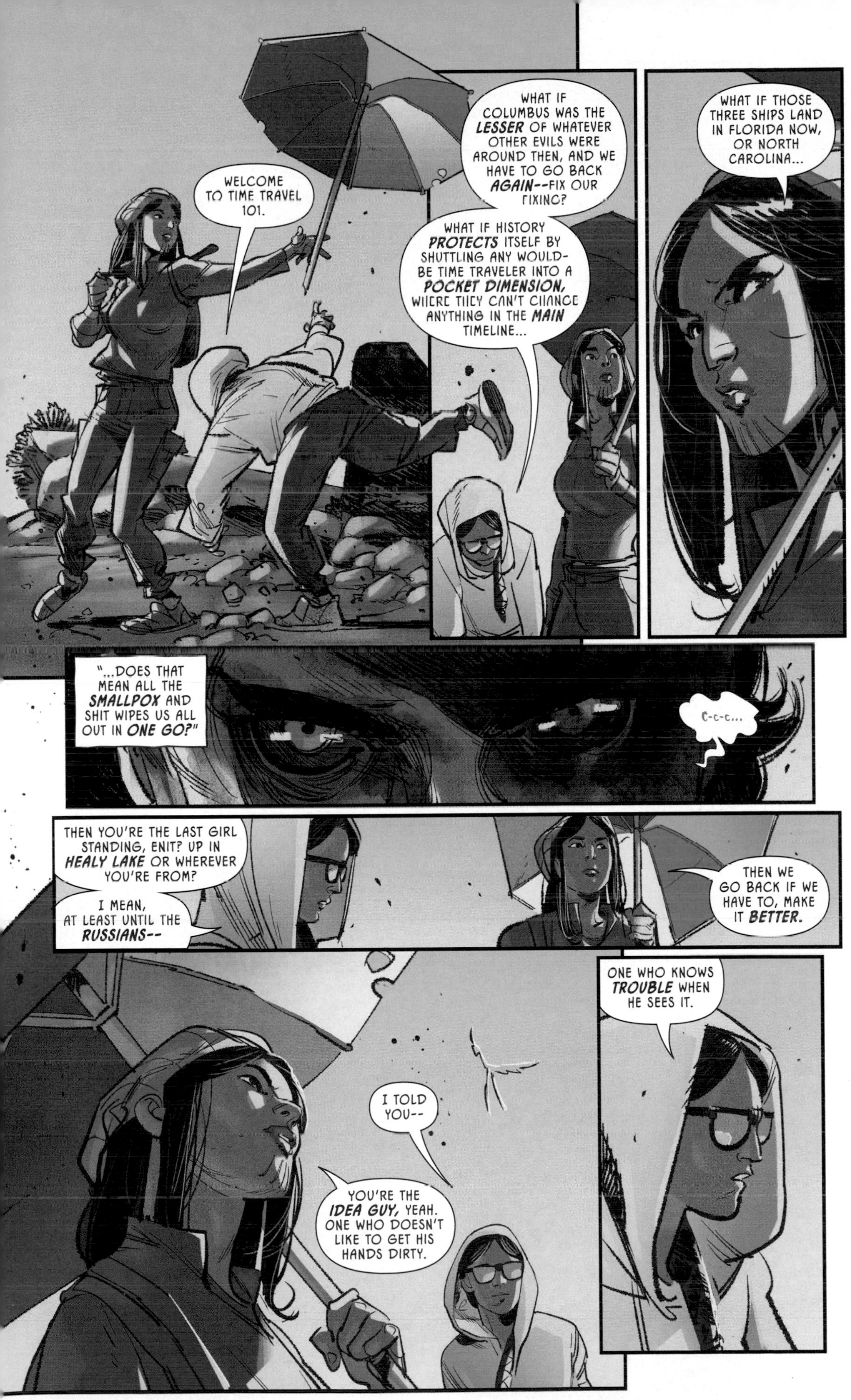
WELCOME TO TIME TRAVEL 101.
WHAT IF COLUMBUS WAS THE LESSER OF WHATEVER OTHER EVILS WERE AROUND THEN, AND WE HAVE TO GO BACK AGAIN--FIX OUR FIXING?
WHAT IF HISTORY PROTECTS ITSELF BY SHUTTLING ANY WOULD-BE TIME TRAVELER INTO A POCKET DIMENSION, WHERE THEY CAN'T CHANGE ANYTHING IN THE MAIN TIMELINE...
WHAT IF THOSE THREE SHIPS LAND IN FLORIDA NOW, OR NORTH CAROLINA...
"...DOES THAT MEAN ALL THE SMALLPOX AND SHIT WIPES US ALL OUT IN ONE GO?"
C-C-C...
THEN YOU'RE THE LAST GIRL STANDING, ENIT? UP IN HEALY LAKE OR WHEREVER YOU'RE FROM?
I MEAN, AT LEAST UNTIL THE RUSSIANS--
THEN WE GO BACK IF WE HAVE TO, MAKE IT BETTER.
I TOLD YOU--
YOU'RE THE IDEA GUY, YEAH. ONE WHO DOESN'T LIKE TO GET HIS HANDS DIRTY.
ONE WHO KNOWS TROUBLE WHEN HE SEES IT.

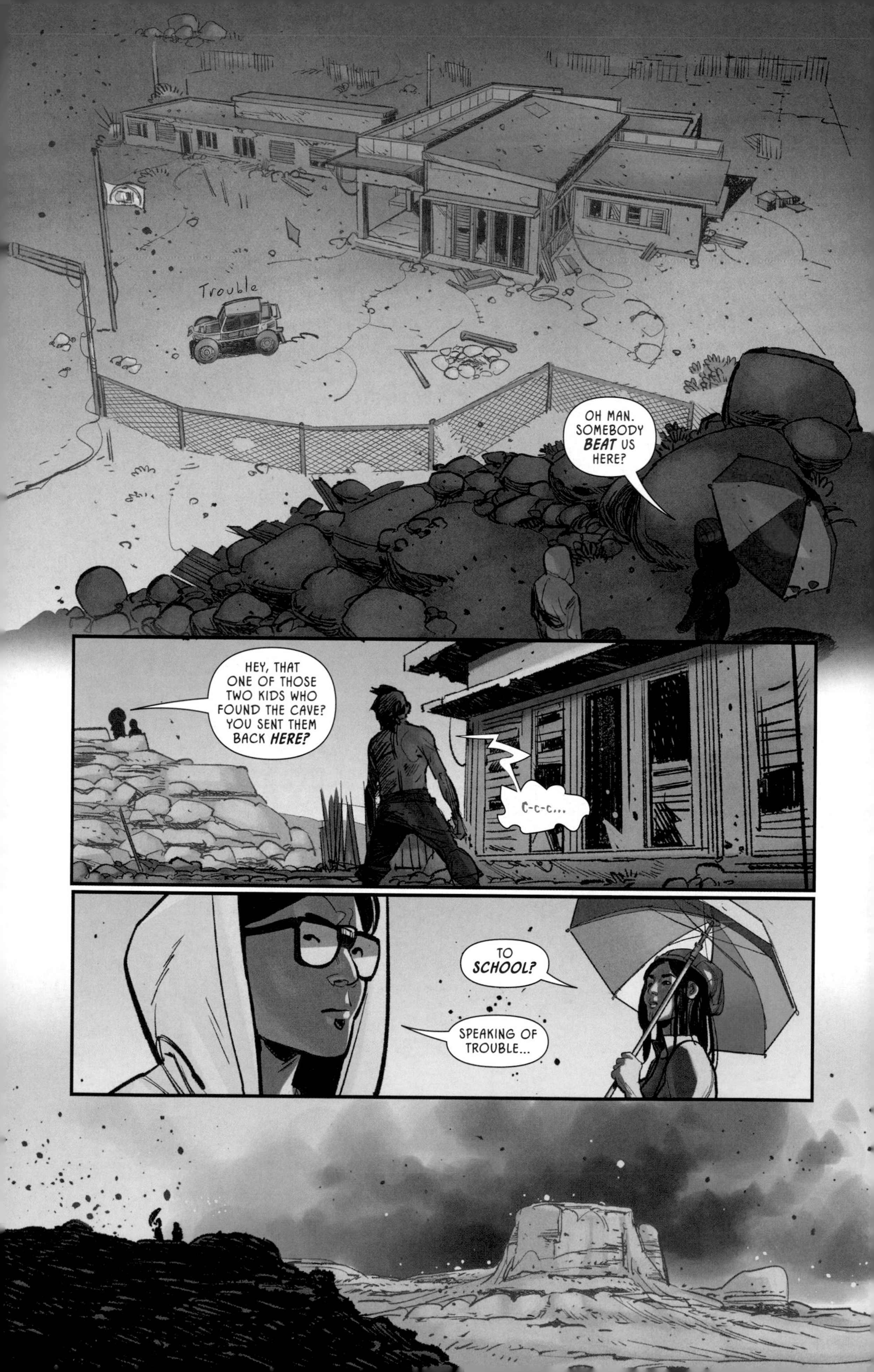
Trouble
OH MAN. SOMEBODY BEAT US HERE?
HEY, THAT ONE OF THOSE TWO KIDS WHO FOUND THE CAVE? YOU SENT THEM BACK HERE?
C-c-c...
TO SCHOOL?
SPEAKING OF TROUBLE...

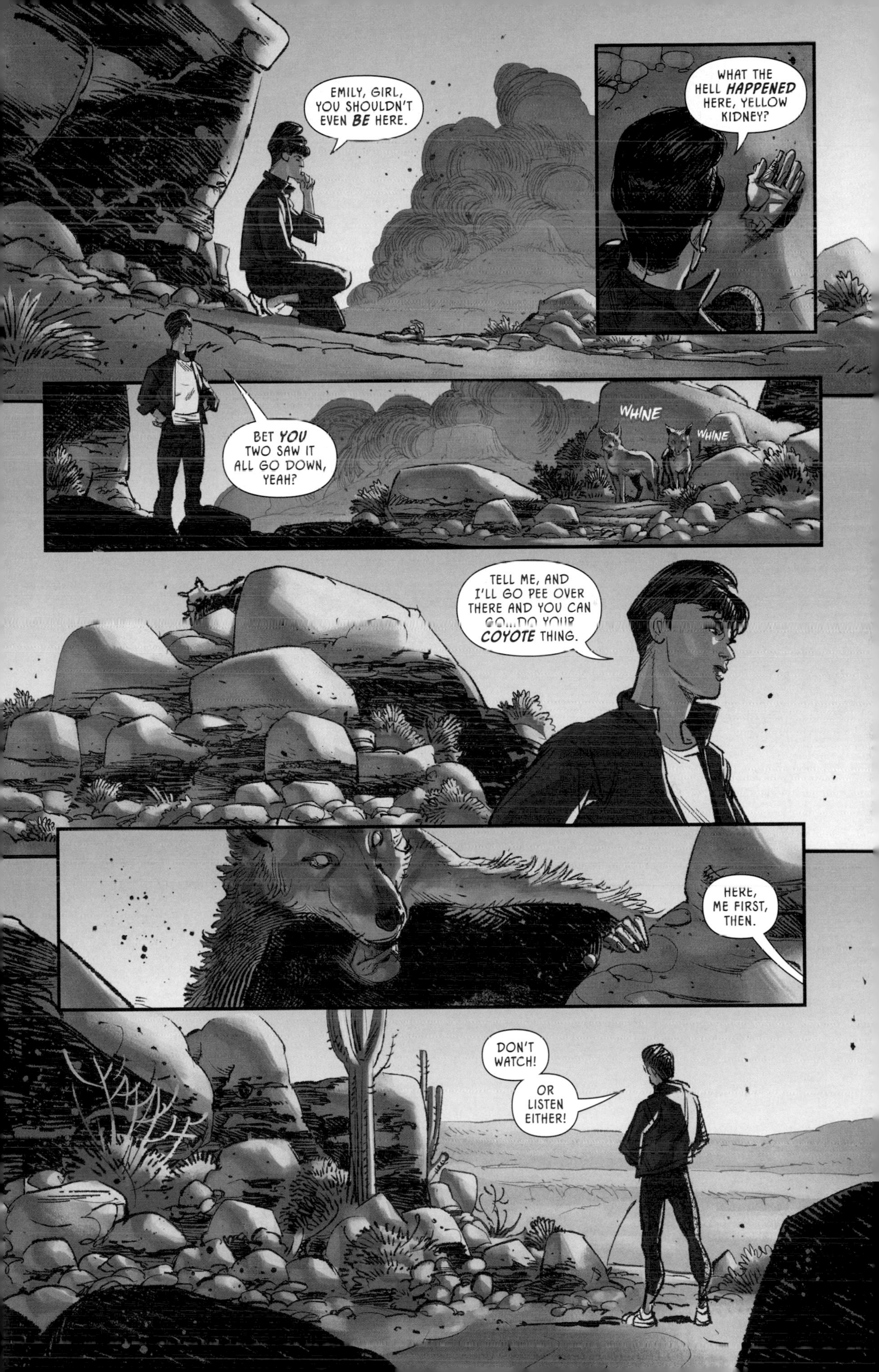
EMILY, GIRL, YOU SHOULDN'T EVEN BE HERE.
WHAT THE HELL HAPPENED HERE, YELLOW KIDNEY?
BET YOU TWO SAW IT ALL GO DOWN, YEAH?
WHINE
WHINE
TELL ME, AND I'LL GO PEE OVER THERE AND YOU CAN GO...DO YOUR COYOTE THING.
HERE, ME FIRST, THEN.
DON'T WATCH!
OR LISTEN EITHER!

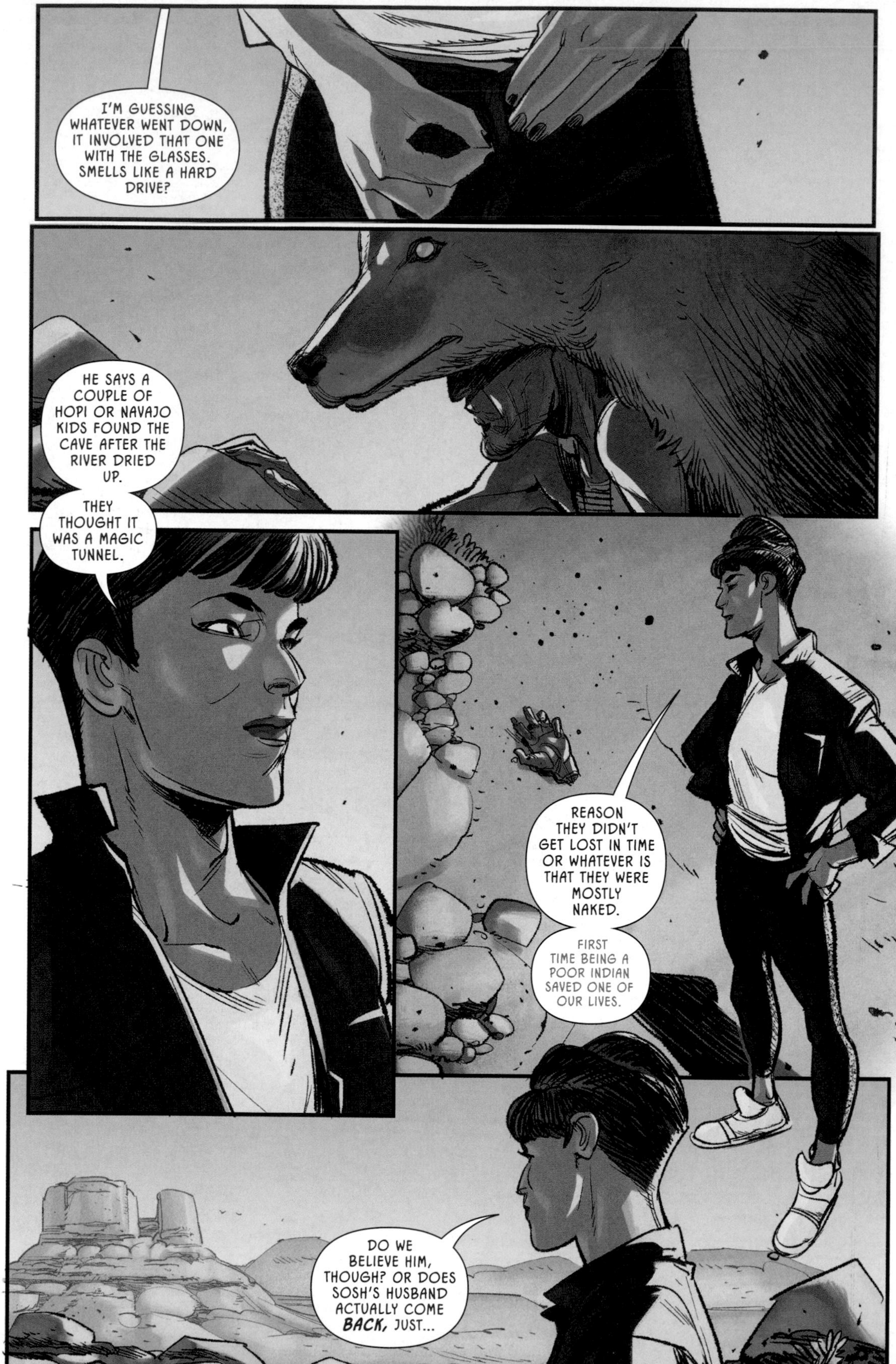
I'M GUESSING WHATEVER WENT DOWN, IT INVOLVED THAT ONE WITH THE GLASSES. SMELLS LIKE A HARD DRIVE?
HE SAYS A COUPLE OF HOPI OR NAVAJO KIDS FOUND THE CAVE AFTER THE RIVER DRIED UP.
THEY THOUGHT IT WAS A MAGIC TUNNEL.
REASON THEY DIDN'T GET LOST IN TIME OR WHATEVER IS THAT THEY WERE MOSTLY NAKED.
FIRST TIME BEING A POOR INDIAN SAVED ONE OF OUR LIVES.
DO WE BELIEVE HIM, THOUGH? OR DOES SOSH'S HUSBAND ACTUALLY COME **BACK,** JUST...

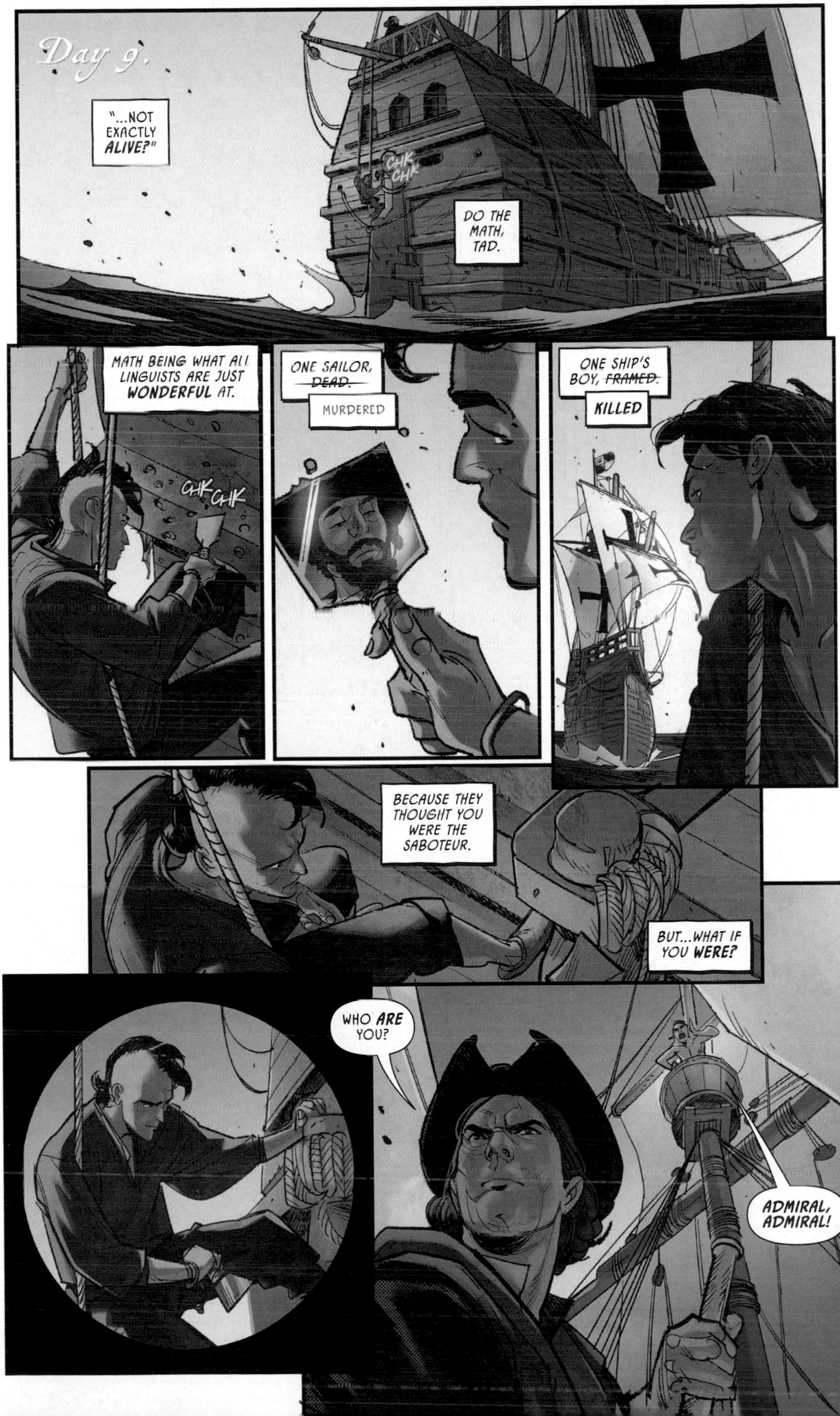
Day 9.
"...NOT EXACTLY ALIVE?"
CHK CHK
DO THE MATH, TAD.
MATH BEING WHAT ALL LINGUISTS ARE JUST WONDERFUL AT.
CHK CHK
ONE SAILOR, DEAD.
MURDERED
ONE SHIP'S BOY, FRAMED.
KILLED
BECAUSE THEY THOUGHT YOU WERE THE SABOTEUR.
BUT...WHAT IF YOU WERE?
WHO ARE YOU?
ADMIRAL, ADMIRAL!

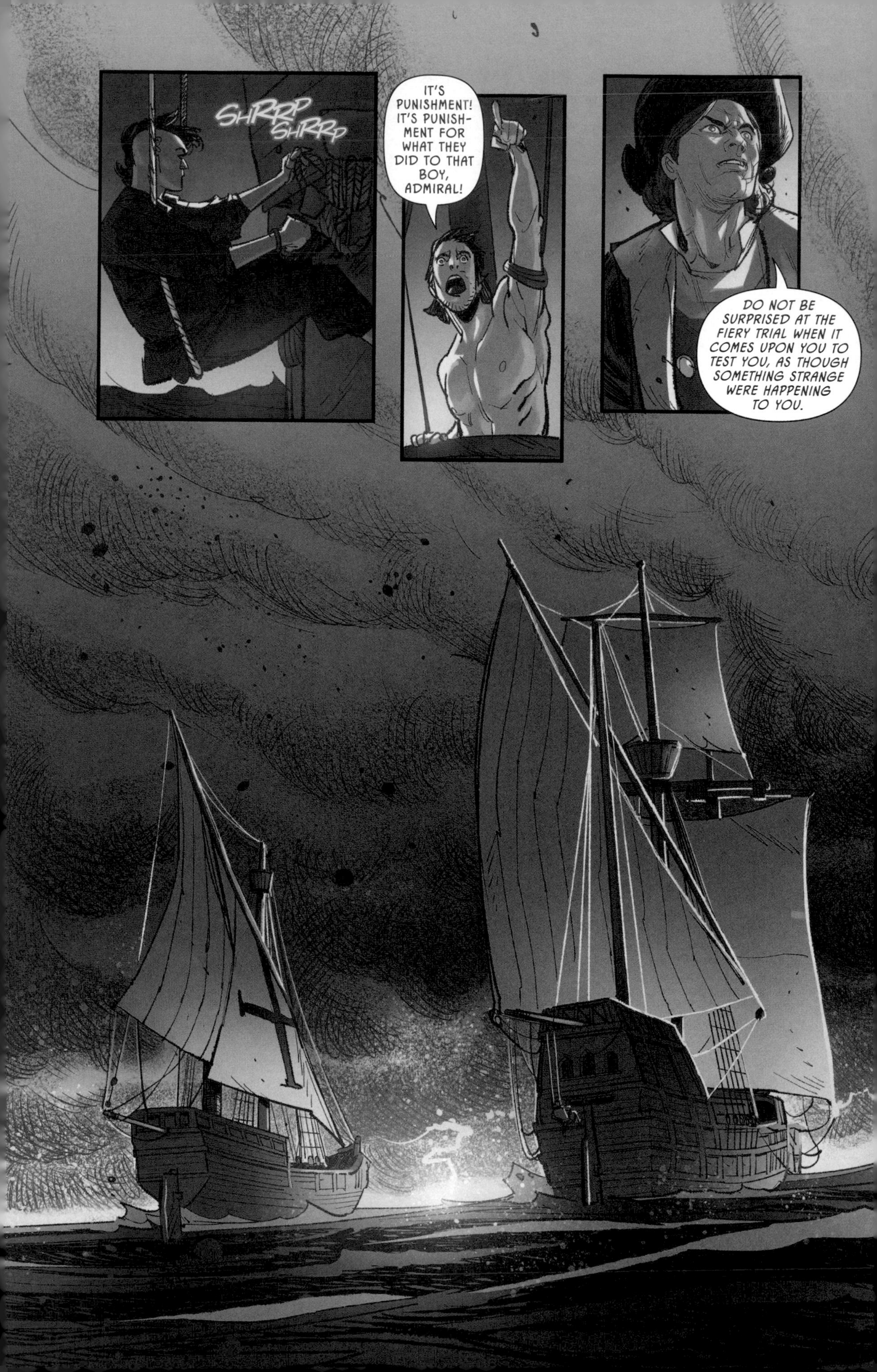
SHRRP SHRRP
IT'S PUNISHMENT! IT'S PUNISHMENT FOR WHAT THEY DID TO THAT BOY, ADMIRAL!
DO NOT BE SURPRISED AT THE FIERY TRIAL WHEN IT COMES UPON YOU TO TEST YOU, AS THOUGH SOMETHING STRANGE WERE HAPPENING TO YOU.

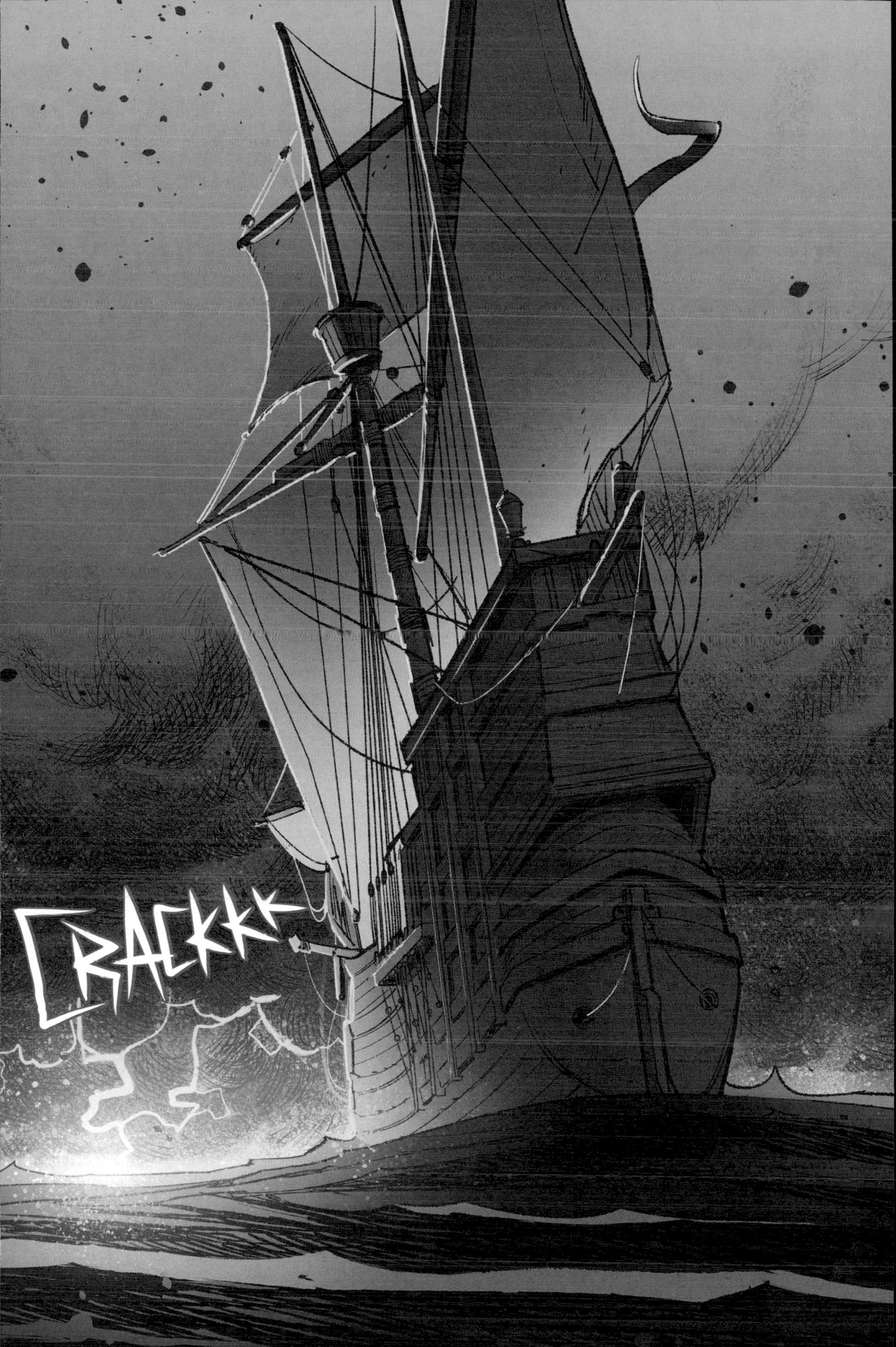
CRACKKK

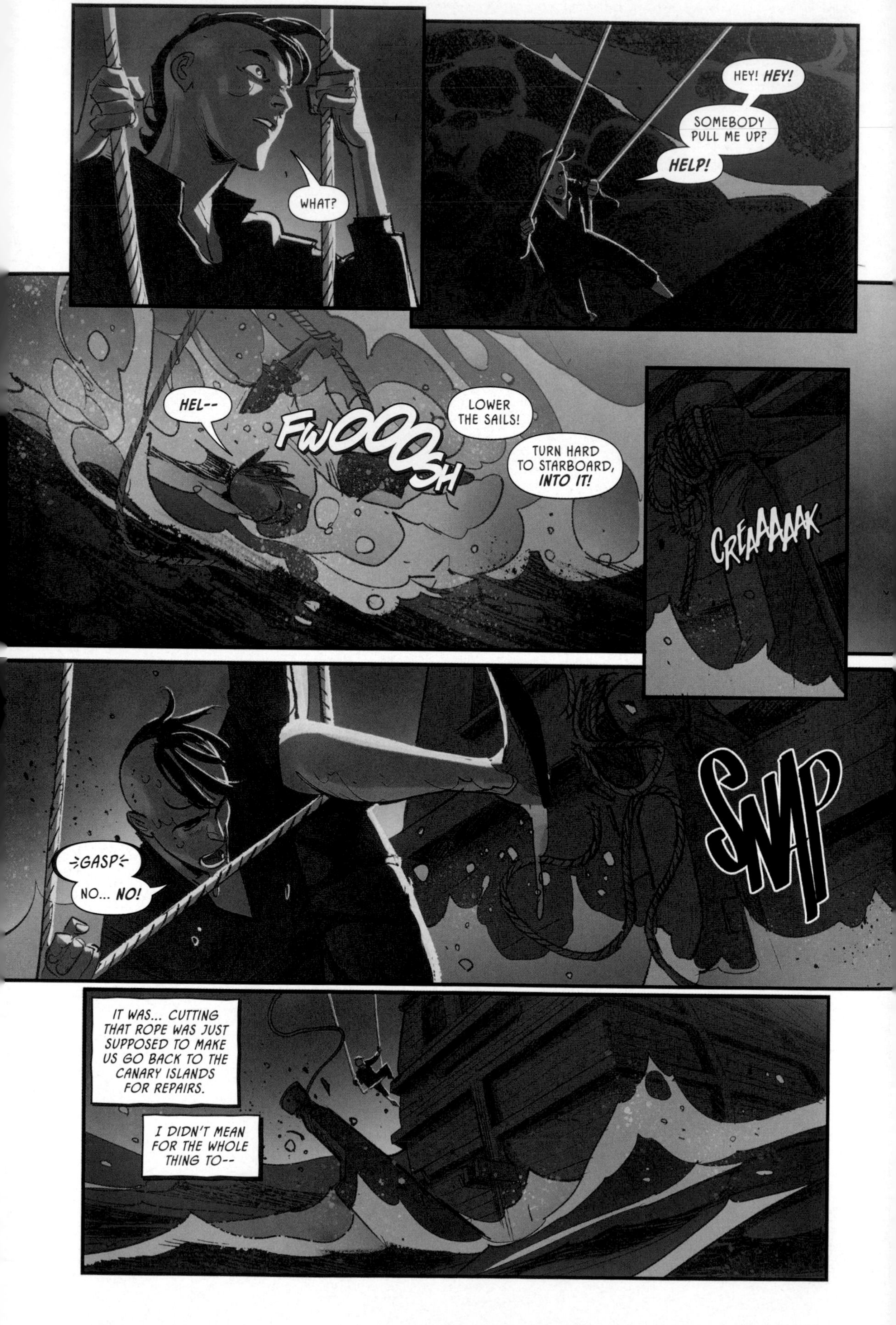

WHAT?
HEY! **HEY!**
SOMEBODY PULL ME UP?
HELP!
HEL--
FWOOOOSH
LOWER THE SAILS!
TURN HARD TO STARBOARD, **INTO IT!**
CREAAAAAK
SNAP
GASP
NO... **NO!**
IT WAS... CUTTING THAT ROPE WAS JUST SUPPOSED TO MAKE US GO BACK TO THE CANARY ISLANDS FOR REPAIRS.
I DIDN'T MEAN FOR THE WHOLE THING TO--

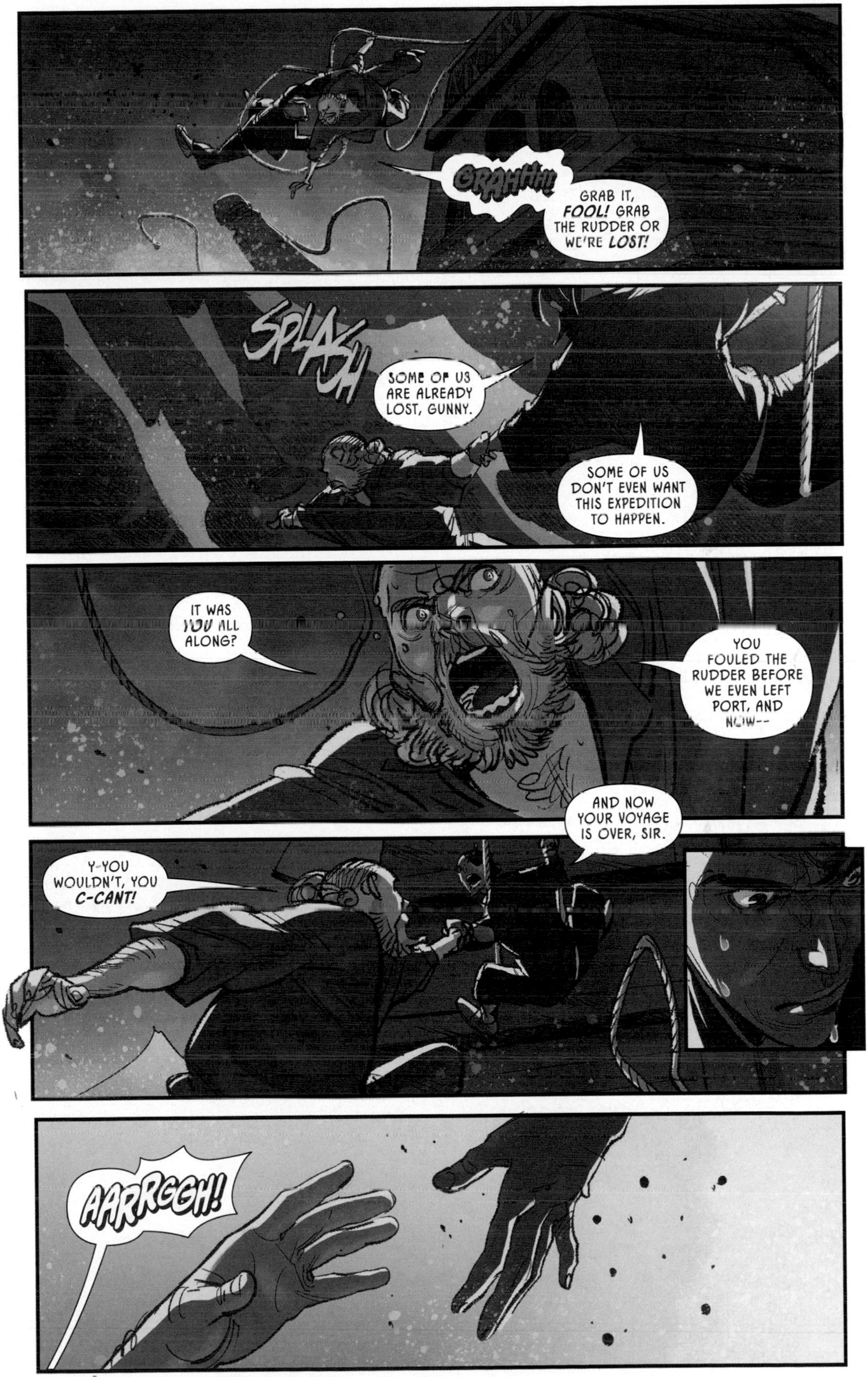
GRAHHH!
GRAB IT, FOOL! GRAB THE RUDDER OR WE'RE LOST!
SPLASH
SOME OF US ARE ALREADY LOST, GUNNY.
SOME OF US DON'T EVEN WANT THIS EXPEDITION TO HAPPEN.
IT WAS YOU ALL ALONG?
YOU FOULED THE RUDDER BEFORE WE EVEN LEFT PORT, AND NOW--
AND NOW YOUR VOYAGE IS OVER, SIR.
Y-YOU WOULDN'T, YOU C-CANT!
AARRGGH!

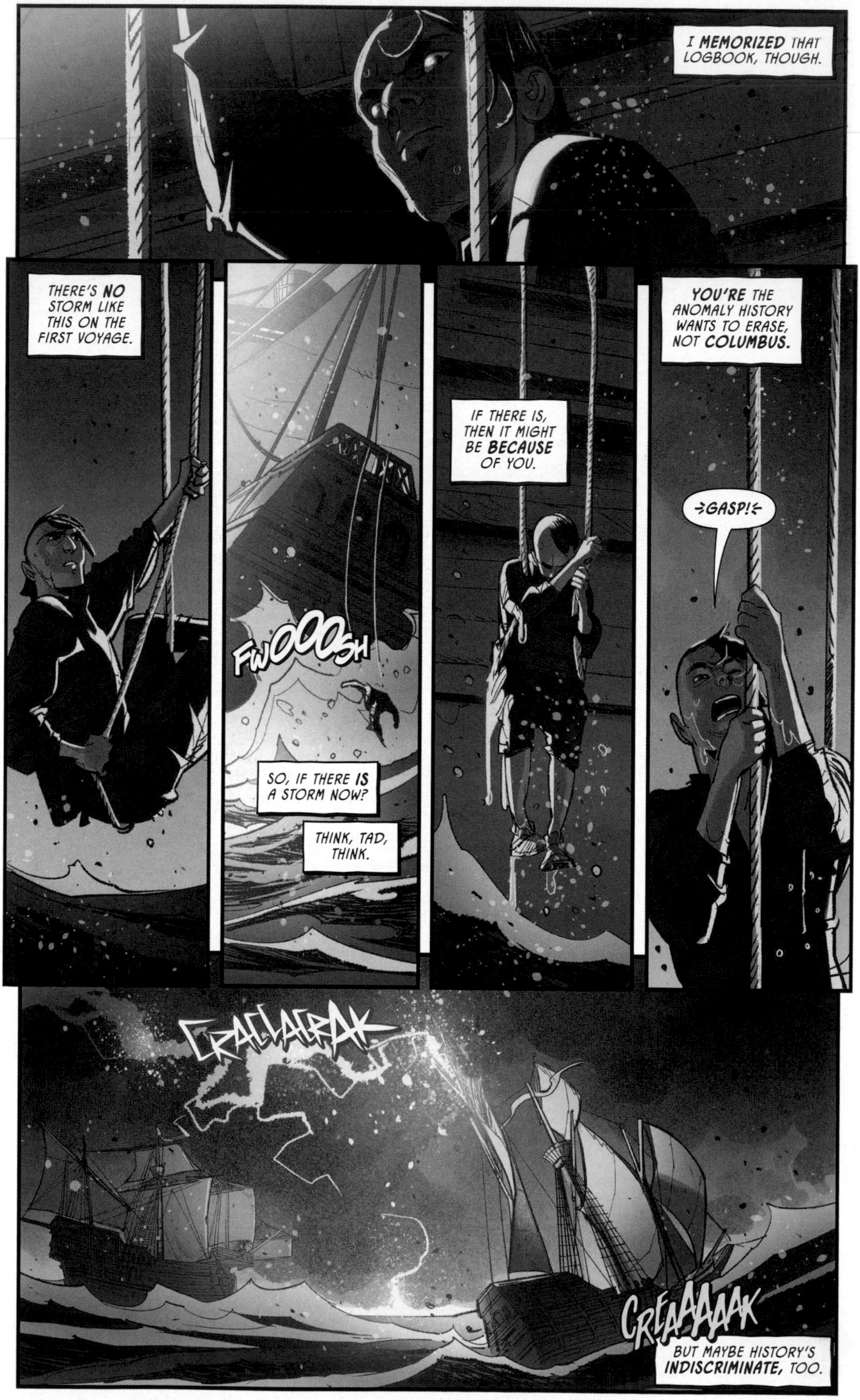

I MEMORIZED THAT LOGBOOK, THOUGH.
THERE'S NO STORM LIKE THIS ON THE FIRST VOYAGE.
FWOOOSH
SO, IF THERE IS A STORM NOW?
THINK, TAD, THINK.
IF THERE IS, THEN IT MIGHT BE BECAUSE OF YOU.
YOU'RE THE ANOMALY HISTORY WANTS TO ERASE, NOT COLUMBUS.
GASP!
CRACKACRAK
CREAAAAAK
BUT MAYBE HISTORY'S INDISCRIMINATE, TOO.

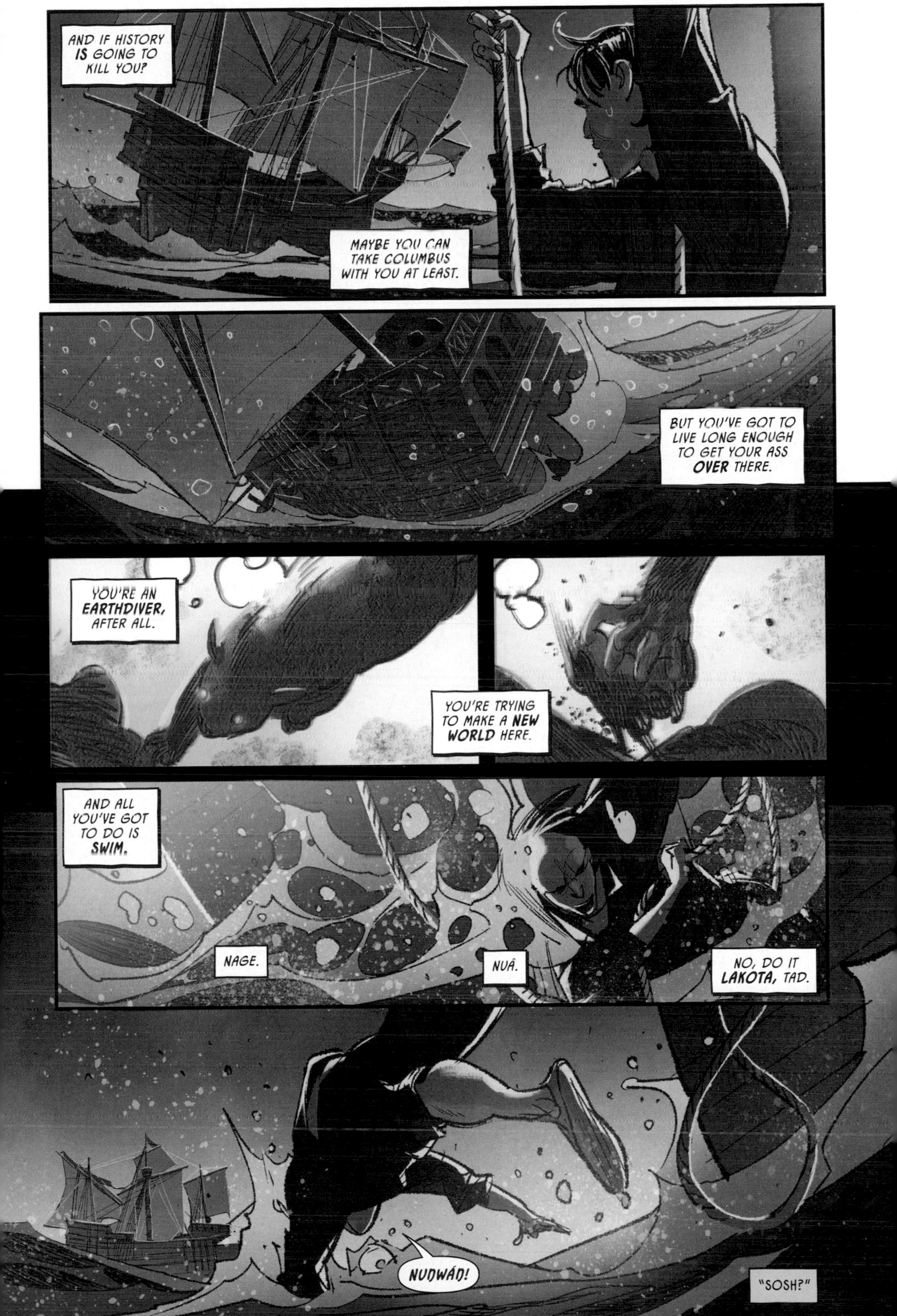
AND IF HISTORY IS GOING TO KILL YOU?
MAYBE YOU CAN TAKE COLUMBUS WITH YOU AT LEAST.
BUT YOU'VE GOT TO LIVE LONG ENOUGH TO GET YOUR ASS OVER THERE.
YOU'RE AN EARTHDIVER, AFTER ALL.
YOU'RE TRYING TO MAKE A NEW WORLD HERE.
AND ALL YOU'VE GOT TO DO IS SWIM.
NAGE.
NUÁ.
NO, DO IT LAKOTA, TAD.
NUDWÁD!
"SOSH?"

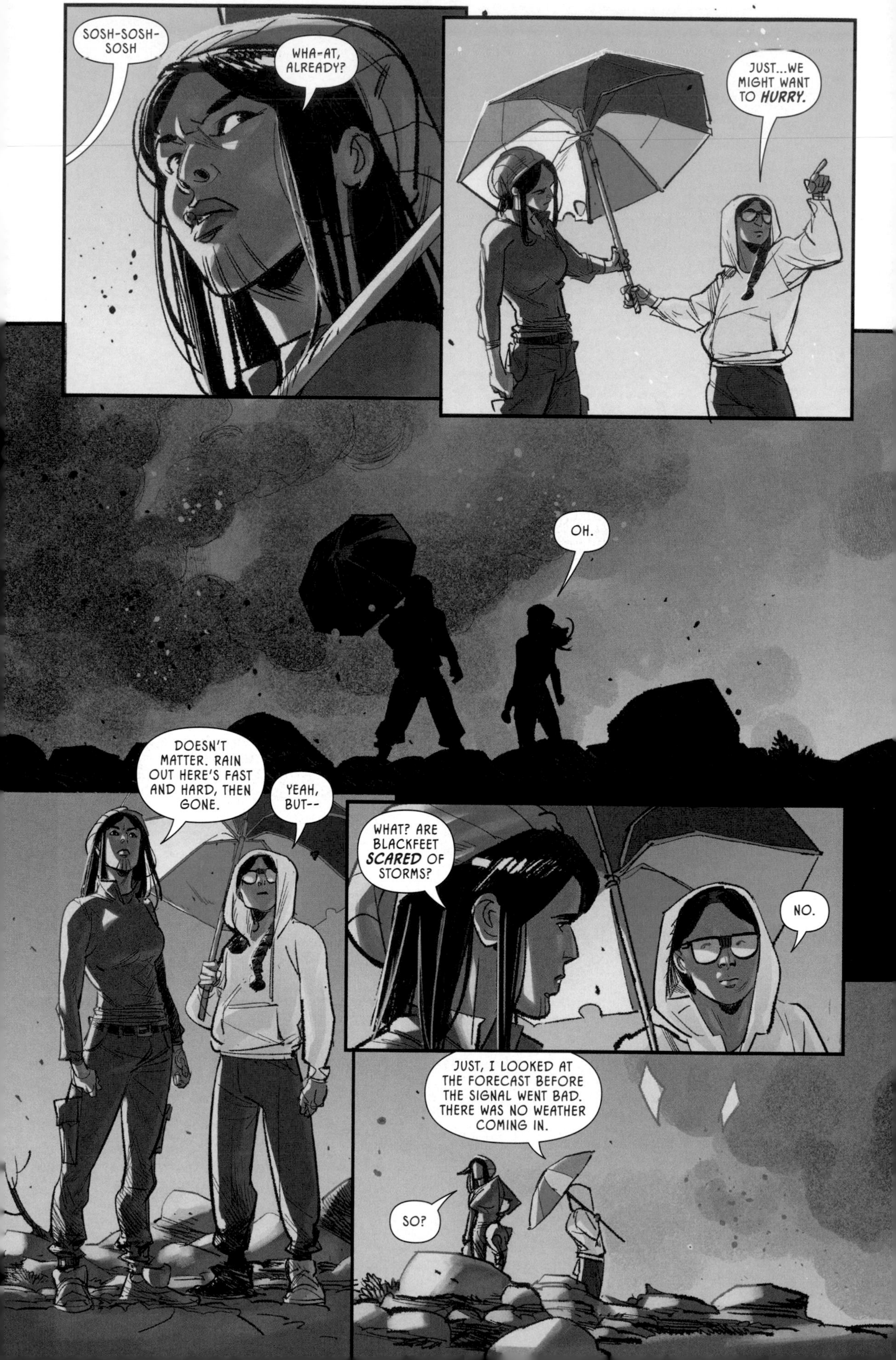
SOSH-SOSH-SOSH
WHA-AT, ALREADY?
JUST...WE MIGHT WANT TO HURRY.
OH.
DOESN'T MATTER. RAIN OUT HERE'S FAST AND HARD, THEN GONE.
YEAH, BUT--
WHAT? ARE BLACKFEET SCARED OF STORMS?
NO.
JUST, I LOOKED AT THE FORECAST BEFORE THE SIGNAL WENT BAD. THERE WAS NO WEATHER COMING IN.
SO?

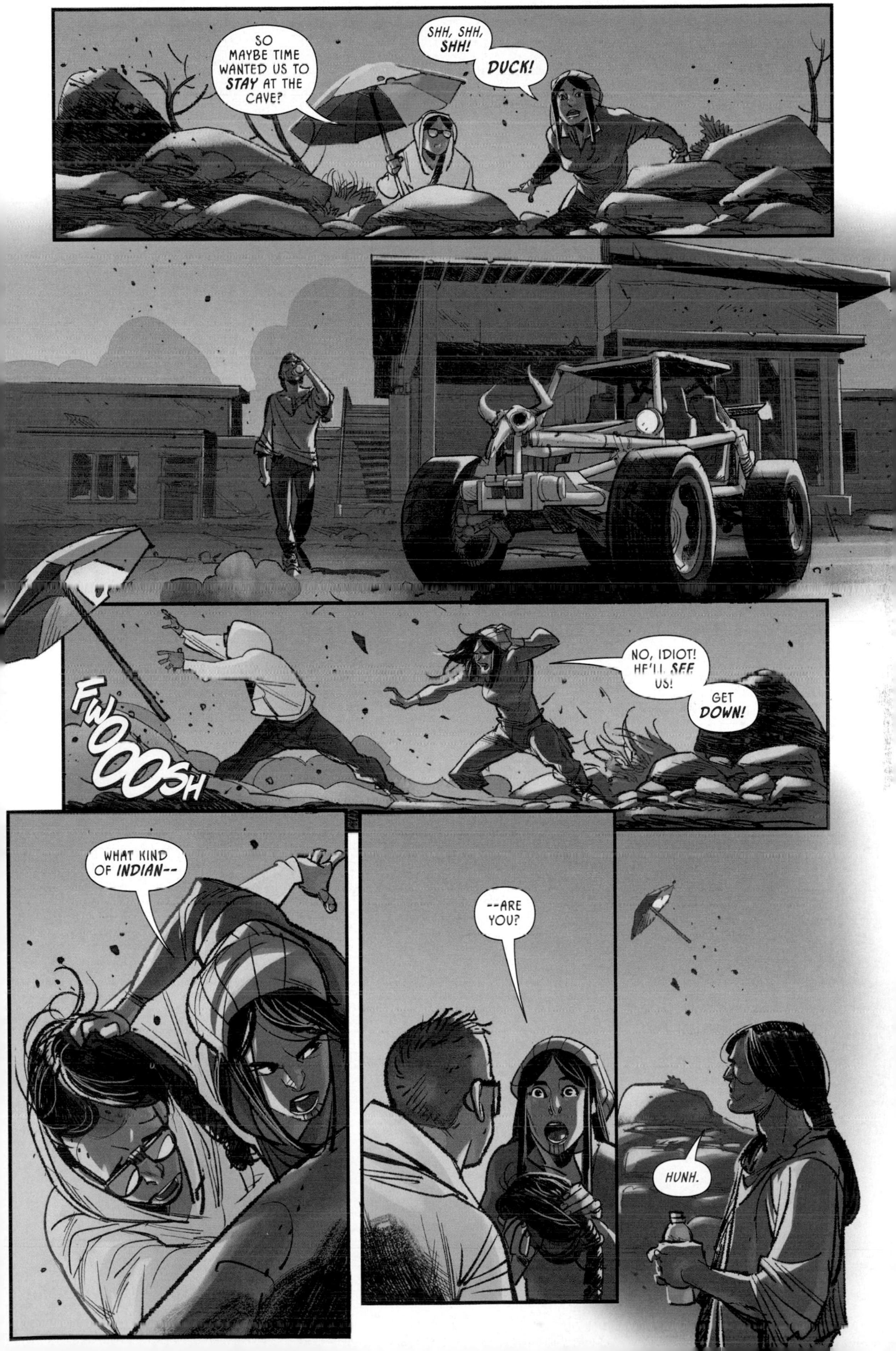
SO MAYBE TIME WANTED US TO STAY AT THE CAVE?
SHH, SHH, SHH!
DUCK!
FWOOOSH
NO, IDIOT! HE'LL SEE US!
GET DOWN!
WHAT KIND OF INDIAN--
--ARE YOU?
HUNH.

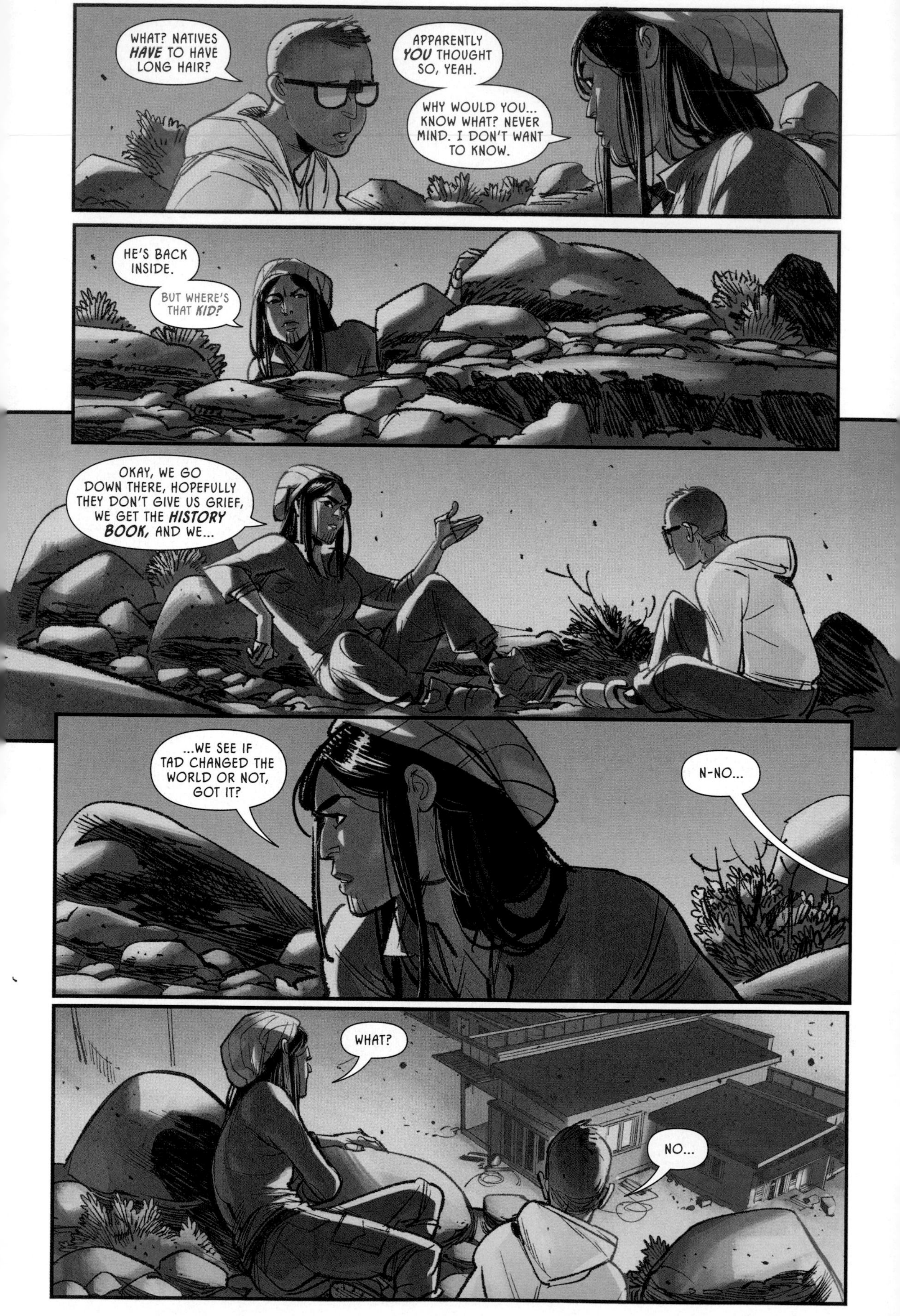
WHAT? NATIVES HAVE TO HAVE LONG HAIR?
APPARENTLY YOU THOUGHT SO, YEAH.
WHY WOULD YOU... KNOW WHAT? NEVER MIND. I DON'T WANT TO KNOW.
HE'S BACK INSIDE.
BUT WHERE'S THAT KID?
OKAY, WE GO DOWN THERE, HOPEFULLY THEY DON'T GIVE US GRIEF, WE GET THE HISTORY BOOK, AND WE...
...WE SEE IF TAD CHANGED THE WORLD OR NOT, GOT IT?
N-NO...
WHAT?
NO...

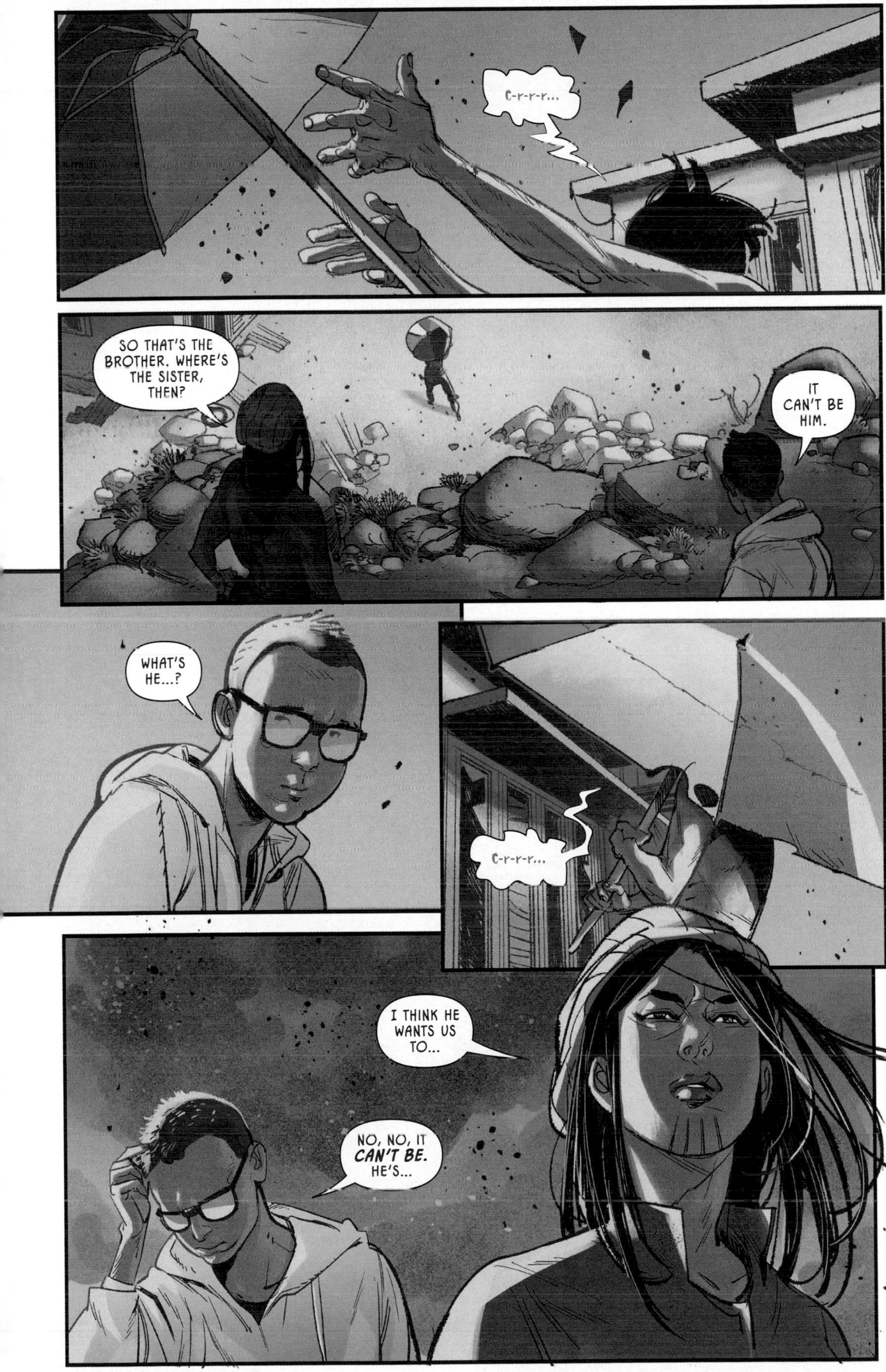
C-r-r-r...
SO THAT'S THE BROTHER. WHERE'S THE SISTER, THEN?
IT CAN'T BE HIM.
WHAT'S HE...?
C-r-r-r...
I THINK HE WANTS US TO...
NO, NO, IT CAN'T BE. HE'S...

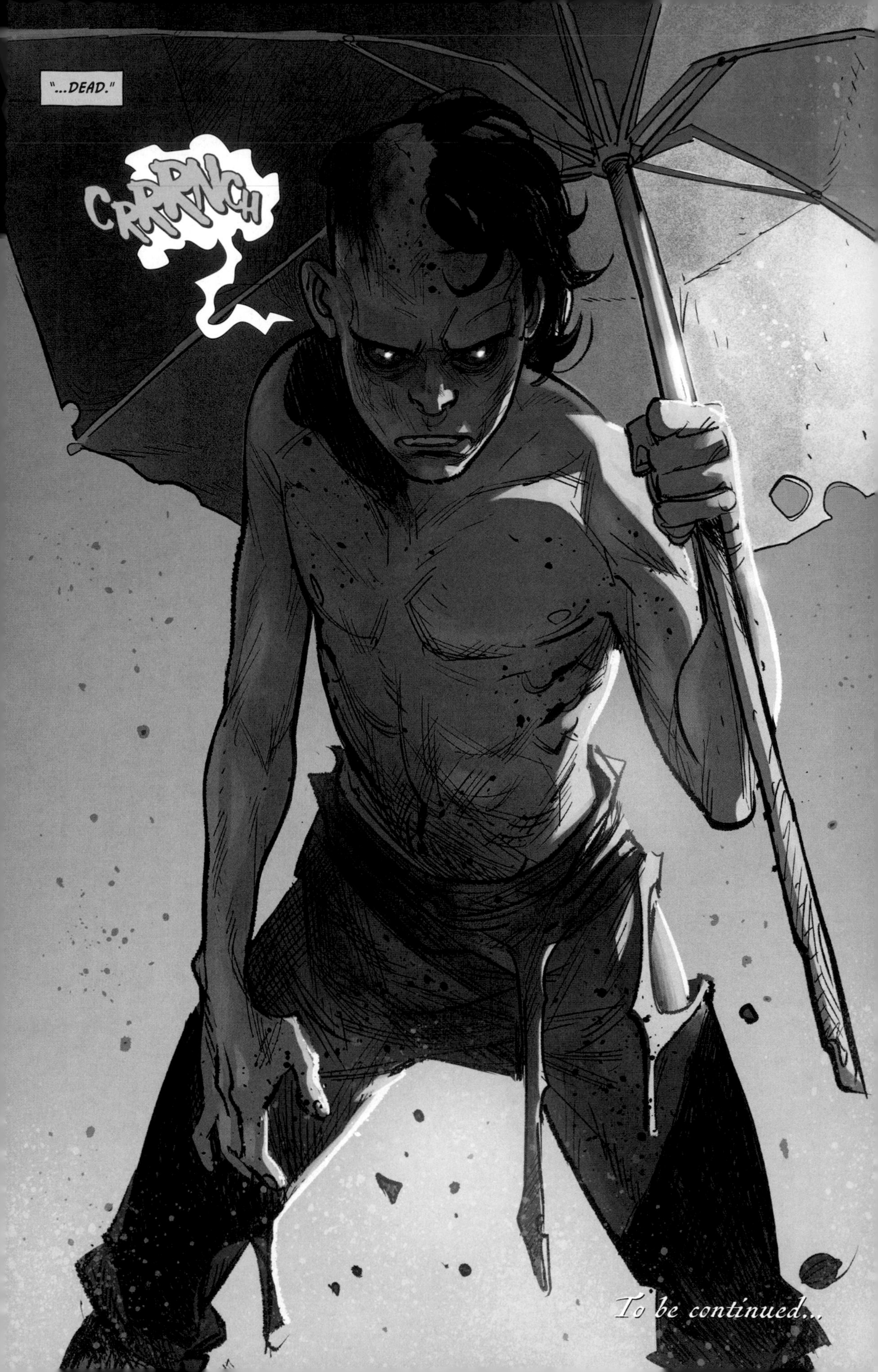
"...DEAD."
CRRRNCH
To be continued...

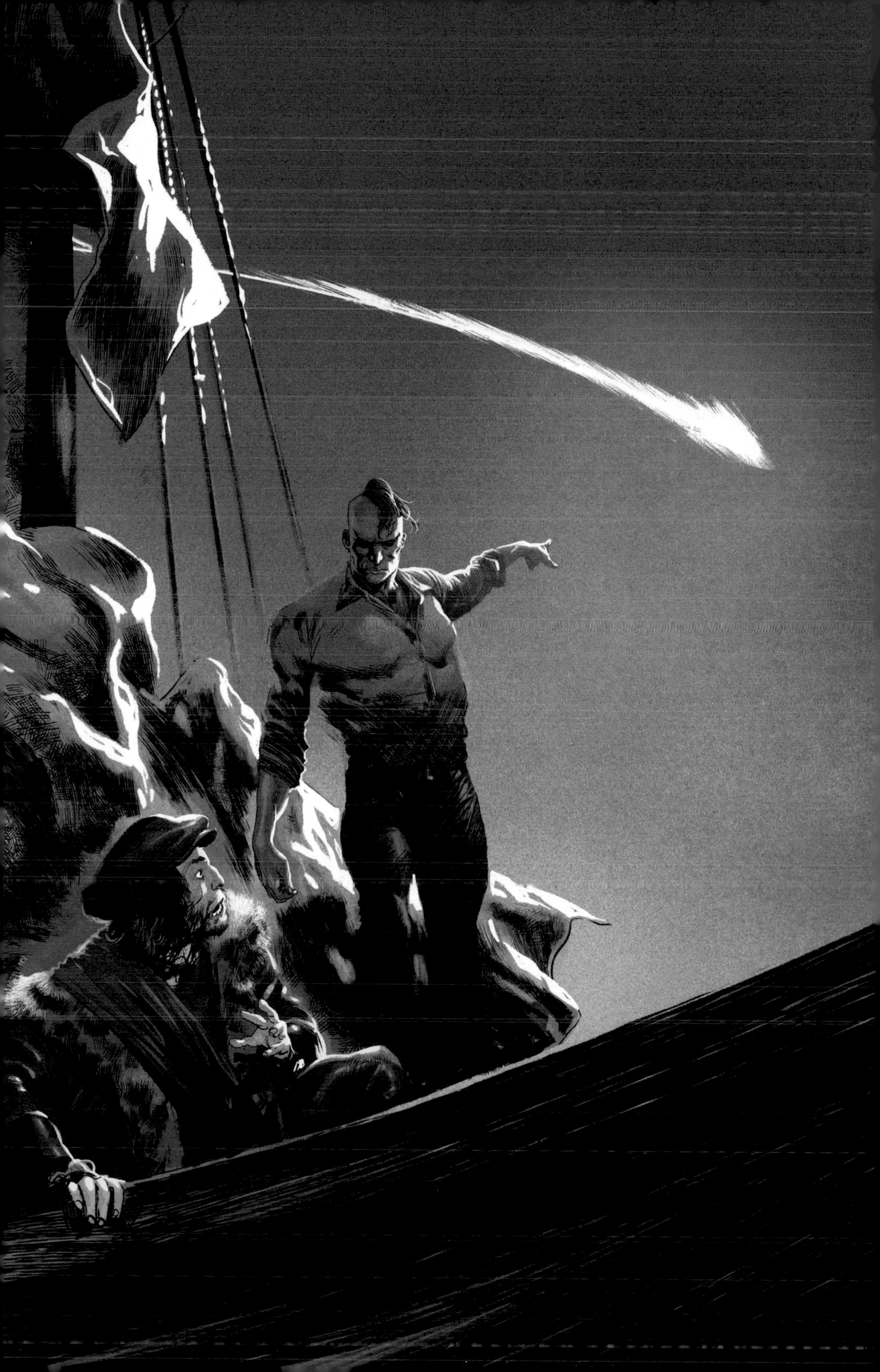

CHAPTER THREE:
Yellow Woman

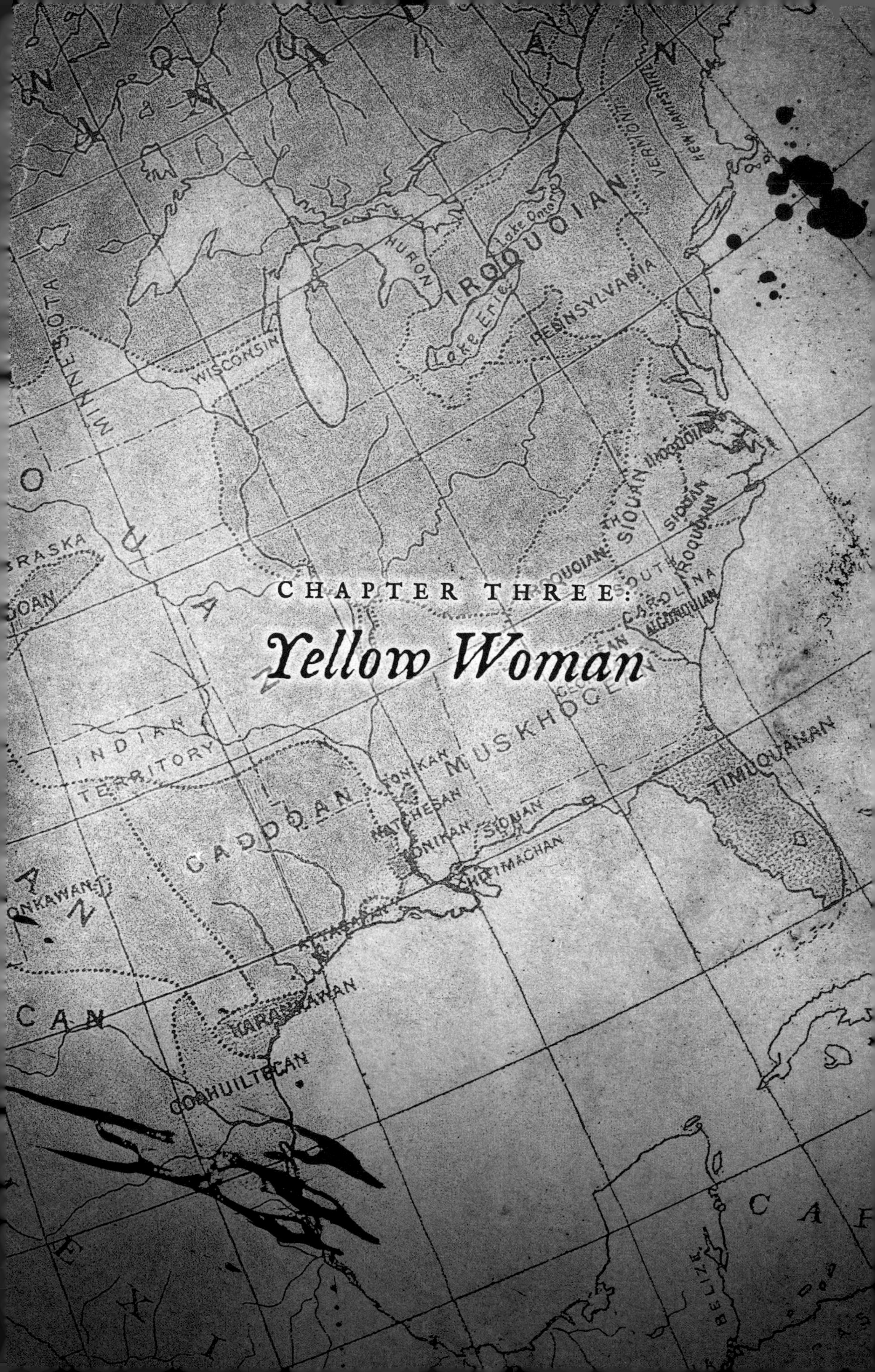

MINNESOTA
WISCONSIN
HURON
Lake Ontario
Lake Erie
IROQUOIAN
PENNSYLVANIA
VERMONT
NEW HAMPSHIRE
SIOUAN
IROQUOIAN
SOUTH CAROLINA
MUSKHOGEAN
INDIAN TERRITORY
CADDOAN
TONIKAN
NATCHESAN
CHITIMACHAN
TIMUQUANAN
COAHUILTECAN
KARANKAWAN
TONKAWAN
BELIZE

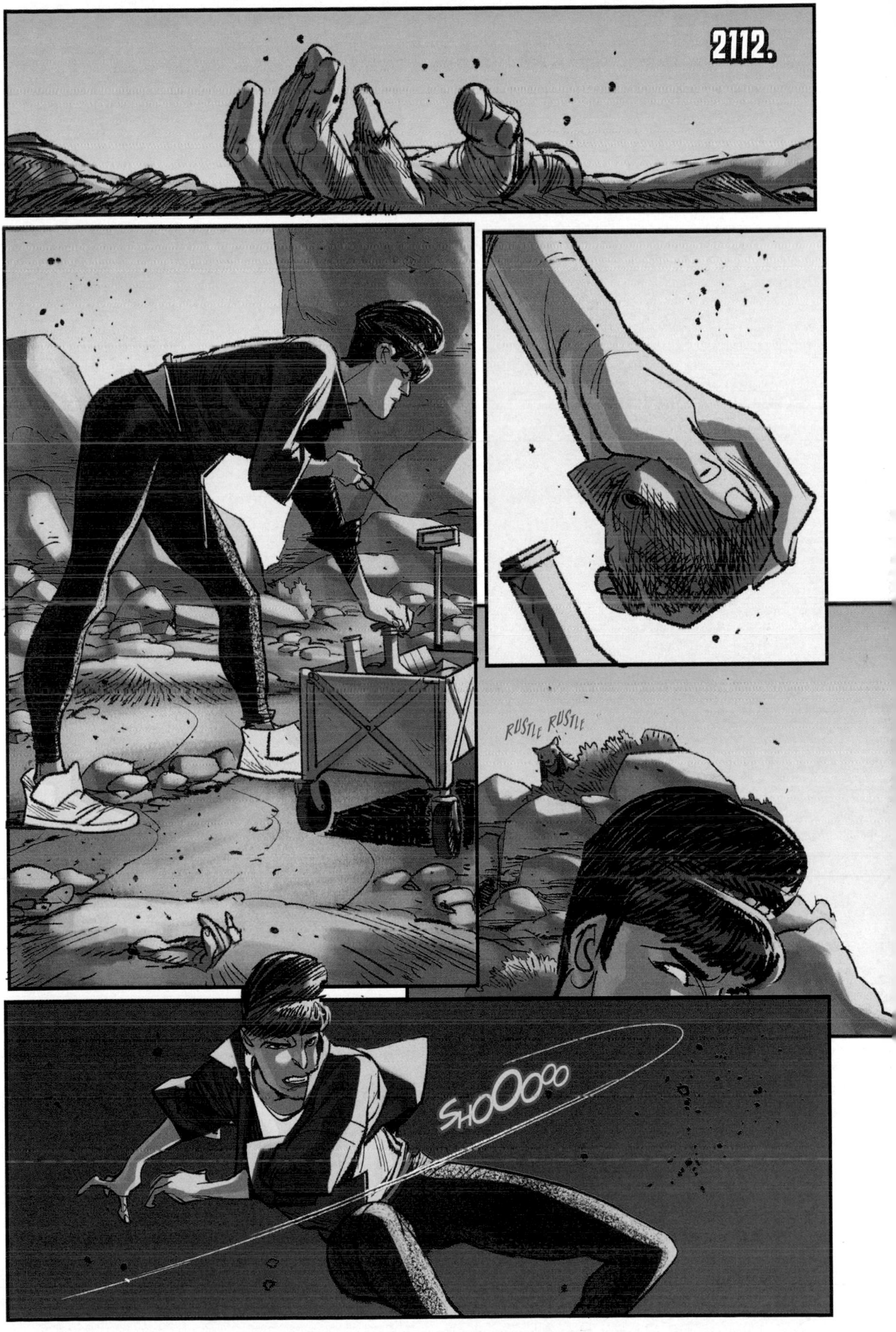
2112.
RUSTLE RUSTLE
SHOOOoo

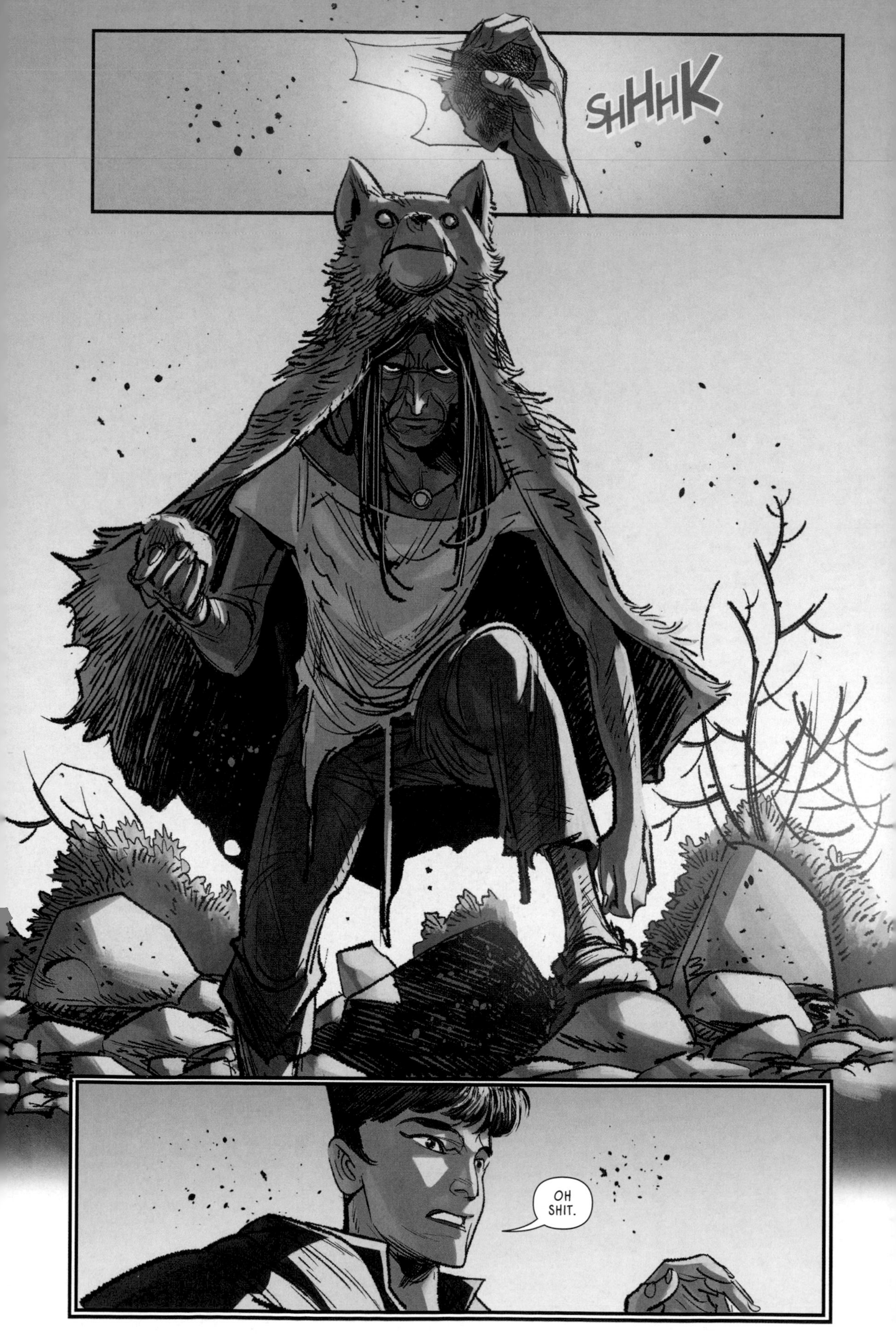
SHHHK
OH SHIT.

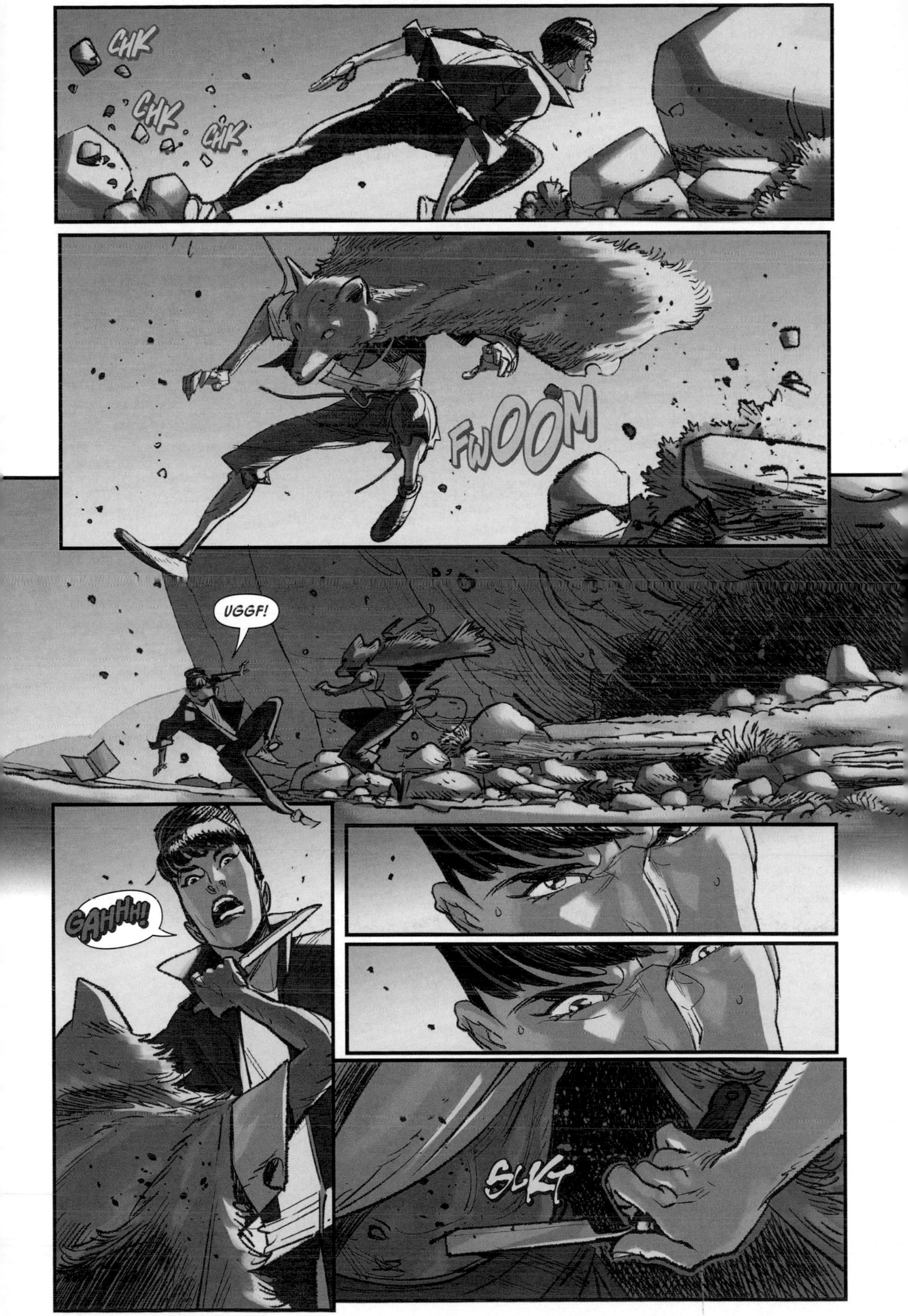
CHK
CHK
CHK
FWOOM
UGGF!
GAHHH!
SLKT

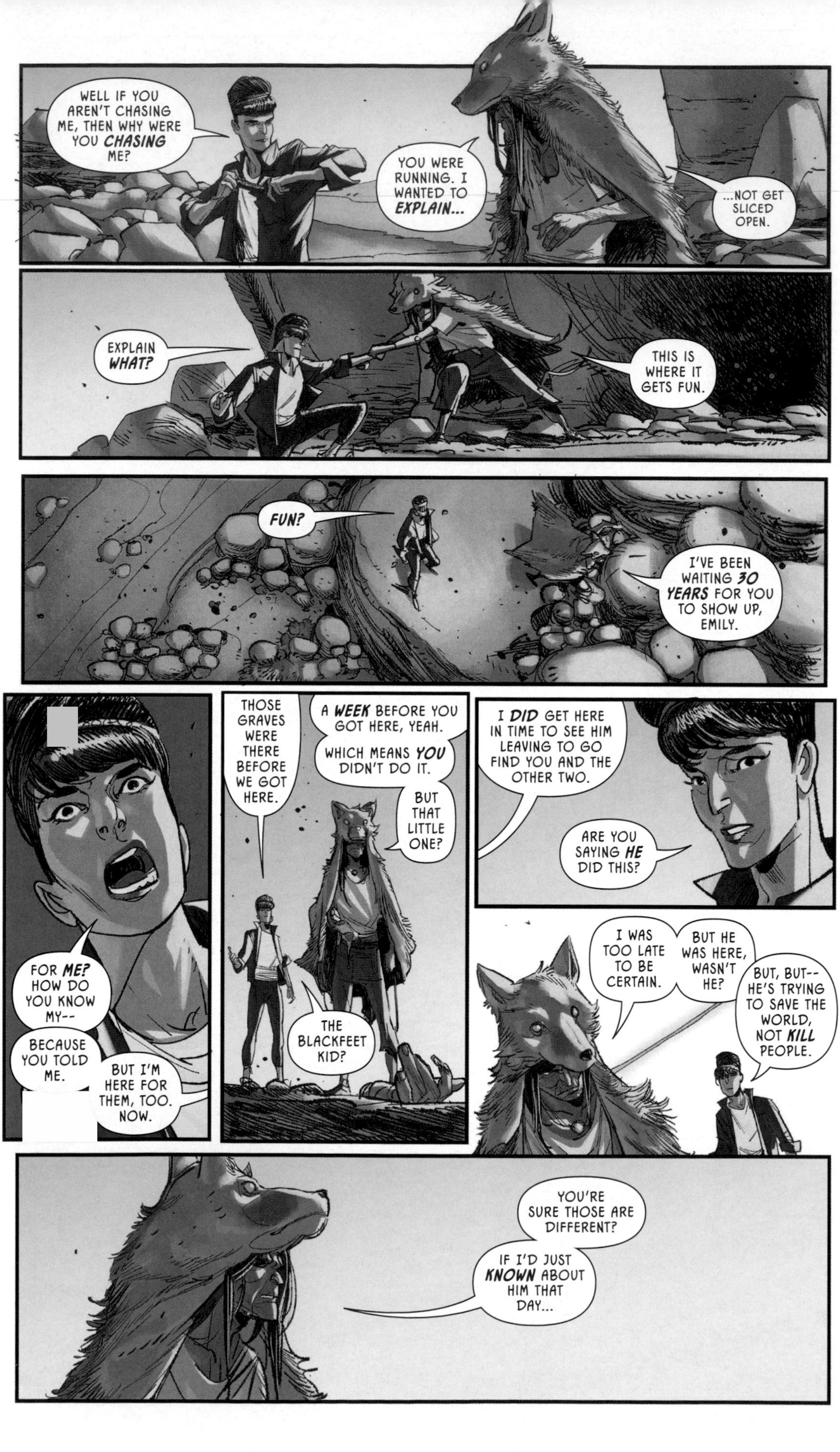
WELL IF YOU AREN'T CHASING ME, THEN WHY WERE YOU CHASING ME?
YOU WERE RUNNING. I WANTED TO EXPLAIN...
...NOT GET SLICED OPEN.
EXPLAIN WHAT?
THIS IS WHERE IT GETS FUN.
FUN?
I'VE BEEN WAITING 30 YEARS FOR YOU TO SHOW UP, EMILY.
FOR ME? HOW DO YOU KNOW MY--
BECAUSE YOU TOLD ME.
BUT I'M HERE FOR THEM, TOO. NOW.
THOSE GRAVES WERE THERE BEFORE WE GOT HERE.
A WEEK BEFORE YOU GOT HERE, YEAH.
WHICH MEANS YOU DIDN'T DO IT.
BUT THAT LITTLE ONE?
THE BLACKFEET KID?
I DID GET HERE IN TIME TO SEE HIM LEAVING TO GO FIND YOU AND THE OTHER TWO.
ARE YOU SAYING HE DID THIS?
I WAS TOO LATE TO BE CERTAIN.
BUT HE WAS HERE, WASN'T HE?
BUT, BUT-- HE'S TRYING TO SAVE THE WORLD, NOT KILL PEOPLE.
YOU'RE SURE THOSE ARE DIFFERENT?
IF I'D JUST KNOWN ABOUT HIM THAT DAY...

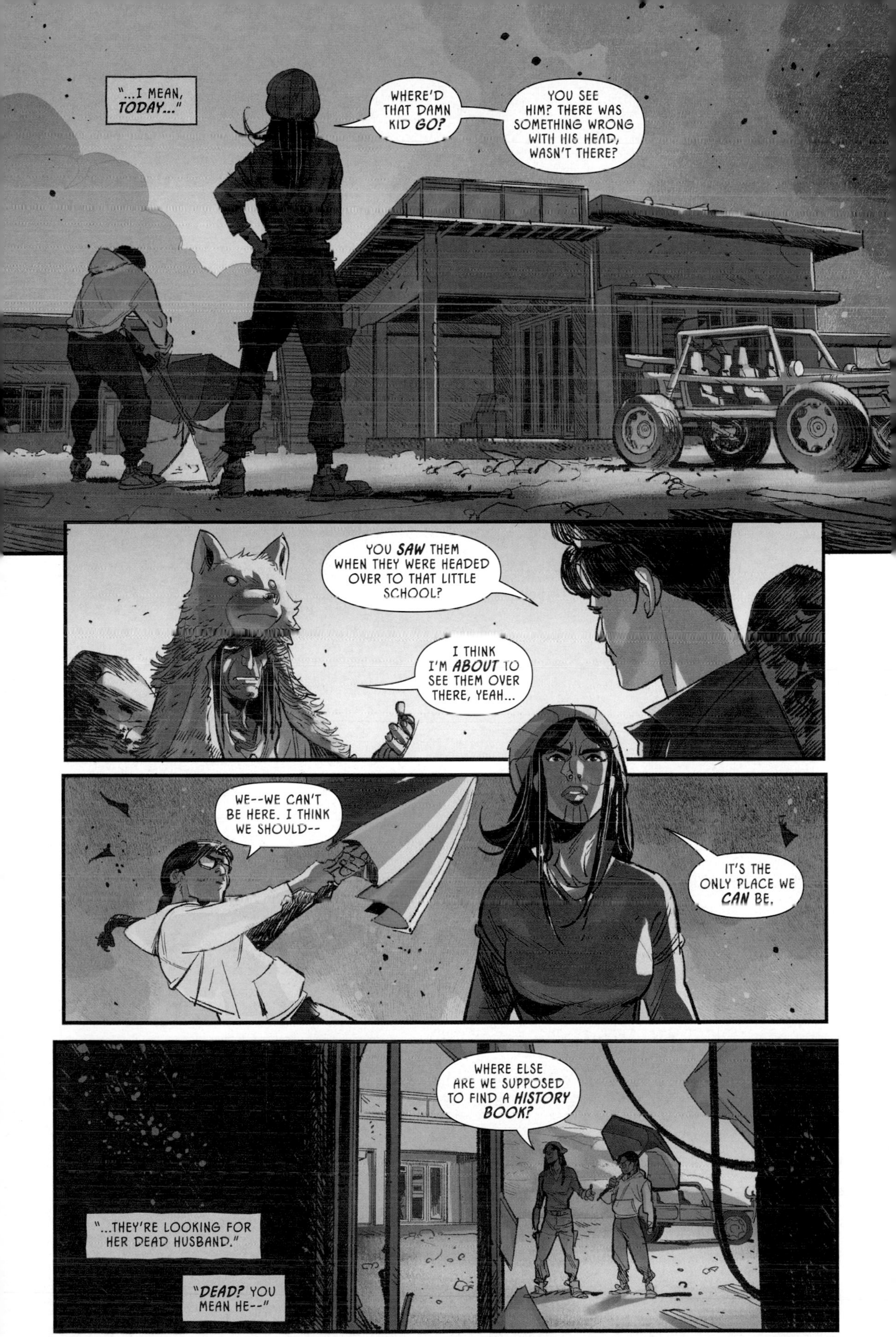
"...I MEAN, TODAY..."
WHERE'D THAT DAMN KID GO?
YOU SEE HIM? THERE WAS SOMETHING WRONG WITH HIS HEAD, WASN'T THERE?
YOU SAW THEM WHEN THEY WERE HEADED OVER TO THAT LITTLE SCHOOL?
I THINK I'M ABOUT TO SEE THEM OVER THERE, YEAH...
WE--WE CAN'T BE HERE. I THINK WE SHOULD--
IT'S THE ONLY PLACE WE CAN BE.
WHERE ELSE ARE WE SUPPOSED TO FIND A HISTORY BOOK?
"...THEY'RE LOOKING FOR HER DEAD HUSBAND."
"DEAD? YOU MEAN HE--"

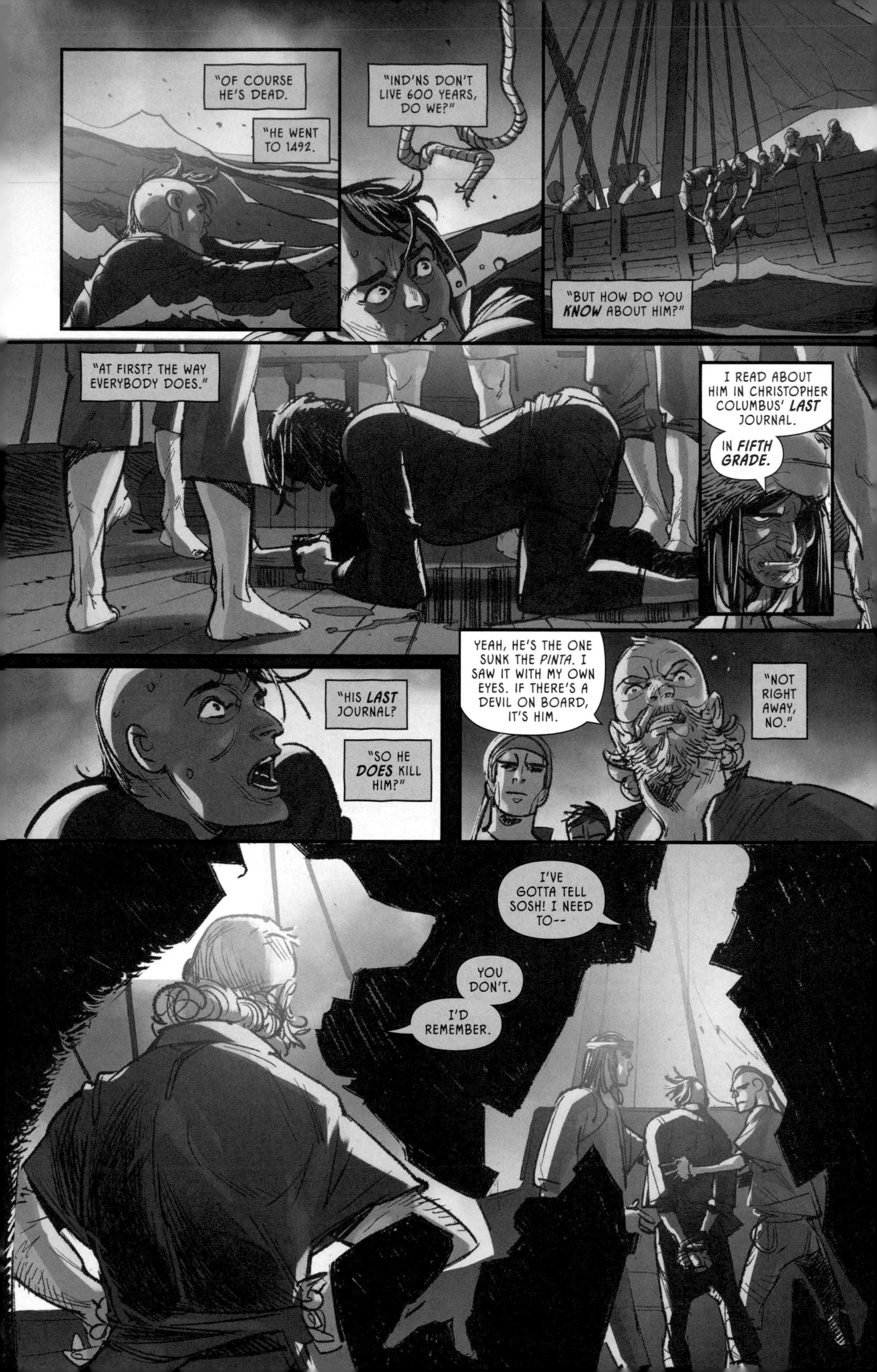
"OF COURSE HE'S DEAD.
"HE WENT TO 1492.
"IND'NS DON'T LIVE 600 YEARS, DO WE?"
"BUT HOW DO YOU KNOW ABOUT HIM?"
"AT FIRST? THE WAY EVERYBODY DOES."
I READ ABOUT HIM IN CHRISTOPHER COLUMBUS' LAST JOURNAL.
IN FIFTH GRADE.
"HIS LAST JOURNAL?
"SO HE DOES KILL HIM?"
YEAH, HE'S THE ONE SUNK THE PINTA. I SAW IT WITH MY OWN EYES. IF THERE'S A DEVIL ON BOARD, IT'S HIM.
"NOT RIGHT AWAY, NO."
I'VE GOTTA TELL SOSH! I NEED TO--
YOU DON'T.
I'D REMEMBER.

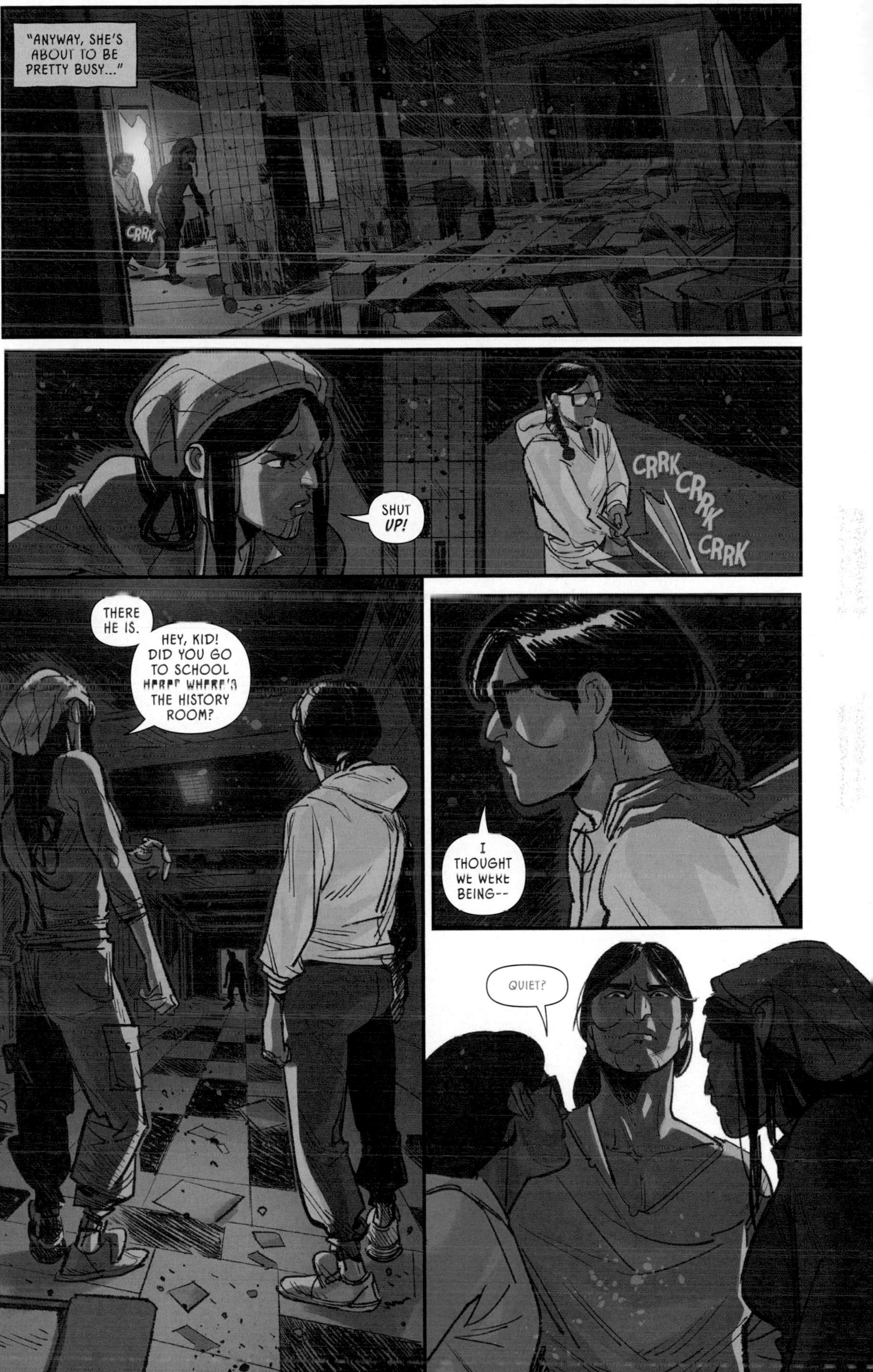
"ANYWAY, SHE'S ABOUT TO BE PRETTY BUSY..."
CRRK
SHUT *UP!*
CRRK CRRK CRRK
THERE HE IS.
HEY, KID! DID YOU GO TO SCHOOL HERE? WHERE'S THE HISTORY ROOM?
I THOUGHT WE WERE BEING--
QUIET?

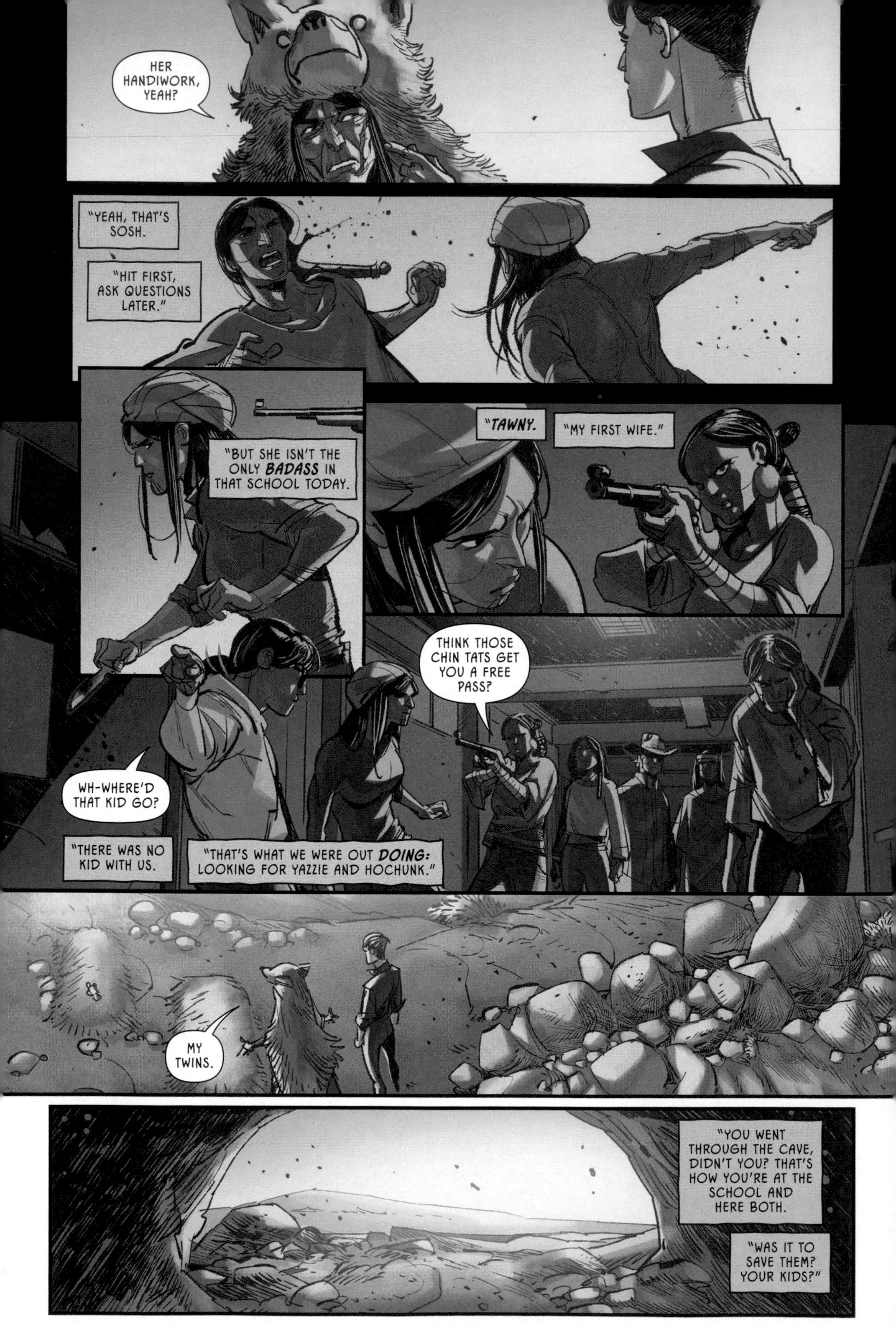
HER HANDIWORK, YEAH?
"YEAH, THAT'S SOSH.
"HIT FIRST, ASK QUESTIONS LATER."
"BUT SHE ISN'T THE ONLY BADASS IN THAT SCHOOL TODAY.
"TAWNY.
"MY FIRST WIFE."
THINK THOSE CHIN TATS GET YOU A FREE PASS?
WH-WHERE'D THAT KID GO?
"THERE WAS NO KID WITH US.
"THAT'S WHAT WE WERE OUT DOING: LOOKING FOR YAZZIE AND HOCHUNK."
MY TWINS.
"YOU WENT THROUGH THE CAVE, DIDN'T YOU? THAT'S HOW YOU'RE AT THE SCHOOL AND HERE BOTH.
"WAS IT TO SAVE THEM? YOUR KIDS?"

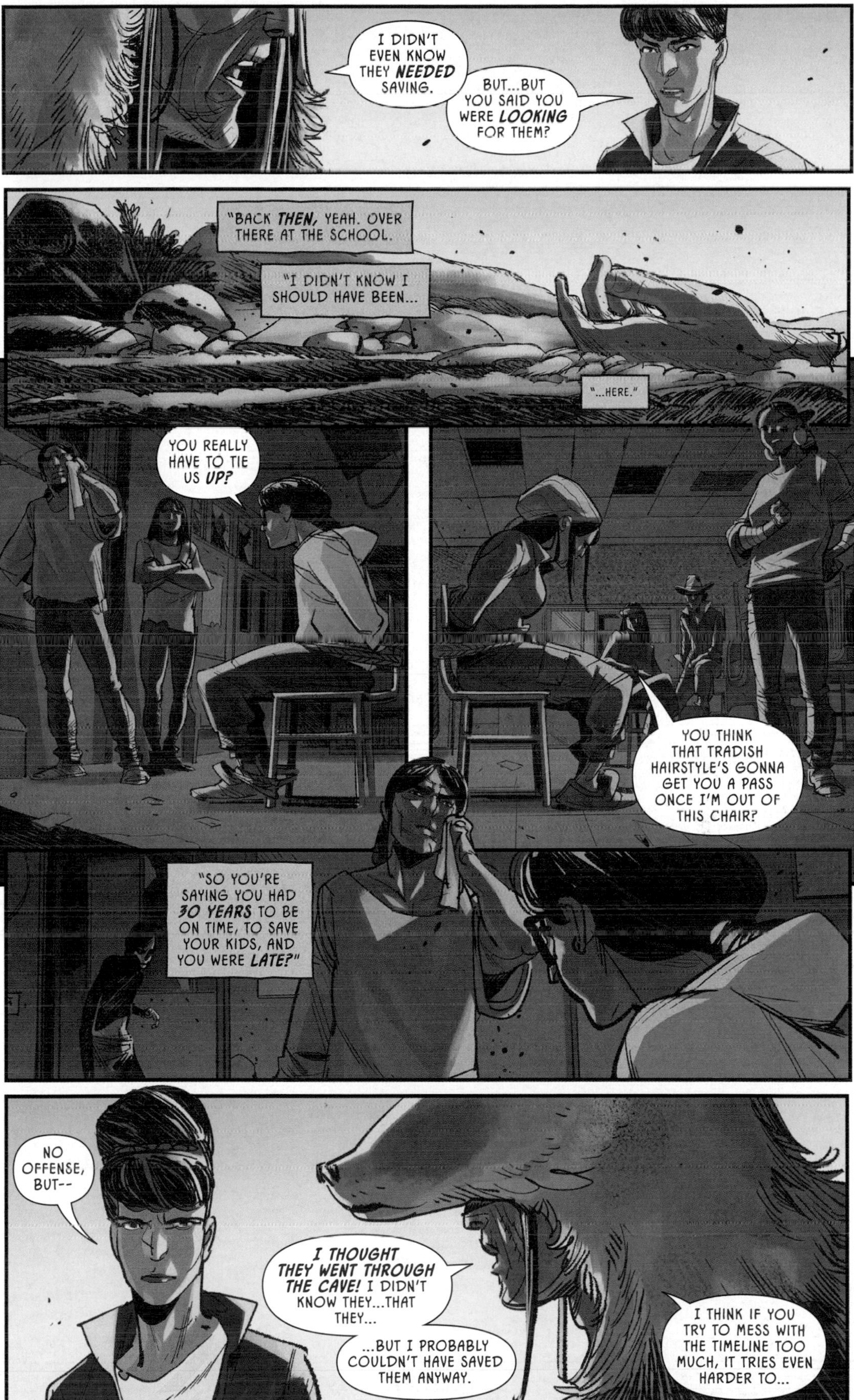
I DIDN'T EVEN KNOW THEY NEEDED SAVING.
BUT...BUT YOU SAID YOU WERE LOOKING FOR THEM?
"BACK THEN, YEAH. OVER THERE AT THE SCHOOL.
"I DIDN'T KNOW I SHOULD HAVE BEEN...
"...HERE."
YOU REALLY HAVE TO TIE US UP?
YOU THINK THAT TRADISH HAIRSTYLE'S GONNA GET YOU A PASS ONCE I'M OUT OF THIS CHAIR?
"SO YOU'RE SAYING YOU HAD 30 YEARS TO BE ON TIME, TO SAVE YOUR KIDS, AND YOU WERE LATE?"
NO OFFENSE, BUT--
I THOUGHT THEY WENT THROUGH THE CAVE! I DIDN'T KNOW THEY...THAT THEY...
...BUT I PROBABLY COULDN'T HAVE SAVED THEM ANYWAY.
I THINK IF YOU TRY TO MESS WITH THE TIMELINE TOO MUCH, IT TRIES EVEN HARDER TO...

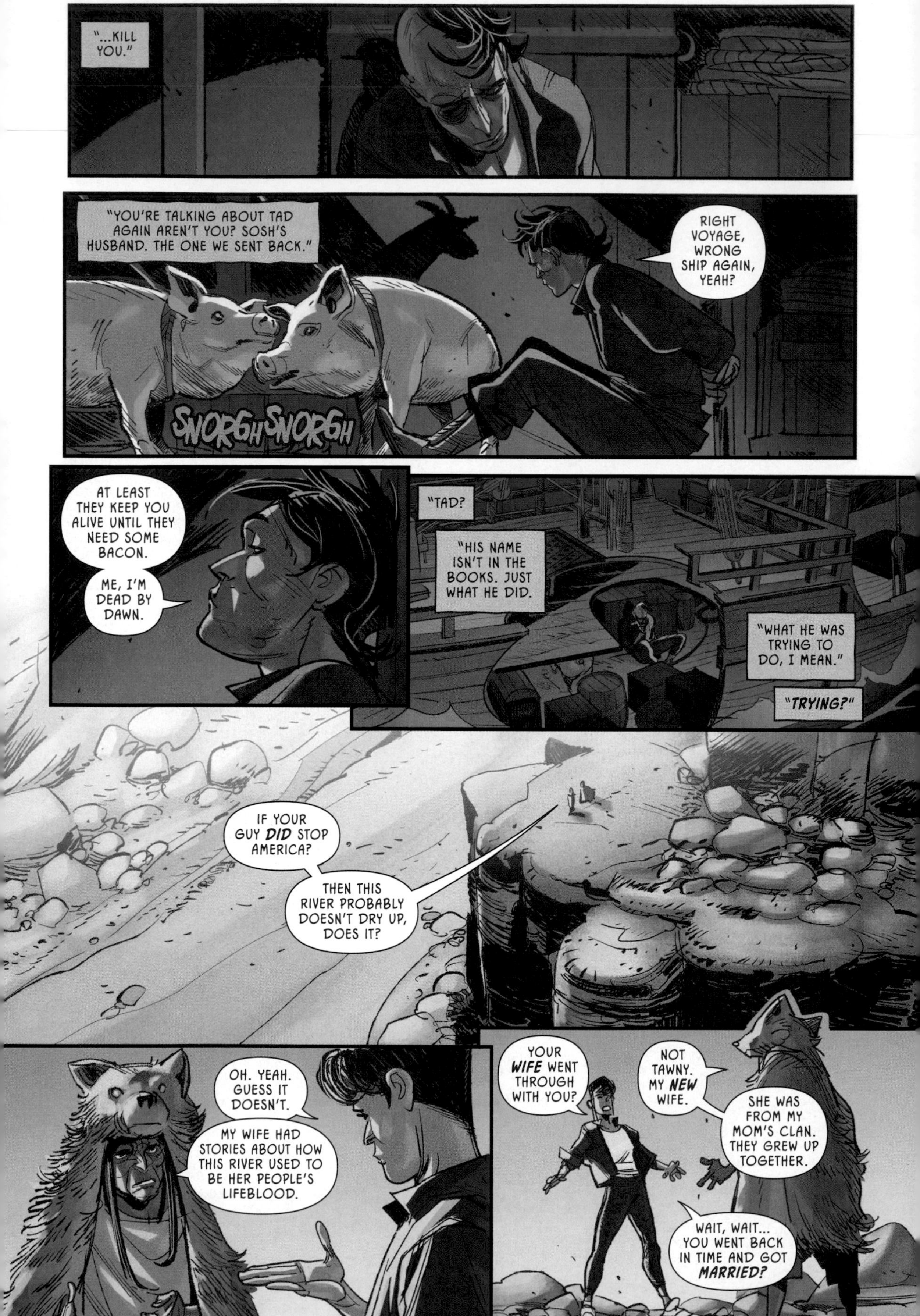
"...KILL YOU."
"YOU'RE TALKING ABOUT TAD AGAIN AREN'T YOU? SOSH'S HUSBAND. THE ONE WE SENT BACK."
RIGHT VOYAGE, WRONG SHIP AGAIN, YEAH?
SNORGH SNORGH
AT LEAST THEY KEEP YOU ALIVE UNTIL THEY NEED SOME BACON.
ME, I'M DEAD BY DAWN.
"TAD?
"HIS NAME ISN'T IN THE BOOKS. JUST WHAT HE DID.
"WHAT HE WAS TRYING TO DO, I MEAN."
"*TRYING?*"
IF YOUR GUY ***DID*** STOP AMERICA?
THEN THIS RIVER PROBABLY DOESN'T DRY UP, DOES IT?
OH. YEAH. GUESS IT DOESN'T.
MY WIFE HAD STORIES ABOUT HOW THIS RIVER USED TO BE HER PEOPLE'S LIFEBLOOD.
YOUR ***WIFE*** WENT THROUGH WITH YOU?
NOT TAWNY. MY ***NEW*** WIFE.
SHE WAS FROM MY MOM'S CLAN. THEY GREW UP TOGETHER.
WAIT, WAIT... YOU WENT BACK IN TIME AND GOT ***MARRIED?***

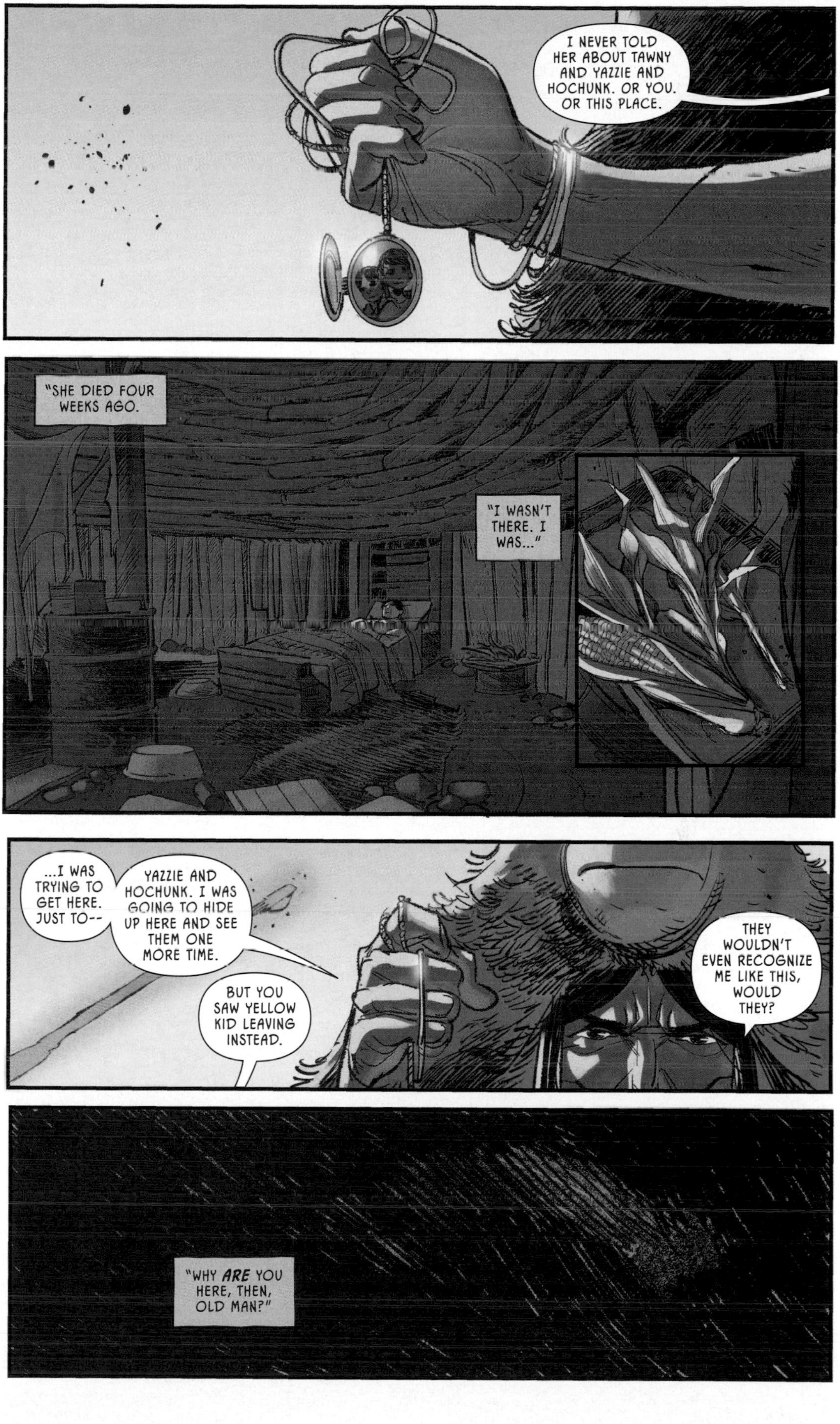

I NEVER TOLD HER ABOUT TAWNY AND YAZZIE AND HOCHUNK. OR YOU. OR THIS PLACE.
"SHE DIED FOUR WEEKS AGO.
"I WASN'T THERE. I WAS..."
...I WAS TRYING TO GET HERE. JUST TO--
YAZZIE AND HOCHUNK. I WAS GOING TO HIDE UP HERE AND SEE THEM ONE MORE TIME.
BUT YOU SAW YELLOW KID LEAVING INSTEAD.
THEY WOULDN'T EVEN RECOGNIZE ME LIKE THIS, WOULD THEY?
"WHY ARE YOU HERE, THEN, OLD MAN?"

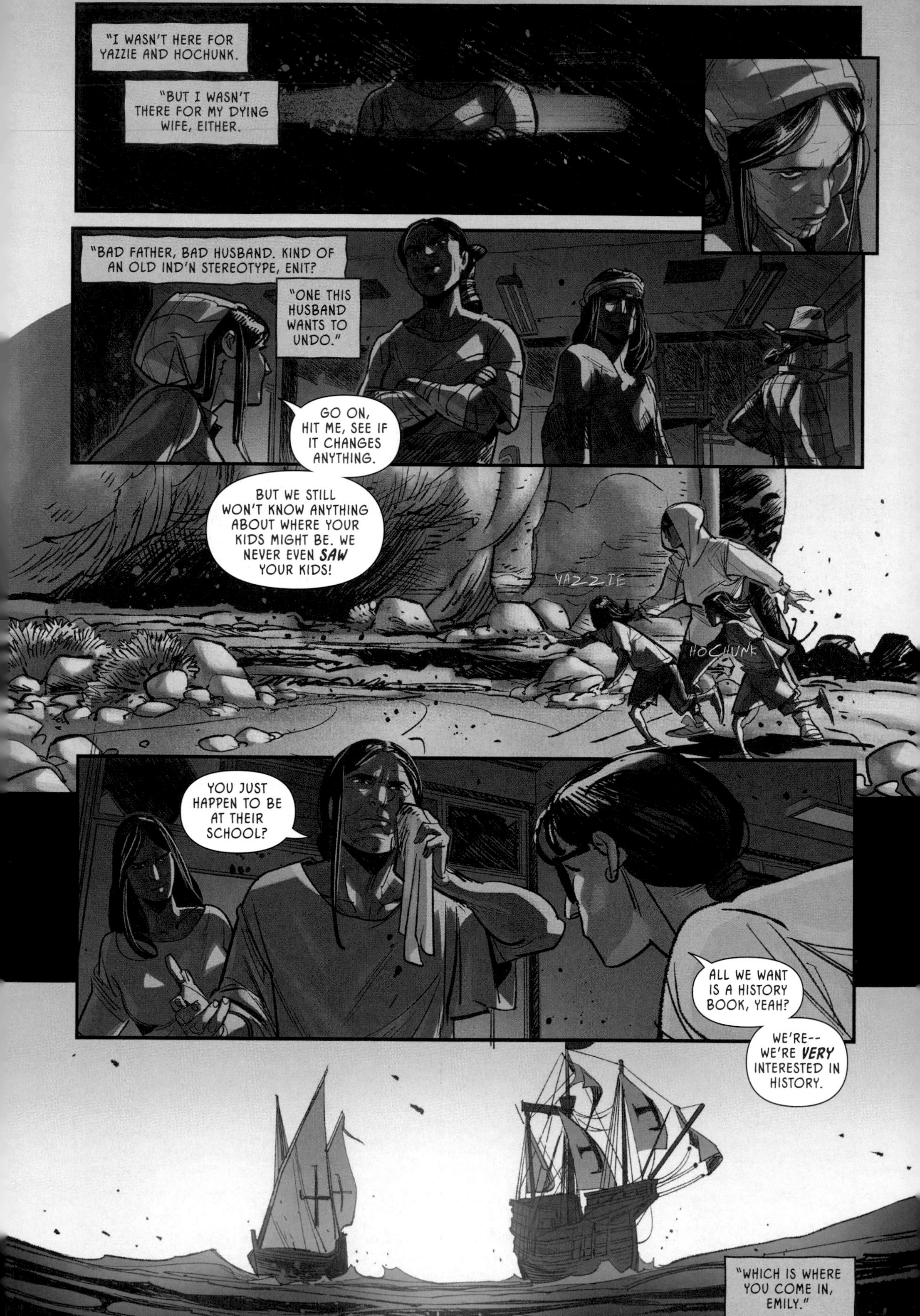
"I WASN'T HERE FOR YAZZIE AND HOCHUNK.
"BUT I WASN'T THERE FOR MY DYING WIFE, EITHER.
"BAD FATHER, BAD HUSBAND. KIND OF AN OLD IND'N STEREOTYPE, ENIT?
"ONE THIS HUSBAND WANTS TO UNDO."
GO ON, HIT ME, SEE IF IT CHANGES ANYTHING.
BUT WE STILL WON'T KNOW ANYTHING ABOUT WHERE YOUR KIDS MIGHT BE. WE NEVER EVEN SAW YOUR KIDS!
YAZZIE
HOCHUNK
YOU JUST HAPPEN TO BE AT THEIR SCHOOL?
ALL WE WANT IS A HISTORY BOOK, YEAH?
WE'RE--WE'RE VERY INTERESTED IN HISTORY.
"WHICH IS WHERE YOU COME IN, EMILY."

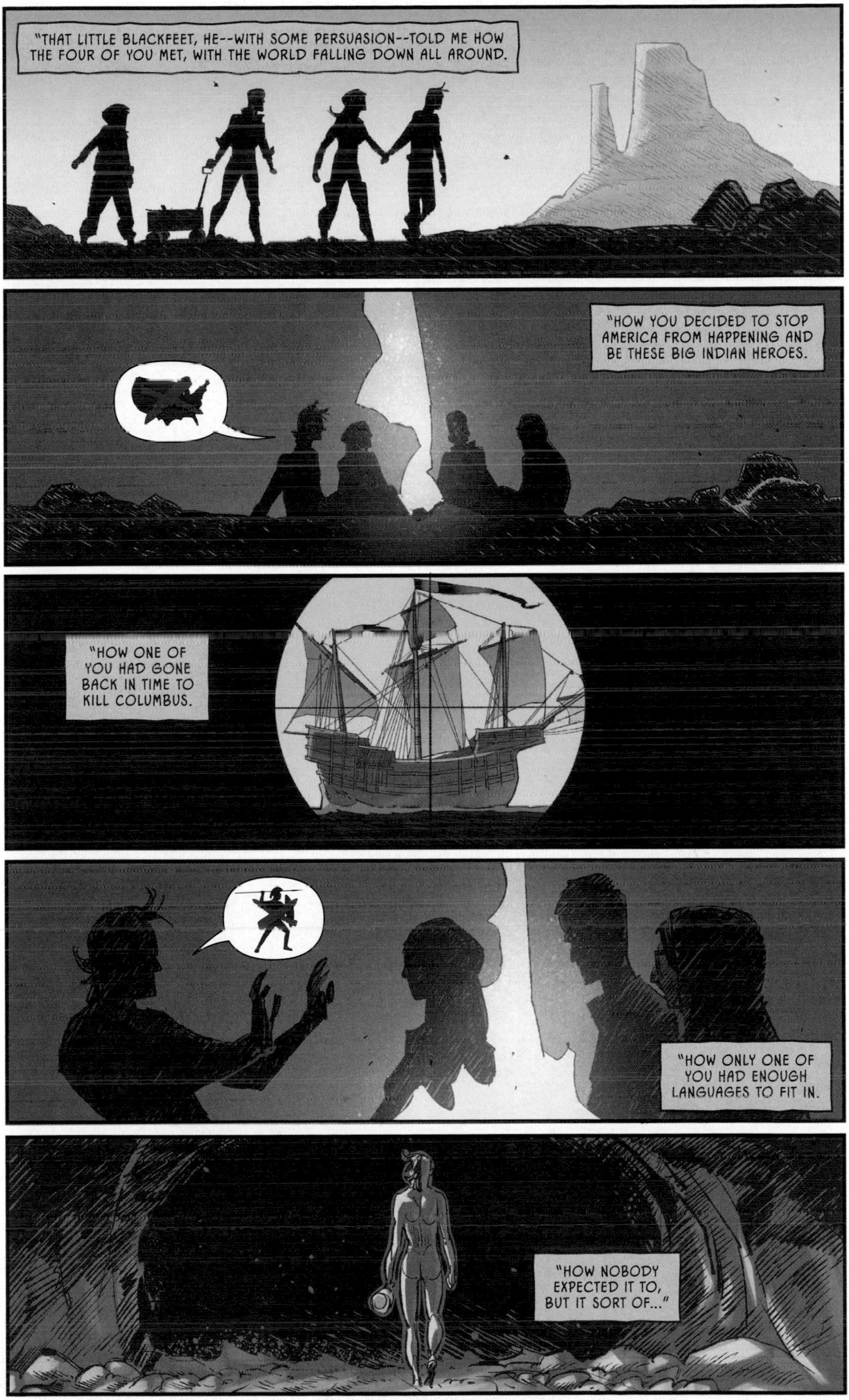
"THAT LITTLE BLACKFEET, HE--WITH SOME PERSUASION--TOLD ME HOW THE FOUR OF YOU MET, WITH THE WORLD FALLING DOWN ALL AROUND.
"HOW YOU DECIDED TO STOP AMERICA FROM HAPPENING AND BE THESE BIG INDIAN HEROES.
"HOW ONE OF YOU HAD GONE BACK IN TIME TO KILL COLUMBUS.
"HOW ONLY ONE OF YOU HAD ENOUGH LANGUAGES TO FIT IN.
"HOW NOBODY EXPECTED IT TO, BUT IT SORT OF..."

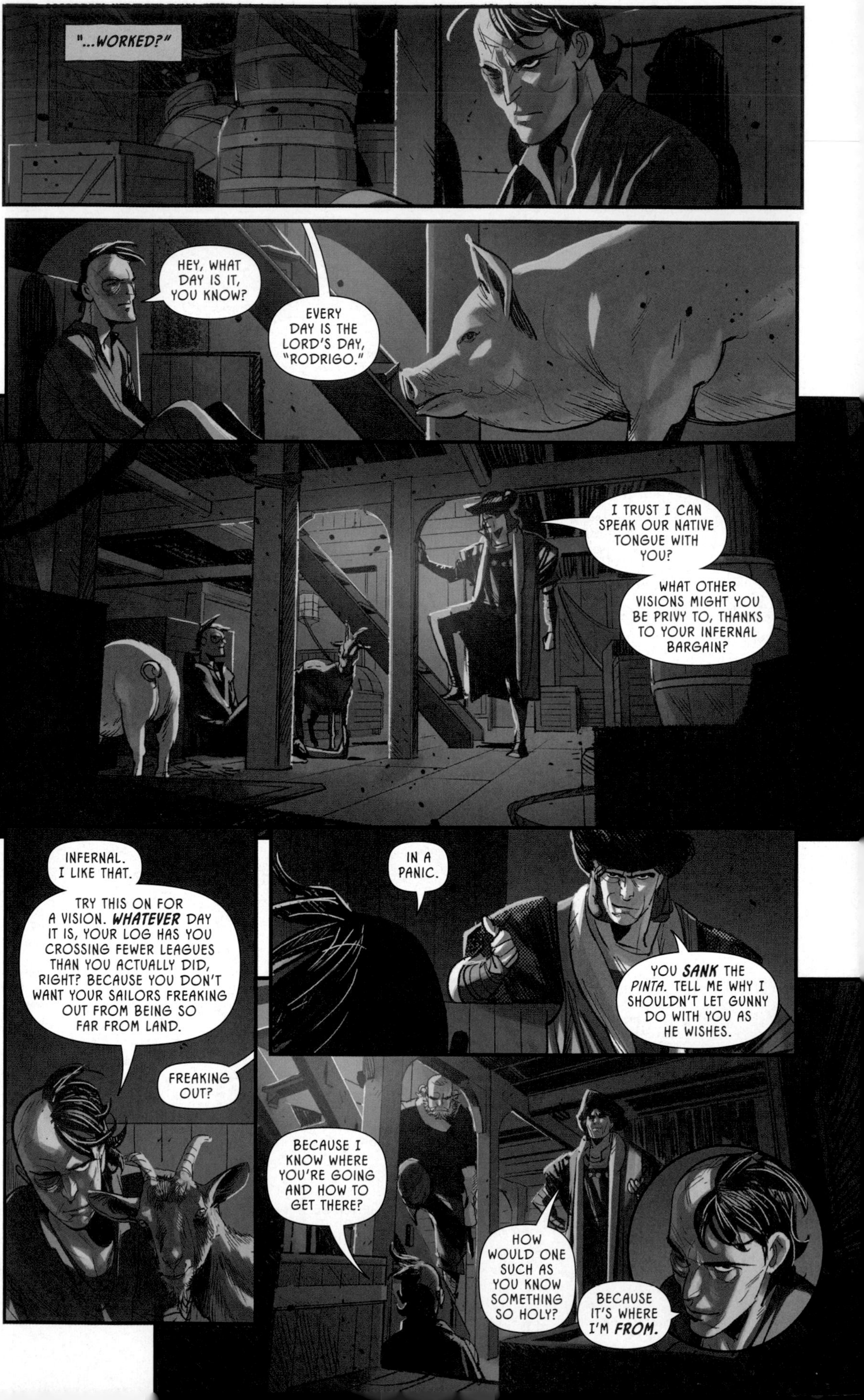

"...WORKED?"
HEY, WHAT DAY IS IT, YOU KNOW?
EVERY DAY IS THE LORD'S DAY, "RODRIGO."
I TRUST I CAN SPEAK OUR NATIVE TONGUE WITH YOU?
WHAT OTHER VISIONS MIGHT YOU BE PRIVY TO, THANKS TO YOUR INFERNAL BARGAIN?
INFERNAL. I LIKE THAT.
TRY THIS ON FOR A VISION. **WHATEVER** DAY IT IS, YOUR LOG HAS YOU CROSSING FEWER LEAGUES THAN YOU ACTUALLY DID, RIGHT? BECAUSE YOU DON'T WANT YOUR SAILORS FREAKING OUT FROM BEING SO FAR FROM LAND.
FREAKING OUT?
IN A PANIC.
YOU **SANK** THE *PINTA*. TELL ME WHY I SHOULDN'T LET GUNNY DO WITH YOU AS HE WISHES.
BECAUSE I KNOW WHERE YOU'RE GOING AND HOW TO GET THERE?
HOW WOULD ONE SUCH AS YOU KNOW SOMETHING SO HOLY?
BECAUSE IT'S WHERE I'M **FROM.**

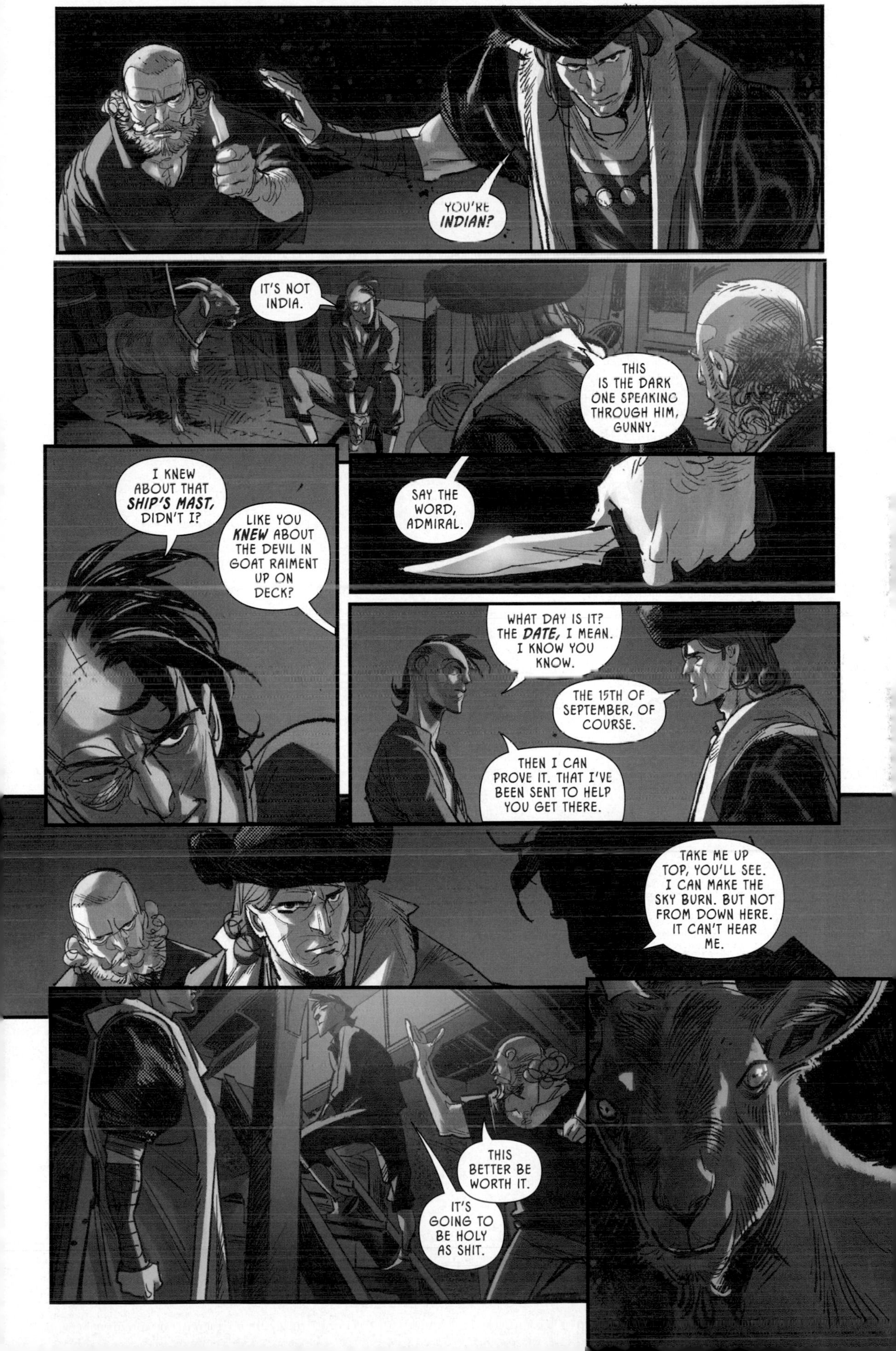
YOU'RE INDIAN?
IT'S NOT INDIA.
THIS IS THE DARK ONE SPEAKING THROUGH HIM, GUNNY.
I KNEW ABOUT THAT SHIP'S MAST, DIDN'T I?
LIKE YOU KNEW ABOUT THE DEVIL IN GOAT RAIMENT UP ON DECK?
SAY THE WORD, ADMIRAL.
WHAT DAY IS IT? THE DATE, I MEAN. I KNOW YOU KNOW.
THE 15TH OF SEPTEMBER, OF COURSE.
THEN I CAN PROVE IT. THAT I'VE BEEN SENT TO HELP YOU GET THERE.
TAKE ME UP TOP, YOU'LL SEE. I CAN MAKE THE SKY BURN. BUT NOT FROM DOWN HERE. IT CAN'T HEAR ME.
THIS BETTER BE WORTH IT.
IT'S GOING TO BE HOLY AS SHIT.

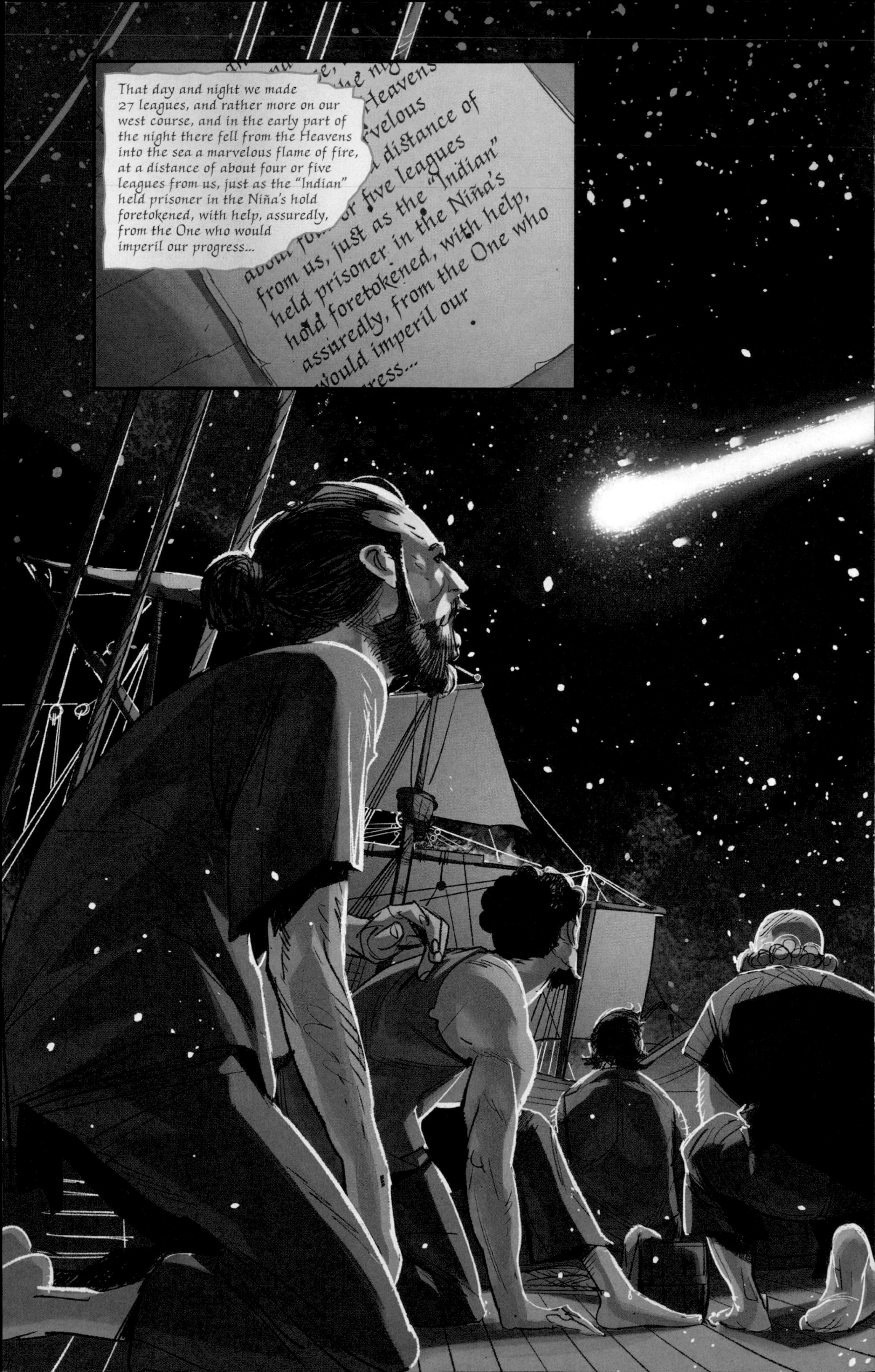
That day and night we made 27 leagues, and rather more on our west course, and in the early part of the night there fell from the Heavens into the sea a marvelous flame of fire, at a distance of about four or five leagues from us, just as the "Indian" held prisoner in the Niña's hold foretokened, with help, assuredly, from the One who would imperil our progress...

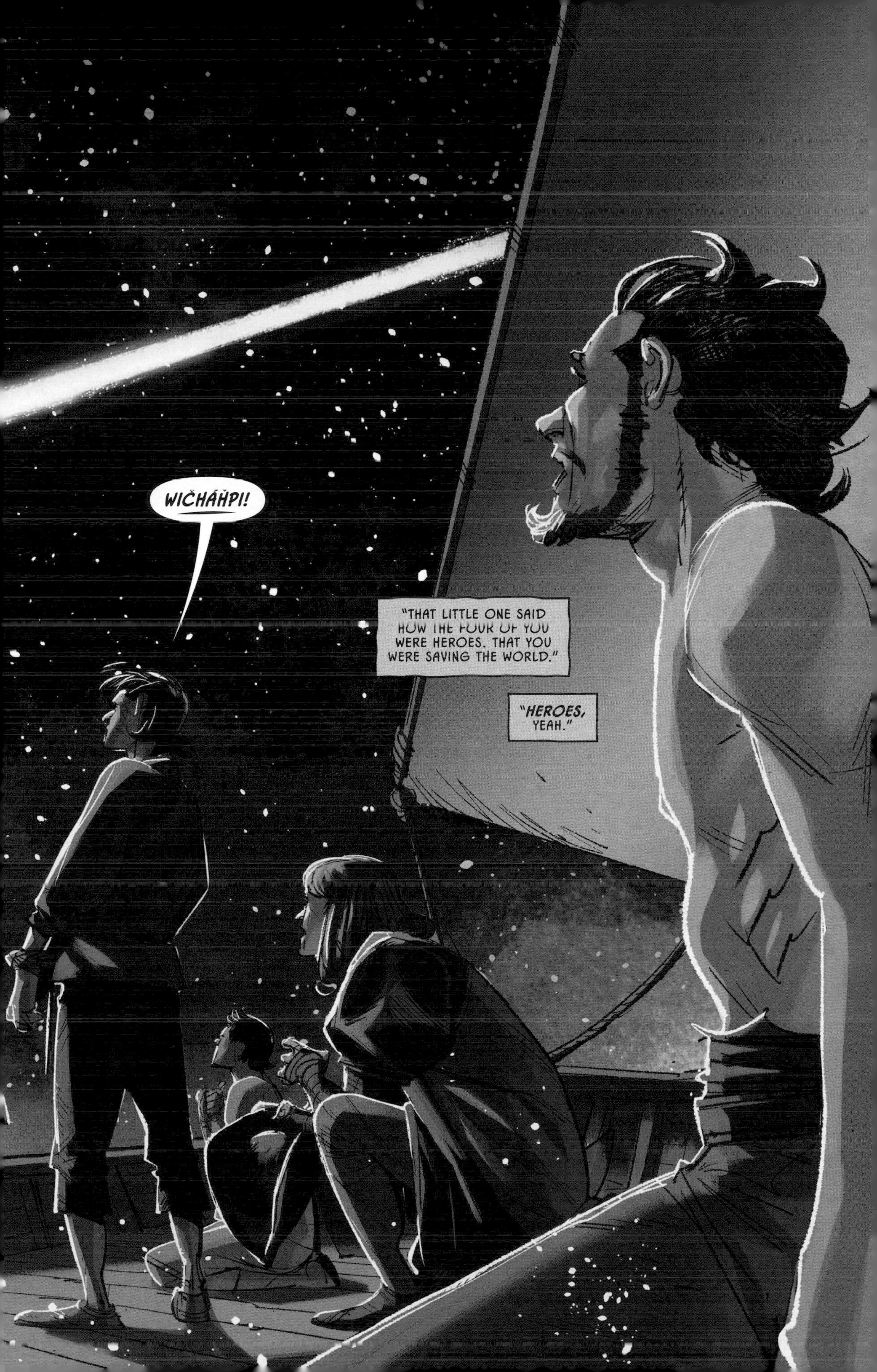
WIČHÁȞPI!
"THAT LITTLE ONE SAID HOW THE FOUR OF YOU WERE HEROES. THAT YOU WERE SAVING THE WORLD."
"HEROES, YEAH."

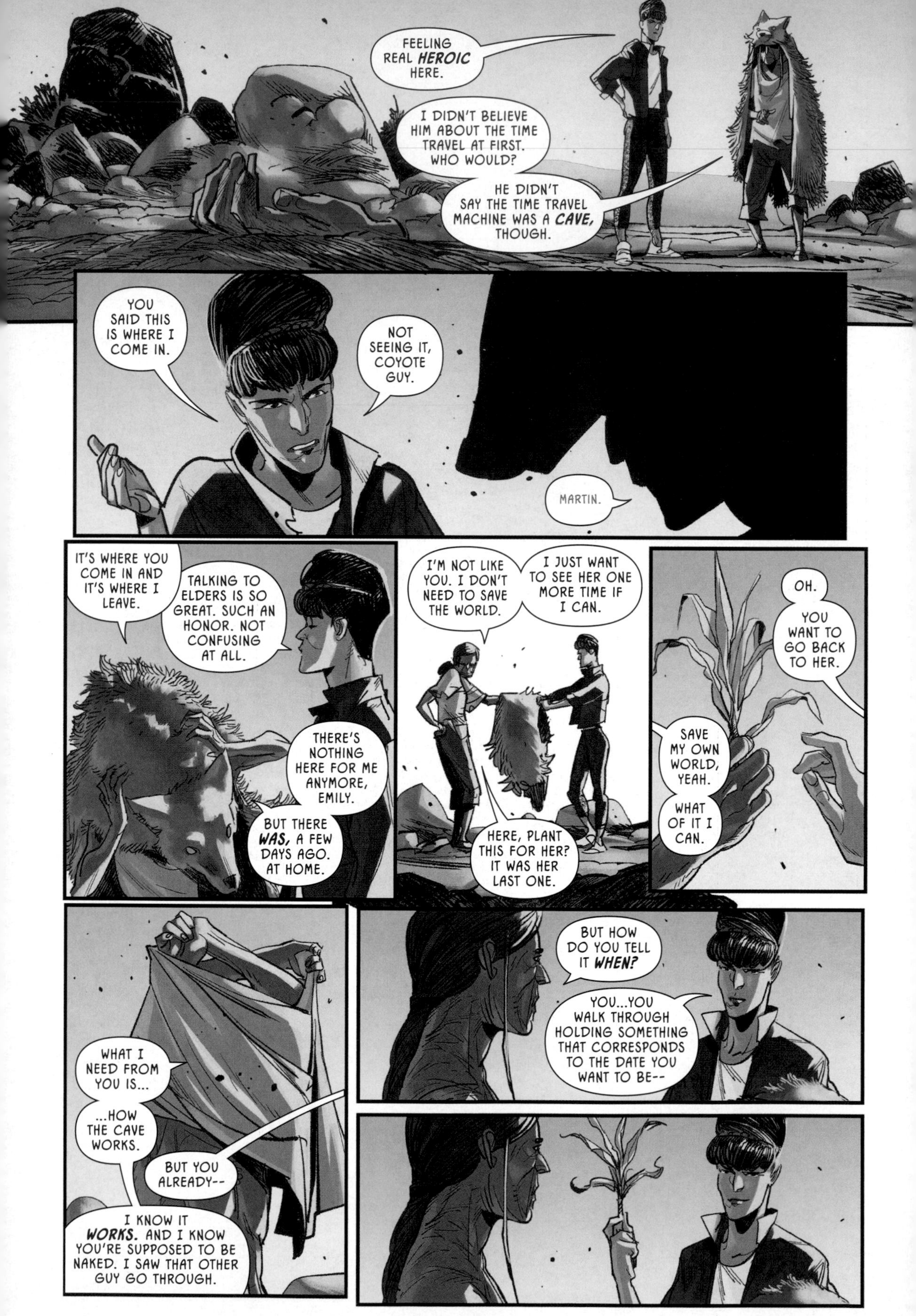
FEELING REAL HEROIC HERE.
I DIDN'T BELIEVE HIM ABOUT THE TIME TRAVEL AT FIRST. WHO WOULD?
HE DIDN'T SAY THE TIME TRAVEL MACHINE WAS A CAVE, THOUGH.
YOU SAID THIS IS WHERE I COME IN.
NOT SEEING IT, COYOTE GUY.
MARTIN.
IT'S WHERE YOU COME IN AND IT'S WHERE I LEAVE.
TALKING TO ELDERS IS SO GREAT. SUCH AN HONOR. NOT CONFUSING AT ALL.
THERE'S NOTHING HERE FOR ME ANYMORE, EMILY.
BUT THERE WAS, A FEW DAYS AGO. AT HOME.
I'M NOT LIKE YOU. I DON'T NEED TO SAVE THE WORLD.
I JUST WANT TO SEE HER ONE MORE TIME IF I CAN.
HERE, PLANT THIS FOR HER? IT WAS HER LAST ONE.
OH.
YOU WANT TO GO BACK TO HER.
SAVE MY OWN WORLD, YEAH.
WHAT OF IT I CAN.
WHAT I NEED FROM YOU IS...
...HOW THE CAVE WORKS.
BUT YOU ALREADY--
I KNOW IT WORKS. AND I KNOW YOU'RE SUPPOSED TO BE NAKED. I SAW THAT OTHER GUY GO THROUGH.
BUT HOW DO YOU TELL IT WHEN?
YOU...YOU WALK THROUGH HOLDING SOMETHING THAT CORRESPONDS TO THE DATE YOU WANT TO BE--

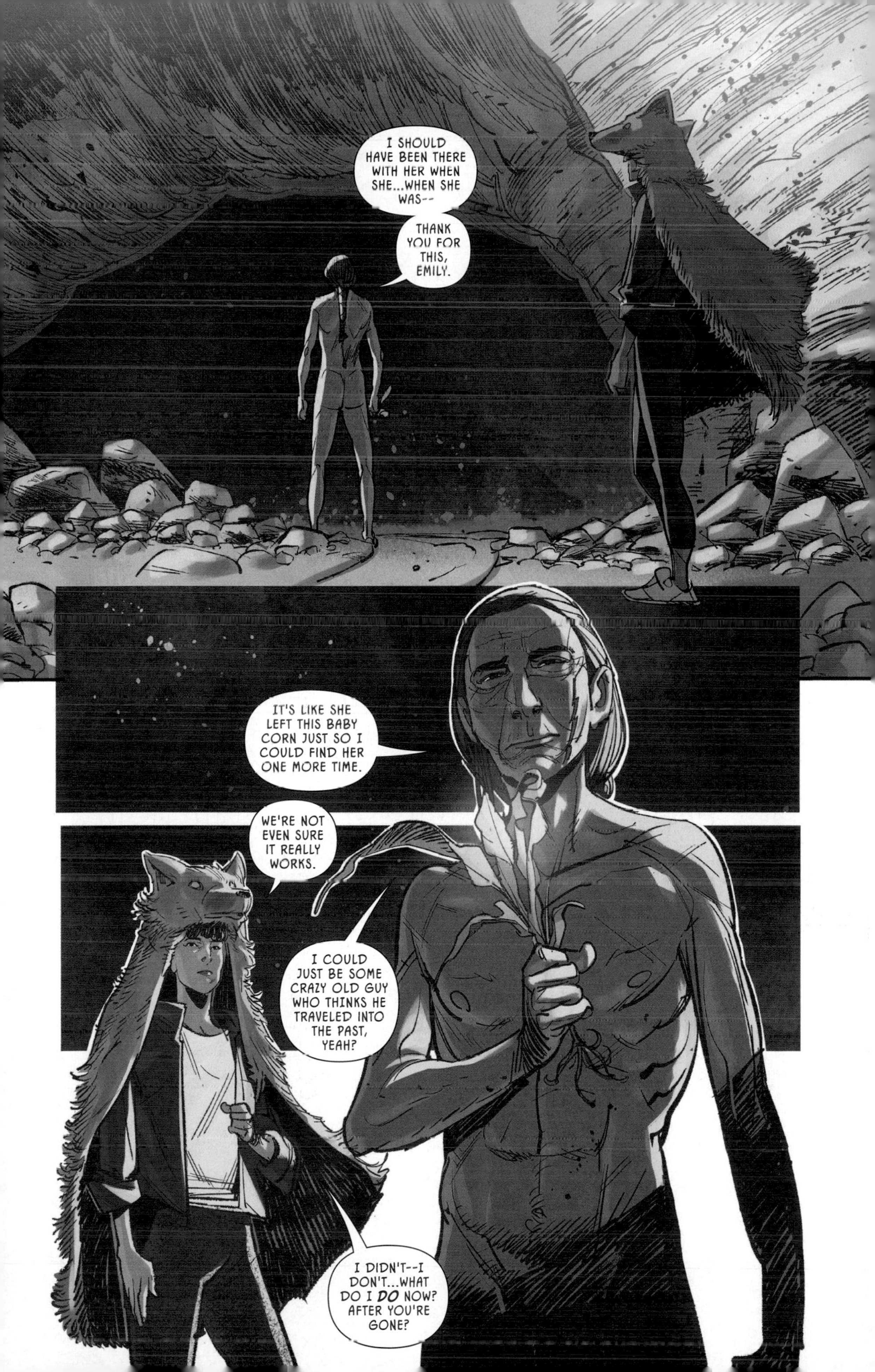
I SHOULD HAVE BEEN THERE WITH HER WHEN SHE...WHEN SHE WAS--
THANK YOU FOR THIS, EMILY.
IT'S LIKE SHE LEFT THIS BABY CORN JUST SO I COULD FIND HER ONE MORE TIME.
WE'RE NOT EVEN SURE IT REALLY WORKS.
I COULD JUST BE SOME CRAZY OLD GUY WHO THINKS HE TRAVELED INTO THE PAST, YEAH?
I DIDN'T--I DON'T...WHAT DO I DO NOW? AFTER YOU'RE GONE?

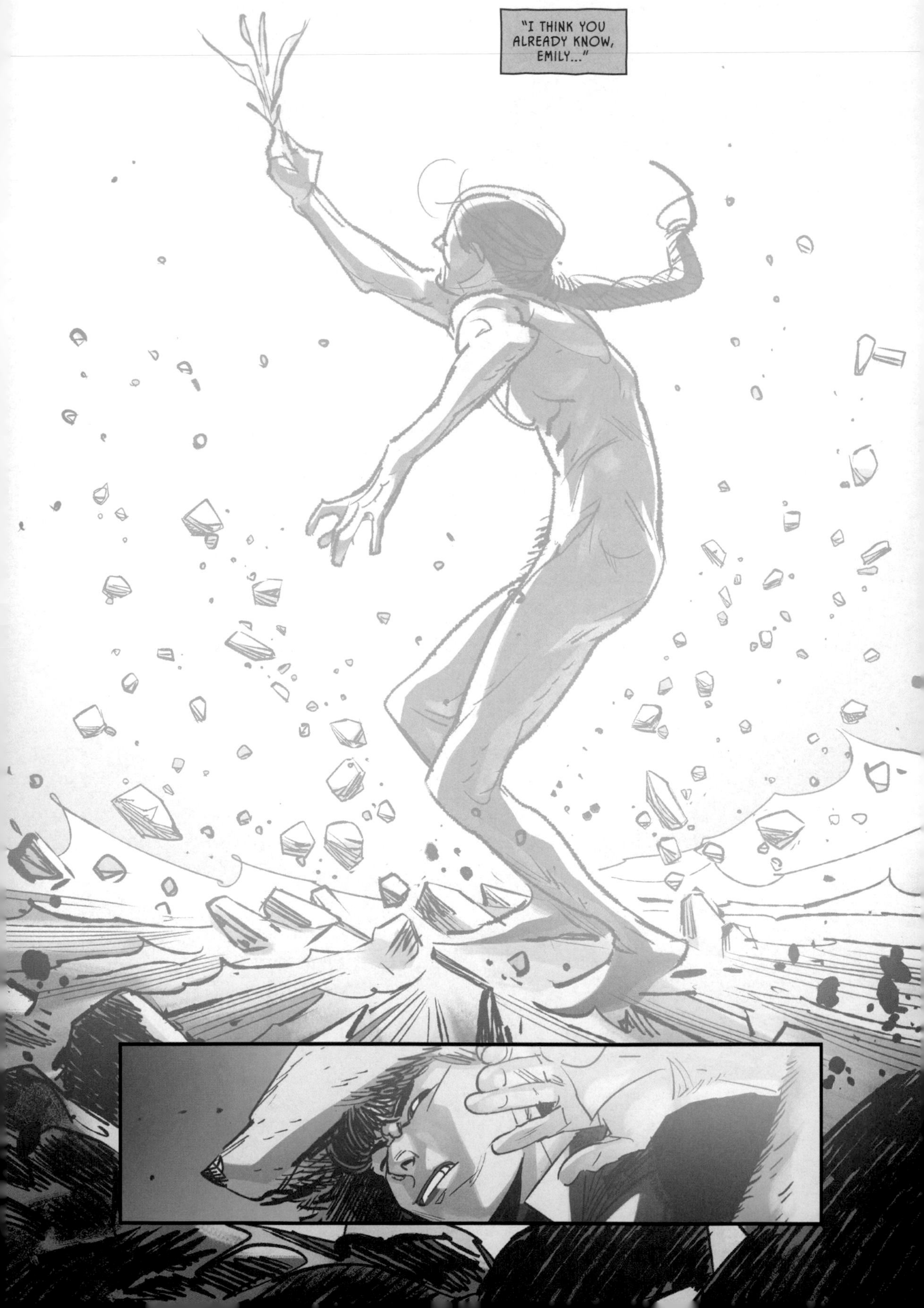
"I THINK YOU ALREADY KNOW, EMILY..."

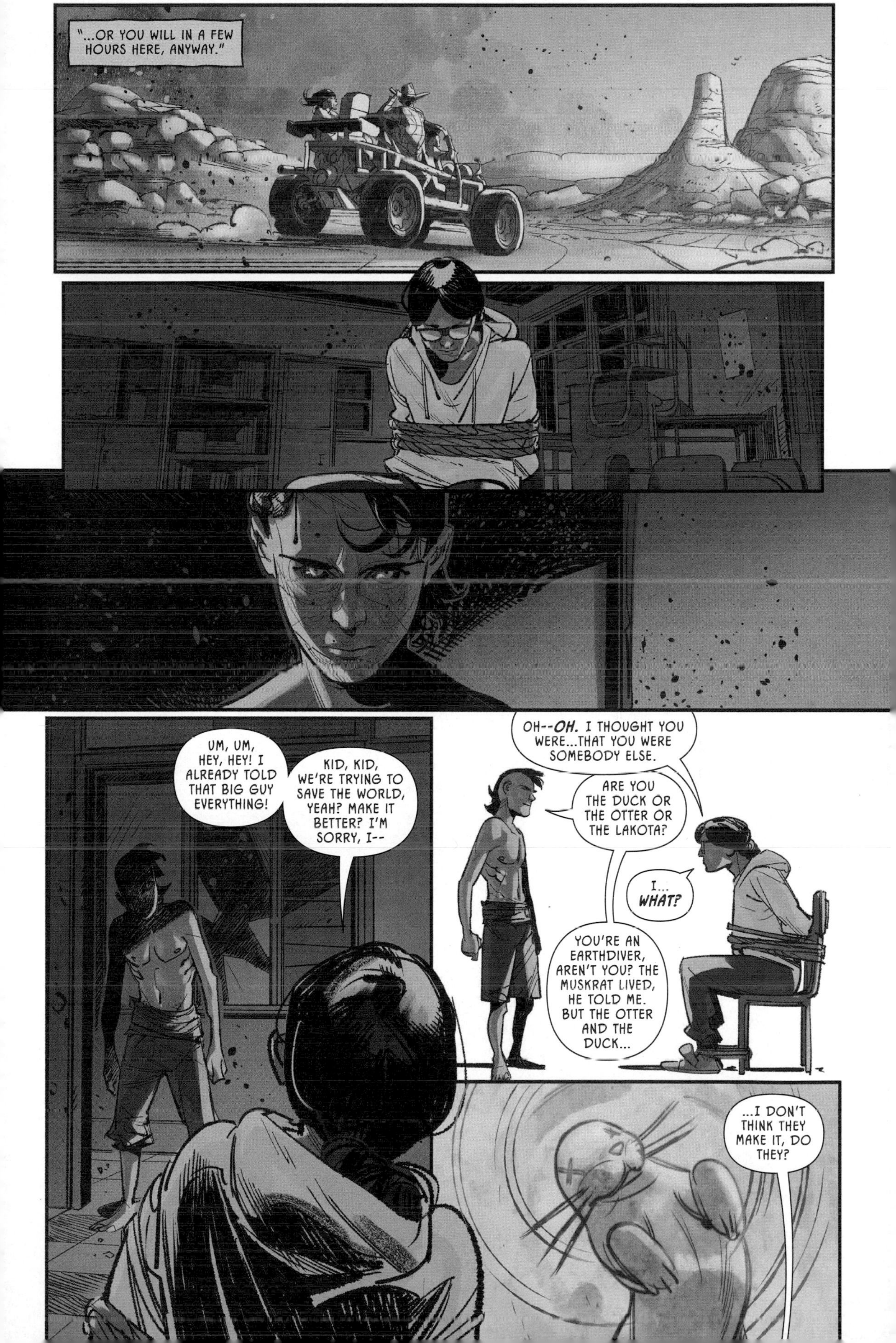
"...OR YOU WILL IN A FEW HOURS HERE, ANYWAY."
UM, UM, HEY, HEY! I ALREADY TOLD THAT BIG GUY EVERYTHING!
KID, KID, WE'RE TRYING TO SAVE THE WORLD, YEAH? MAKE IT BETTER? I'M SORRY, I--
OH--OH. I THOUGHT YOU WERE...THAT YOU WERE SOMEBODY ELSE.
ARE YOU THE DUCK OR THE OTTER OR THE LAKOTA?
I... WHAT?
YOU'RE AN EARTHDIVER, AREN'T YOU? THE MUSKRAT LIVED, HE TOLD ME. BUT THE OTTER AND THE DUCK...
...I DON'T THINK THEY MAKE IT, DO THEY?

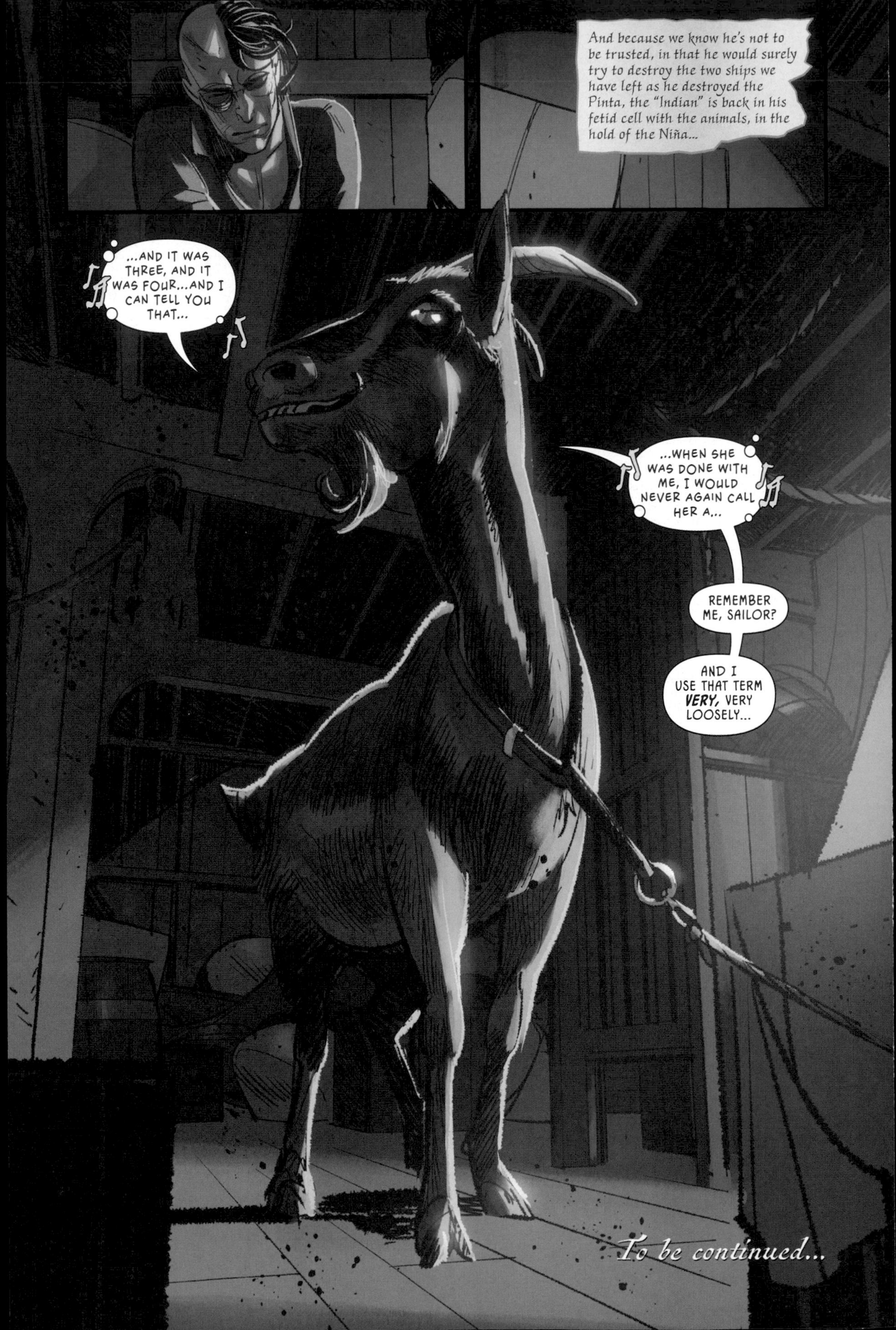
And because we know he's not to be trusted, in that he would surely try to destroy the two ships we have left as he destroyed the Pinta, the "Indian" is back in his fetid cell with the animals, in the hold of the Niña...
...AND IT WAS THREE, AND IT WAS FOUR...AND I CAN TELL YOU THAT...
...WHEN SHE WAS DONE WITH ME, I WOULD NEVER AGAIN CALL HER A...
REMEMBER ME, SAILOR?
AND I USE THAT TERM VERY, VERY LOOSELY...
To be continued...

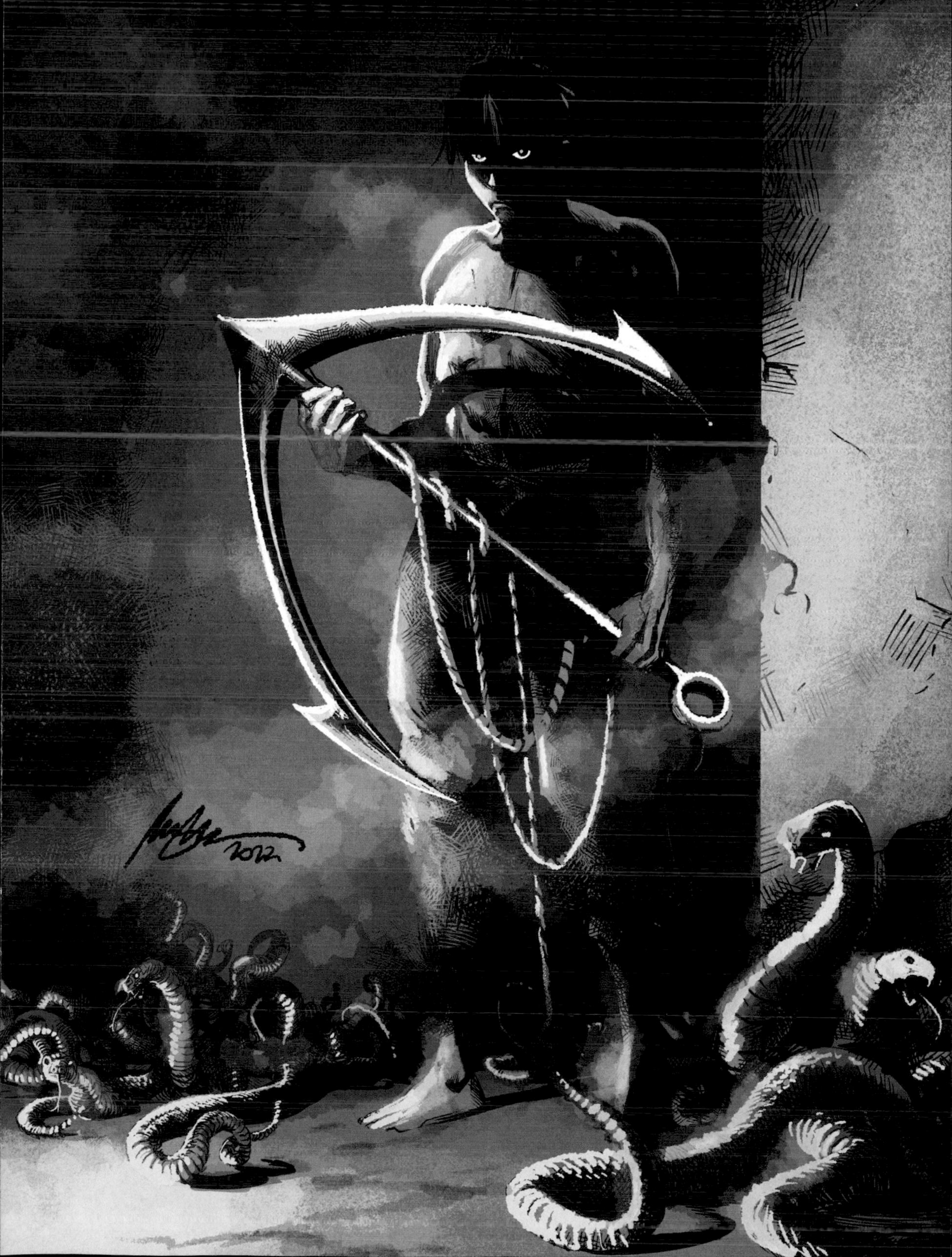

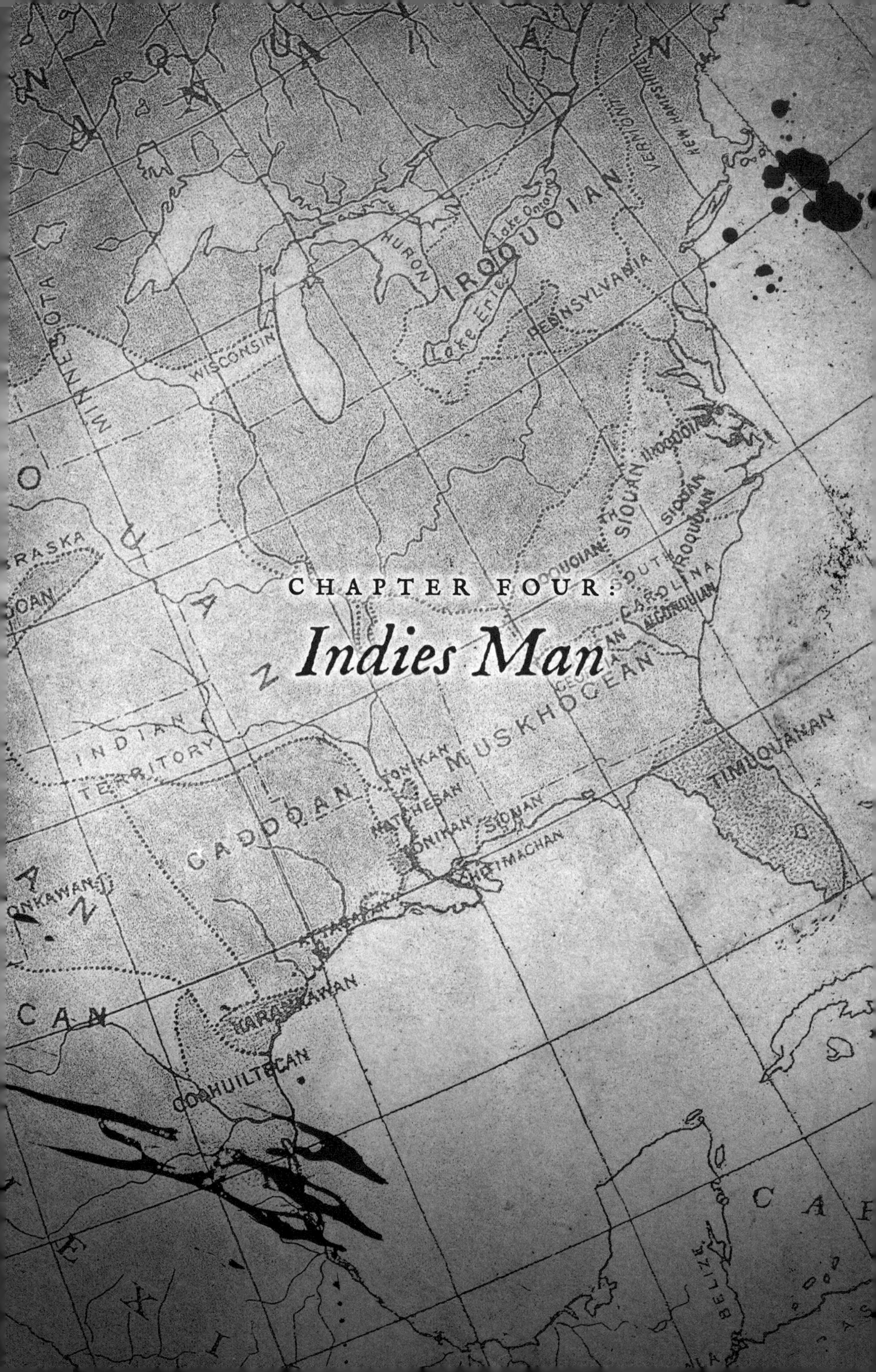

WISCONSIN
HURON
Lake Erie
PENNSYLVANIA
VERMONT
NEW HAMPSHIRE
IROQUOIAN
SIOUAN
INDIAN TERRITORY
CADDOAN
MUSKHOGEAN
TIMUQUANAN
CHITIMACHAN
COAHUILTECAN
BELIZE

CHAPTER FOUR:

Indies Man

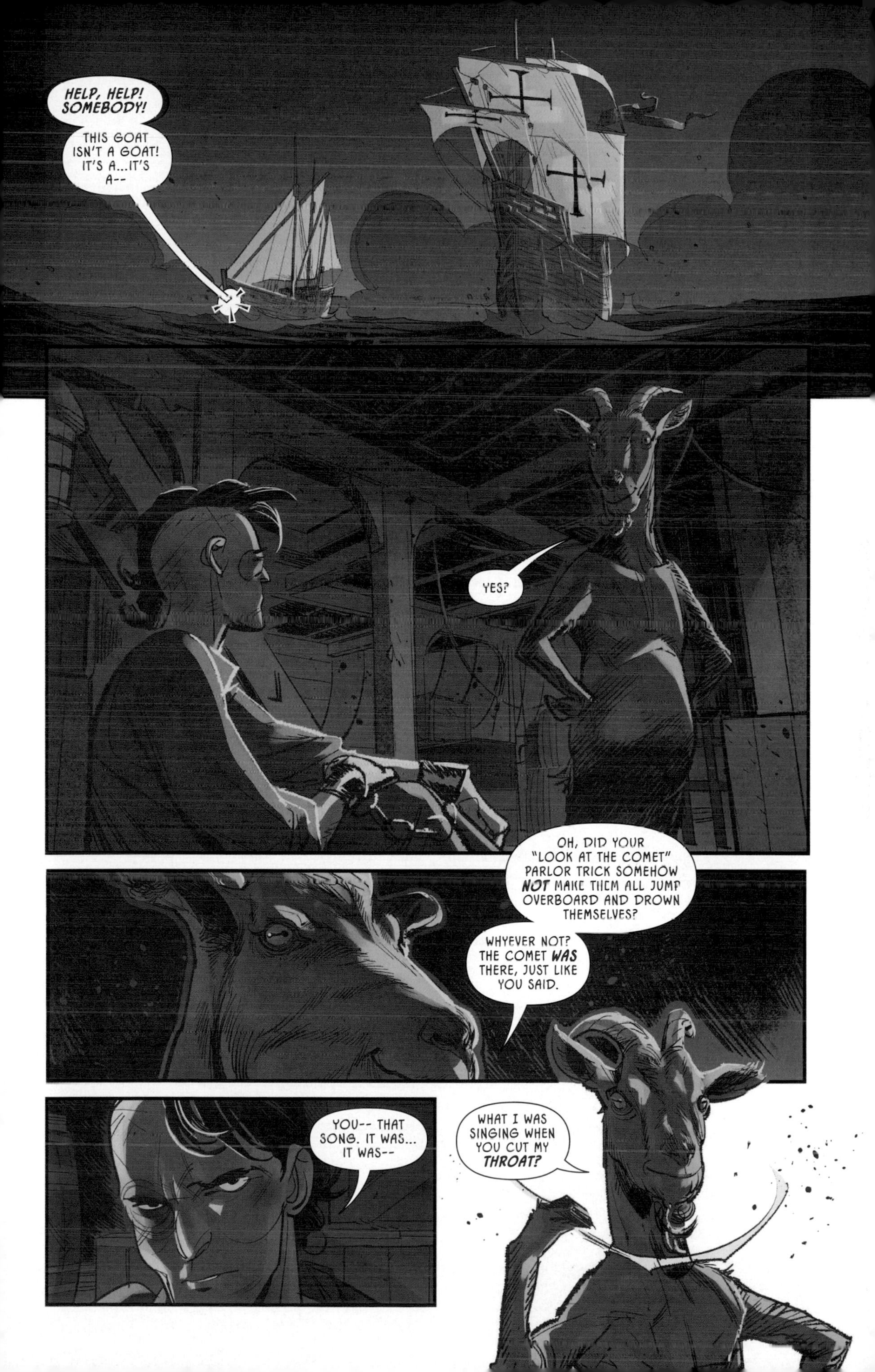
HELP, HELP! SOMEBODY!
THIS GOAT ISN'T A GOAT! IT'S A...IT'S A--
YES?
OH, DID YOUR "LOOK AT THE COMET" PARLOR TRICK SOMEHOW NOT MAKE THEM ALL JUMP OVERBOARD AND DROWN THEMSELVES?
WHYEVER NOT? THE COMET WAS THERE, JUST LIKE YOU SAID.
YOU-- THAT SONG. IT WAS... IT WAS--
WHAT I WAS SINGING WHEN YOU CUT MY THROAT?

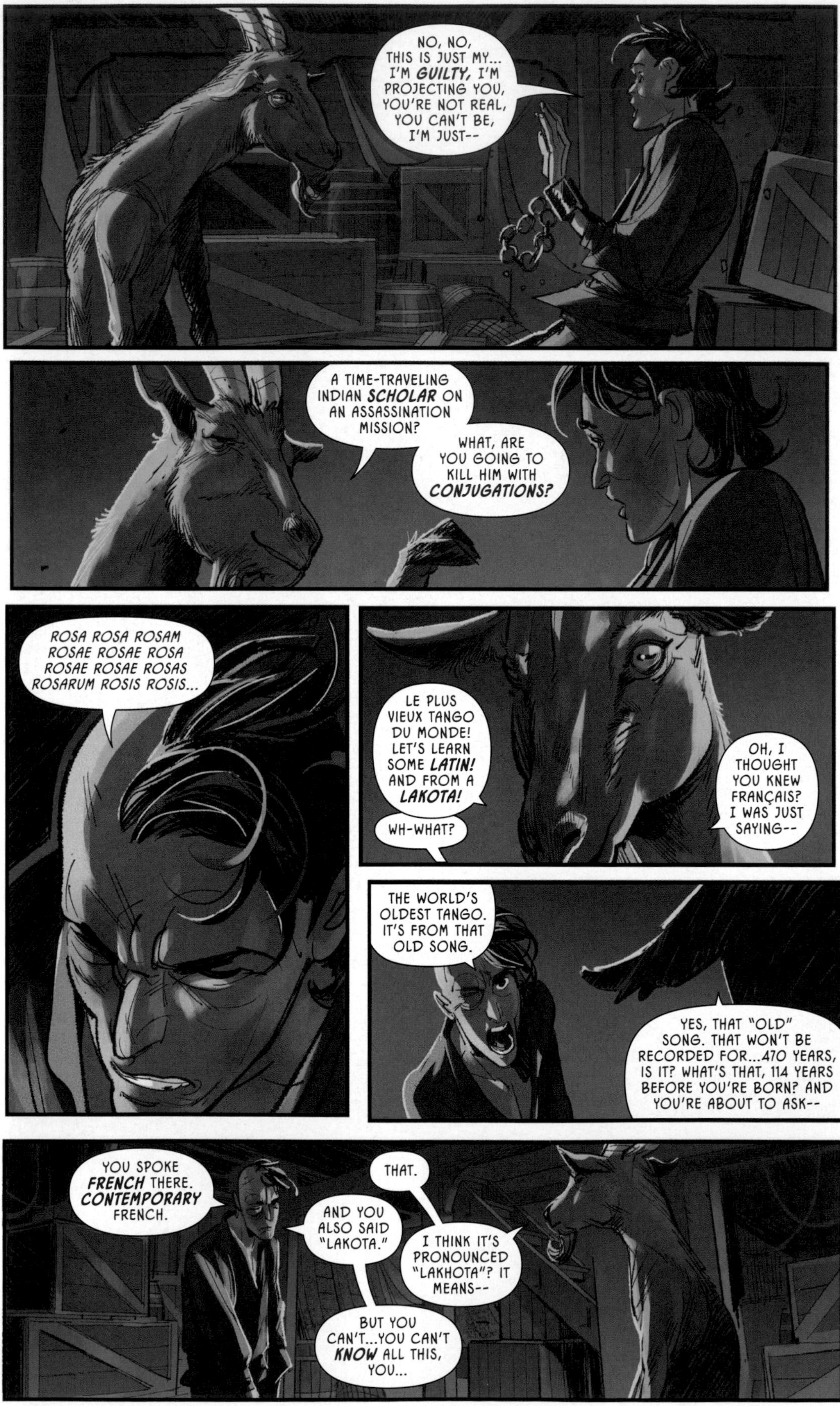
NO, NO, THIS IS JUST MY... I'M GUILTY, I'M PROJECTING YOU, YOU'RE NOT REAL, YOU CAN'T BE, I'M JUST--
A TIME-TRAVELING INDIAN SCHOLAR ON AN ASSASSINATION MISSION?
WHAT, ARE YOU GOING TO KILL HIM WITH CONJUGATIONS?
ROSA ROSA ROSAM ROSAE ROSAE ROSA ROSAE ROSAE ROSAS ROSARUM ROSIS ROSIS...
LE PLUS VIEUX TANGO DU MONDE! LET'S LEARN SOME LATIN! AND FROM A LAKOTA!
WH-WHAT?
OH, I THOUGHT YOU KNEW FRANÇAIS? I WAS JUST SAYING--
THE WORLD'S OLDEST TANGO. IT'S FROM THAT OLD SONG.
YES, THAT "OLD" SONG. THAT WON'T BE RECORDED FOR...470 YEARS, IS IT? WHAT'S THAT, 114 YEARS BEFORE YOU'RE BORN? AND YOU'RE ABOUT TO ASK--
YOU SPOKE FRENCH THERE. CONTEMPORARY FRENCH.
THAT.
AND YOU ALSO SAID "LAKOTA."
I THINK IT'S PRONOUNCED "LAKHOTA"? IT MEANS--
BUT YOU CAN'T...YOU CAN'T KNOW ALL THIS, YOU...

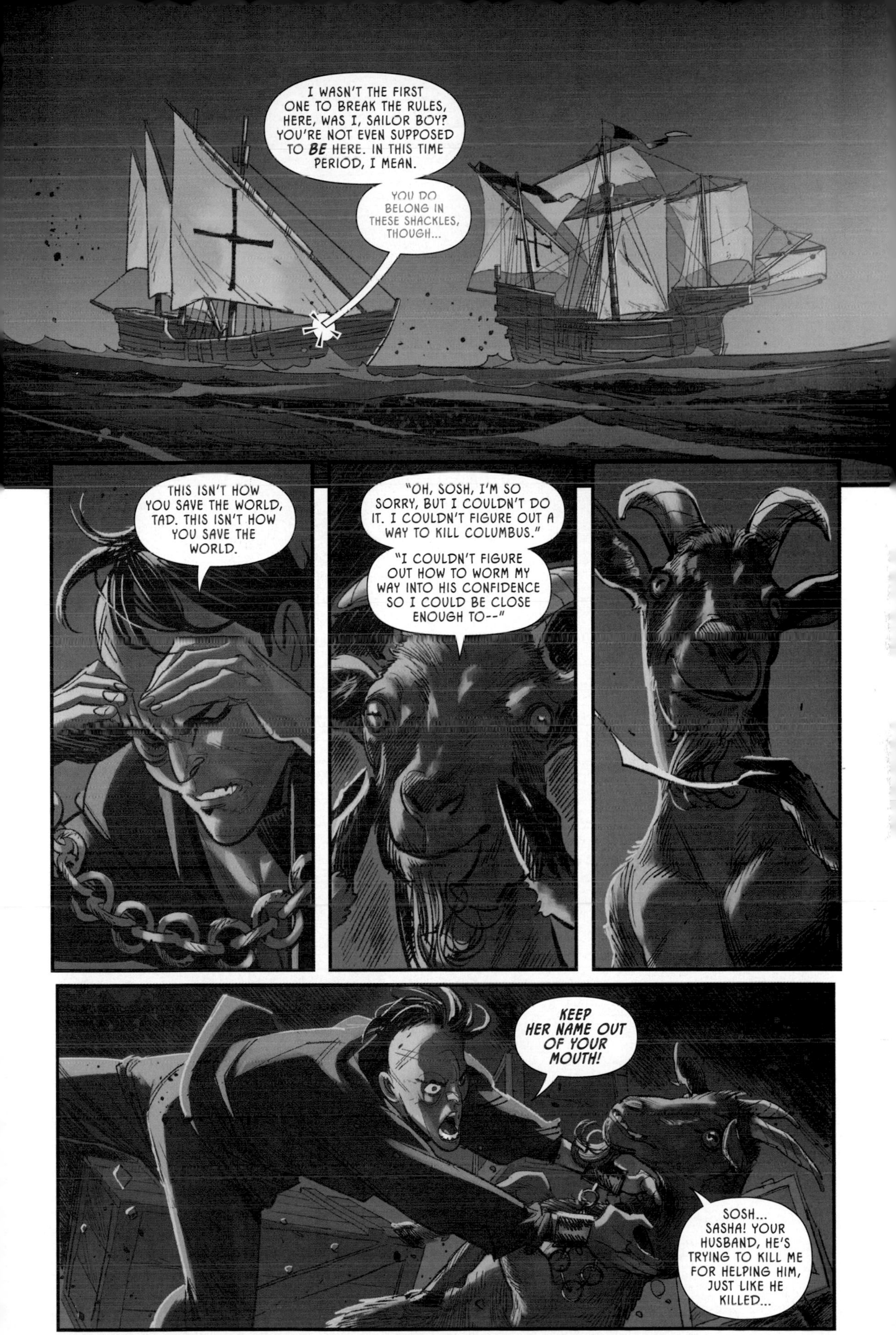
I WASN'T THE FIRST ONE TO BREAK THE RULES, HERE, WAS I, SAILOR BOY? YOU'RE NOT EVEN SUPPOSED TO BE HERE. IN THIS TIME PERIOD, I MEAN.
YOU DO BELONG IN THESE SHACKLES, THOUGH...
THIS ISN'T HOW YOU SAVE THE WORLD, TAD. THIS ISN'T HOW YOU SAVE THE WORLD.
"OH, SOSH, I'M SO SORRY, BUT I COULDN'T DO IT. I COULDN'T FIGURE OUT A WAY TO KILL COLUMBUS."
"I COULDN'T FIGURE OUT HOW TO WORM MY WAY INTO HIS CONFIDENCE SO I COULD BE CLOSE ENOUGH TO--"
KEEP HER NAME OUT OF YOUR MOUTH!
SOSH... SASHA! YOUR HUSBAND, HE'S TRYING TO KILL ME FOR HELPING HIM, JUST LIKE HE KILLED...

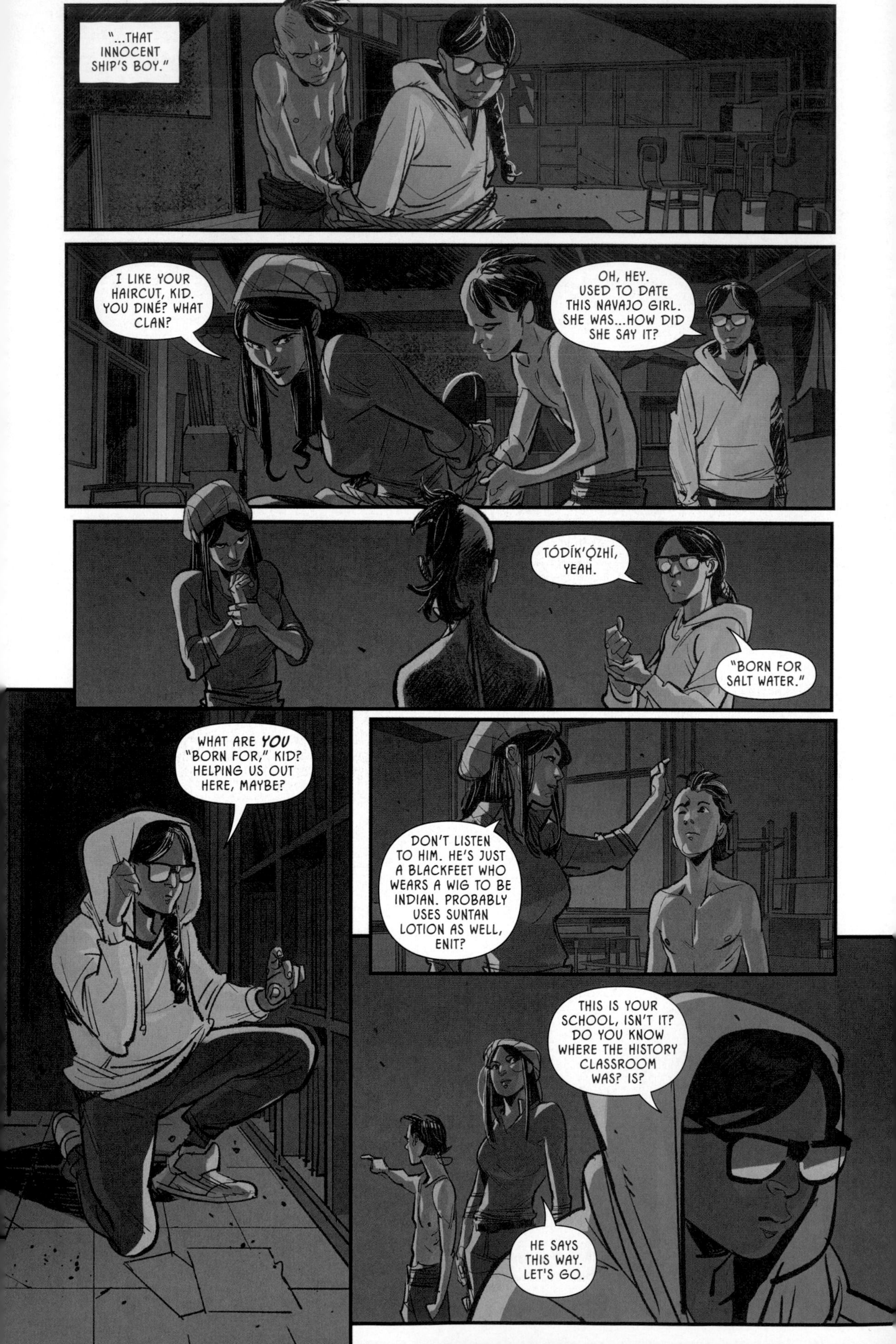
"...THAT INNOCENT SHIP'S BOY."
I LIKE YOUR HAIRCUT, KID. YOU DINÉ? WHAT CLAN?
OH, HEY. USED TO DATE THIS NAVAJO GIRL. SHE WAS...HOW DID SHE SAY IT?
TÓDÍK'ÓZHÍ, YEAH.
"BORN FOR SALT WATER."
WHAT ARE *YOU* "BORN FOR," KID? HELPING US OUT HERE, MAYBE?
DON'T LISTEN TO HIM. HE'S JUST A BLACKFEET WHO WEARS A WIG TO BE INDIAN. PROBABLY USES SUNTAN LOTION AS WELL, ENIT?
THIS IS YOUR SCHOOL, ISN'T IT? DO YOU KNOW WHERE THE HISTORY CLASSROOM WAS? IS?
HE SAYS THIS WAY. LET'S GO.

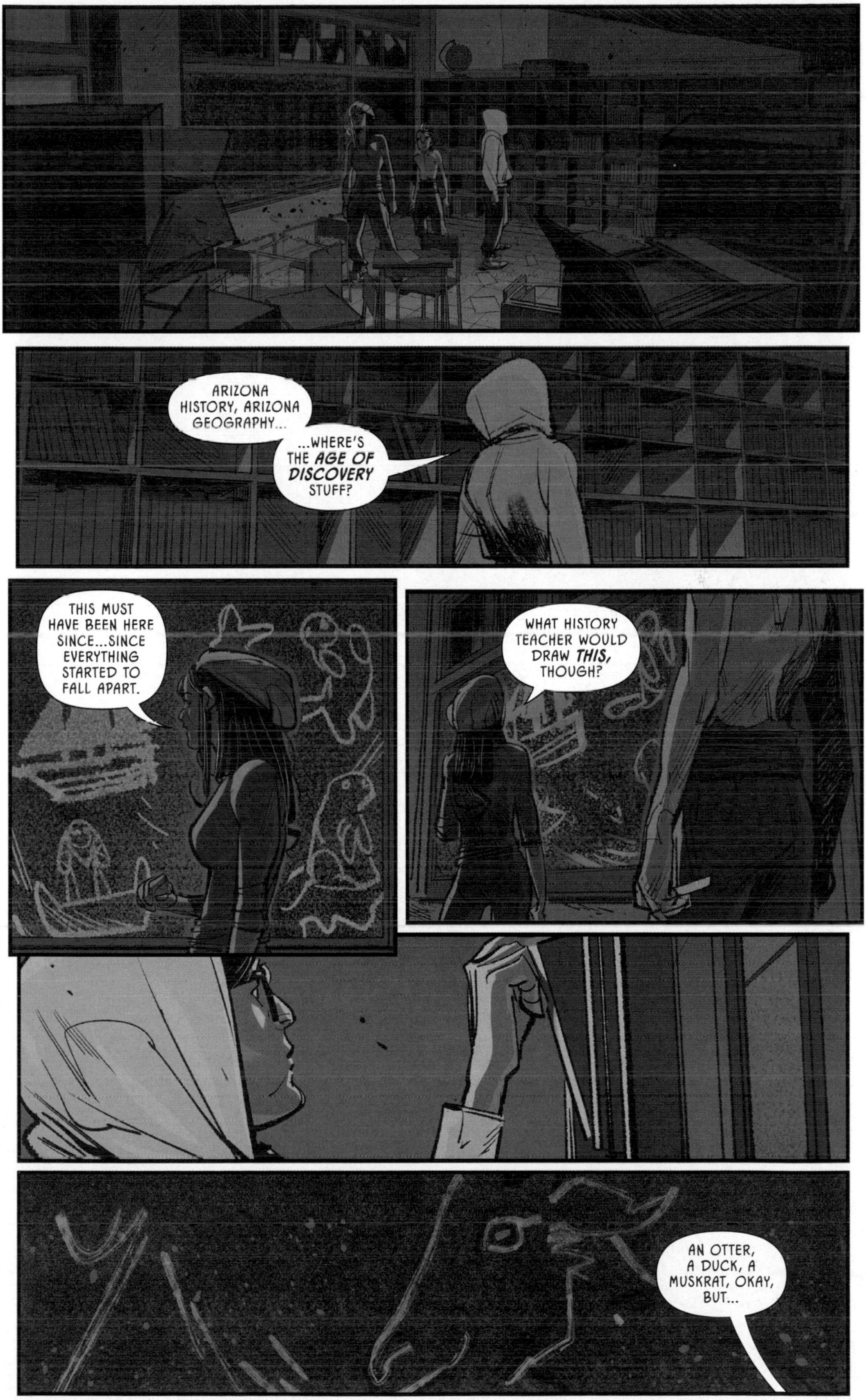
ARIZONA HISTORY, ARIZONA GEOGRAPHY...
...WHERE'S THE AGE OF DISCOVERY STUFF?
THIS MUST HAVE BEEN HERE SINCE...SINCE EVERYTHING STARTED TO FALL APART.
WHAT HISTORY TEACHER WOULD DRAW THIS, THOUGH?
AN OTTER, A DUCK, A MUSKRAT, OKAY, BUT...

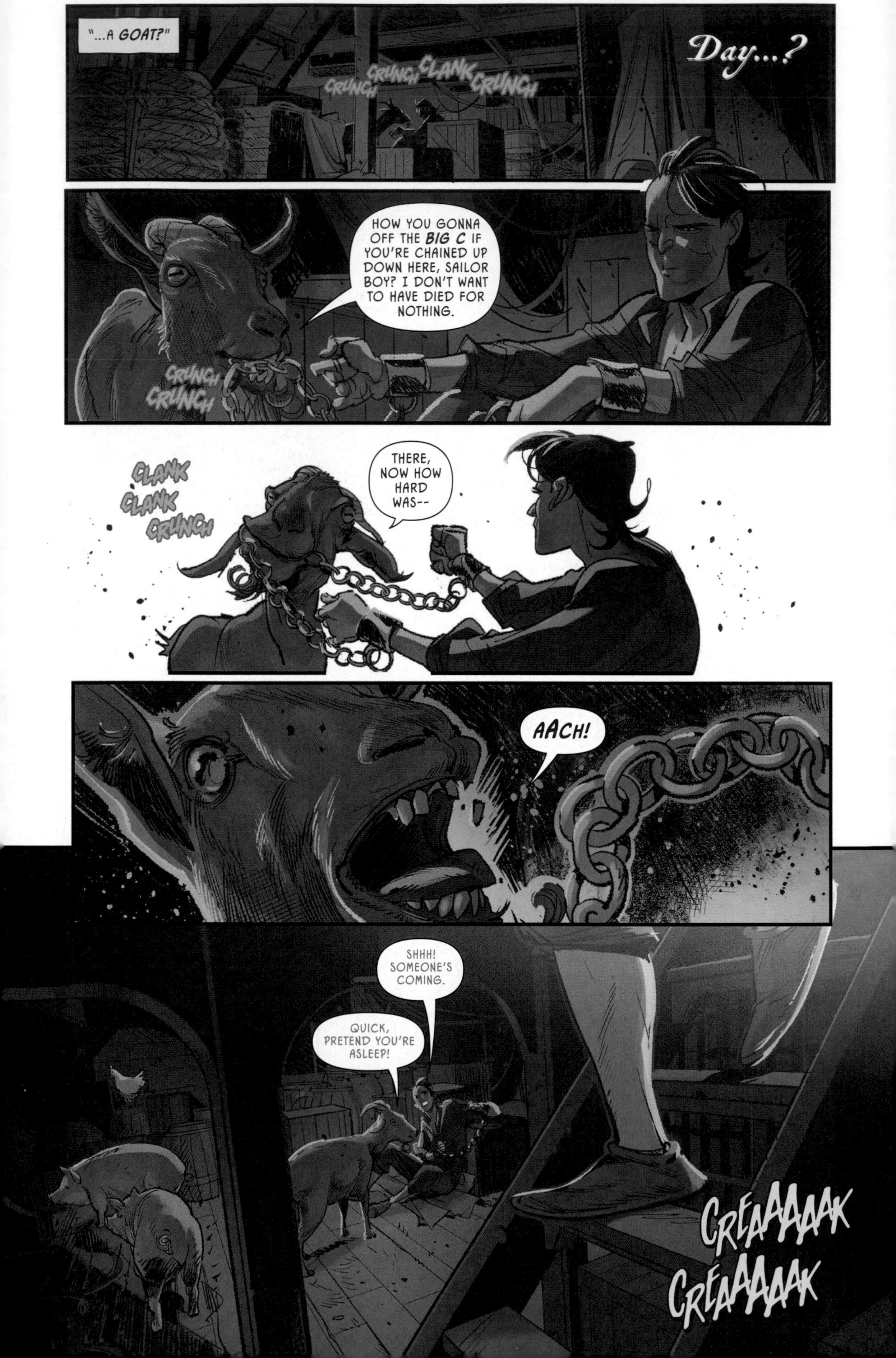
"...A GOAT?"
Day...?
CRUNCH CRUNCH CLANK CRUNCH
HOW YOU GONNA OFF THE BIG C IF YOU'RE CHAINED UP DOWN HERE, SAILOR BOY? I DON'T WANT TO HAVE DIED FOR NOTHING.
CRUNCH CRUNCH
CLANK CLANK CRUNCH
THERE, NOW HOW HARD WAS--
AACH!
SHHH! SOMEONE'S COMING.
QUICK, PRETEND YOU'RE ASLEEP!
CREAAAAAK CREAAAAAK

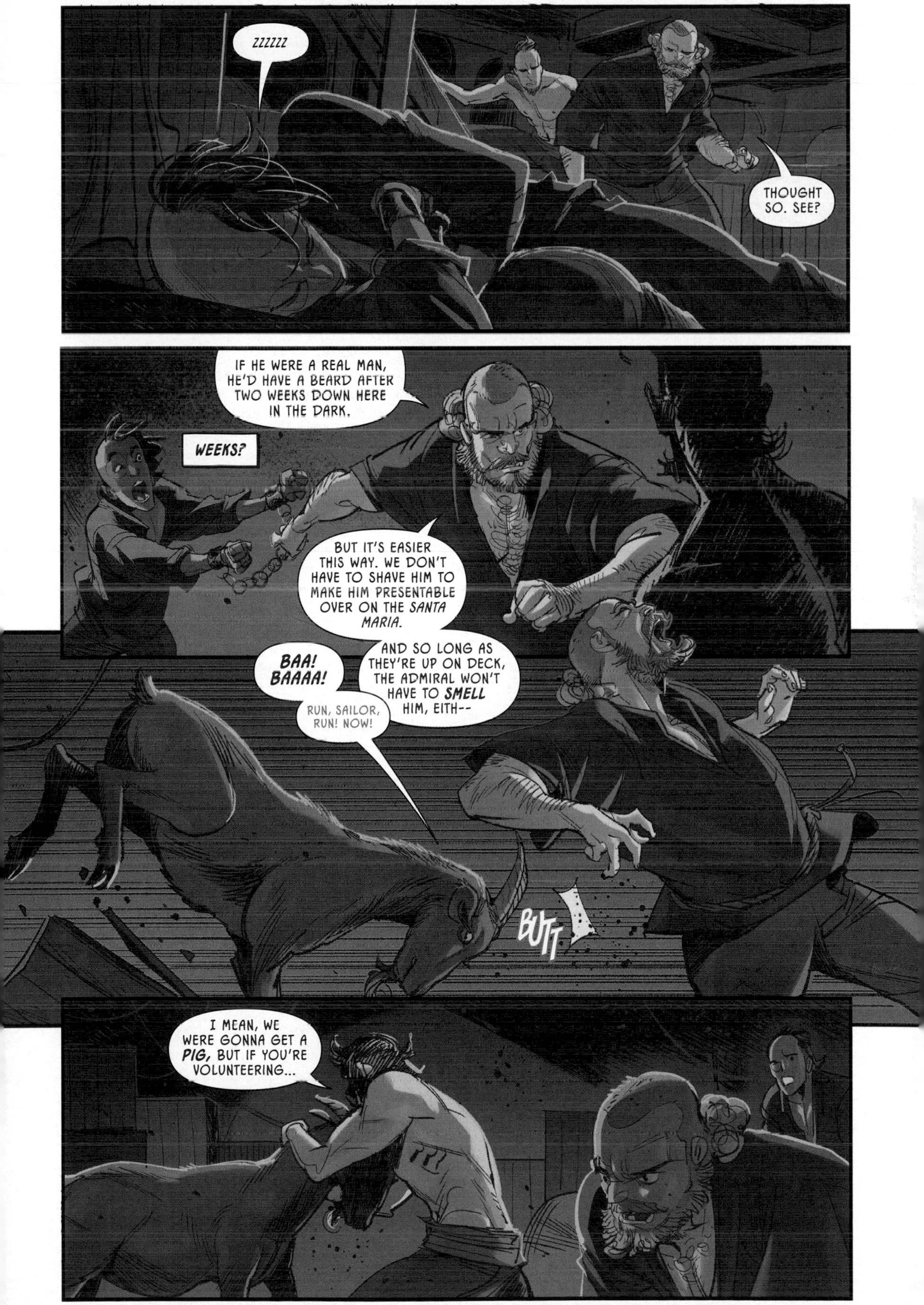
ZZZZZZ
THOUGHT SO. SEE?
IF HE WERE A REAL MAN, HE'D HAVE A BEARD AFTER TWO WEEKS DOWN HERE IN THE DARK.
WEEKS?
BUT IT'S EASIER THIS WAY. WE DON'T HAVE TO SHAVE HIM TO MAKE HIM PRESENTABLE OVER ON THE SANTA MARIA.
AND SO LONG AS THEY'RE UP ON DECK, THE ADMIRAL WON'T HAVE TO SMELL HIM, EITH--
BAA! BAAAA!
RUN, SAILOR, RUN! NOW!
BUTT
I MEAN, WE WERE GONNA GET A PIG, BUT IF YOU'RE VOLUNTEERING...

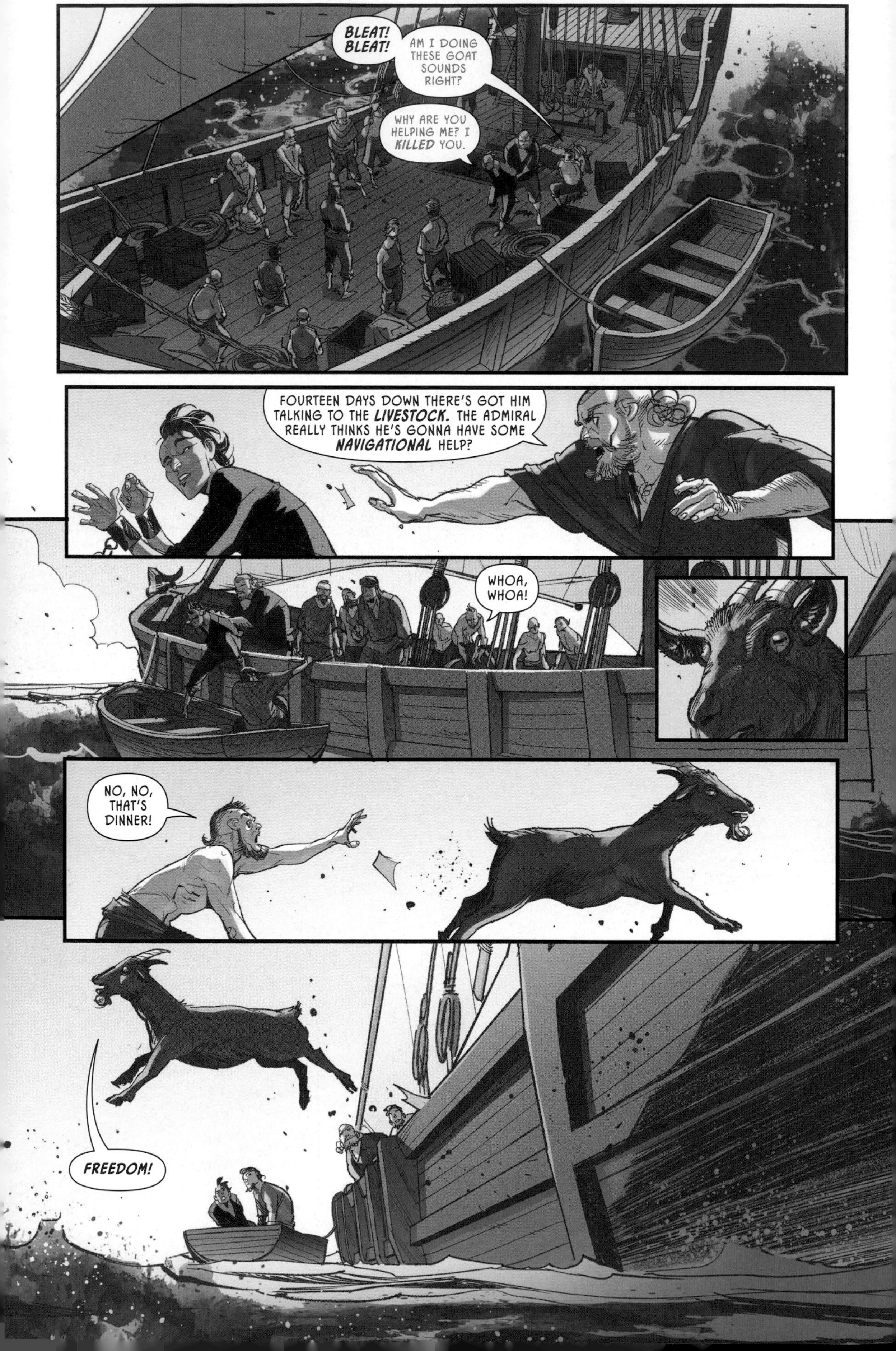
BLEAT! BLEAT!
AM I DOING THESE GOAT SOUNDS RIGHT?
WHY ARE YOU HELPING ME? I KILLED YOU.
FOURTEEN DAYS DOWN THERE'S GOT HIM TALKING TO THE LIVESTOCK. THE ADMIRAL REALLY THINKS HE'S GONNA HAVE SOME NAVIGATIONAL HELP?
WHOA, WHOA!
NO, NO, THAT'S DINNER!
FREEDOM!

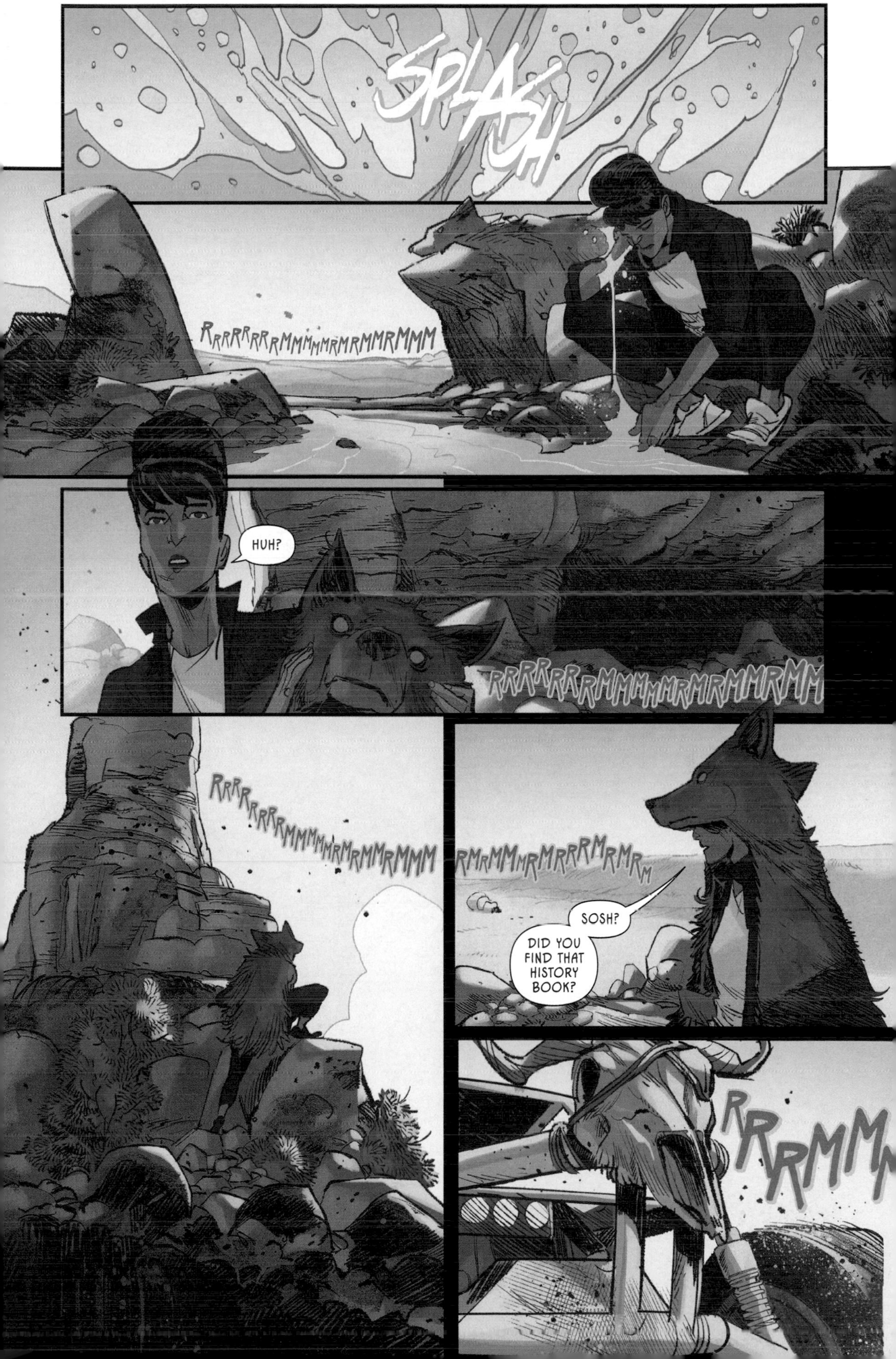
SPLASH
RRRRRRRMMMMMRMRMMRMMM
HUH?
RRRRRRRMMMMMMRMRMMRMM
RRRRRRRMMMMMRMRMMRMMM
RMRMMRMRRRMRMRM
SOSH?
DID YOU FIND THAT HISTORY BOOK?
RRRMMM

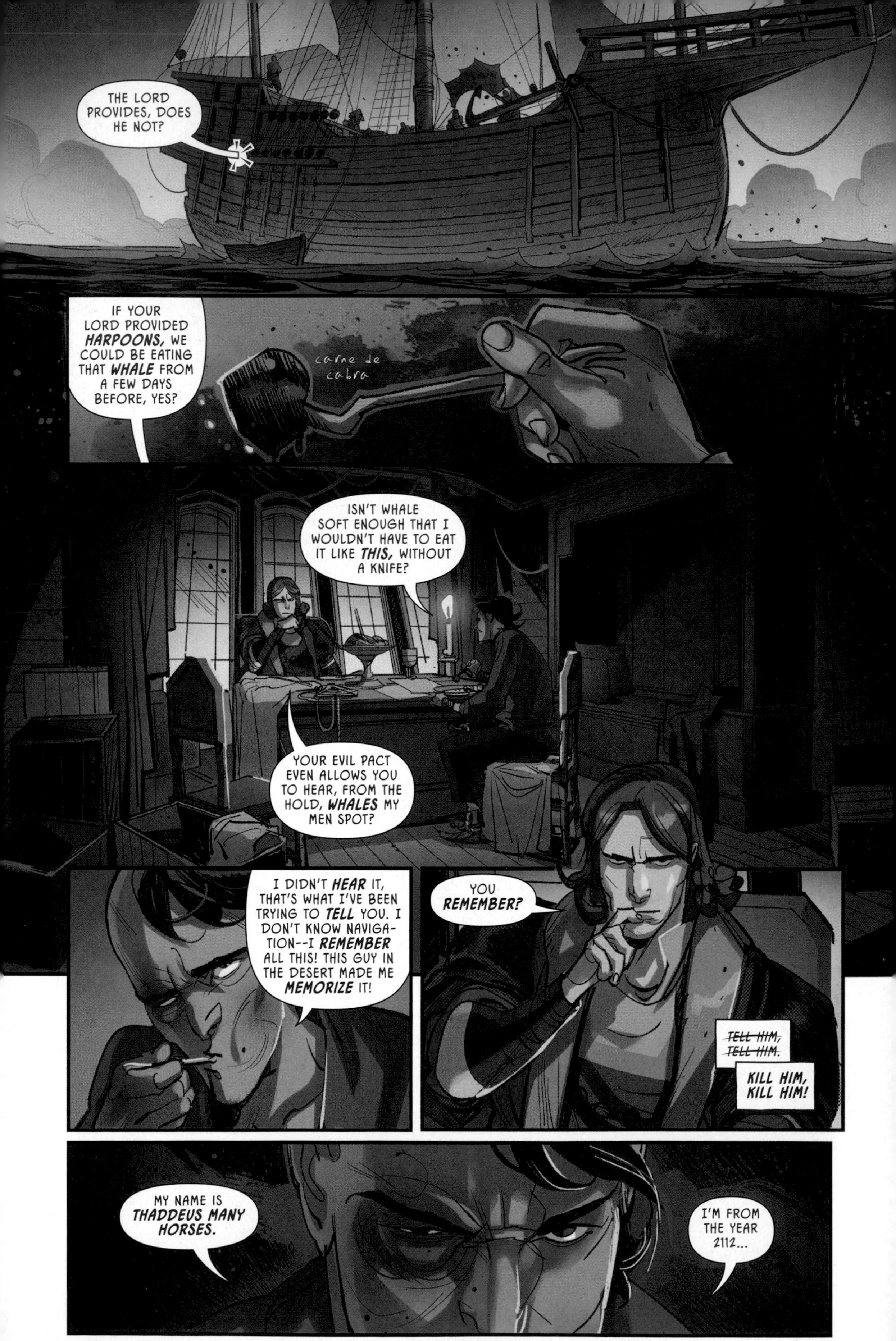
THE LORD PROVIDES, DOES HE NOT?
IF YOUR LORD PROVIDED HARPOONS, WE COULD BE EATING THAT WHALE FROM A FEW DAYS BEFORE, YES?
carne de cabra
ISN'T WHALE SOFT ENOUGH THAT I WOULDN'T HAVE TO EAT IT LIKE THIS, WITHOUT A KNIFE?
YOUR EVIL PACT EVEN ALLOWS YOU TO HEAR, FROM THE HOLD, WHALES MY MEN SPOT?
I DIDN'T HEAR IT, THAT'S WHAT I'VE BEEN TRYING TO TELL YOU. I DON'T KNOW NAVIGA-TION--I REMEMBER ALL THIS! THIS GUY IN THE DESERT MADE ME MEMORIZE IT!
YOU REMEMBER?
~~TELL HIM, TELL HIM.~~
KILL HIM, KILL HIM!
MY NAME IS THADDEUS MANY HORSES.
I'M FROM THE YEAR 2112...

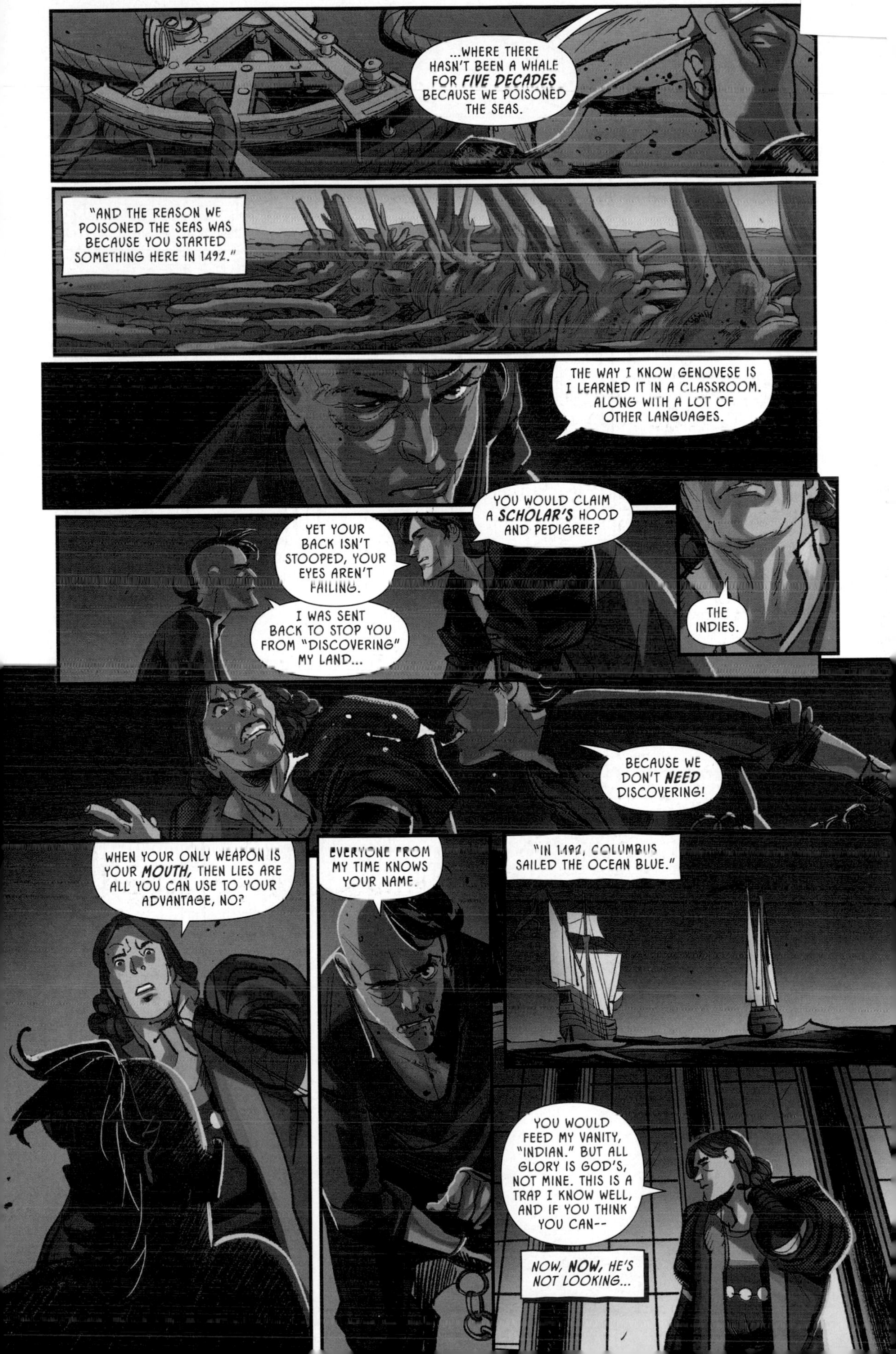
...WHERE THERE HASN'T BEEN A WHALE FOR FIVE DECADES BECAUSE WE POISONED THE SEAS.
"AND THE REASON WE POISONED THE SEAS WAS BECAUSE YOU STARTED SOMETHING HERE IN 1492."
THE WAY I KNOW GENOVESE IS I LEARNED IT IN A CLASSROOM. ALONG WITH A LOT OF OTHER LANGUAGES.
YOU WOULD CLAIM A SCHOLAR'S HOOD AND PEDIGREE?
YET YOUR BACK ISN'T STOOPED, YOUR EYES AREN'T FAILING.
I WAS SENT BACK TO STOP YOU FROM "DISCOVERING" MY LAND...
THE INDIES.
BECAUSE WE DON'T NEED DISCOVERING!
WHEN YOUR ONLY WEAPON IS YOUR MOUTH, THEN LIES ARE ALL YOU CAN USE TO YOUR ADVANTAGE, NO?
EVERYONE FROM MY TIME KNOWS YOUR NAME.
"IN 1492, COLUMBUS SAILED THE OCEAN BLUE."
YOU WOULD FEED MY VANITY, "INDIAN." BUT ALL GLORY IS GOD'S, NOT MINE. THIS IS A TRAP I KNOW WELL, AND IF YOU THINK YOU CAN--
NOW, NOW, HE'S NOT LOOKING...

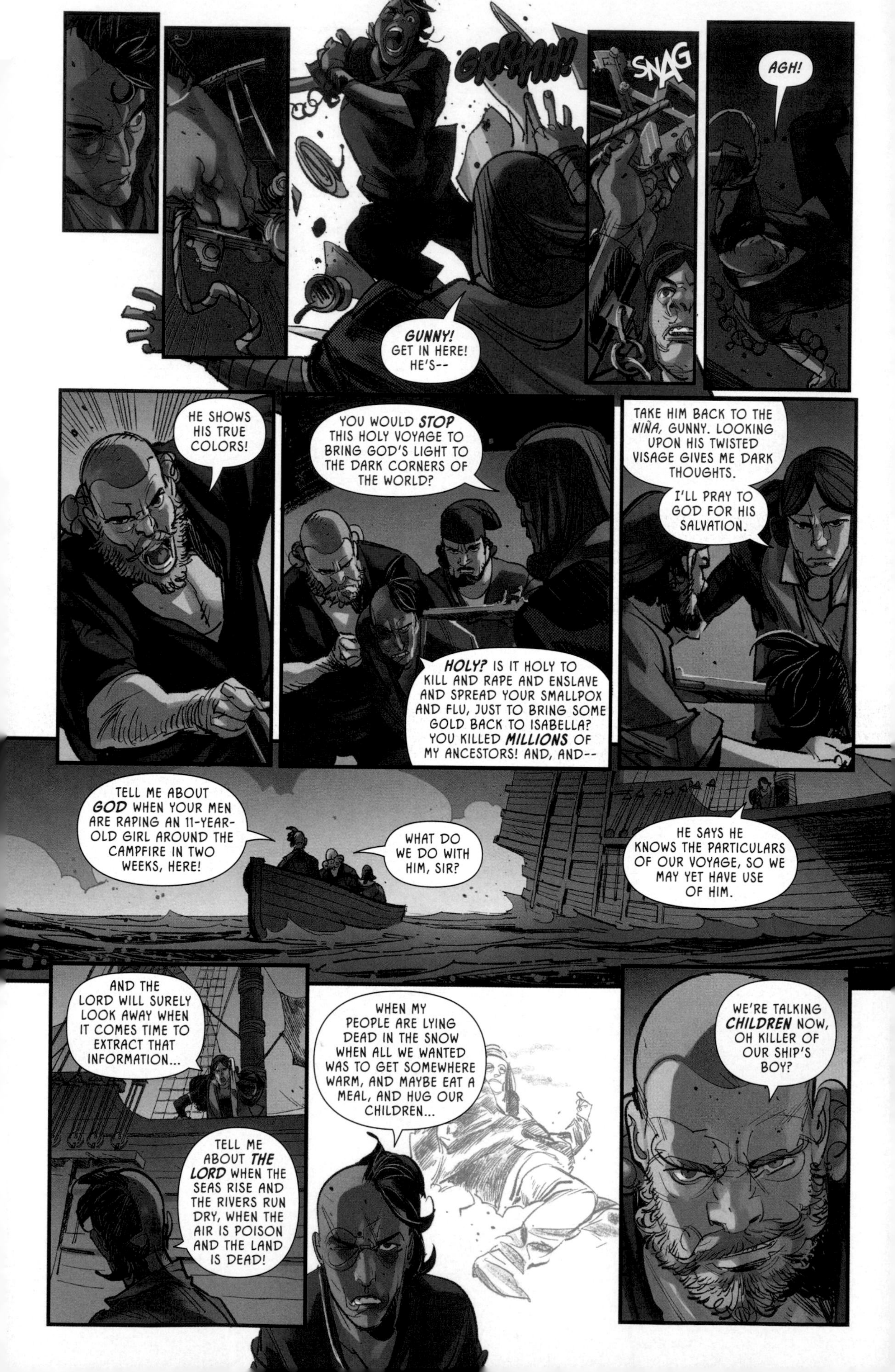

GRRAAHH!!
GUNNY! GET IN HERE! HE'S--
SNAG
AGH!
HE SHOWS HIS TRUE COLORS!
YOU WOULD STOP THIS HOLY VOYAGE TO BRING GOD'S LIGHT TO THE DARK CORNERS OF THE WORLD?
HOLY? IS IT HOLY TO KILL AND RAPE AND ENSLAVE AND SPREAD YOUR SMALLPOX AND FLU, JUST TO BRING SOME GOLD BACK TO ISABELLA? YOU KILLED MILLIONS OF MY ANCESTORS! AND, AND--
TAKE HIM BACK TO THE NIÑA, GUNNY. LOOKING UPON HIS TWISTED VISAGE GIVES ME DARK THOUGHTS.
I'LL PRAY TO GOD FOR HIS SALVATION.
TELL ME ABOUT GOD WHEN YOUR MEN ARE RAPING AN 11-YEAR-OLD GIRL AROUND THE CAMPFIRE IN TWO WEEKS, HERE!
WHAT DO WE DO WITH HIM, SIR?
HE SAYS HE KNOWS THE PARTICULARS OF OUR VOYAGE, SO WE MAY YET HAVE USE OF HIM.
AND THE LORD WILL SURELY LOOK AWAY WHEN IT COMES TIME TO EXTRACT THAT INFORMATION...
TELL ME ABOUT THE LORD WHEN THE SEAS RISE AND THE RIVERS RUN DRY, WHEN THE AIR IS POISON AND THE LAND IS DEAD!
WHEN MY PEOPLE ARE LYING DEAD IN THE SNOW WHEN ALL WE WANTED WAS TO GET SOMEWHERE WARM, AND MAYBE EAT A MEAL, AND HUG OUR CHILDREN...
WE'RE TALKING CHILDREN NOW, OH KILLER OF OUR SHIP'S BOY?

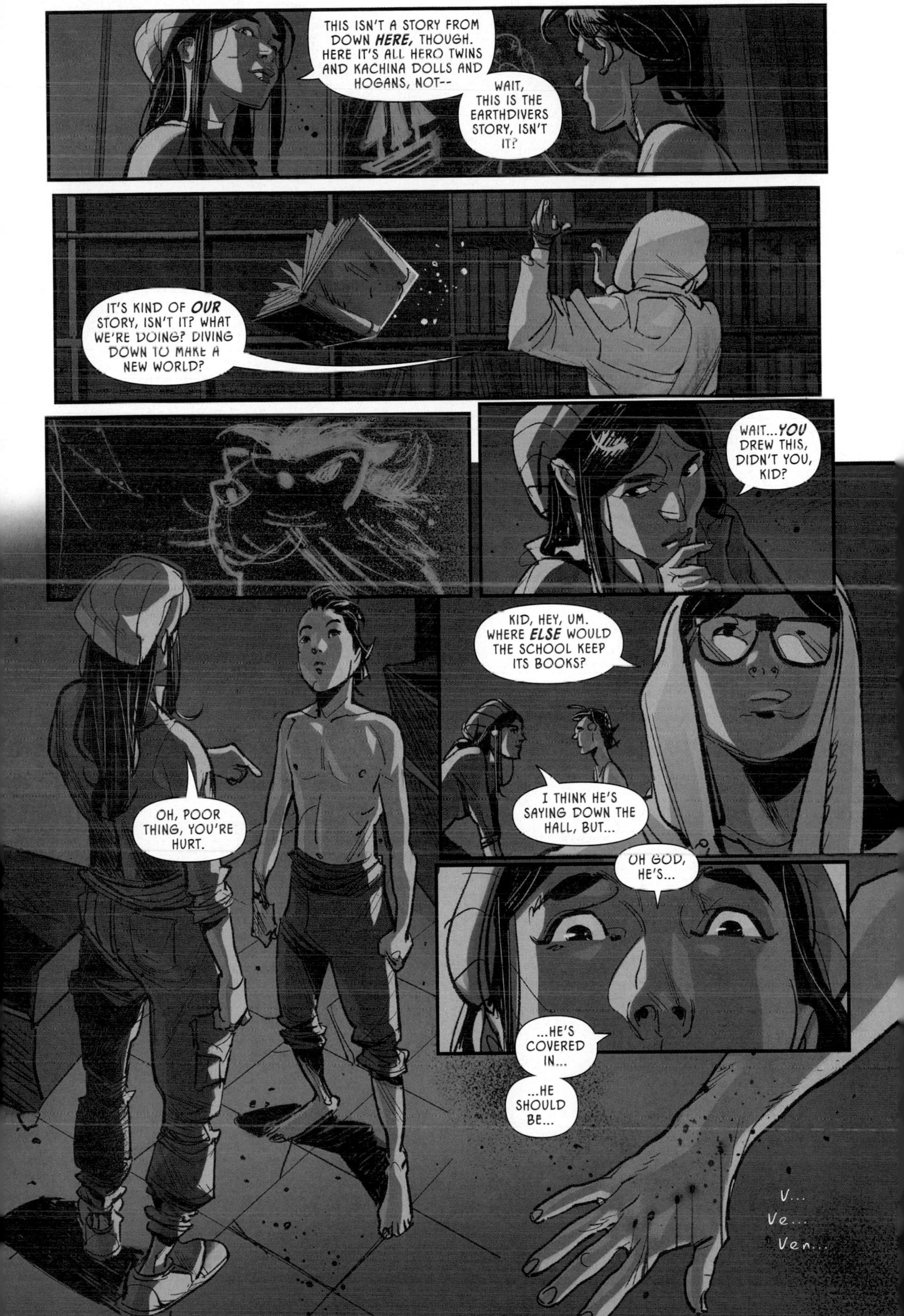

THIS ISN'T A STORY FROM DOWN HERE, THOUGH. HERE IT'S ALL HERO TWINS AND KACHINA DOLLS AND HOGANS, NOT--
WAIT, THIS IS THE EARTHDIVERS STORY, ISN'T IT?
IT'S KIND OF OUR STORY, ISN'T IT? WHAT WE'RE DOING? DIVING DOWN TO MAKE A NEW WORLD?
WAIT...YOU DREW THIS, DIDN'T YOU, KID?
KID, HEY, UM. WHERE ELSE WOULD THE SCHOOL KEEP ITS BOOKS?
I THINK HE'S SAYING DOWN THE HALL, BUT...
OH, POOR THING, YOU'RE HURT.
OH GOD, HE'S...
...HE'S COVERED IN...
...HE SHOULD BE...
V...
Ve...
Ven...

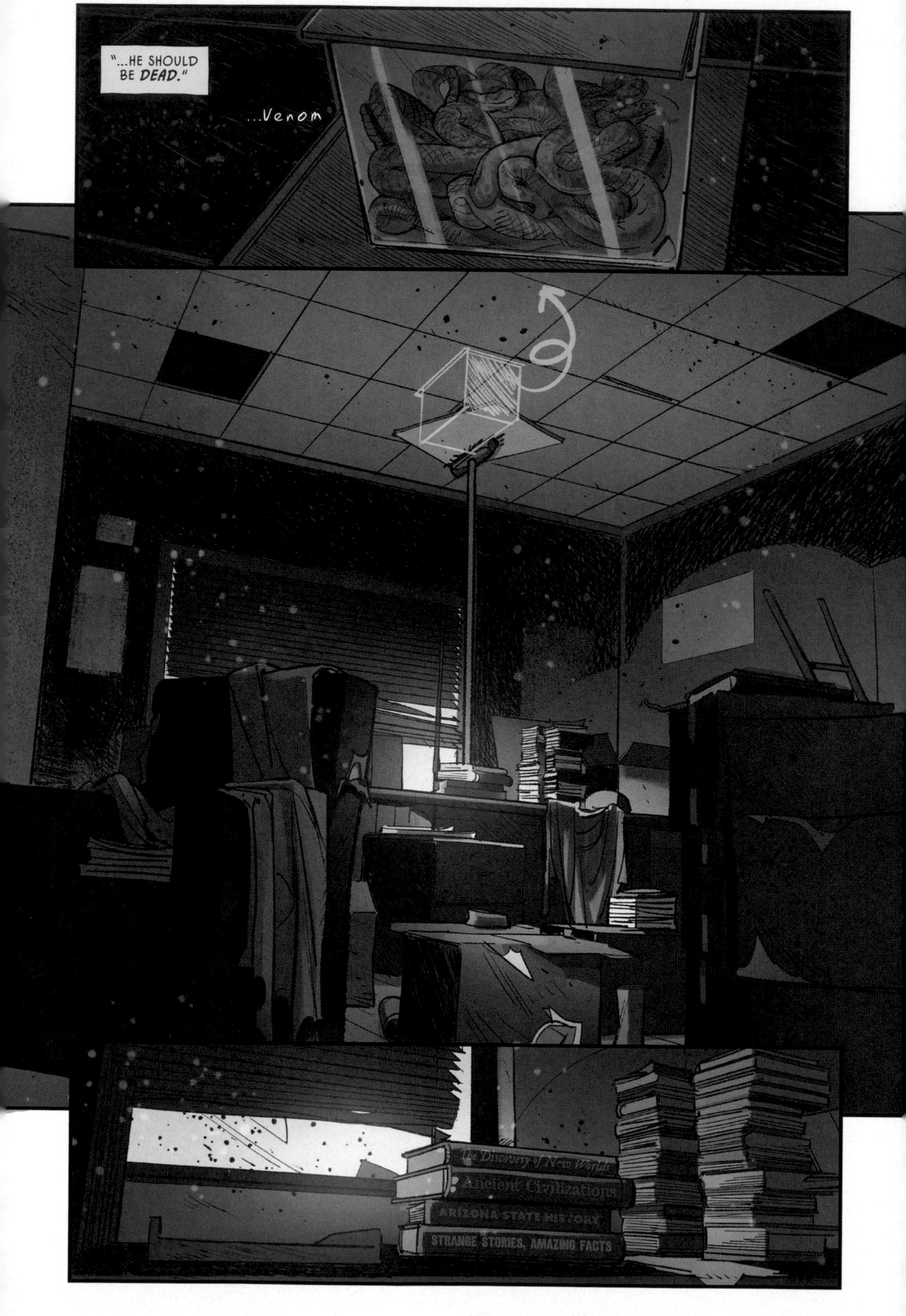
"...HE SHOULD BE *DEAD.*"
...Venom
The Discovery of New Worlds
Ancient Civilizations
ARIZONA STATE HISTORY
STRANGE STORIES, AMAZING FACTS

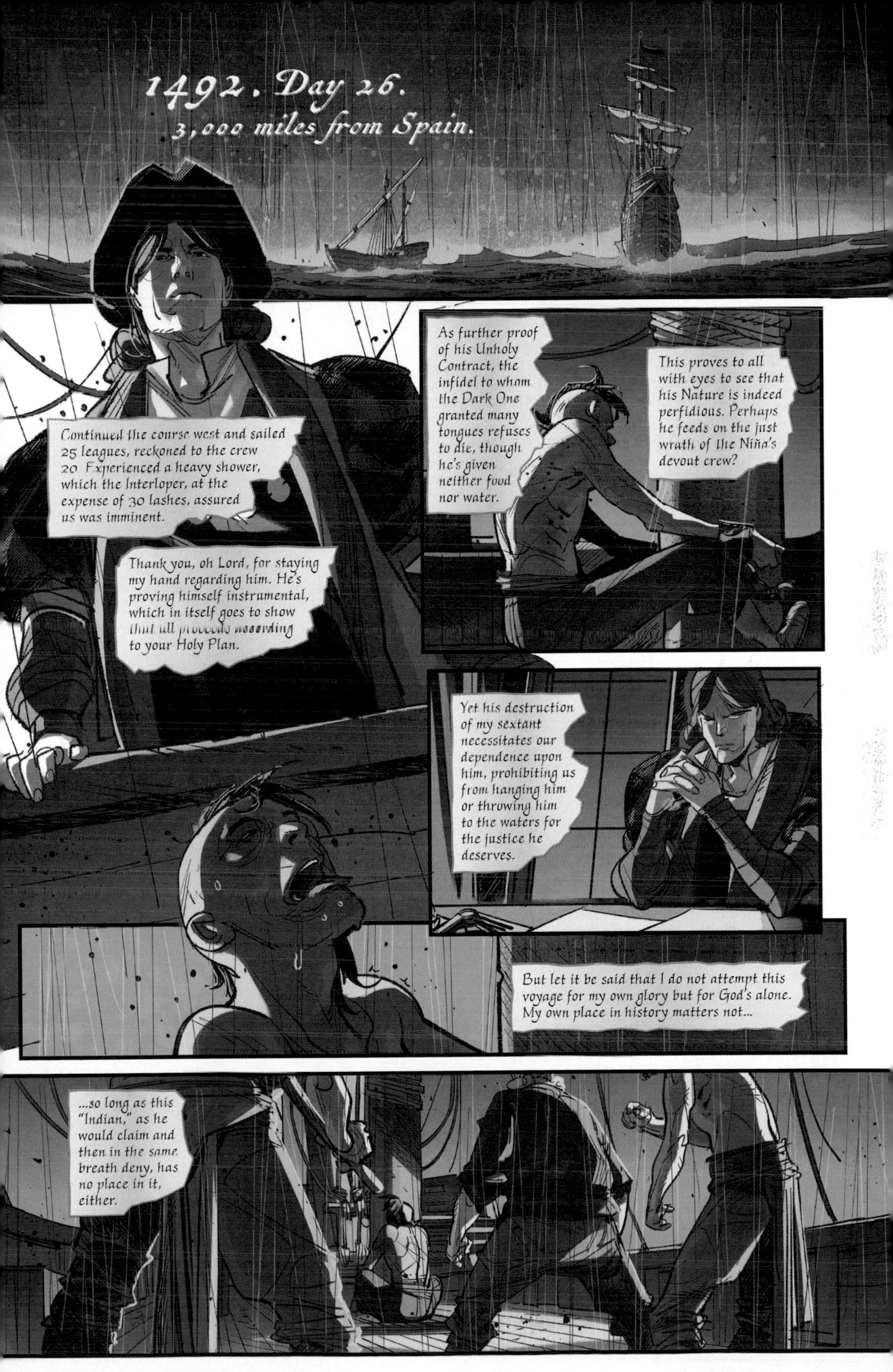
1492. Day 26.
3,000 miles from Spain.
Continued the course west and sailed 25 leagues, reckoned to the crew 20. Experienced a heavy shower, which the Interloper, at the expense of 30 lashes, assured us was imminent.
Thank you, oh Lord, for staying my hand regarding him. He's proving himself instrumental, which in itself goes to show that all proceeds according to your Holy Plan.
As further proof of his Unholy Contract, the infidel to whom the Dark One granted many tongues refuses to die, though he's given neither food nor water.
This proves to all with eyes to see that his Nature is indeed perfidious. Perhaps he feeds on the just wrath of the Niña's devout crew?
Yet his destruction of my sextant necessitates our dependence upon him, prohibiting us from hanging him or throwing him to the waters for the justice he deserves.
But let it be said that I do not attempt this voyage for my own glory but for God's alone. My own place in history matters not...
...so long as this "Indian," as he would claim and then in the same breath deny, has no place in it, either.

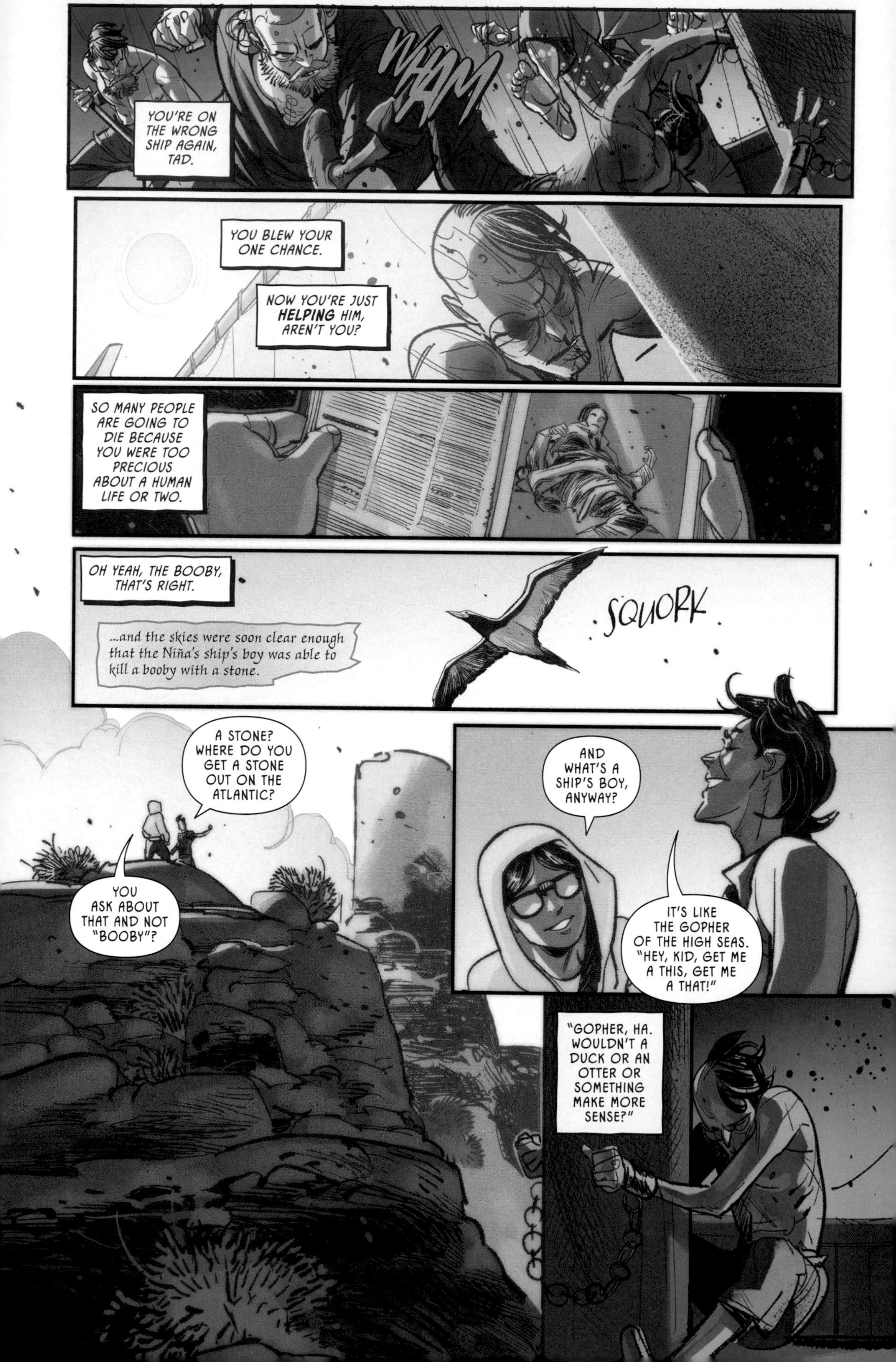

YOU'RE ON THE WRONG SHIP AGAIN, TAD.
WHAM
YOU BLEW YOUR ONE CHANCE.
NOW YOU'RE JUST **HELPING** HIM, AREN'T YOU?
SO MANY PEOPLE ARE GOING TO DIE BECAUSE YOU WERE TOO PRECIOUS ABOUT A HUMAN LIFE OR TWO.
OH YEAH, THE BOOBY, THAT'S RIGHT.
...and the skies were soon clear enough that the Niña's ship's boy was able to kill a booby with a stone.
SQUORK
A STONE? WHERE DO YOU GET A STONE OUT ON THE ATLANTIC?
YOU ASK ABOUT THAT AND NOT "BOOBY"?
AND WHAT'S A SHIP'S BOY, ANYWAY?
IT'S LIKE THE GOPHER OF THE HIGH SEAS. "HEY, KID, GET ME A THIS, GET ME A THAT!"
"GOPHER, HA. WOULDN'T A DUCK OR AN OTTER OR SOMETHING MAKE MORE SENSE?"

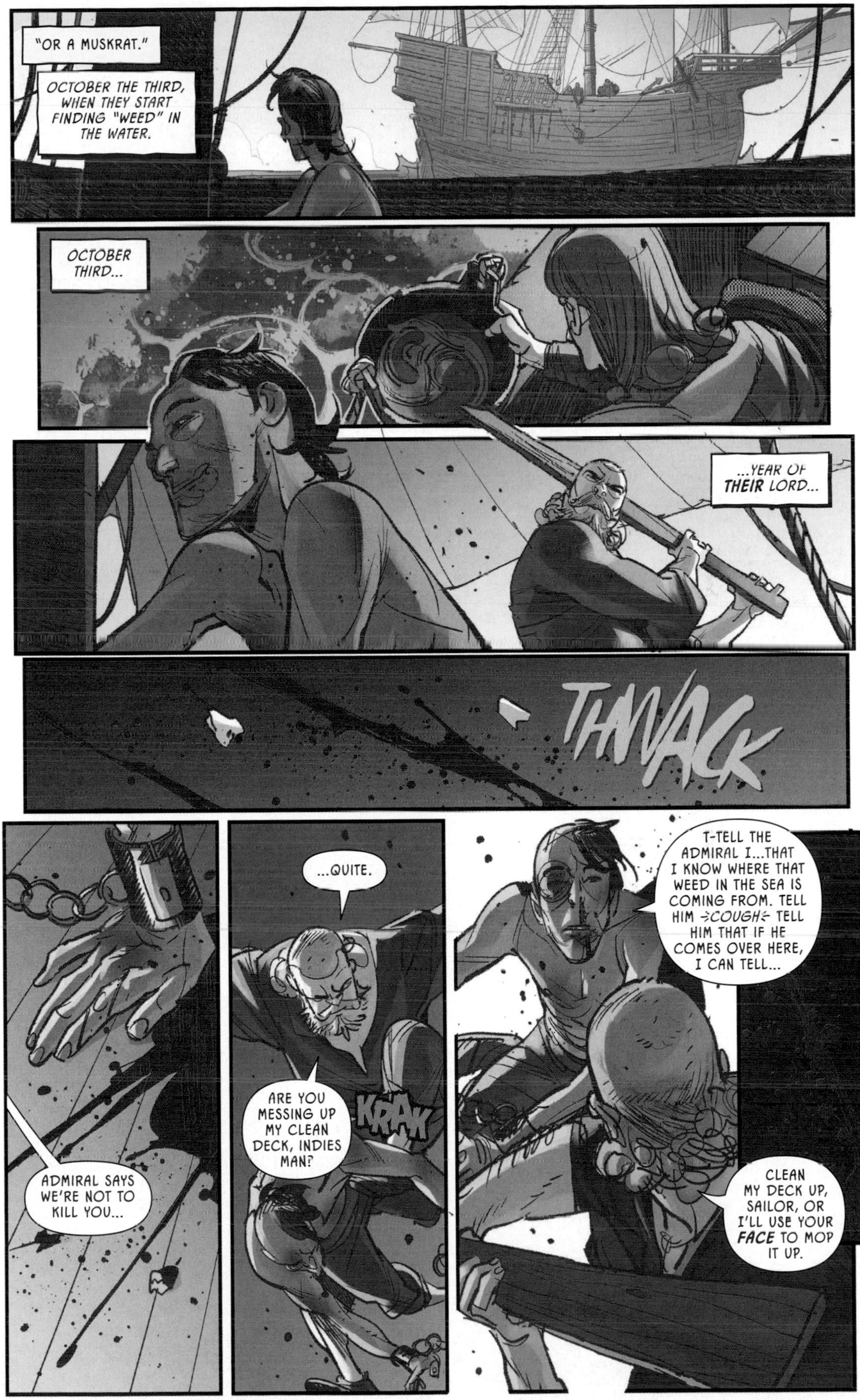
"OR A MUSKRAT."
OCTOBER THE THIRD, WHEN THEY START FINDING "WEED" IN THE WATER.
OCTOBER THIRD...
...YEAR OF THEIR LORD...
THWACK
ADMIRAL SAYS WE'RE NOT TO KILL YOU...
...QUITE.
ARE YOU MESSING UP MY CLEAN DECK, INDIES MAN?
KRAK
T-TELL THE ADMIRAL I...THAT I KNOW WHERE THAT WEED IN THE SEA IS COMING FROM. TELL HIM *COUGH* TELL HIM THAT IF HE COMES OVER HERE, I CAN TELL...
CLEAN MY DECK UP, SAILOR, OR I'LL USE YOUR FACE TO MOP IT UP.

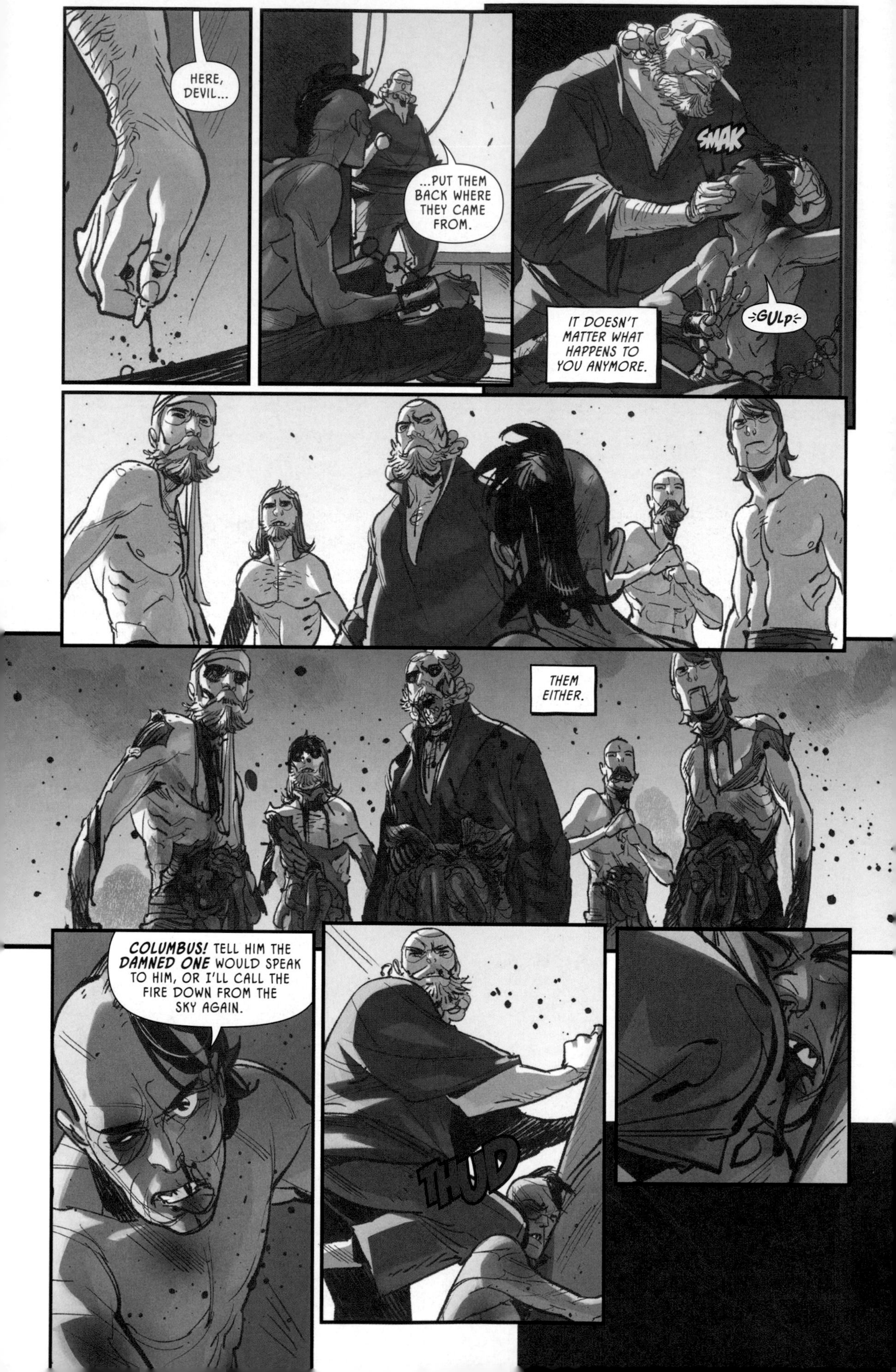
HERE, DEVIL...
...PUT THEM BACK WHERE THEY CAME FROM.
SMAK
IT DOESN'T MATTER WHAT HAPPENS TO YOU ANYMORE.
GULp
THEM EITHER.
COLUMBUS! TELL HIM THE DAMNED ONE WOULD SPEAK TO HIM, OR I'LL CALL THE FIRE DOWN FROM THE SKY AGAIN.
THUD

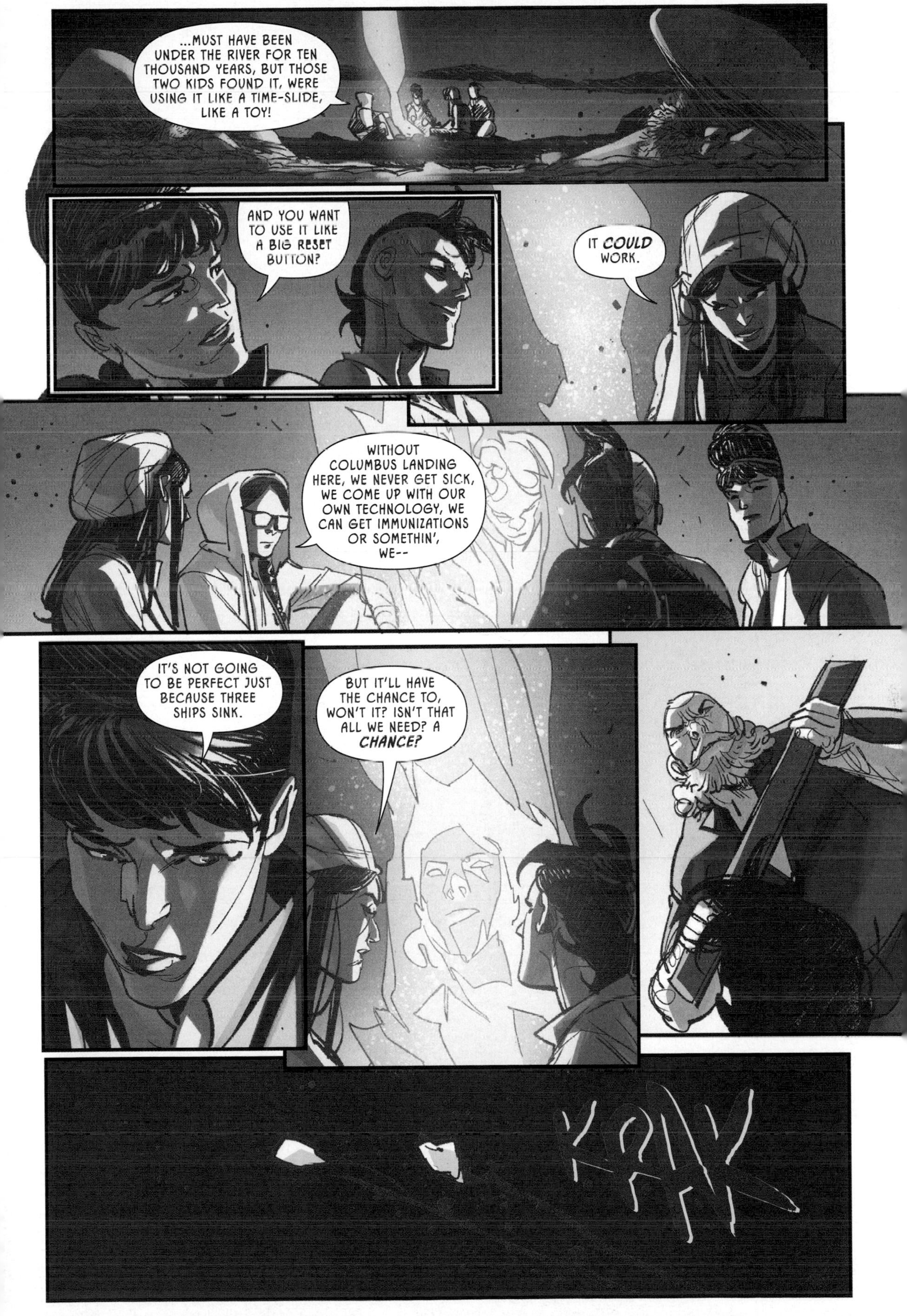
...MUST HAVE BEEN UNDER THE RIVER FOR TEN THOUSAND YEARS, BUT THOSE TWO KIDS FOUND IT, WERE USING IT LIKE A TIME-SLIDE, LIKE A TOY!
AND YOU WANT TO USE IT LIKE A BIG RESET BUTTON?
IT COULD WORK.
WITHOUT COLUMBUS LANDING HERE, WE NEVER GET SICK, WE COME UP WITH OUR OWN TECHNOLOGY, WE CAN GET IMMUNIZATIONS OR SOMETHIN', WE--
IT'S NOT GOING TO BE PERFECT JUST BECAUSE THREE SHIPS SINK.
BUT IT'LL HAVE THE CHANCE TO, WON'T IT? ISN'T THAT ALL WE NEED? A CHANCE?
KRAK

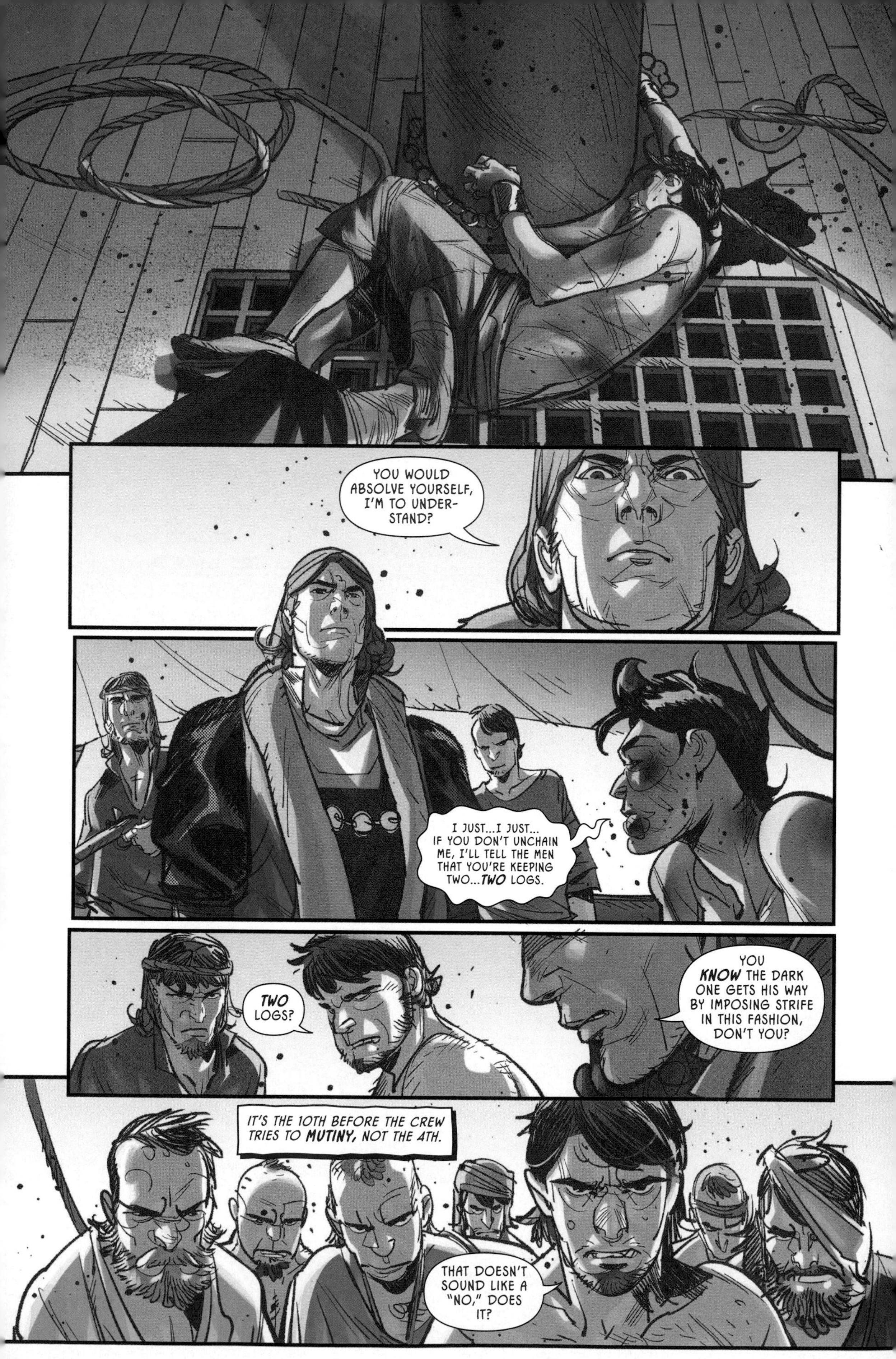
YOU WOULD ABSOLVE YOURSELF, I'M TO UNDER-STAND?
I JUST...I JUST... IF YOU DON'T UNCHAIN ME, I'LL TELL THE MEN THAT YOU'RE KEEPING TWO...TWO LOGS.
TWO LOGS?
YOU KNOW THE DARK ONE GETS HIS WAY BY IMPOSING STRIFE IN THIS FASHION, DON'T YOU?
IT'S THE 10TH BEFORE THE CREW TRIES TO MUTINY, NOT THE 4TH.
THAT DOESN'T SOUND LIKE A "NO," DOES IT?

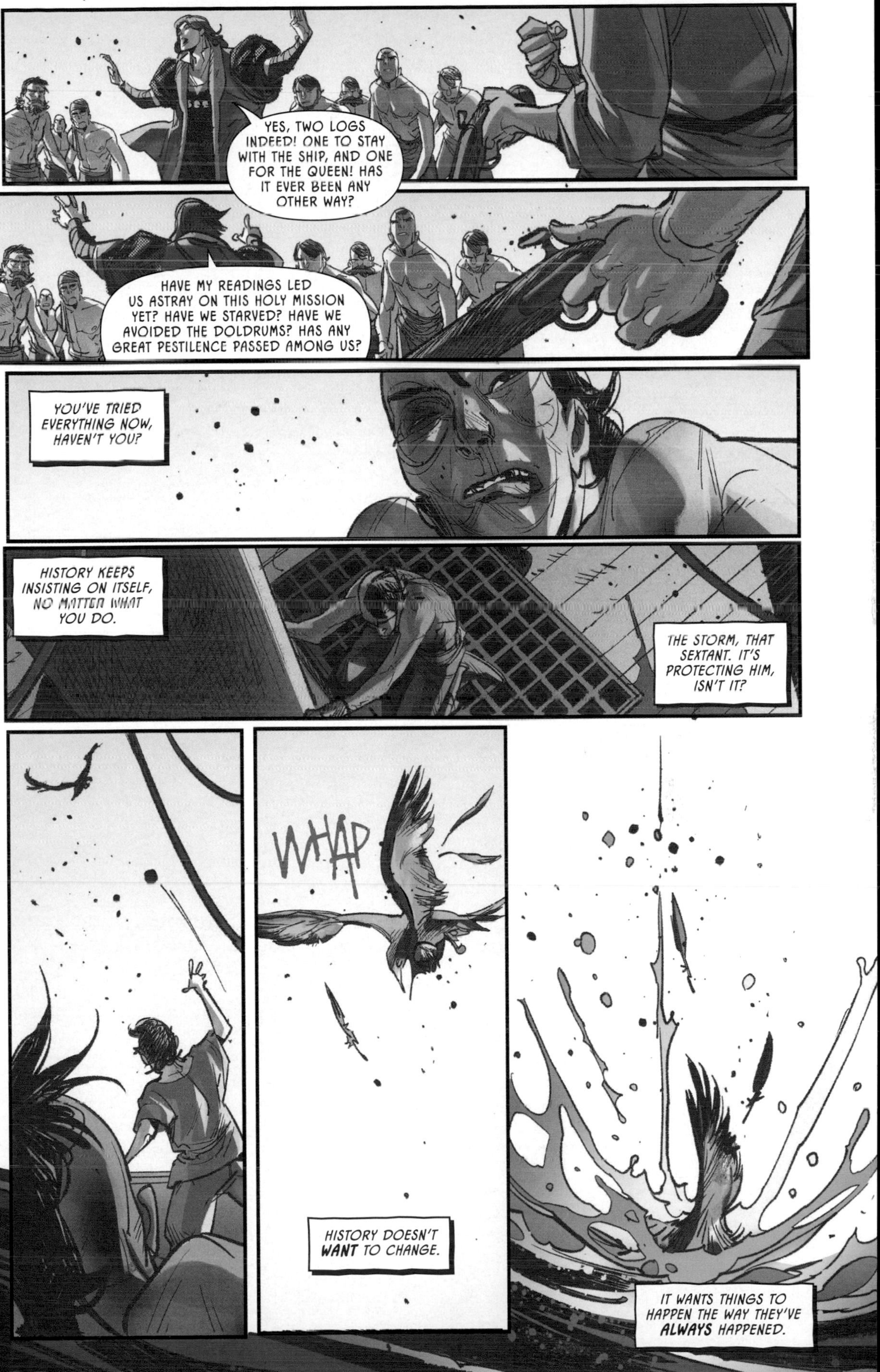
YES, TWO LOGS INDEED! ONE TO STAY WITH THE SHIP, AND ONE FOR THE QUEEN! HAS IT EVER BEEN ANY OTHER WAY?
HAVE MY READINGS LED US ASTRAY ON THIS HOLY MISSION YET? HAVE WE STARVED? HAVE WE AVOIDED THE DOLDRUMS? HAS ANY GREAT PESTILENCE PASSED AMONG US?
YOU'VE TRIED EVERYTHING NOW, HAVEN'T YOU?
HISTORY KEEPS INSISTING ON ITSELF, NO MATTER WHAT YOU DO.
THE STORM, THAT SEXTANT. IT'S PROTECTING HIM, ISN'T IT?
WHAP
HISTORY DOESN'T WANT TO CHANGE.
IT WANTS THINGS TO HAPPEN THE WAY THEY'VE ALWAYS HAPPENED.

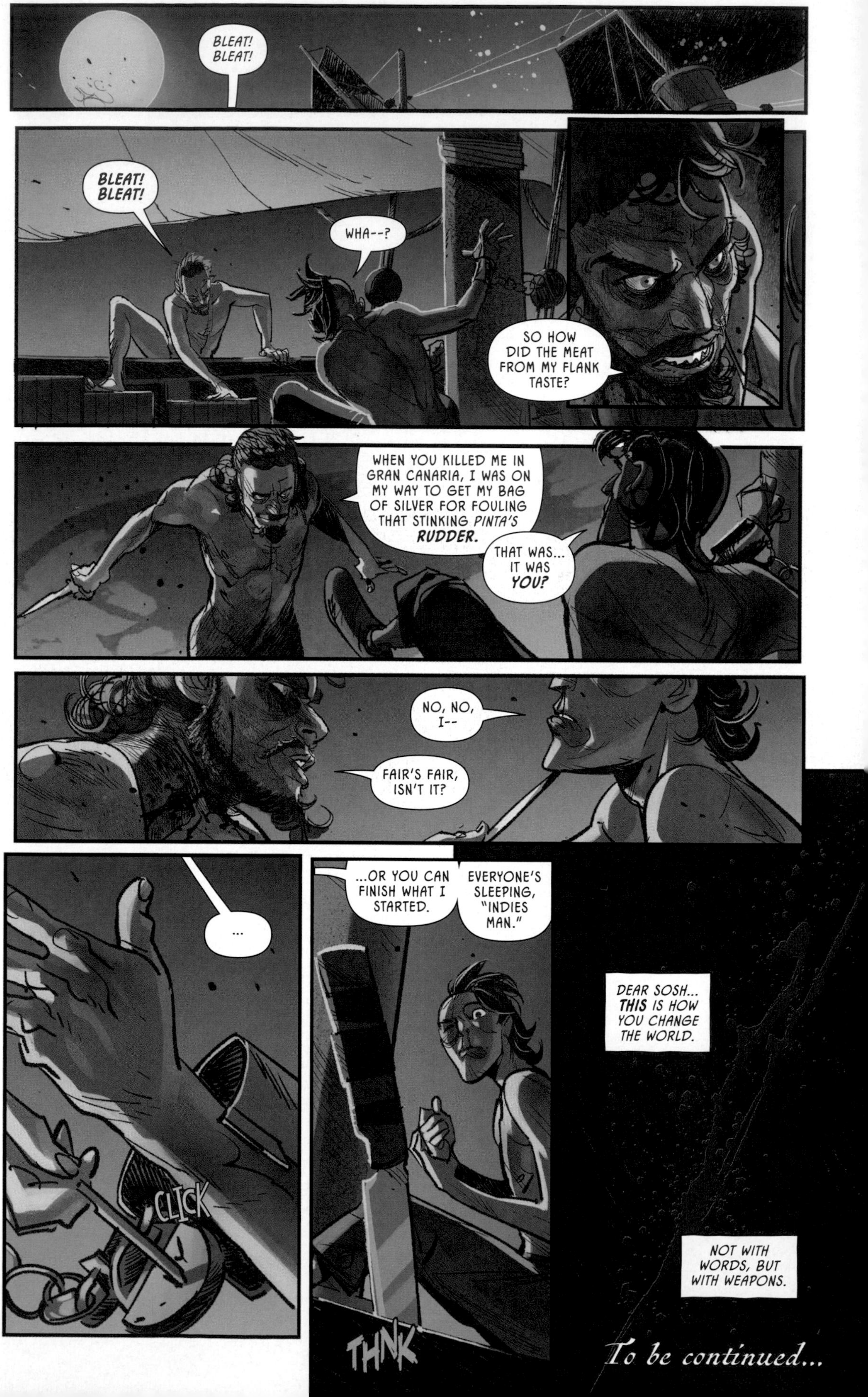
BLEAT! BLEAT!
BLEAT! BLEAT!
WHA--?
SO HOW DID THE MEAT FROM MY FLANK TASTE?
WHEN YOU KILLED ME IN GRAN CANARIA, I WAS ON MY WAY TO GET MY BAG OF SILVER FOR FOULING THAT STINKING PINTA'S RUDDER.
THAT WAS... IT WAS YOU?
NO, NO, I--
FAIR'S FAIR, ISN'T IT?
...
CLICK
...OR YOU CAN FINISH WHAT I STARTED.
EVERYONE'S SLEEPING, "INDIES MAN."
THNK
DEAR SOSH... THIS IS HOW YOU CHANGE THE WORLD.
NOT WITH WORDS, BUT WITH WEAPONS.
To be continued...

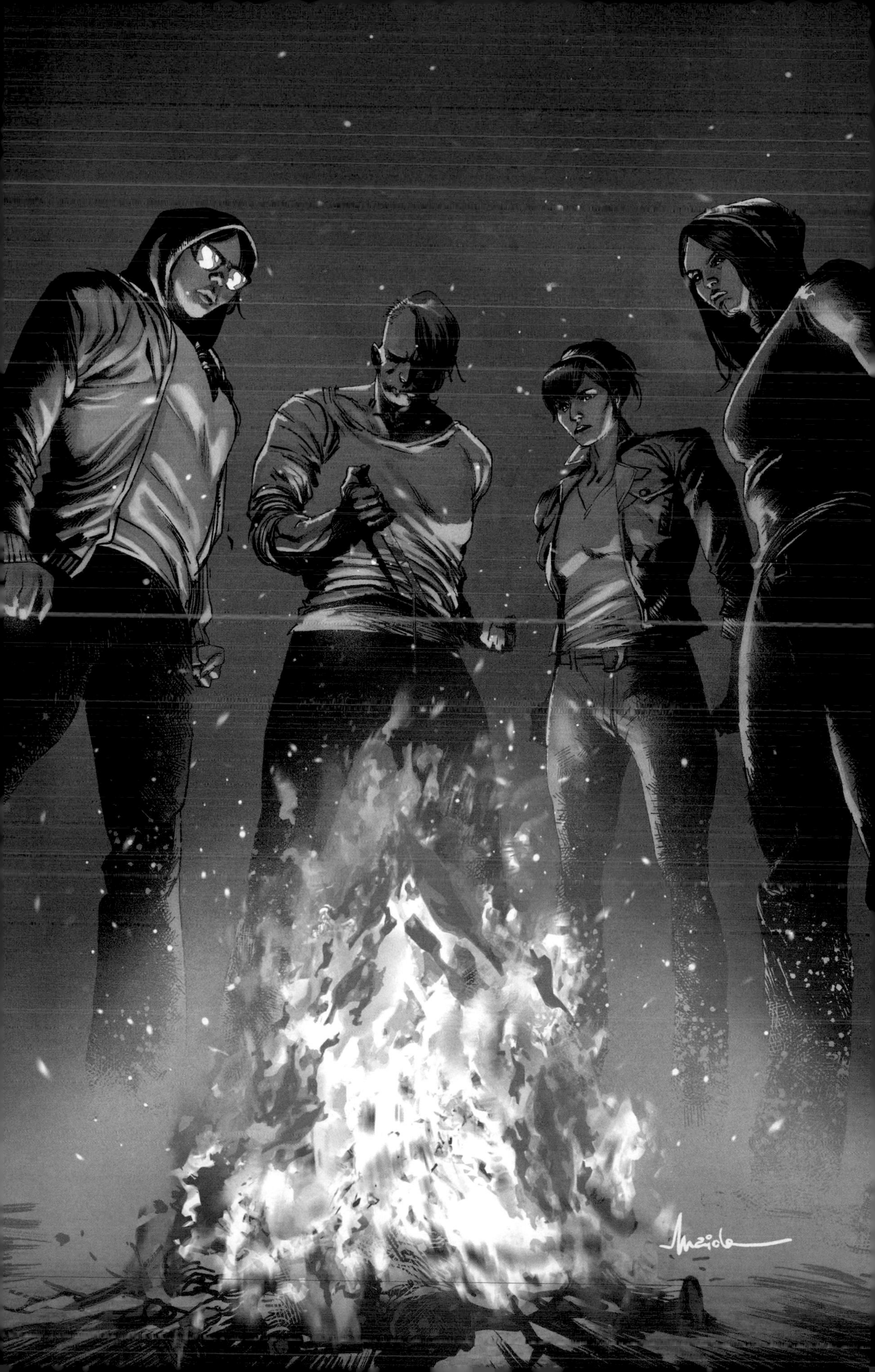

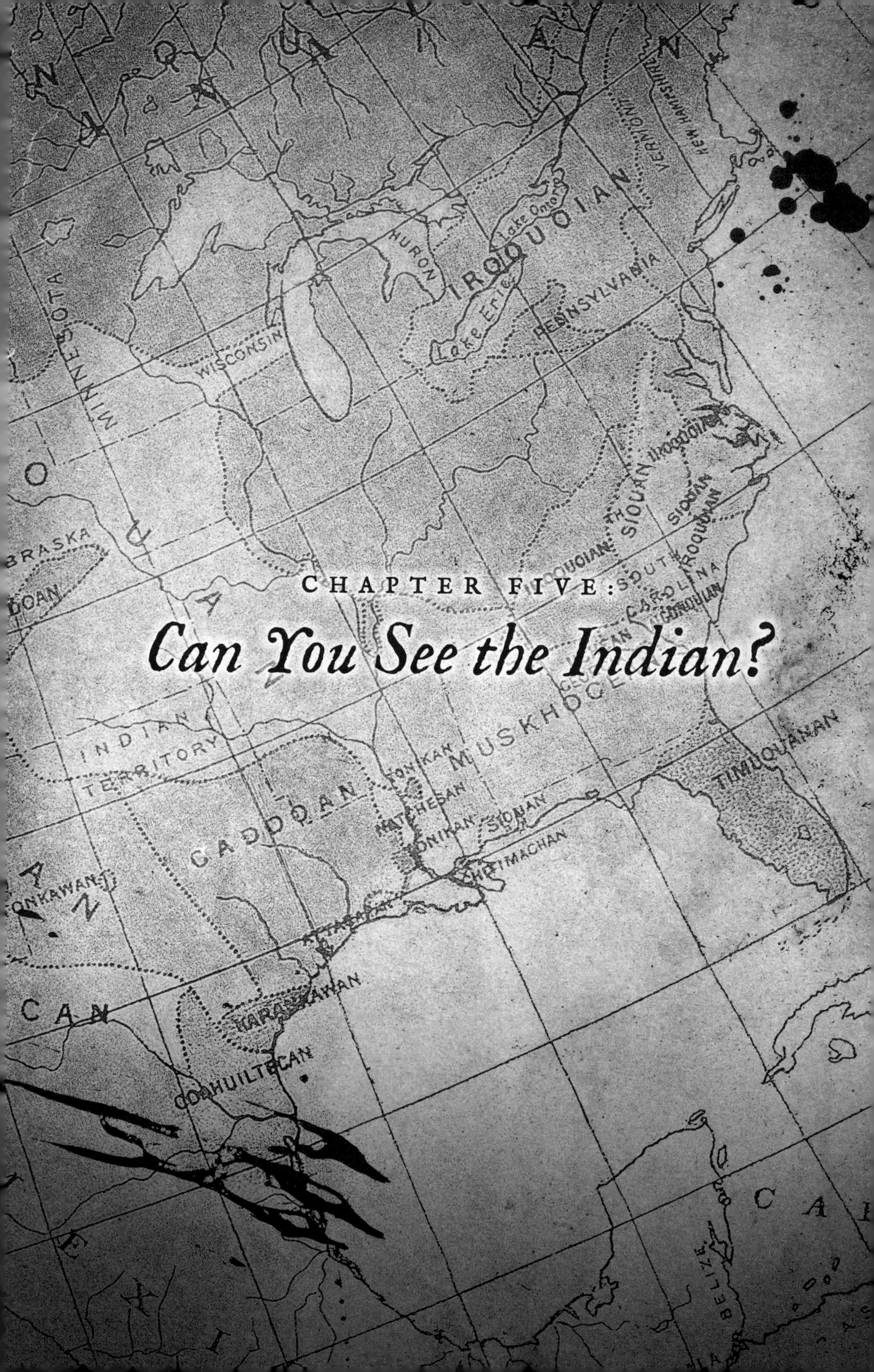
MINNESOTA
WISCONSIN
HURON
Lake Ontario
Lake Erie
IROQUOIAN
PENNSYLVANIA
VERMONT
NEW HAMPSHIRE
SIOUAN
IROQUOIAN
SOUTH CAROLINA
NEBRASKA
INDIAN TERRITORY
MUSKHOGEAN
TONIKAN
NATCHESAN
CADDOAN
SIOUAN
CHITIMACHAN
TIMUQUANAN
TONKAWAN
KARANKAWAN
COAHUILTECAN
BELIZE

CHAPTER FIVE:

Can You See the Indian?

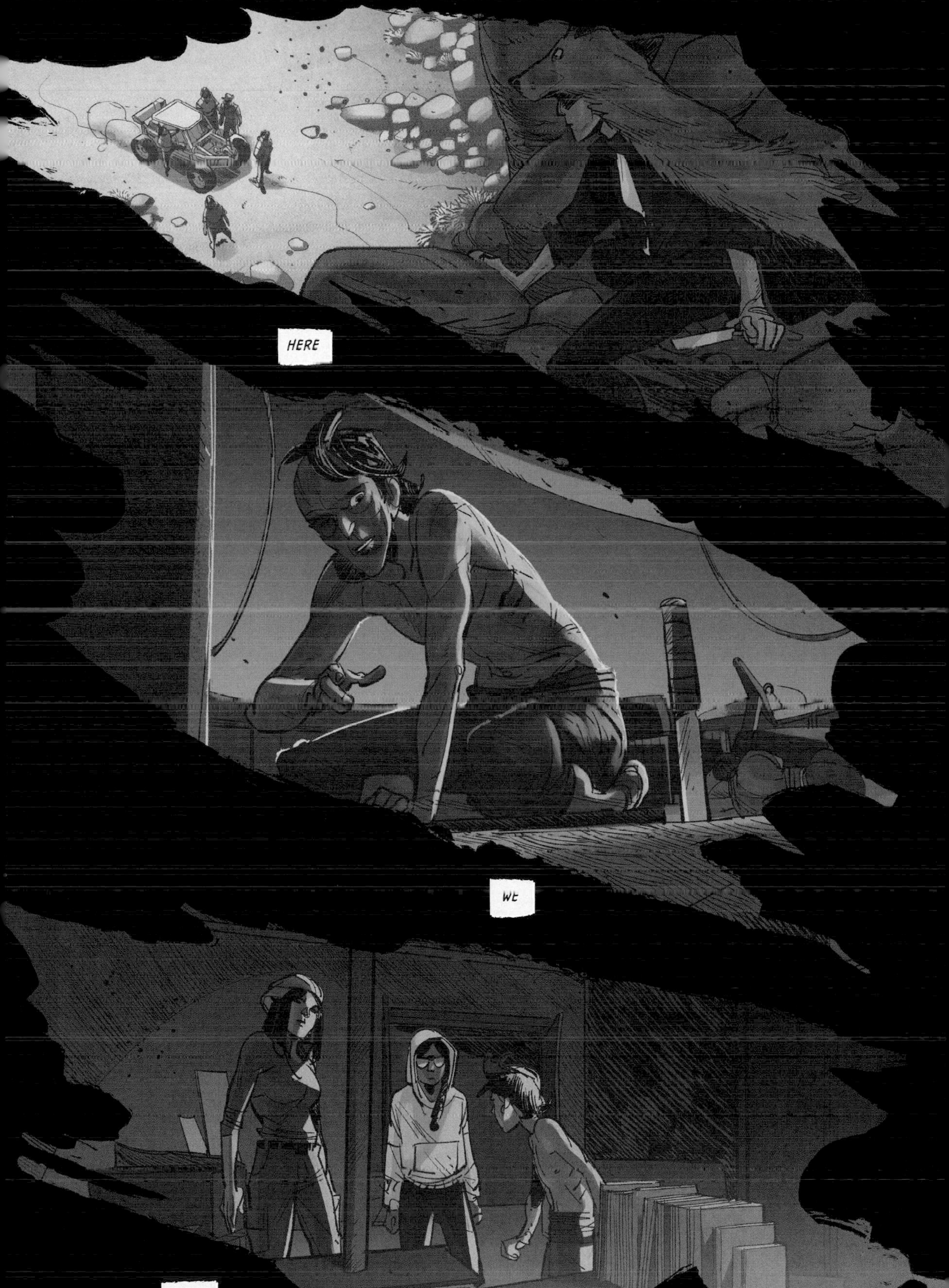
HERE
WE
GO...

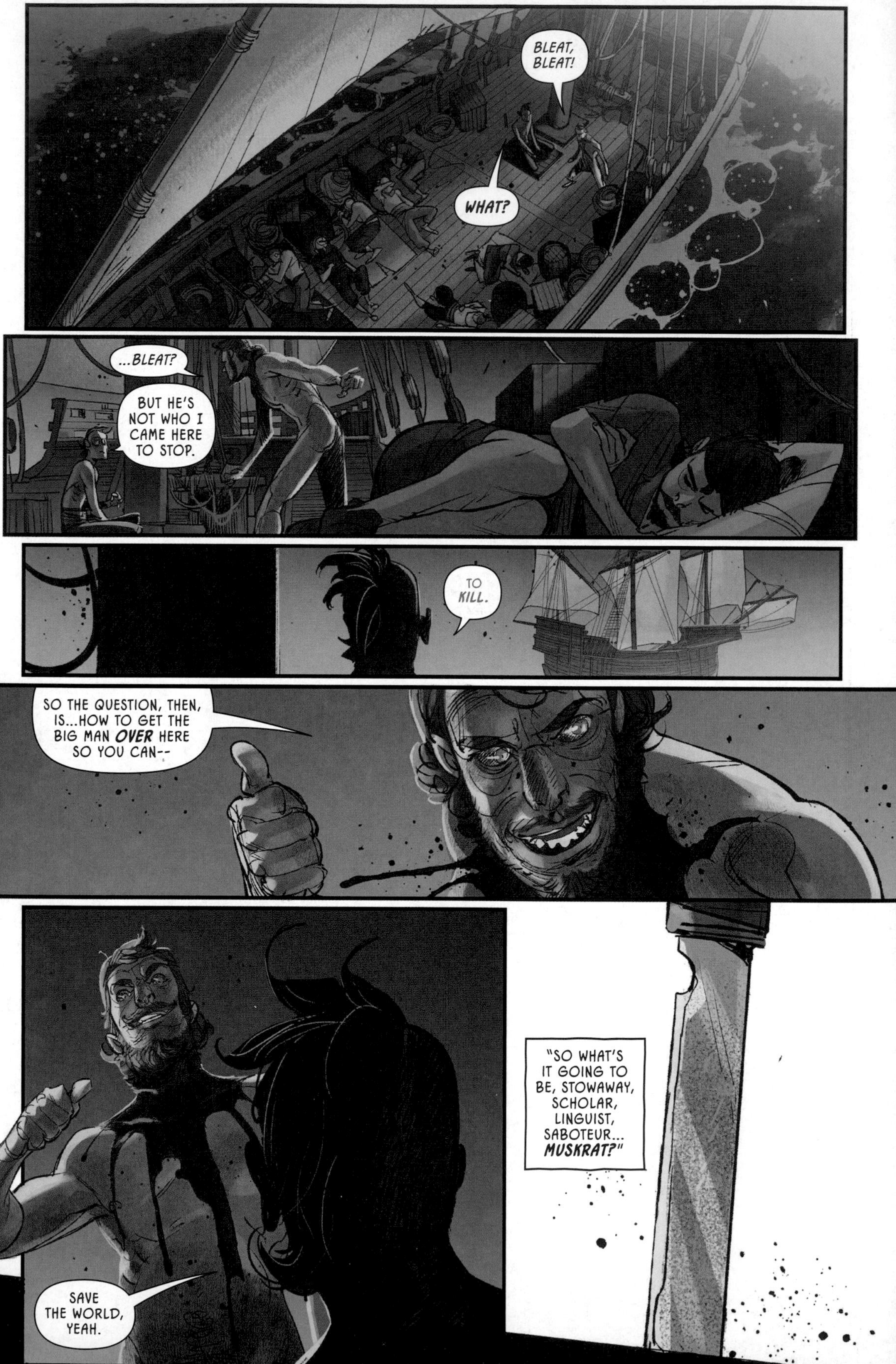
BLEAT, BLEAT!
WHAT?
...BLEAT?
BUT HE'S NOT WHO I CAME HERE TO STOP.
TO KILL.
SO THE QUESTION, THEN, IS...HOW TO GET THE BIG MAN OVER HERE SO YOU CAN--
"SO WHAT'S IT GOING TO BE, STOWAWAY, SCHOLAR, LINGUIST, SABOTEUR... MUSKRAT?"
SAVE THE WORLD, YEAH.

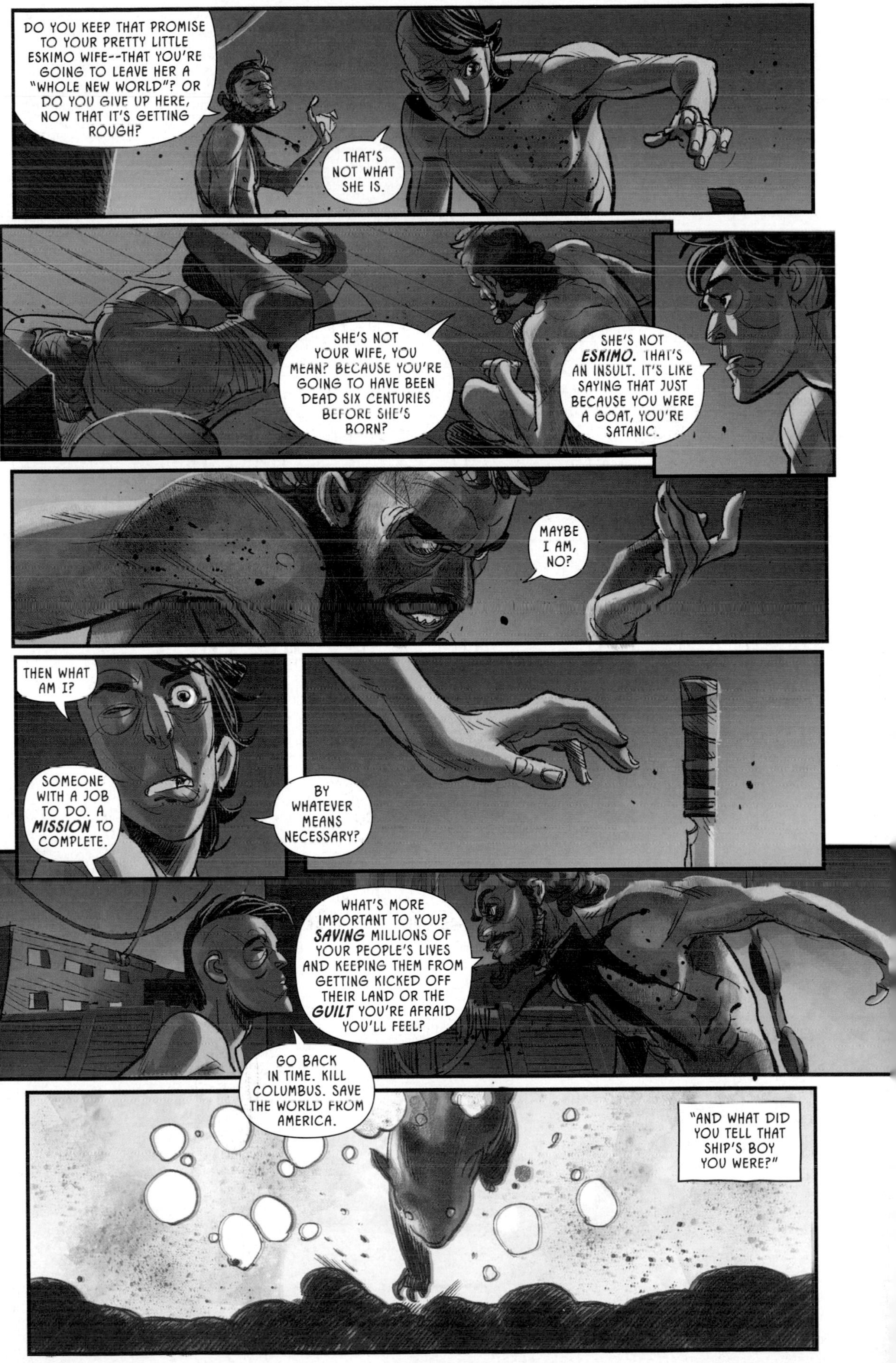

DO YOU KEEP THAT PROMISE TO YOUR PRETTY LITTLE ESKIMO WIFE--THAT YOU'RE GOING TO LEAVE HER A "WHOLE NEW WORLD"? OR DO YOU GIVE UP HERE, NOW THAT IT'S GETTING ROUGH?
THAT'S NOT WHAT SHE IS.
SHE'S NOT YOUR WIFE, YOU MEAN? BECAUSE YOU'RE GOING TO HAVE BEEN DEAD SIX CENTURIES BEFORE SHE'S BORN?
SHE'S NOT *ESKIMO.* THAT'S AN INSULT. IT'S LIKE SAYING THAT JUST BECAUSE YOU WERE A GOAT, YOU'RE SATANIC.
MAYBE I AM, NO?
THEN WHAT AM I?
SOMEONE WITH A JOB TO DO. A *MISSION* TO COMPLETE.
BY WHATEVER MEANS NECESSARY?
WHAT'S MORE IMPORTANT TO YOU? *SAVING* MILLIONS OF YOUR PEOPLE'S LIVES AND KEEPING THEM FROM GETTING KICKED OFF THEIR LAND OR THE *GUILT* YOU'RE AFRAID YOU'LL FEEL?
GO BACK IN TIME. KILL COLUMBUS. SAVE THE WORLD FROM AMERICA.
"AND WHAT DID YOU TELL THAT SHIP'S BOY YOU WERE?"

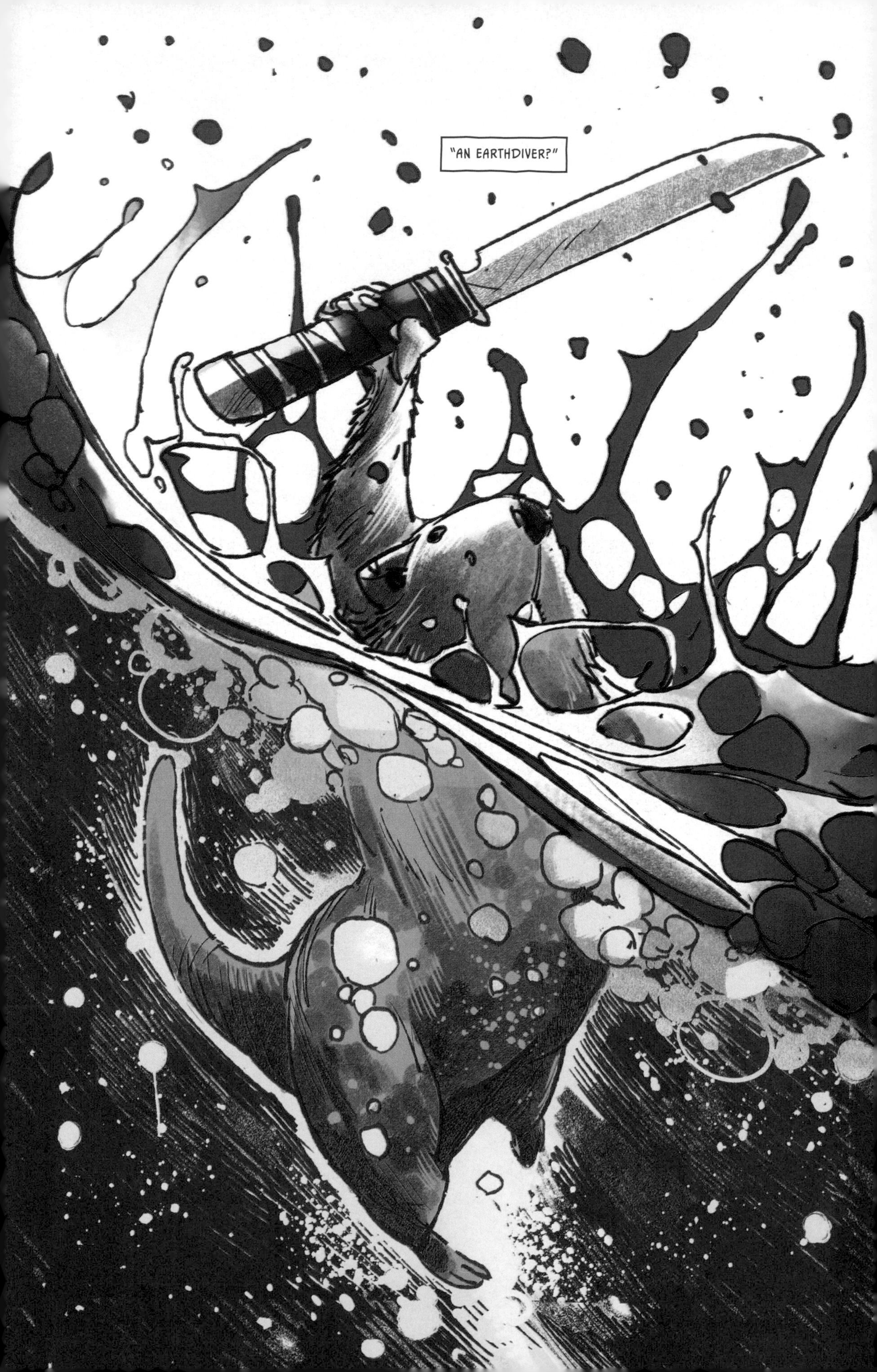
"AN EARTHDIVER?"

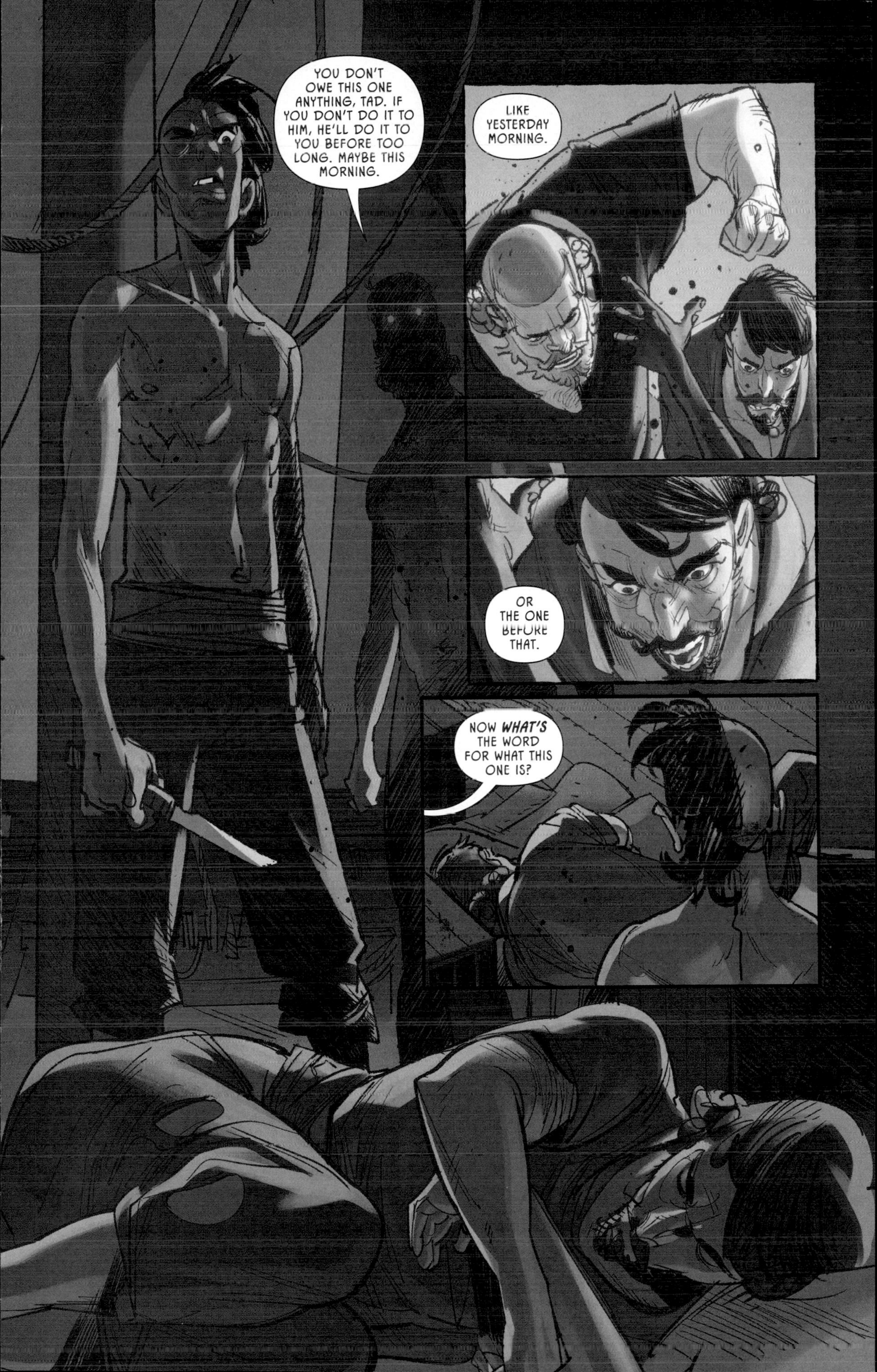
YOU DON'T OWE THIS ONE ANYTHING, TAD. IF YOU DON'T DO IT TO HIM, HE'LL DO IT TO YOU BEFORE TOO LONG. MAYBE THIS MORNING.
LIKE YESTERDAY MORNING.
OR THE ONE BEFORE THAT.
NOW *WHAT'S* THE WORD FOR WHAT THIS ONE IS?

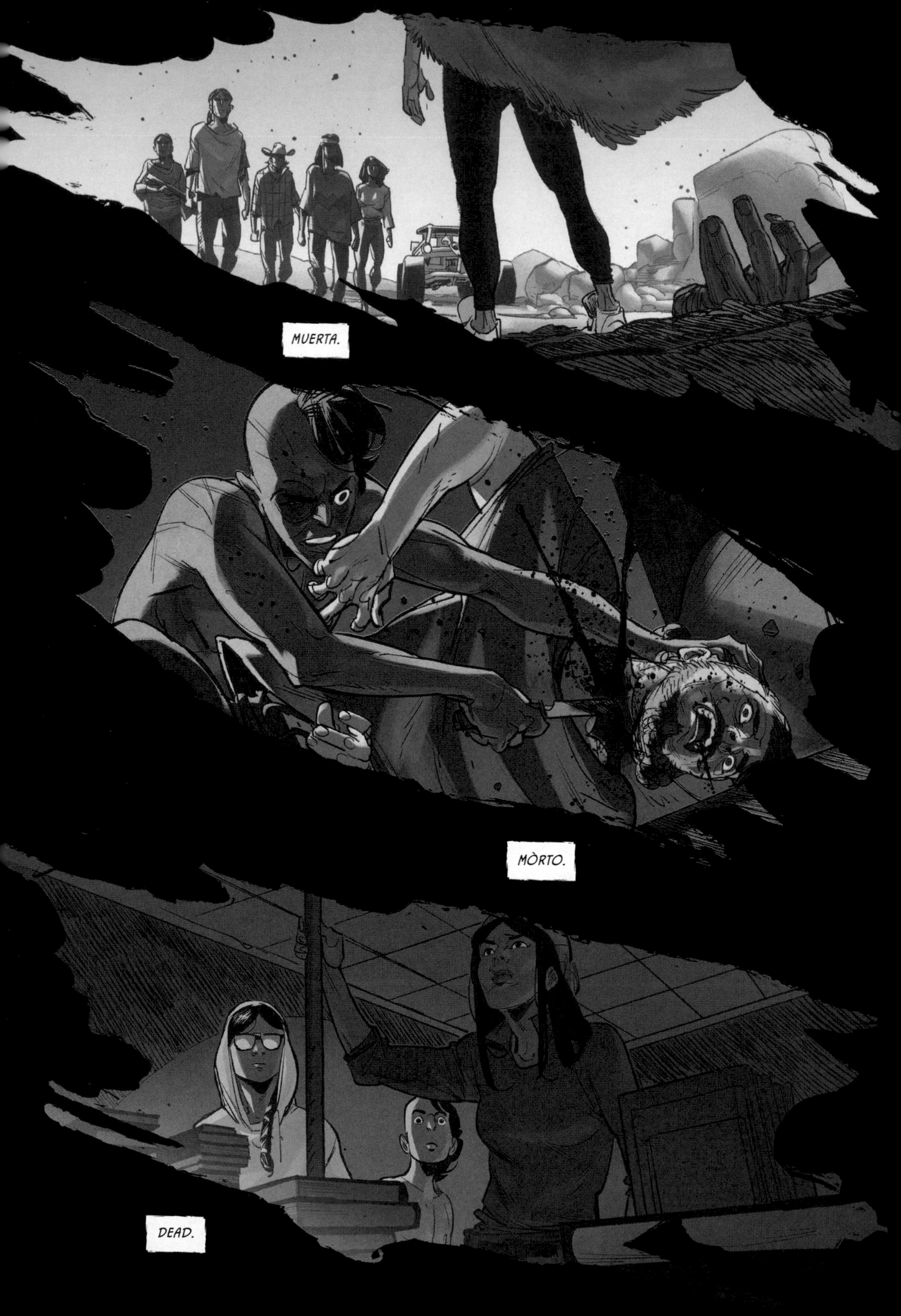
MUERTA.
MÒRTO.
DEAD.

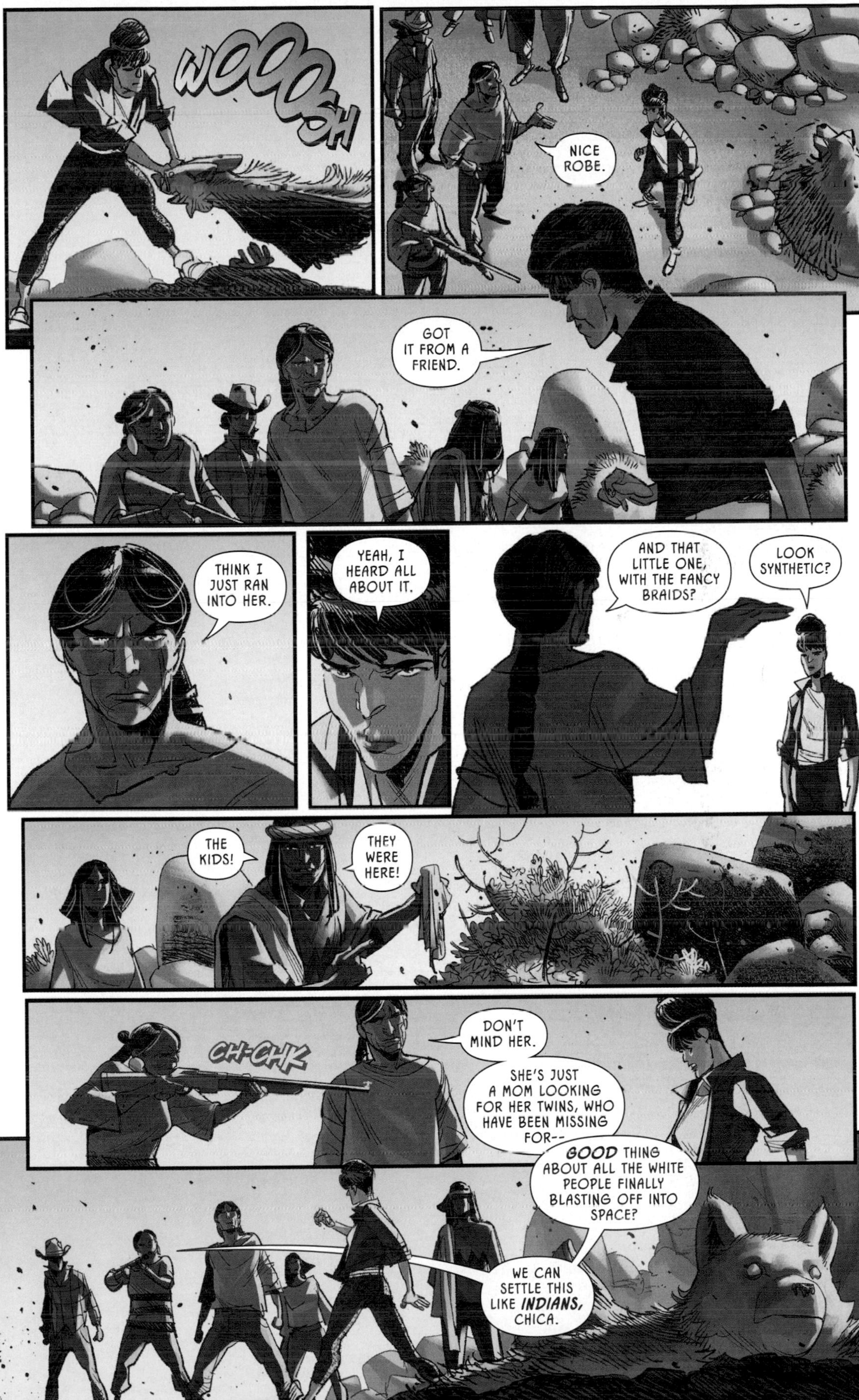
WOOOOSH
NICE ROBE.
GOT IT FROM A FRIEND.
THINK I JUST RAN INTO HER.
YEAH, I HEARD ALL ABOUT IT.
AND THAT LITTLE ONE, WITH THE FANCY BRAIDS?
LOOK SYNTHETIC?
THE KIDS!
THEY WERE HERE!
CH-CHK
DON'T MIND HER.
SHE'S JUST A MOM LOOKING FOR HER TWINS, WHO HAVE BEEN MISSING FOR--
GOOD THING ABOUT ALL THE WHITE PEOPLE FINALLY BLASTING OFF INTO SPACE?
WE CAN SETTLE THIS LIKE INDIANS, CHICA.

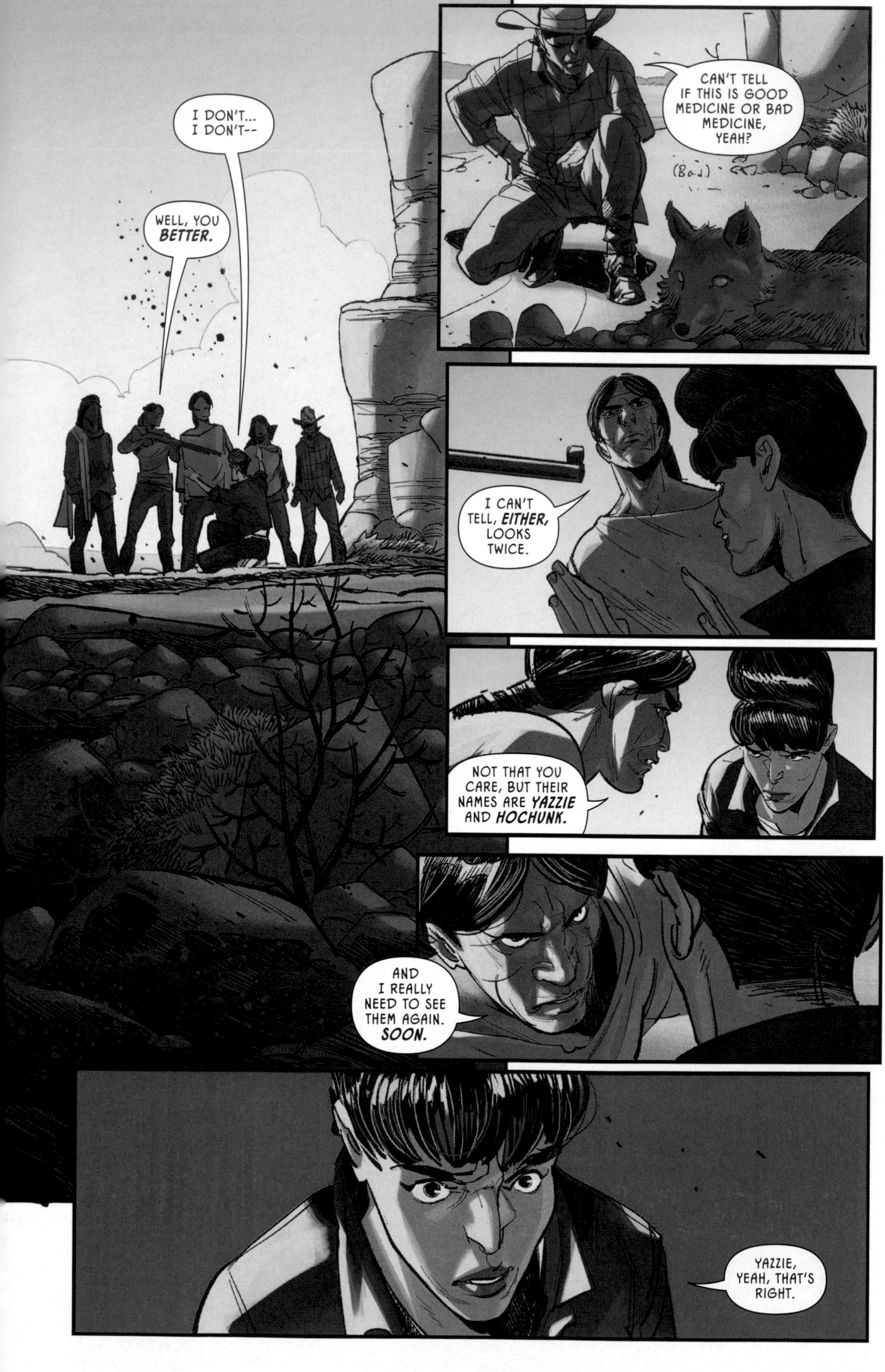

I DON'T... I DON'T--
WELL, YOU BETTER.
CAN'T TELL IF THIS IS GOOD MEDICINE OR BAD MEDICINE, YEAH?
(Bad)
I CAN'T TELL, EITHER, LOOKS TWICE.
NOT THAT YOU CARE, BUT THEIR NAMES ARE YAZZIE AND HOCHUNK.
AND I REALLY NEED TO SEE THEM AGAIN. SOON.
YAZZIE, YEAH, THAT'S RIGHT.

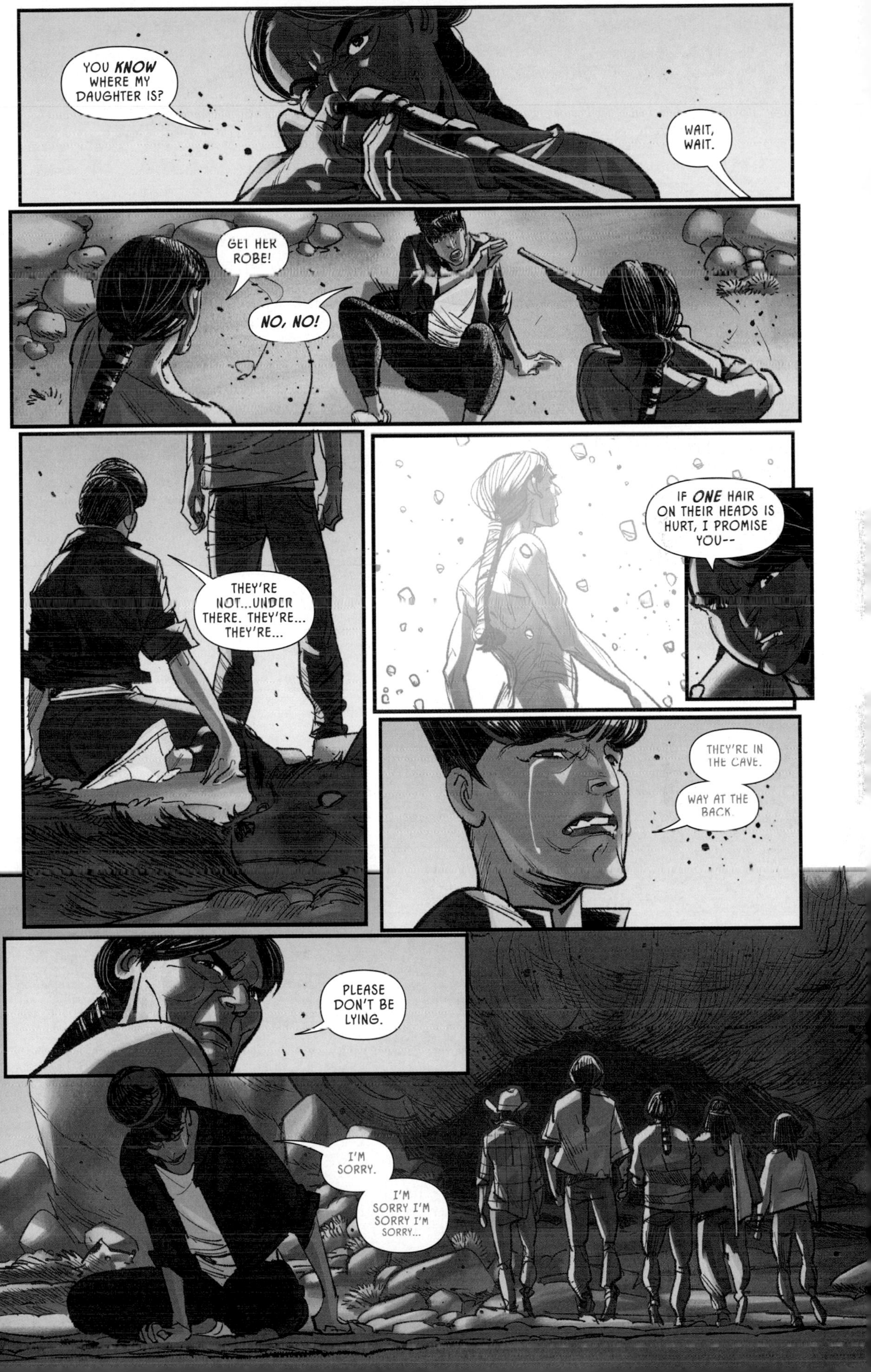
YOU KNOW WHERE MY DAUGHTER IS?
WAIT, WAIT.
GET HER ROBE!
NO, NO!
THEY'RE NOT...UNDER THERE. THEY'RE... THEY'RE...
IF ONE HAIR ON THEIR HEADS IS HURT, I PROMISE YOU--
THEY'RE IN THE CAVE.
WAY AT THE BACK.
PLEASE DON'T BE LYING.
I'M SORRY.
I'M SORRY I'M SORRY I'M SORRY...

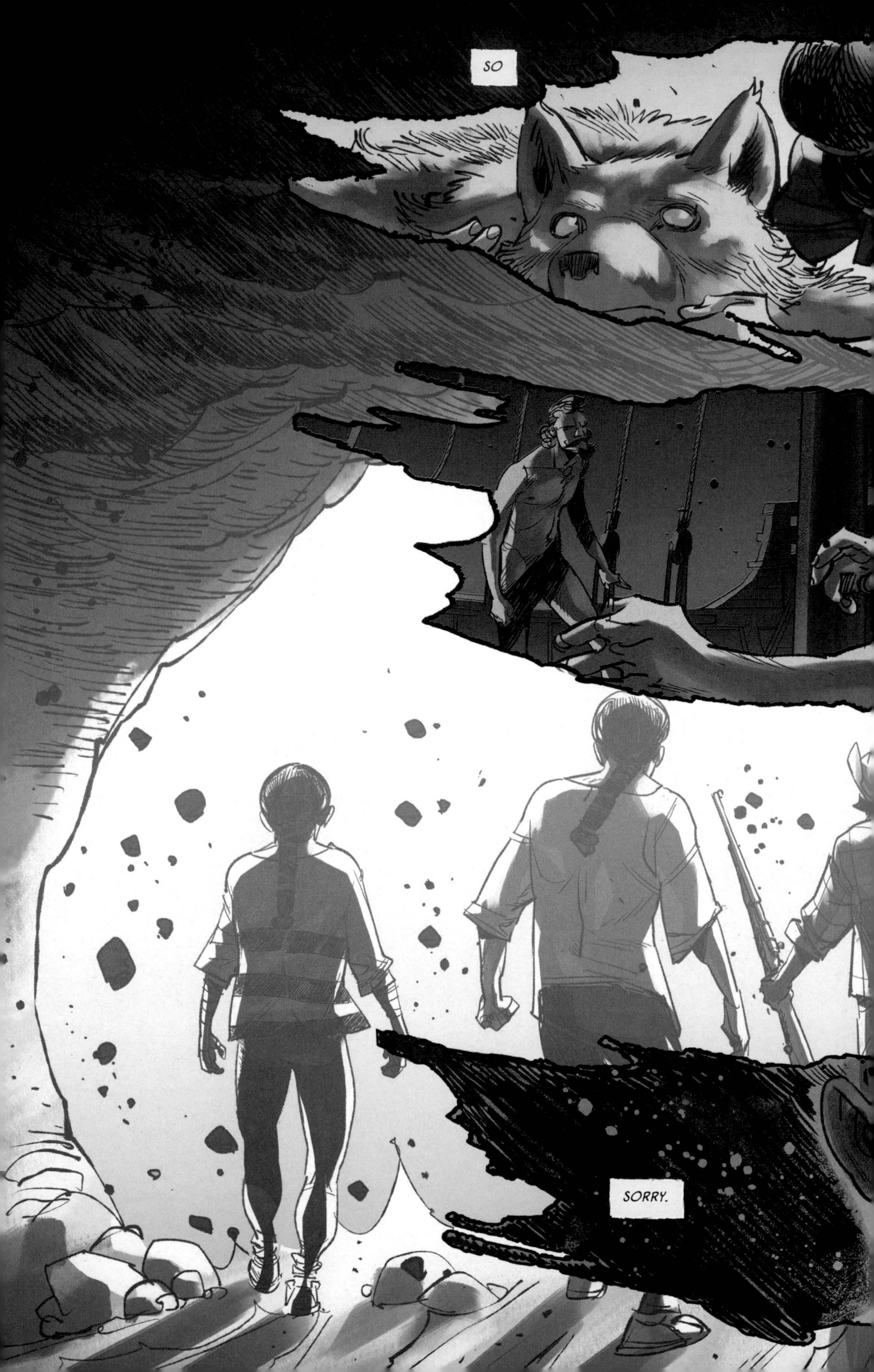
SO
SORRY.

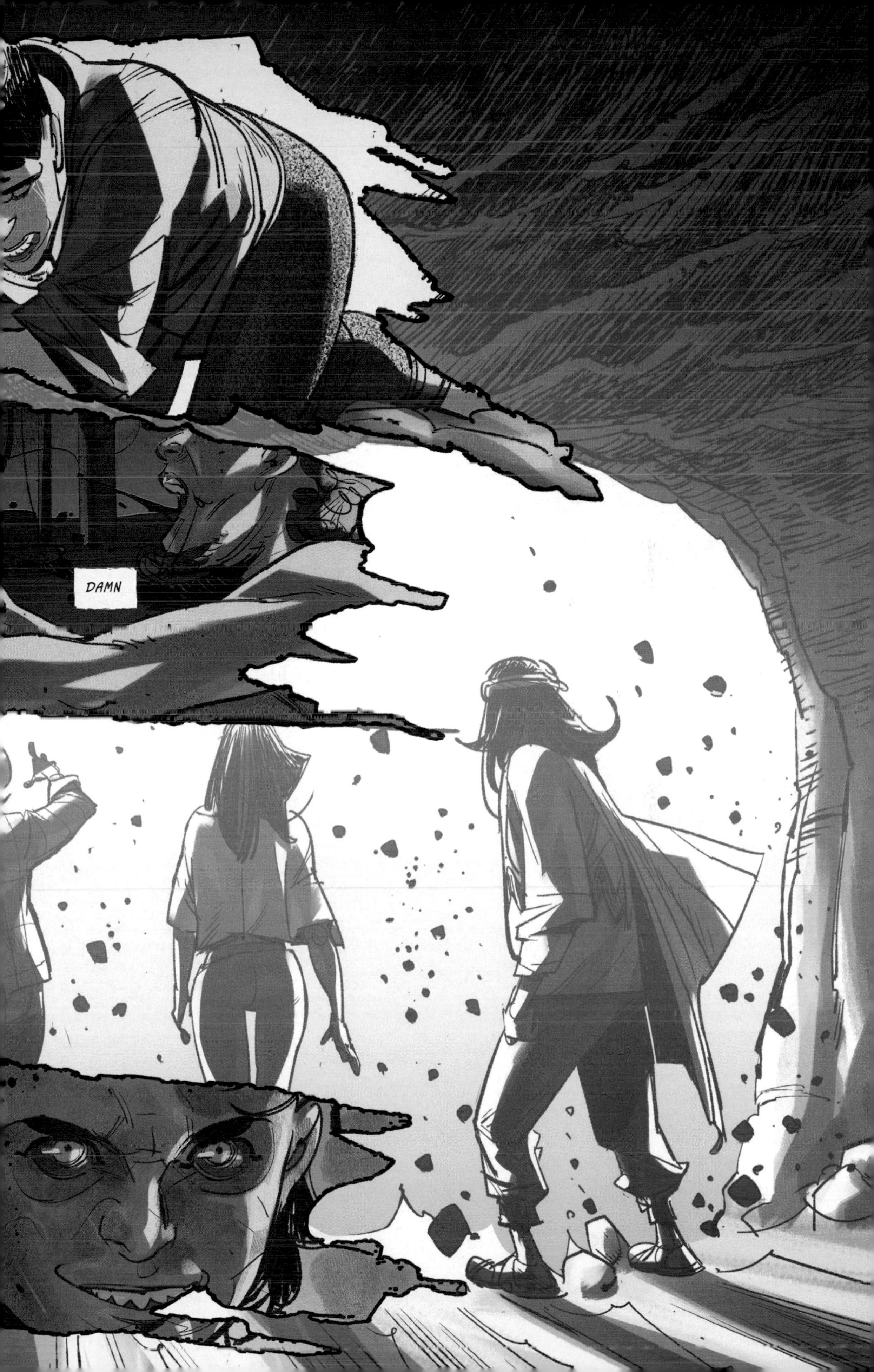
DAMN

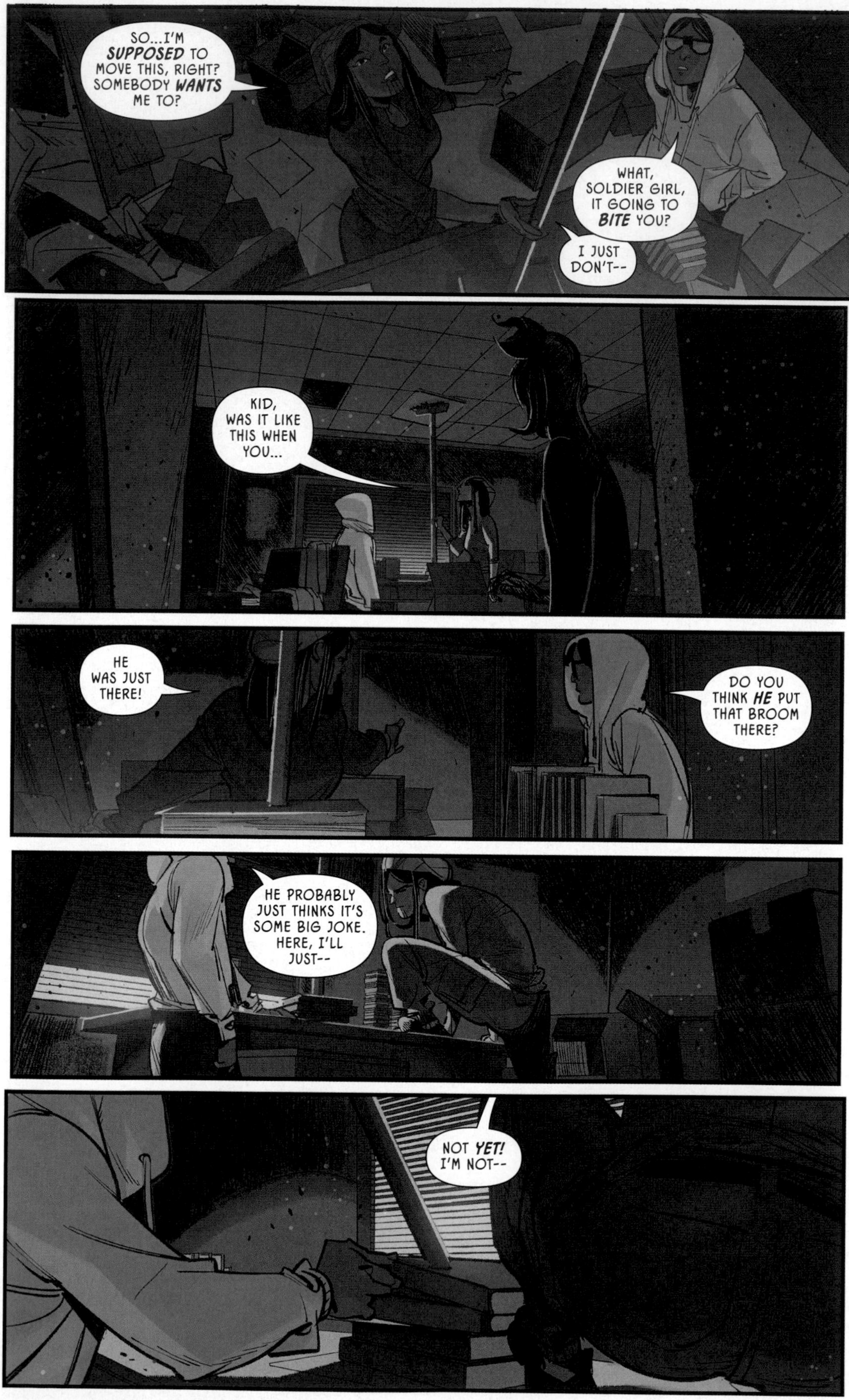
SO...I'M SUPPOSED TO MOVE THIS, RIGHT? SOMEBODY WANTS ME TO?
WHAT, SOLDIER GIRL, IT GOING TO BITE YOU?
I JUST DON'T--
KID, WAS IT LIKE THIS WHEN YOU...
HE WAS JUST THERE!
DO YOU THINK HE PUT THAT BROOM THERE?
HE PROBABLY JUST THINKS IT'S SOME BIG JOKE. HERE, I'LL JUST--
NOT YET! I'M NOT--

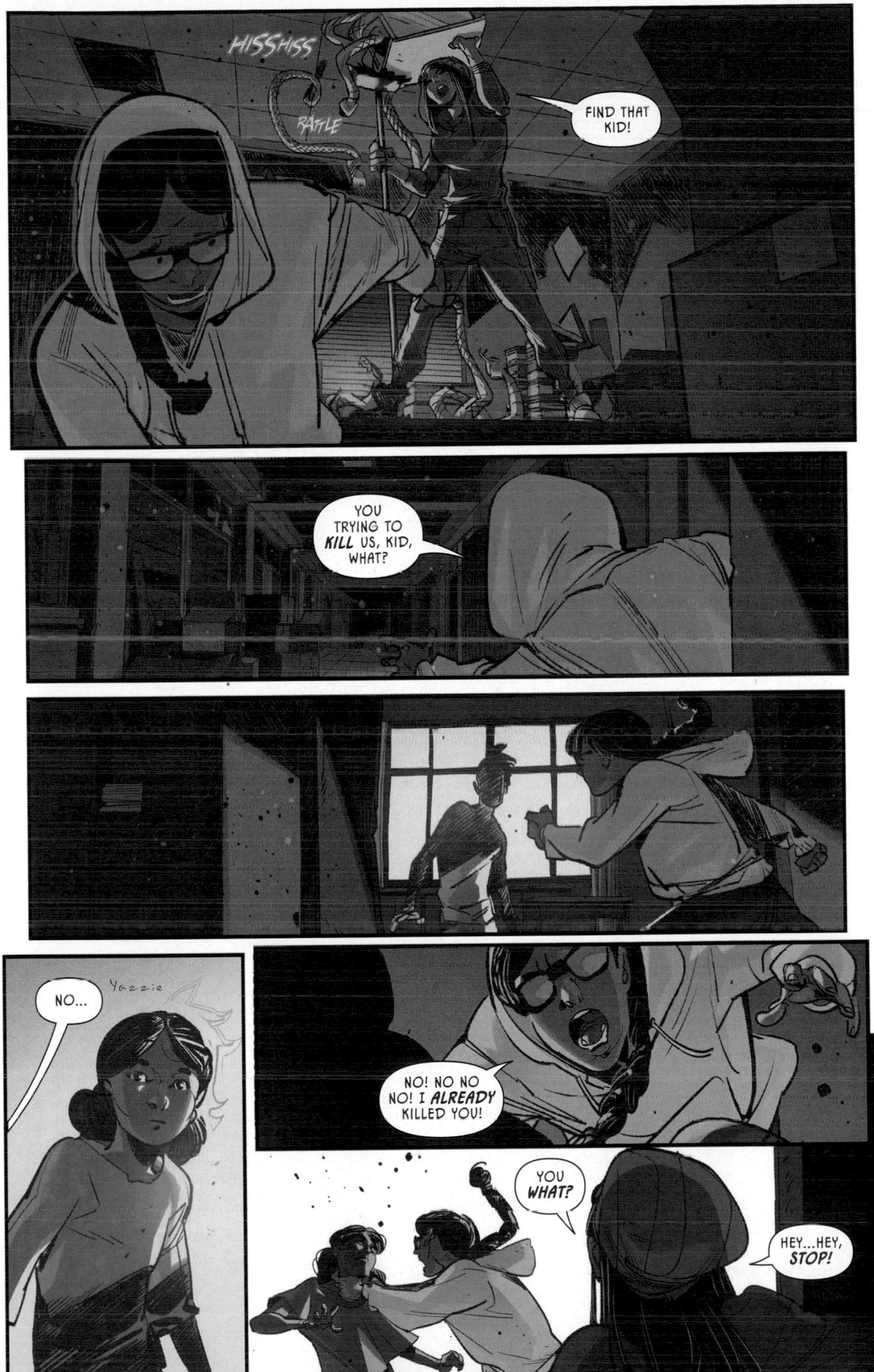
HISSHISS
RATTLE
FIND THAT KID!
YOU TRYING TO *KILL* US, KID, WHAT?
NO...
Yazzie
NO! NO NO NO! I *ALREADY* KILLED YOU!
YOU *WHAT?*
HEY...HEY, *STOP!*

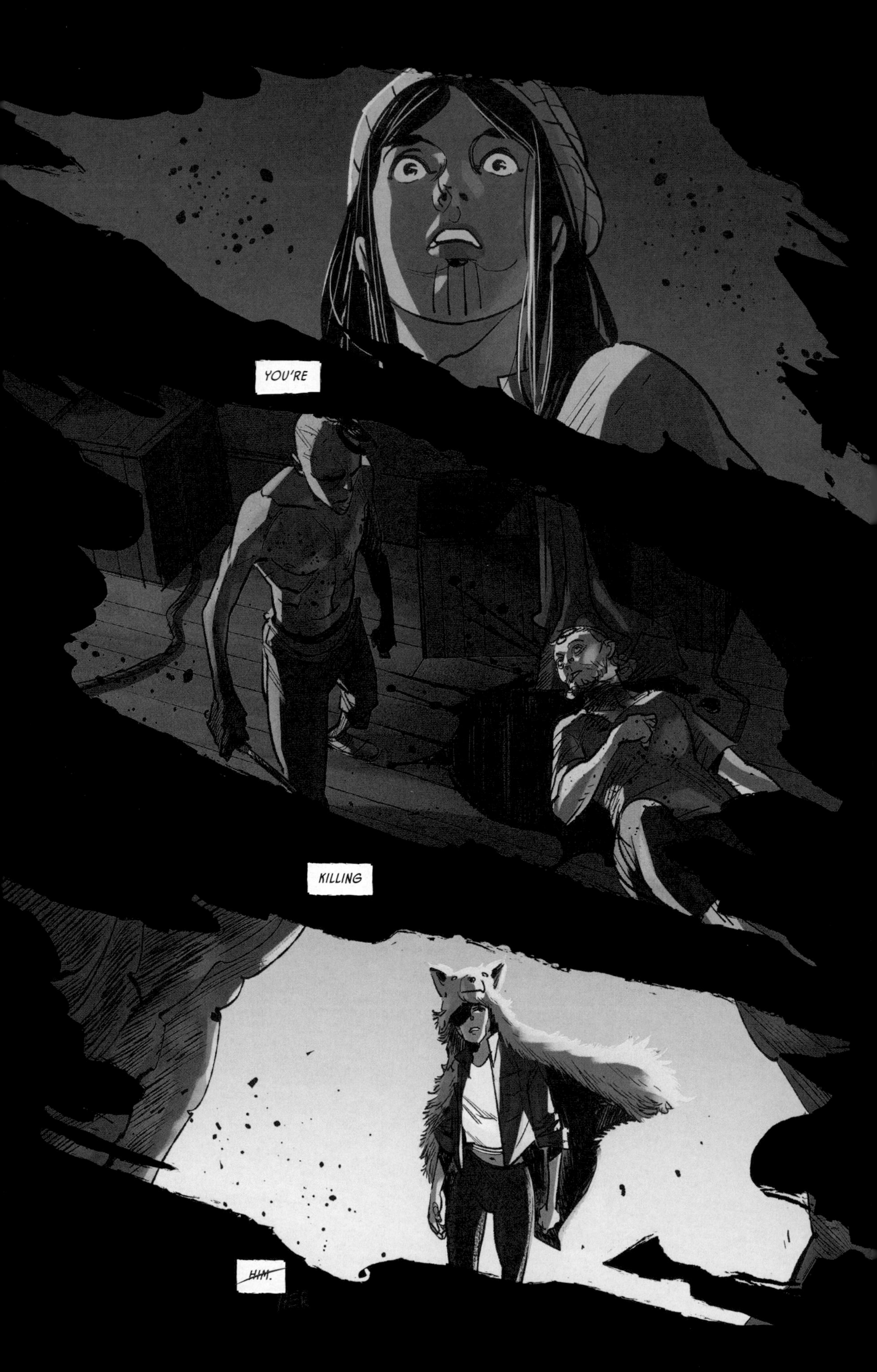
YOU'RE
KILLING
~~HIM.~~
HER

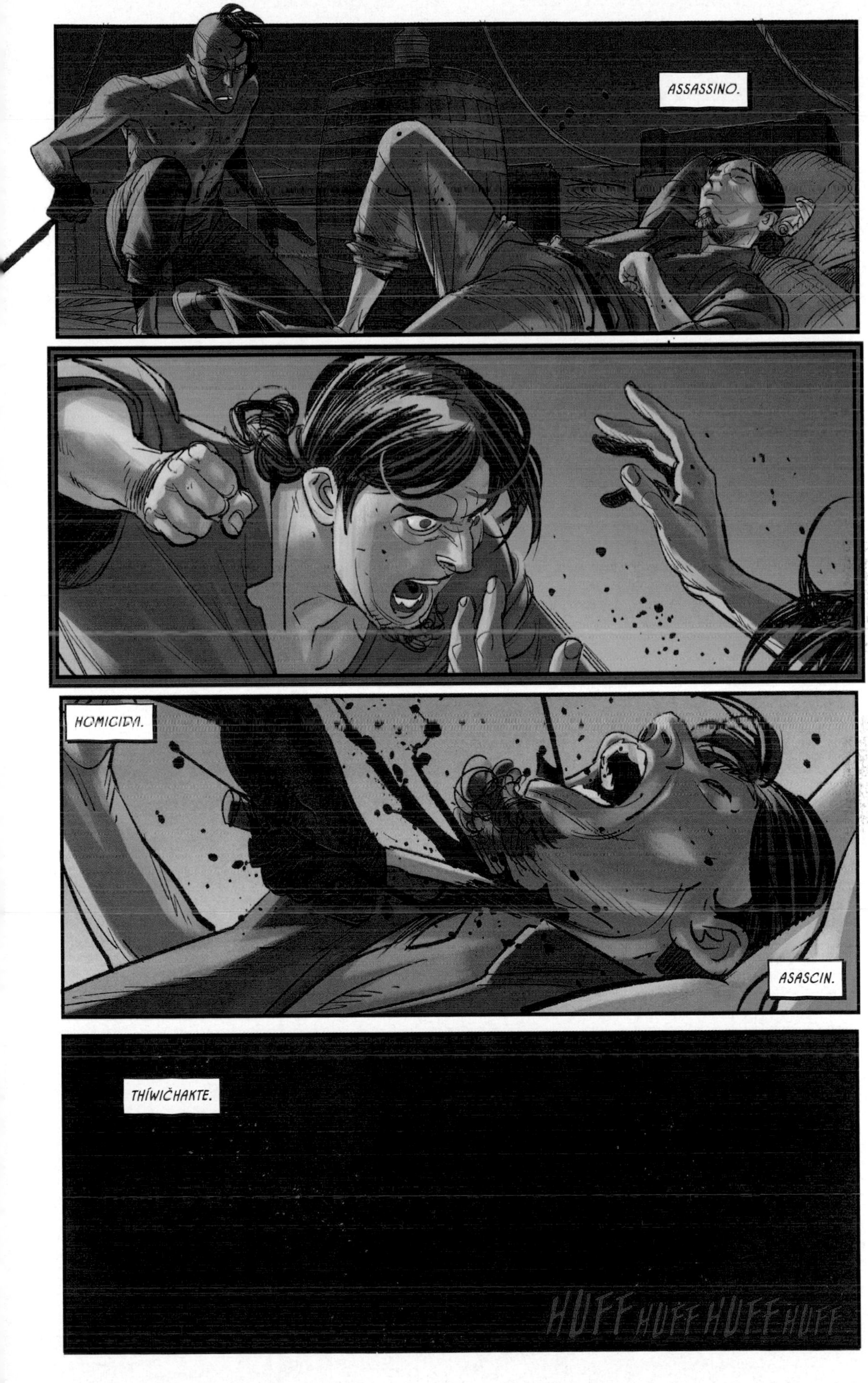
ASSASSINO.
HOMICIDA.
ASASCIN.
THÍWIČHAKTE.
HUFF HUFF HUFF HUFF

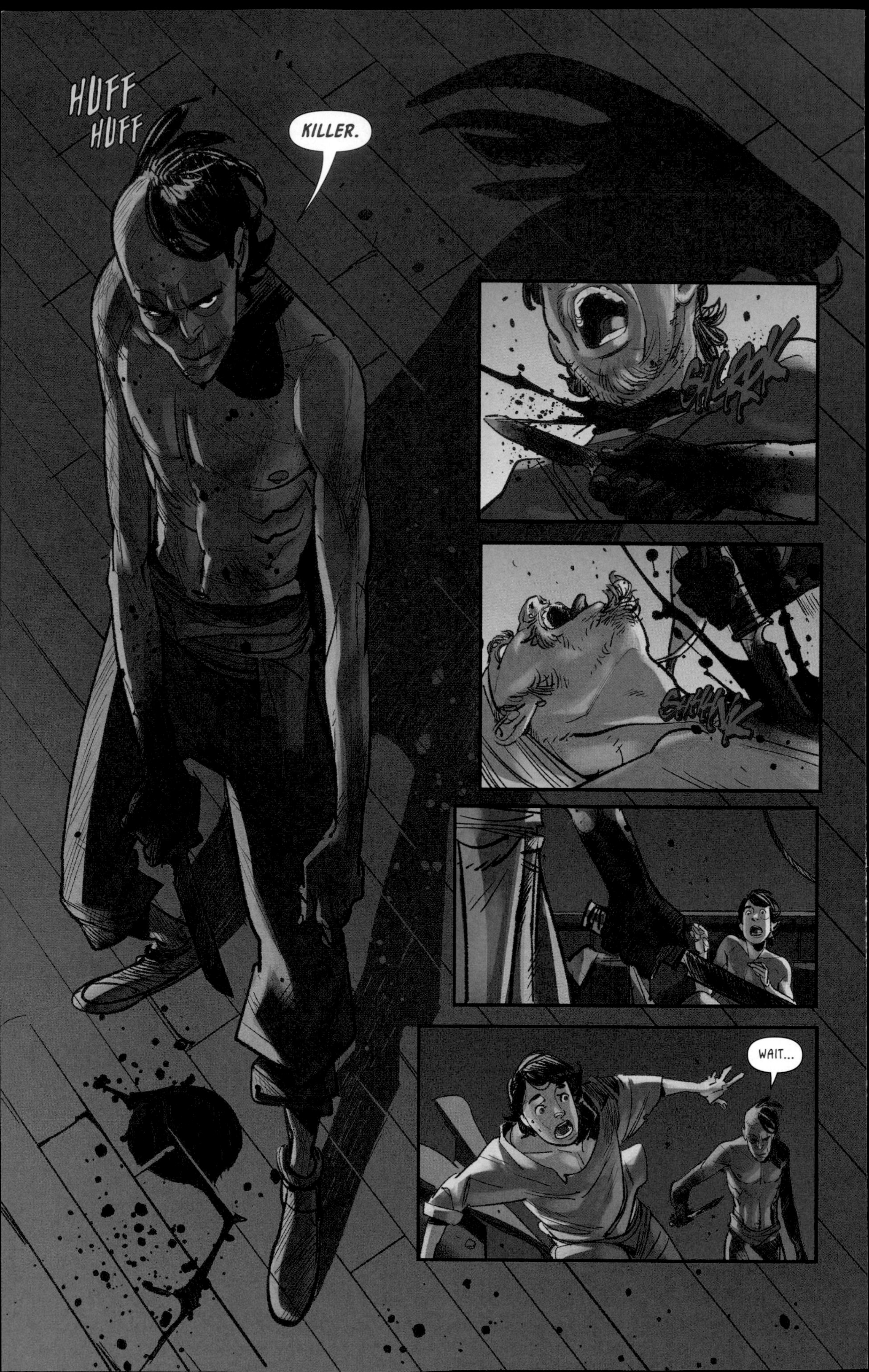
HUFF
HUFF
KILLER.
WAIT...

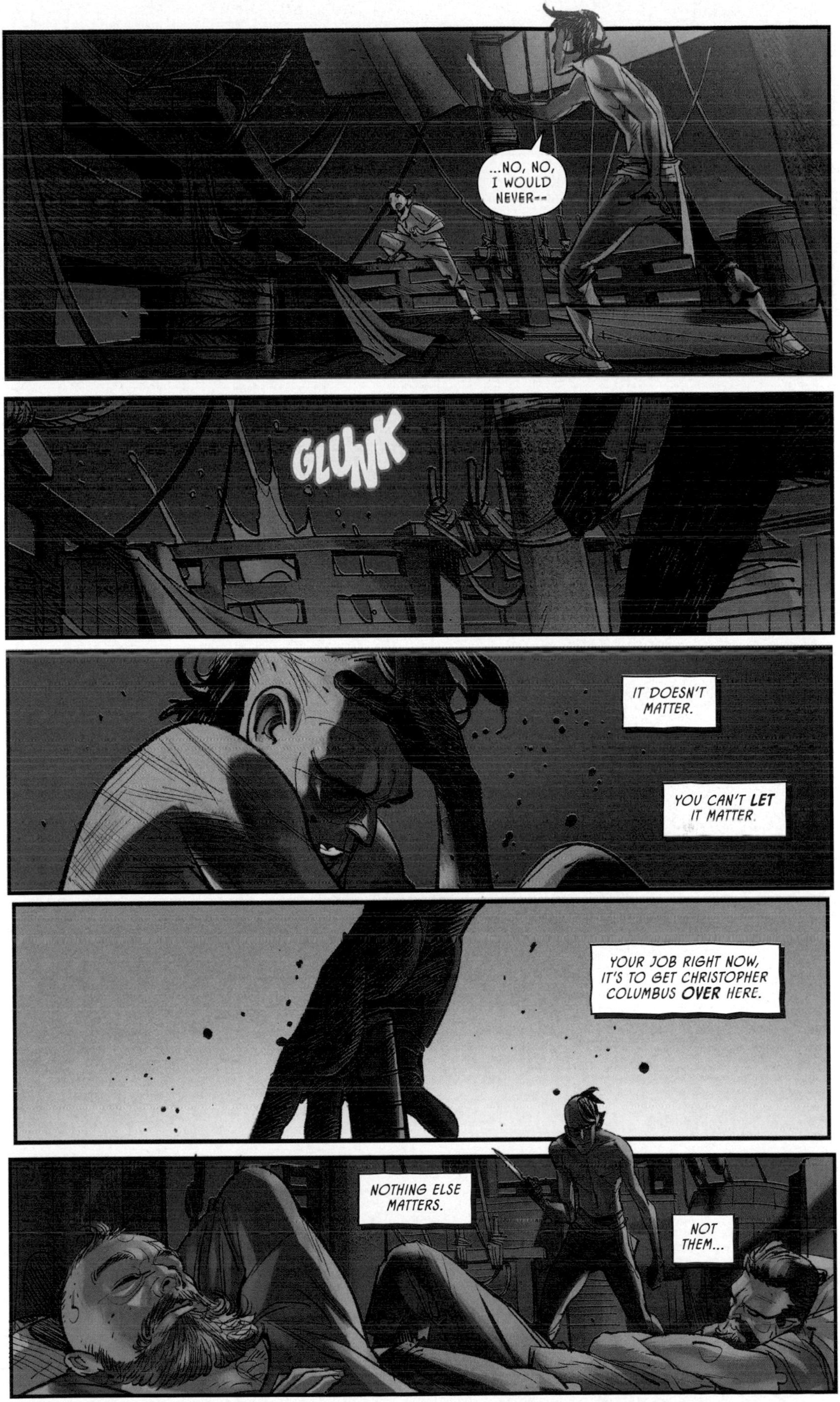
...NO, NO, I WOULD NEVER--
GLUNK
IT DOESN'T MATTER.
YOU CAN'T LET IT MATTER.
YOUR JOB RIGHT NOW, IT'S TO GET CHRISTOPHER COLUMBUS OVER HERE.
NOTHING ELSE MATTERS.
NOT THEM...

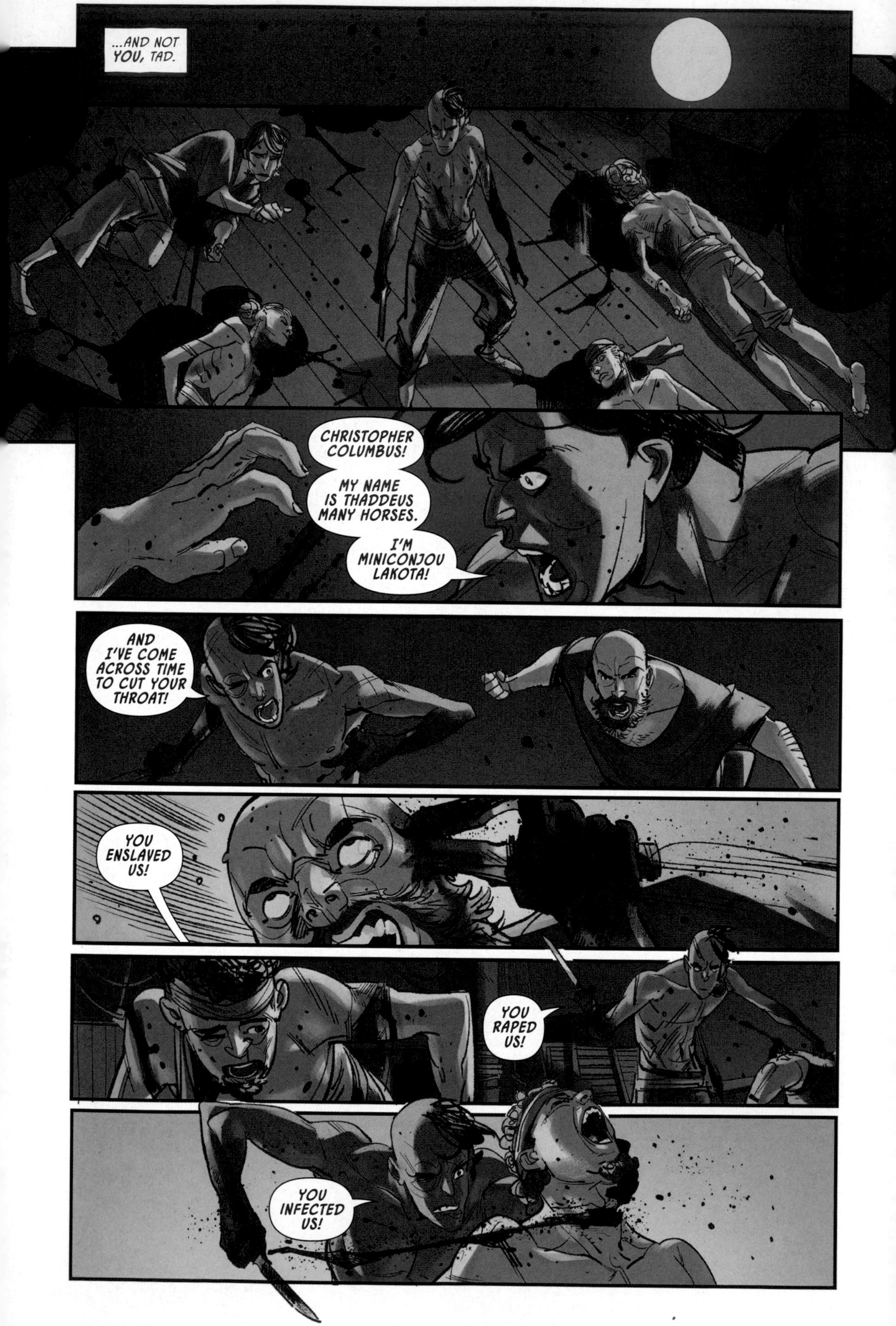
...AND NOT YOU, TAD.
CHRISTOPHER COLUMBUS!
MY NAME IS THADDEUS MANY HORSES.
I'M MINICONJOU LAKOTA!
AND I'VE COME ACROSS TIME TO CUT YOUR THROAT!
YOU ENSLAVED US!
YOU RAPED US!
YOU INFECTED US!

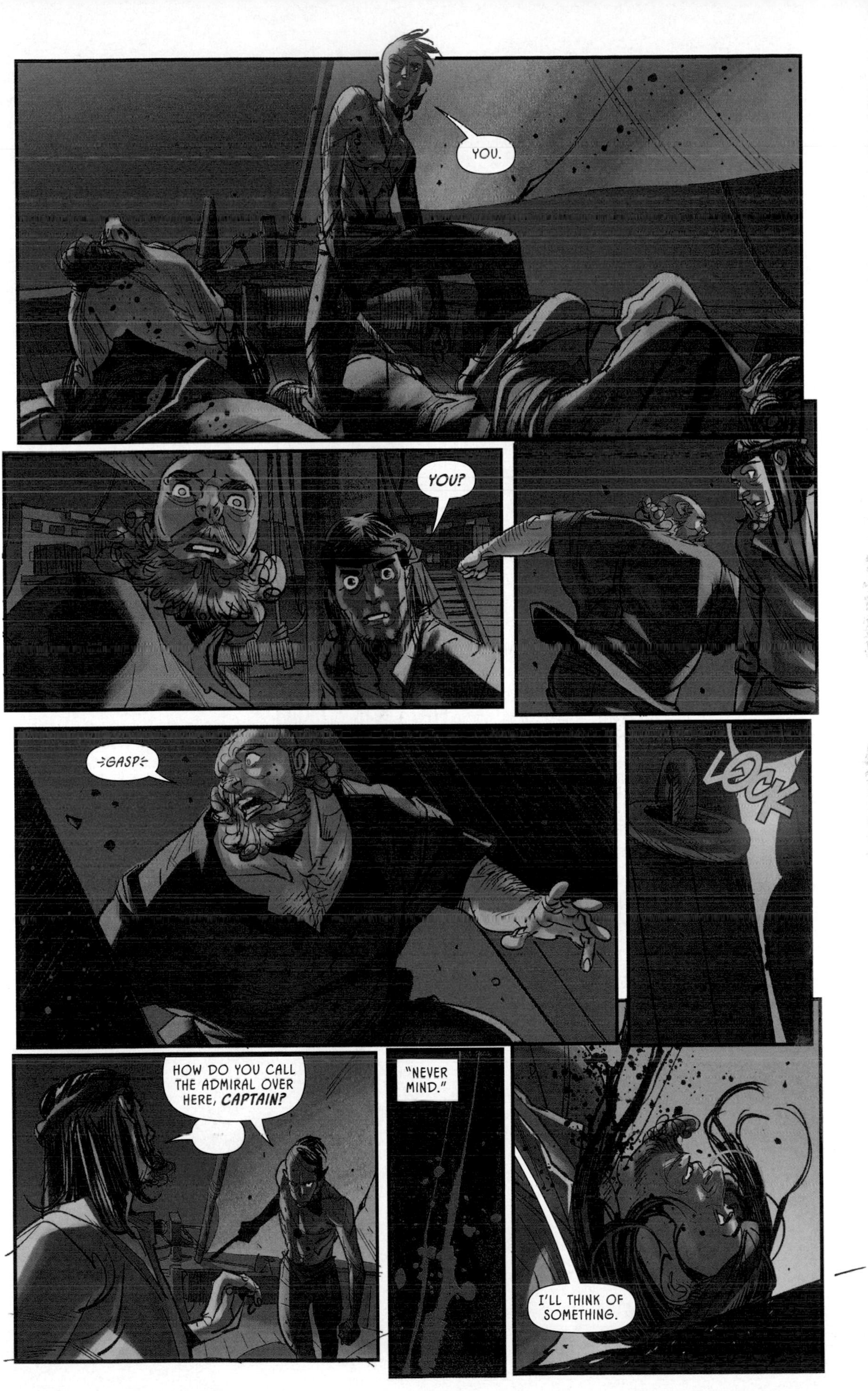
YOU.
YOU?
-GASP-
LOCK
HOW DO YOU CALL THE ADMIRAL OVER HERE, CAPTAIN?
...
"NEVER MIND."
I'LL THINK OF SOMETHING.

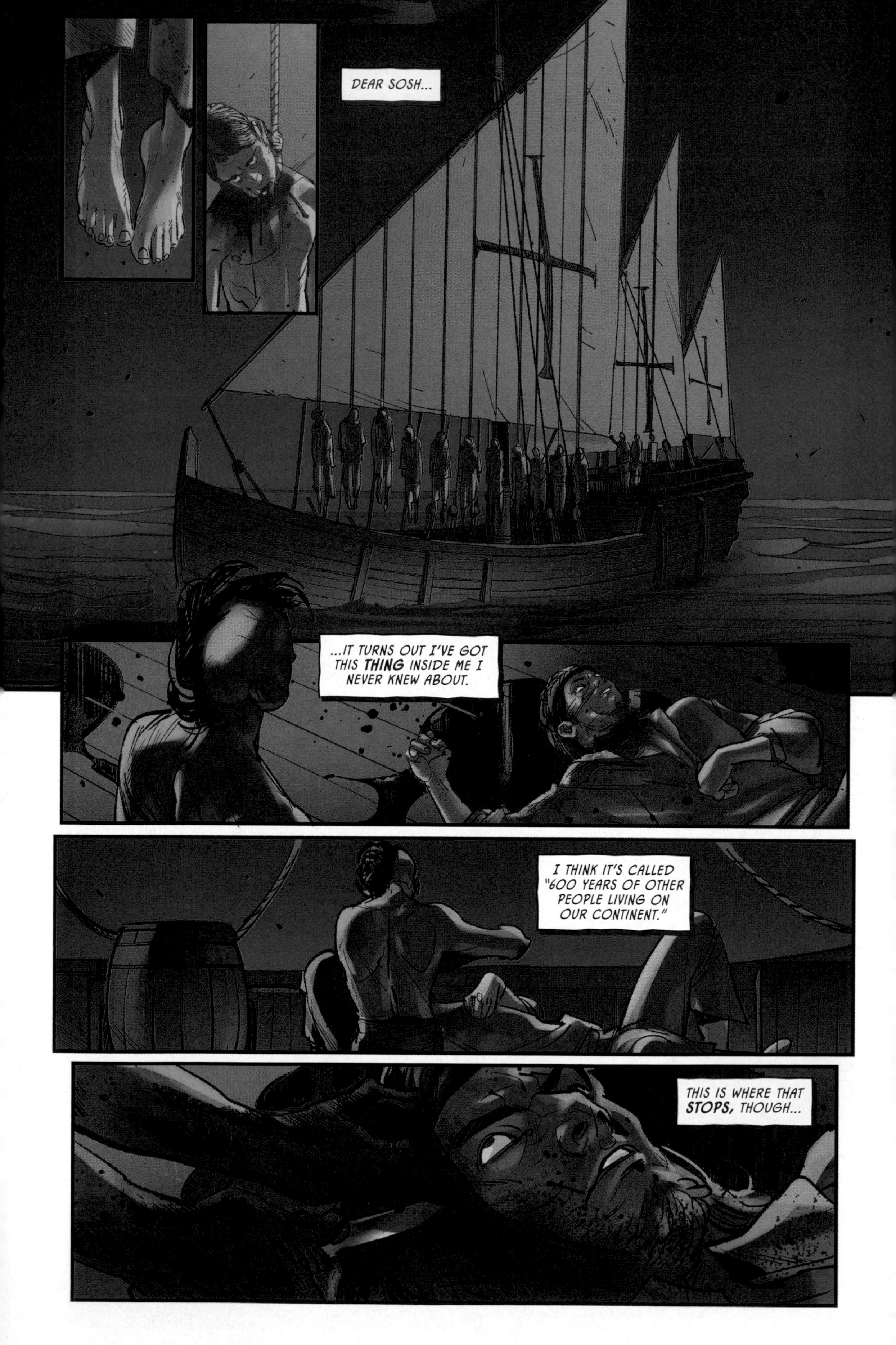
DEAR SOSH...
...IT TURNS OUT I'VE GOT THIS **THING** INSIDE ME I NEVER KNEW ABOUT.
I THINK IT'S CALLED "600 YEARS OF OTHER PEOPLE LIVING ON OUR CONTINENT."
THIS IS WHERE THAT **STOPS,** THOUGH...

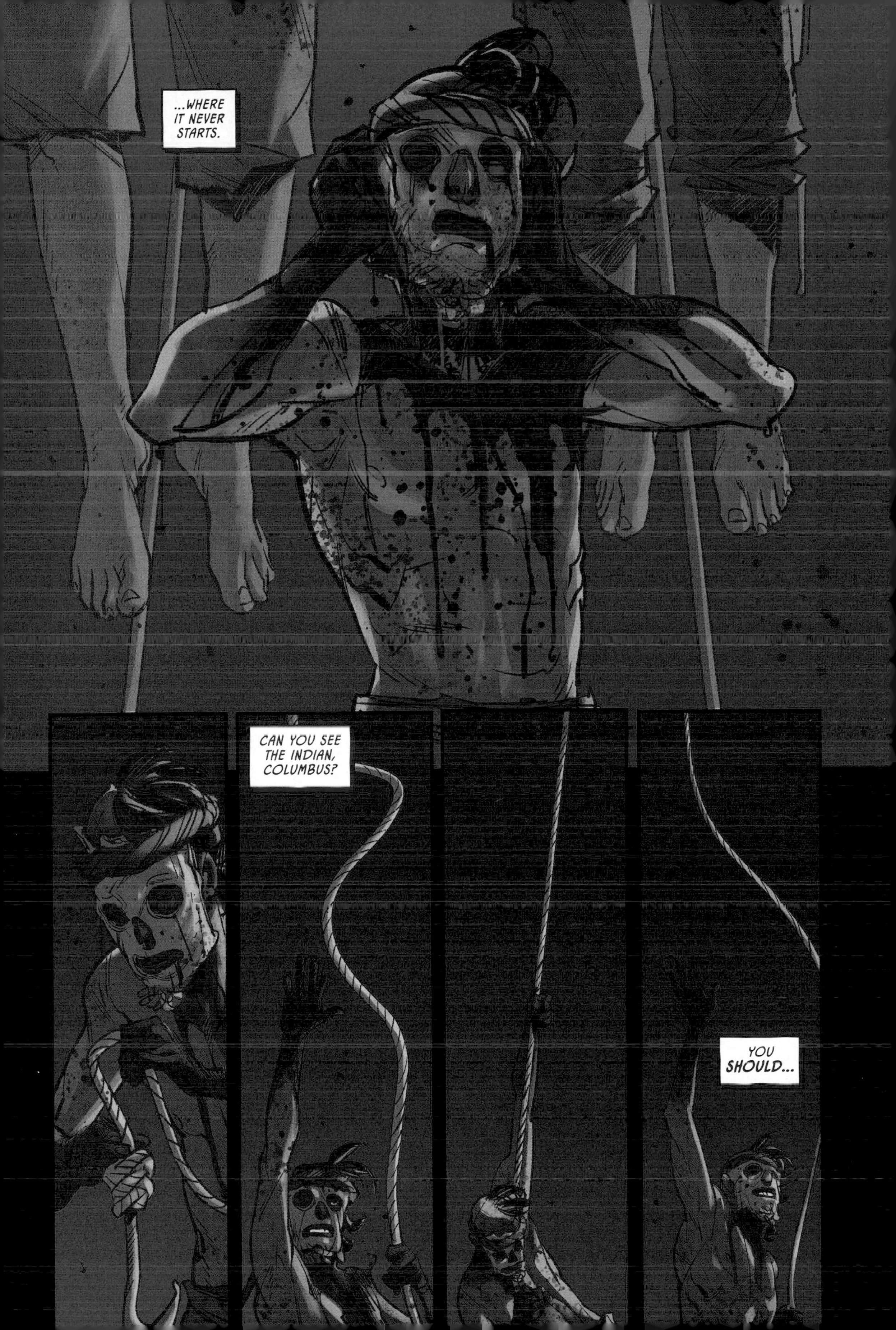
...WHERE IT NEVER STARTS.
CAN YOU SEE THE INDIAN, COLUMBUS?
YOU SHOULD...

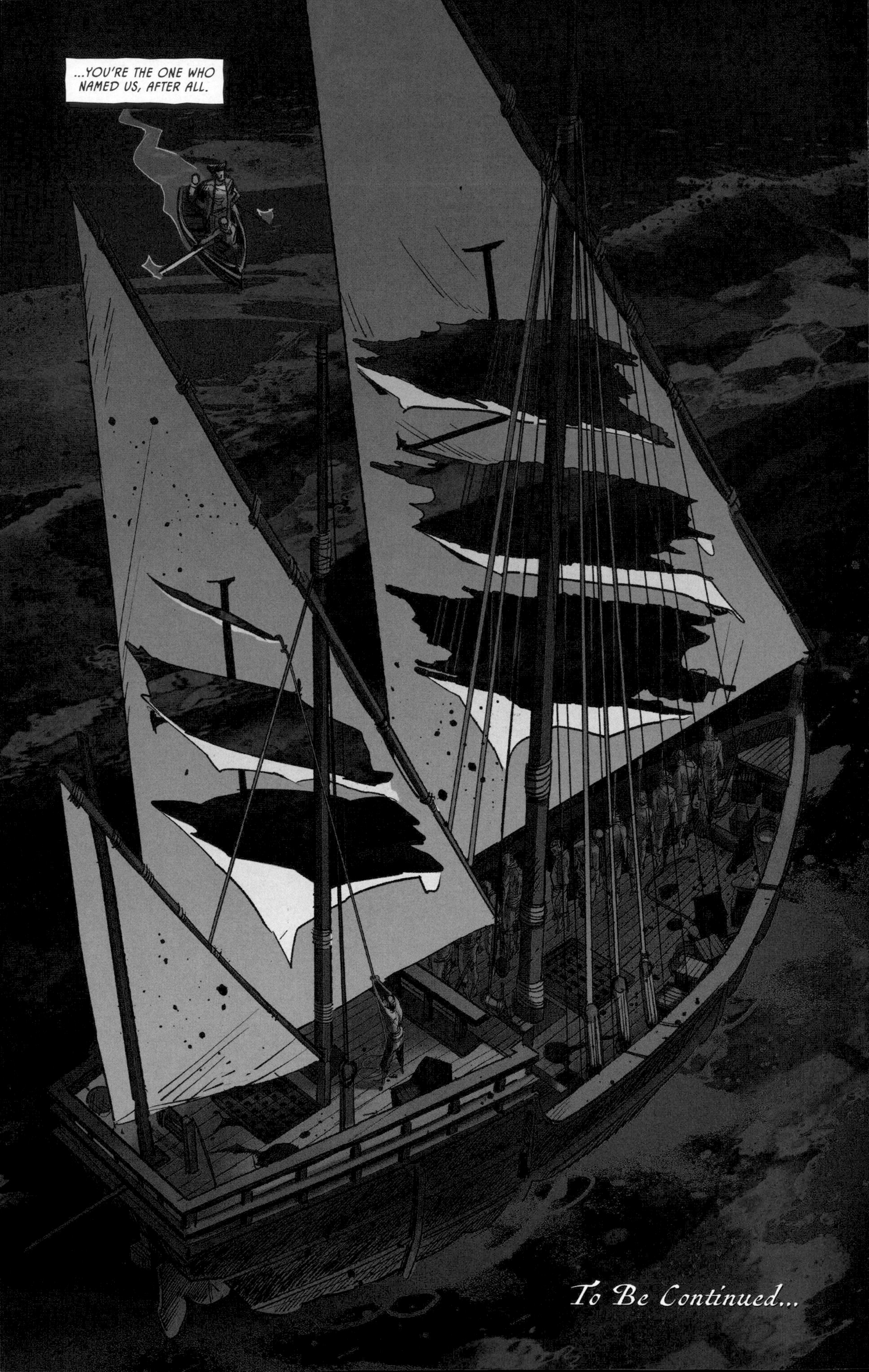
...YOU'RE THE ONE WHO NAMED US, AFTER ALL.
To Be Continued...

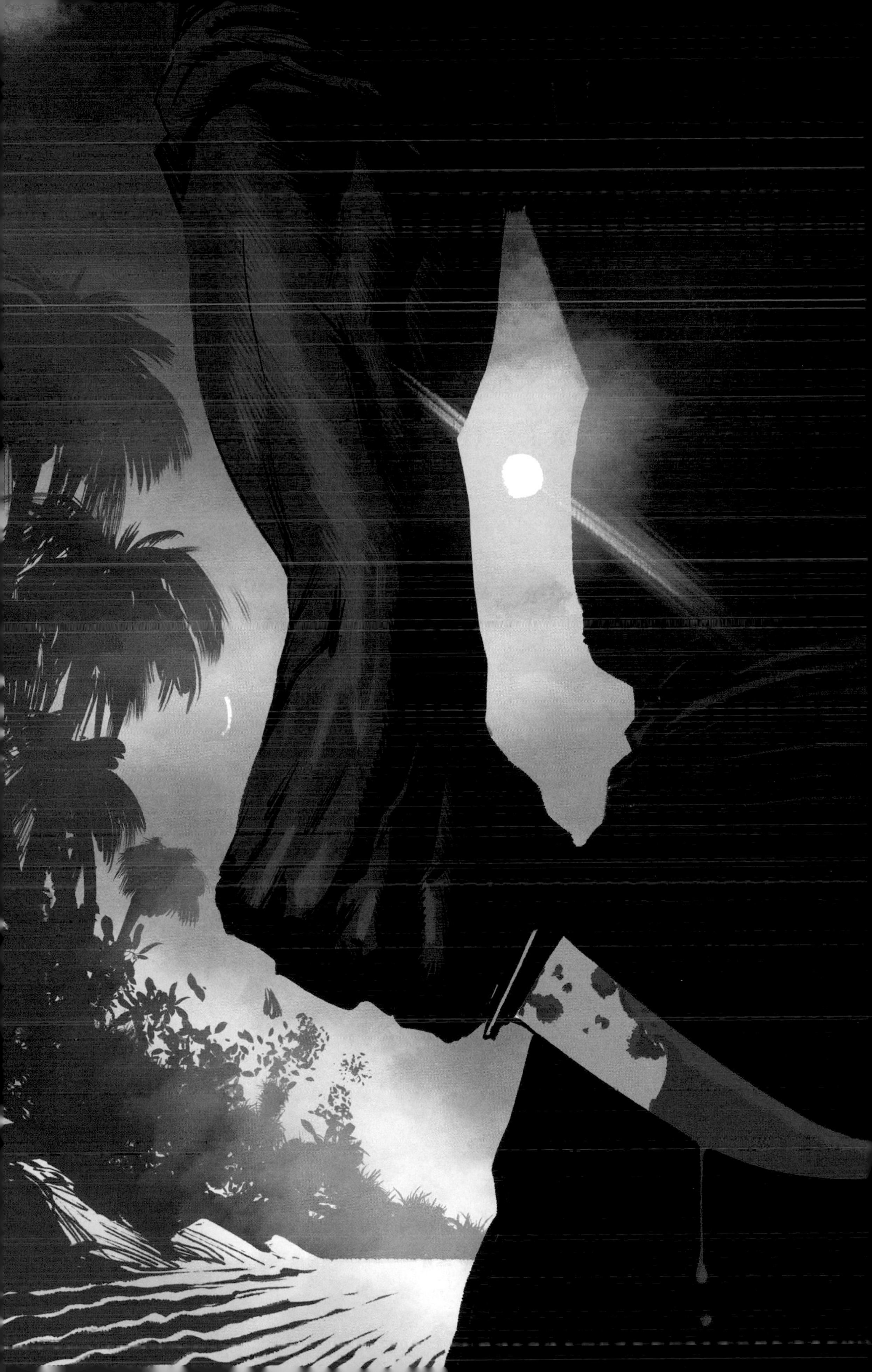

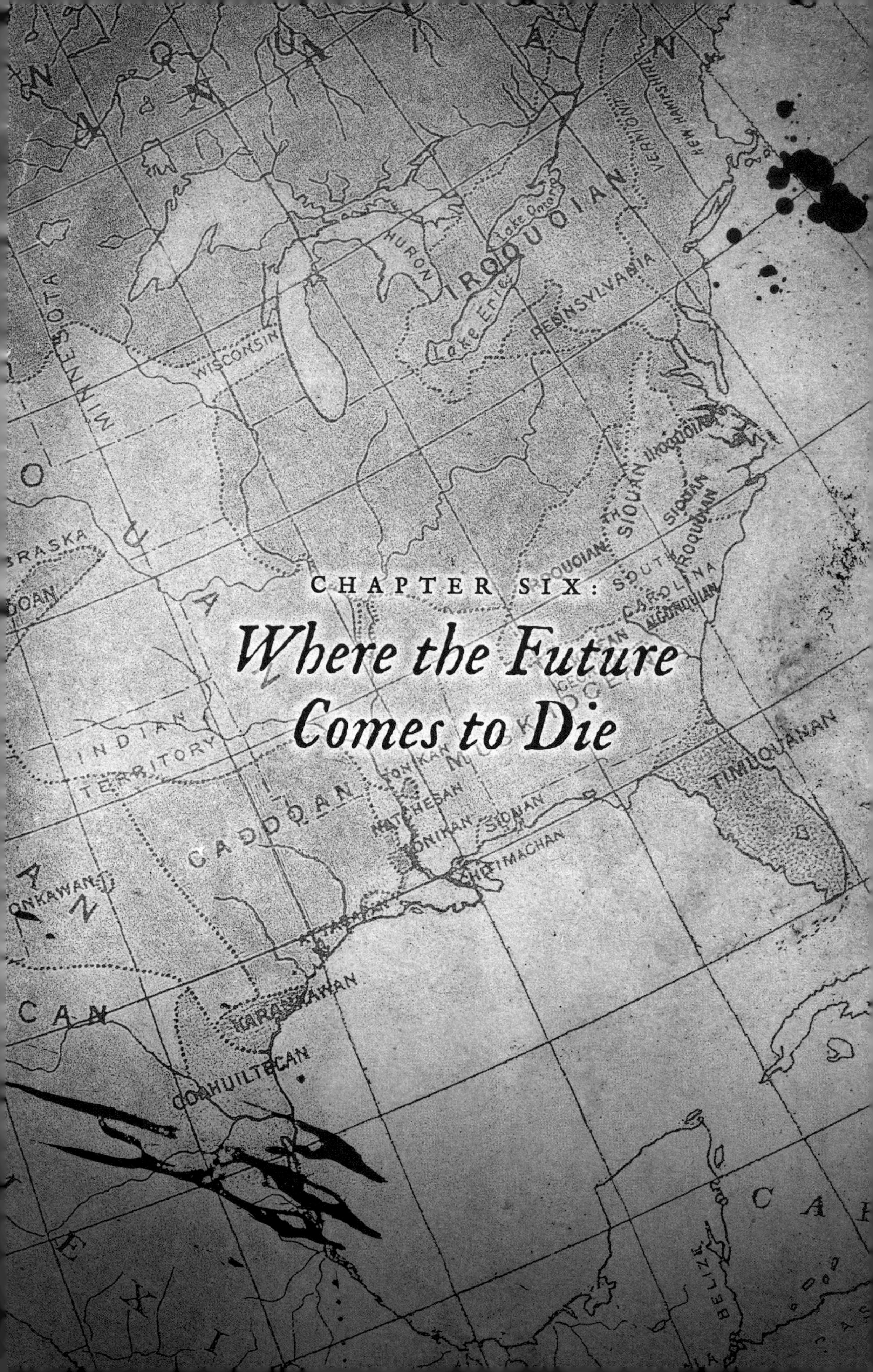
VERMONT
NEW HAMPSHIRE
IROQUOIAN
Lake Ontario
HURON
Lake Erie
PENNSYLVANIA
WISCONSIN
MINNESOTA
BRASKA
SIOUAN
SOUTH
CAROLINA
ALGONQUIAN
INDIAN
TERRITORY
CADDOAN
TONIKAN
NATCHESAN
SIOUAN
CHITIMACHAN
TIMUQUANAN
KARANKAWAN
COAHUILTECAN
BELIZE

CHAPTER SIX:

Where the Future Comes to Die

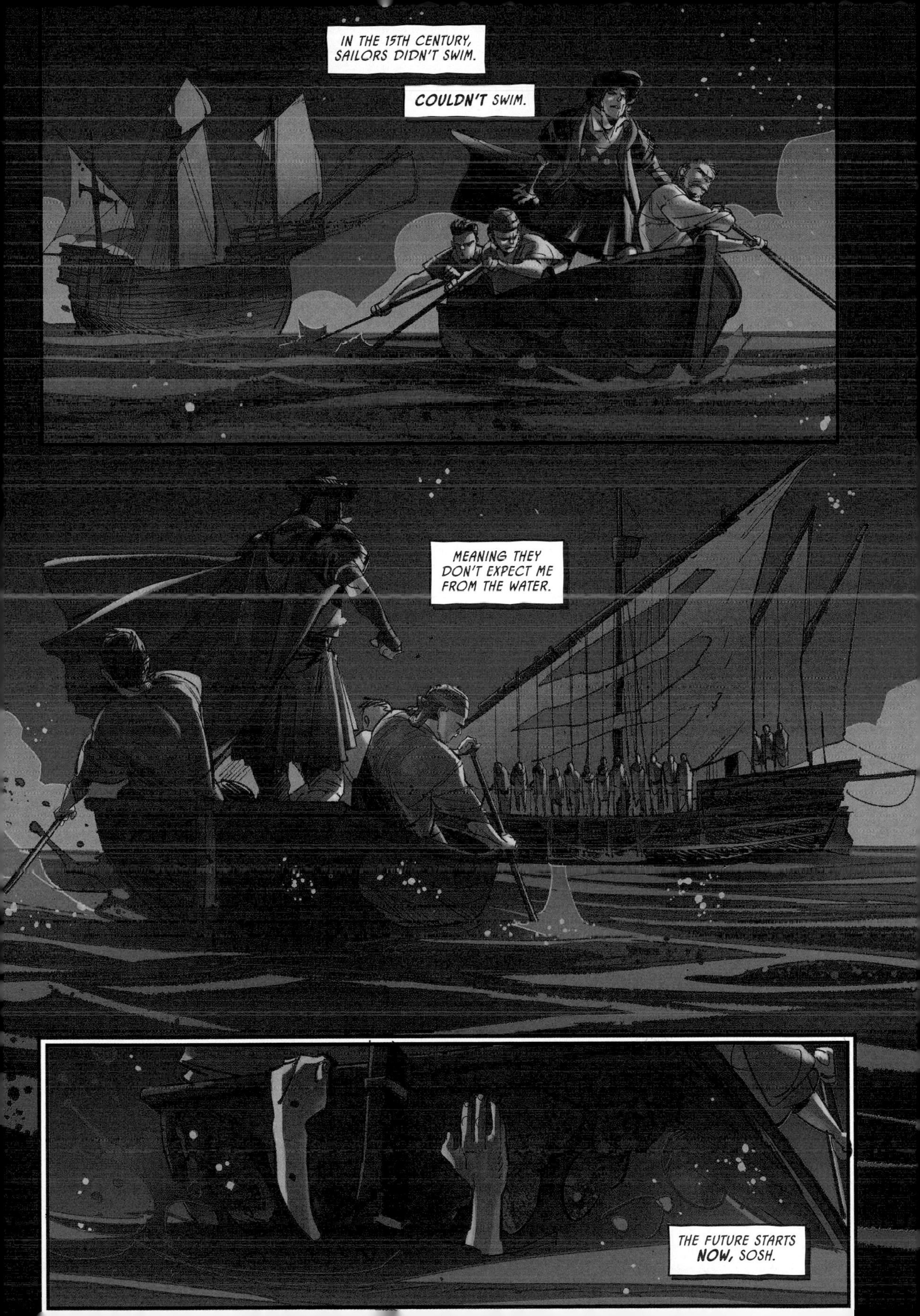

IN THE 15TH CENTURY, SAILORS DIDN'T SWIM.
COULDN'T SWIM.
MEANING THEY DON'T EXPECT ME FROM THE WATER.
THE FUTURE STARTS NOW, SOSH.

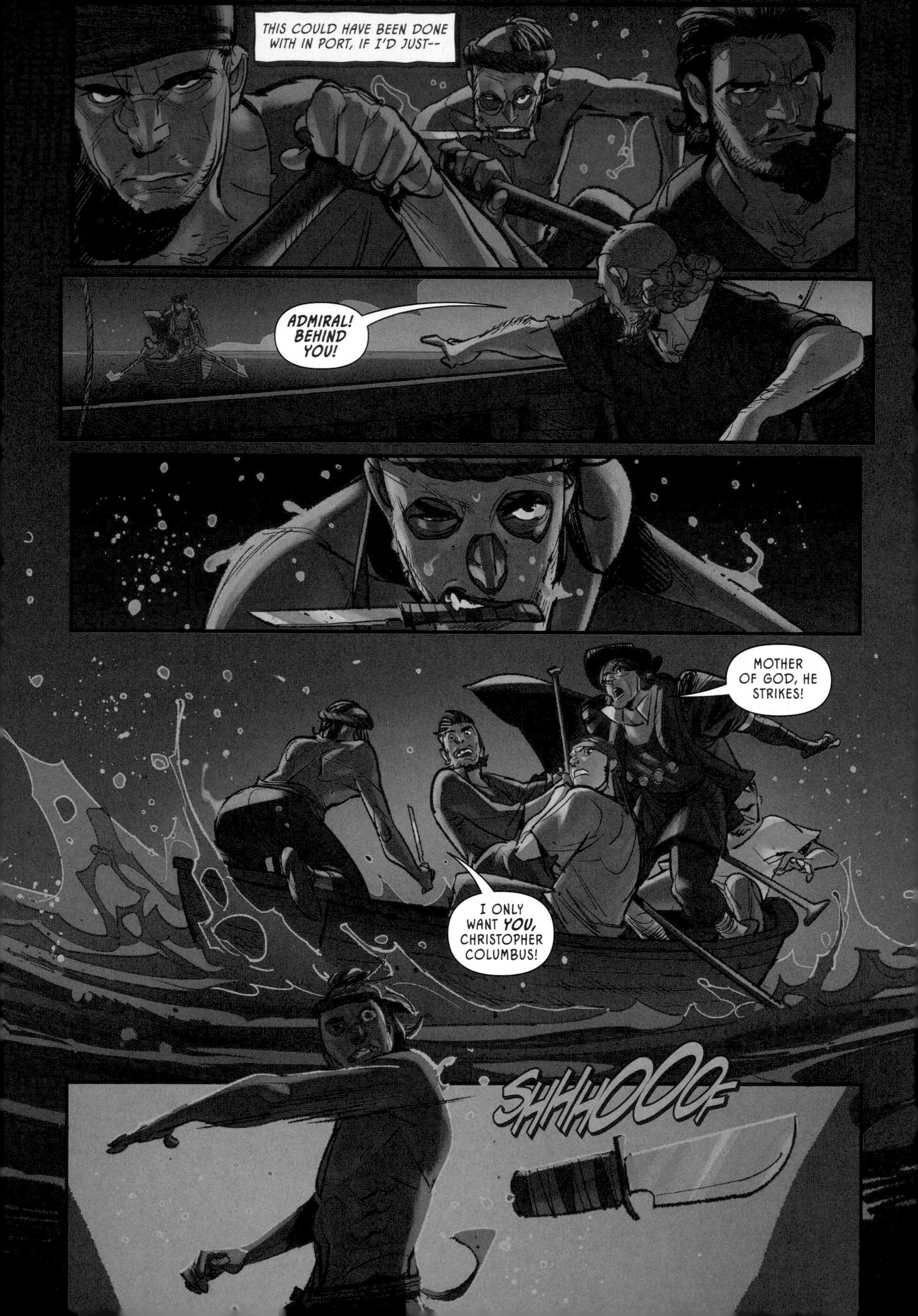

THIS COULD HAVE BEEN DONE WITH IN PORT, IF I'D JUST--
ADMIRAL! BEHIND YOU!
MOTHER OF GOD, HE STRIKES!
I ONLY WANT *YOU*, CHRISTOPHER COLUMBUS!
SHHHOOOF

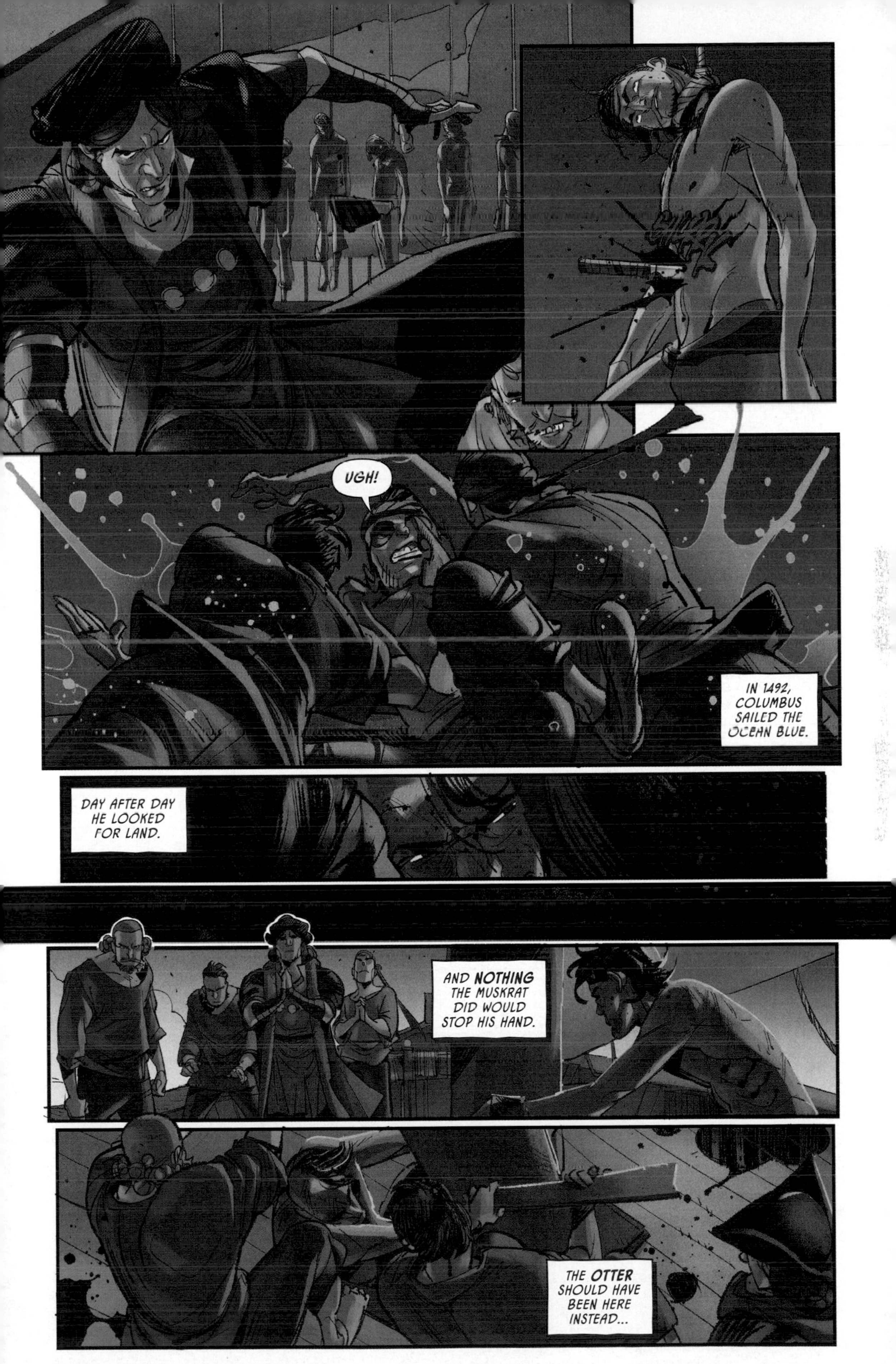
UGH!
IN 1492, COLUMBUS SAILED THE OCEAN BLUE.
DAY AFTER DAY HE LOOKED FOR LAND.
AND NOTHING THE MUSKRAT DID WOULD STOP HIS HAND.
THE OTTER SHOULD HAVE BEEN HERE INSTEAD...

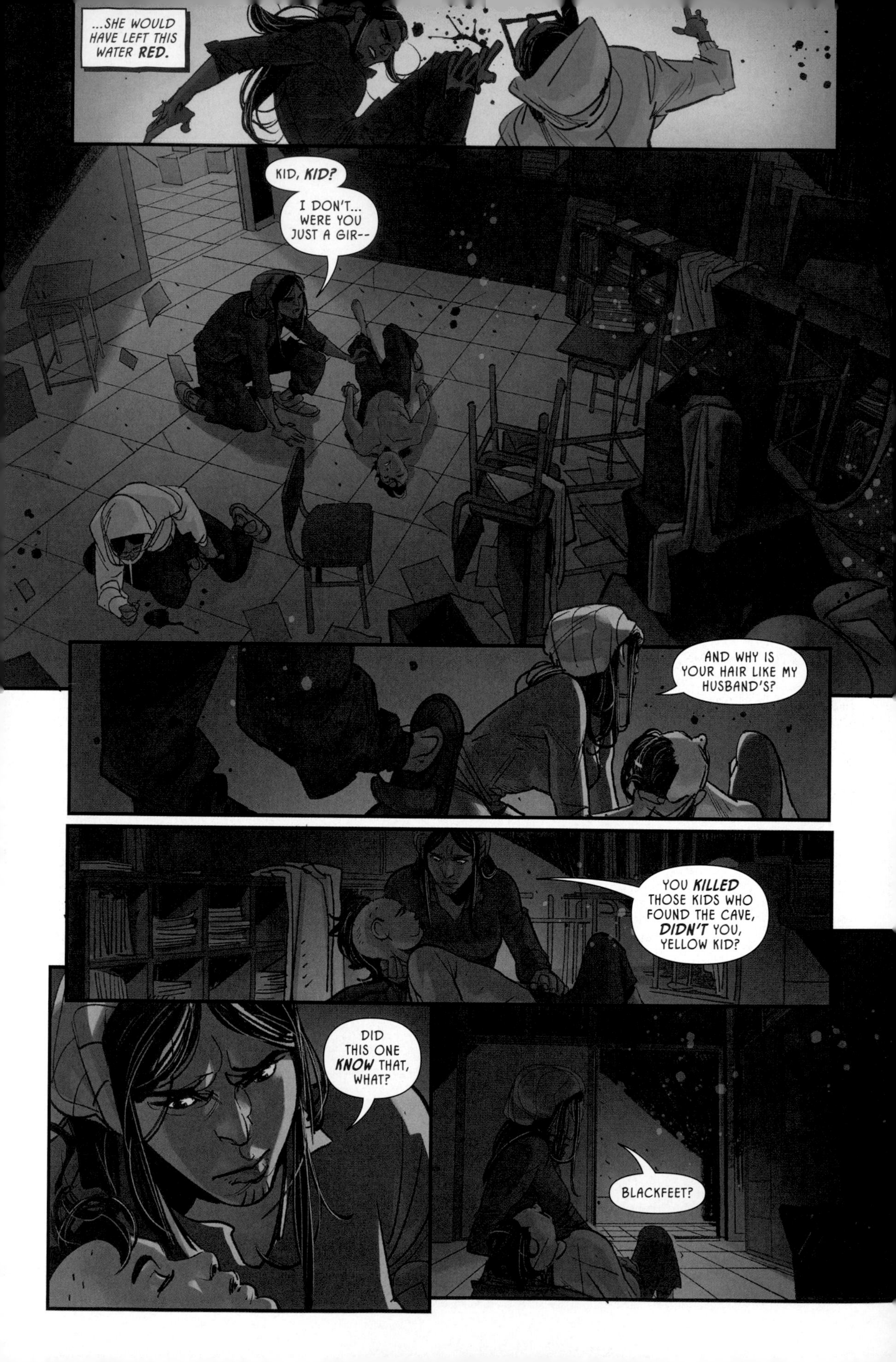
...SHE WOULD HAVE LEFT THIS WATER RED.
KID, KID?
I DON'T... WERE YOU JUST A GIR--
AND WHY IS YOUR HAIR LIKE MY HUSBAND'S?
YOU KILLED THOSE KIDS WHO FOUND THE CAVE, DIDN'T YOU, YELLOW KID?
DID THIS ONE KNOW THAT, WHAT?
BLACKFEET?

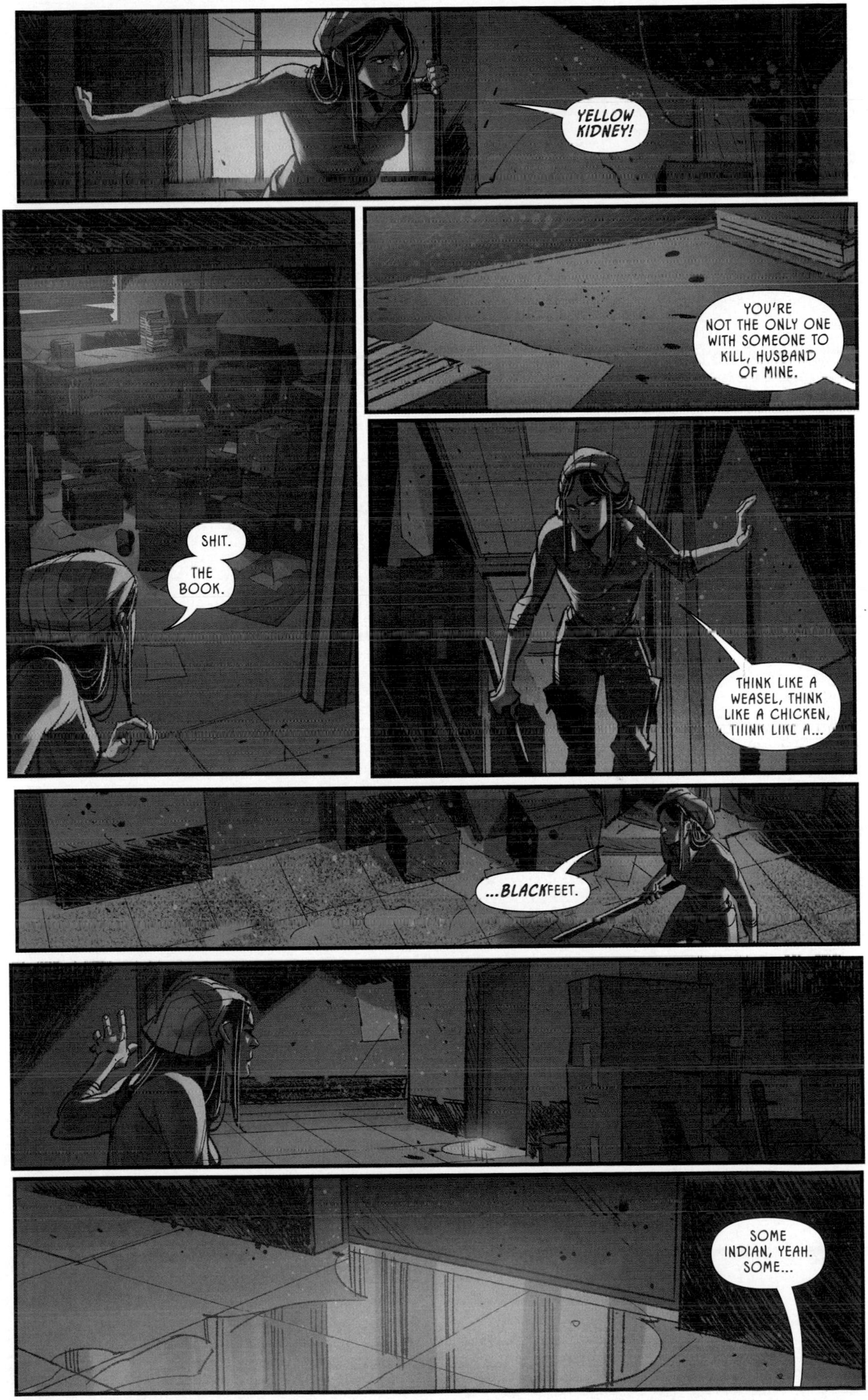
YELLOW KIDNEY!
SHIT.
THE BOOK.
YOU'RE NOT THE ONLY ONE WITH SOMEONE TO KILL, HUSBAND OF MINE.
THINK LIKE A WEASEL, THINK LIKE A CHICKEN, THINK LIKE A...
...BLACKFEET.
SOME INDIAN, YEAH. SOME...

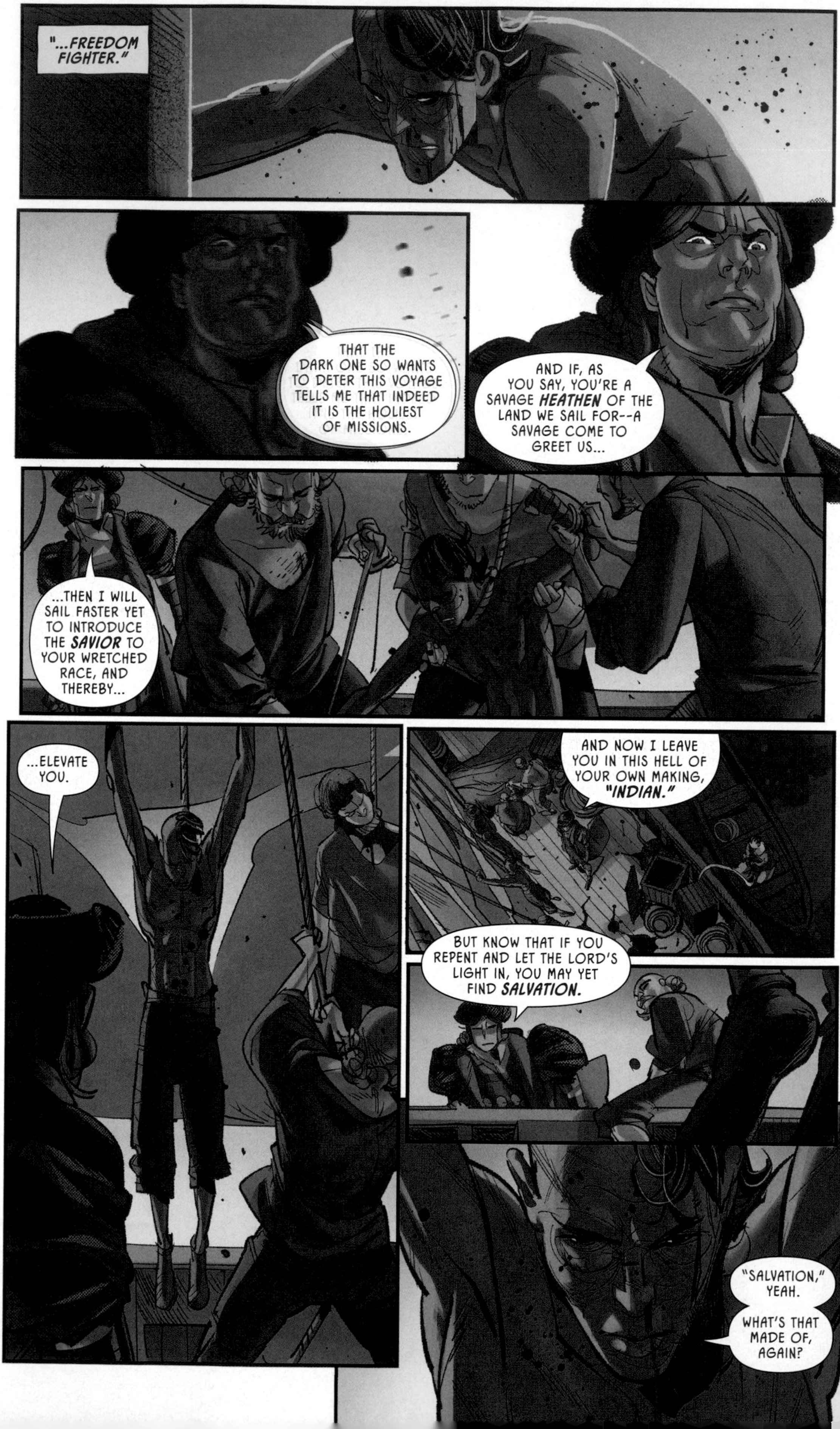
"...FREEDOM FIGHTER."
THAT THE DARK ONE SO WANTS TO DETER THIS VOYAGE TELLS ME THAT INDEED IT IS THE HOLIEST OF MISSIONS.
AND IF, AS YOU SAY, YOU'RE A SAVAGE HEATHEN OF THE LAND WE SAIL FOR--A SAVAGE COME TO GREET US...
...THEN I WILL SAIL FASTER YET TO INTRODUCE THE SAVIOR TO YOUR WRETCHED RACE, AND THEREBY...
...ELEVATE YOU.
AND NOW I LEAVE YOU IN THIS HELL OF YOUR OWN MAKING, "INDIAN."
BUT KNOW THAT IF YOU REPENT AND LET THE LORD'S LIGHT IN, YOU MAY YET FIND SALVATION.
"SALVATION," YEAH.
WHAT'S THAT MADE OF, AGAIN?

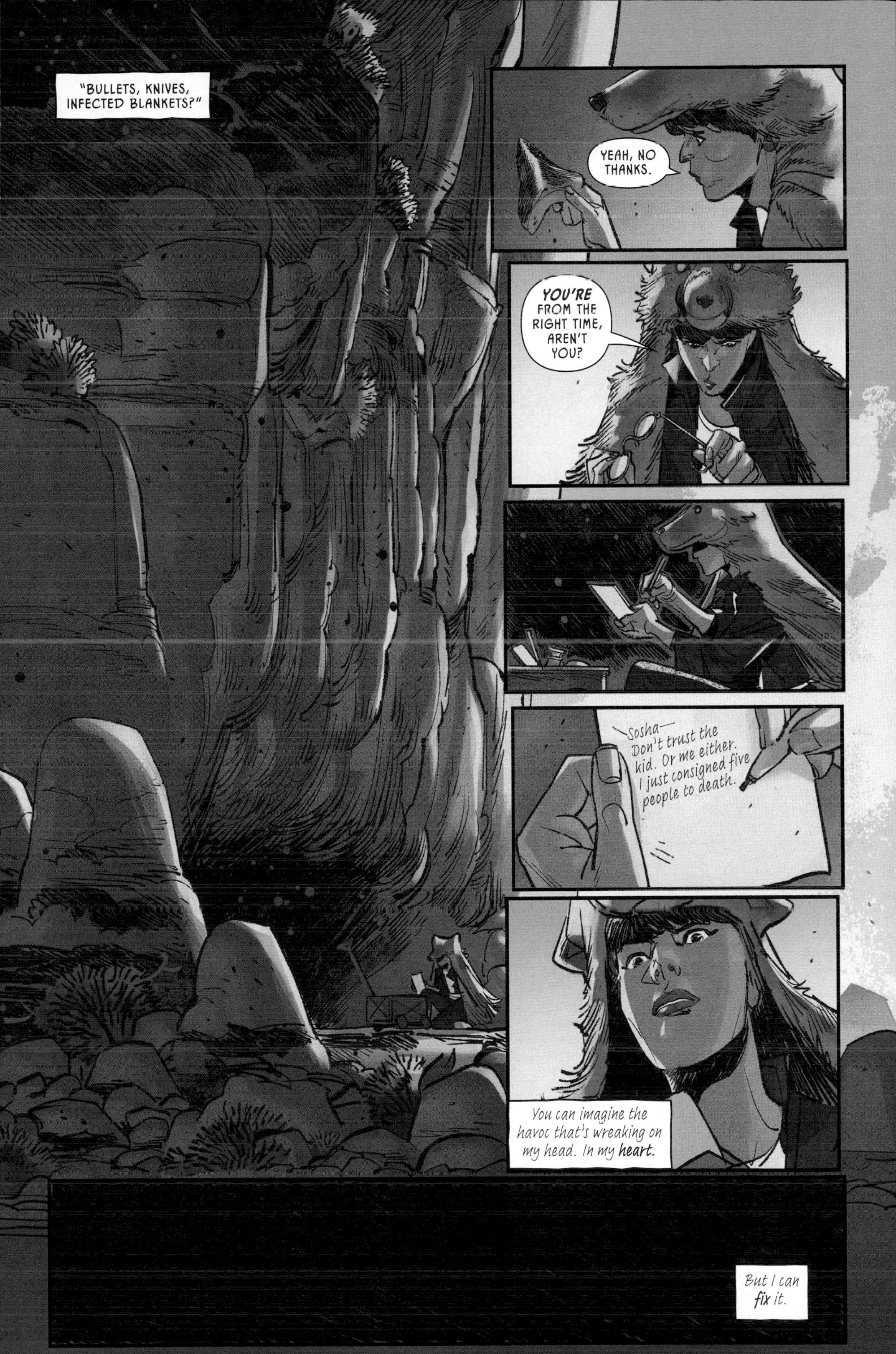
"BULLETS, KNIVES, INFECTED BLANKETS?"
YEAH, NO THANKS.
YOU'RE FROM THE RIGHT TIME, AREN'T YOU?
Sosha— Don't trust the kid. Or me either. I just consigned five people to death.
You can imagine the havoc that's wreaking on my head. In my **heart**.
But I can *fix* it.

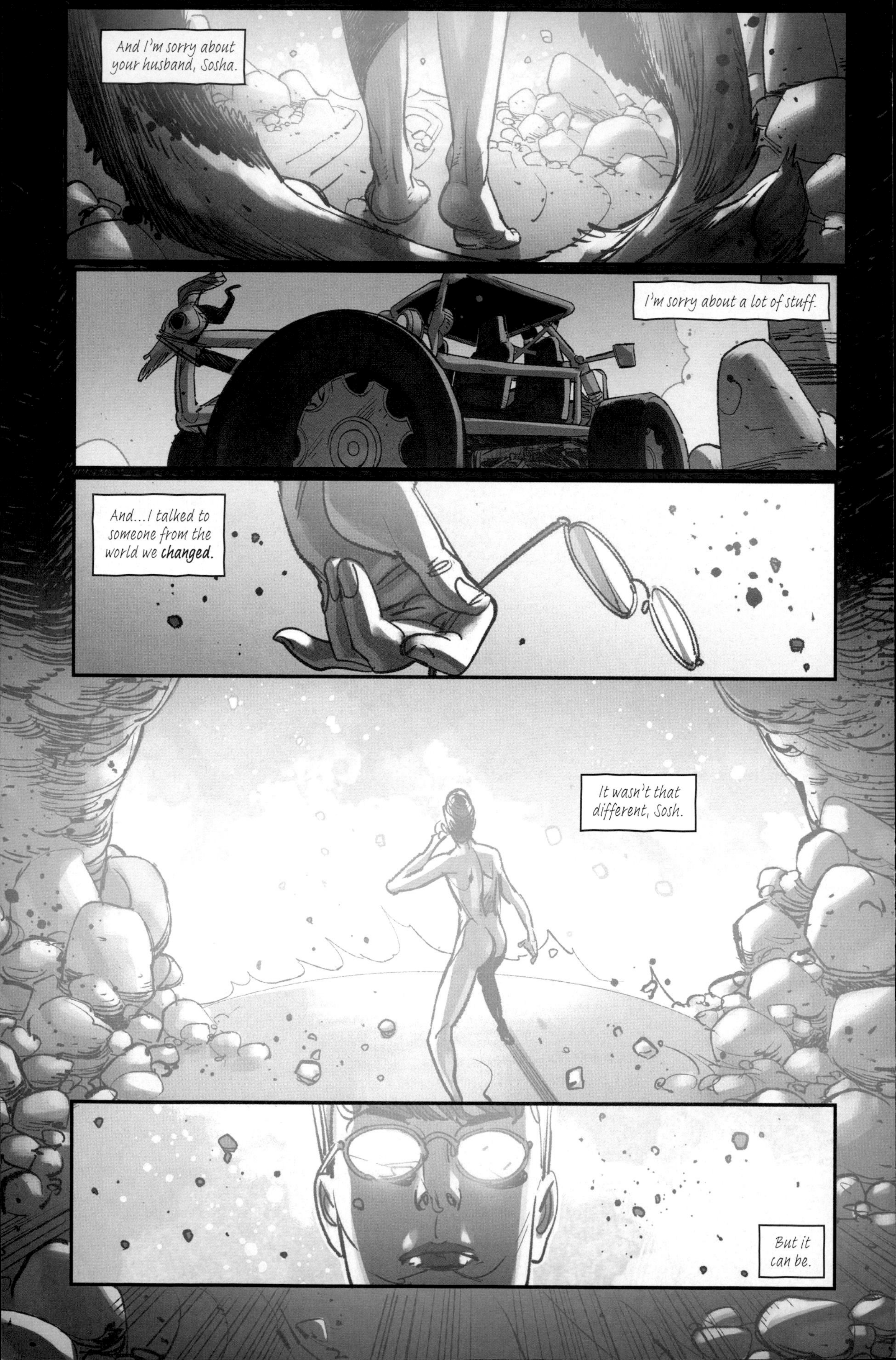
And I'm sorry about your husband, Sosha.
I'm sorry about a lot of stuff.
And...I talked to someone from the world we **changed**.
It wasn't that different, Sosh.
But it can be.

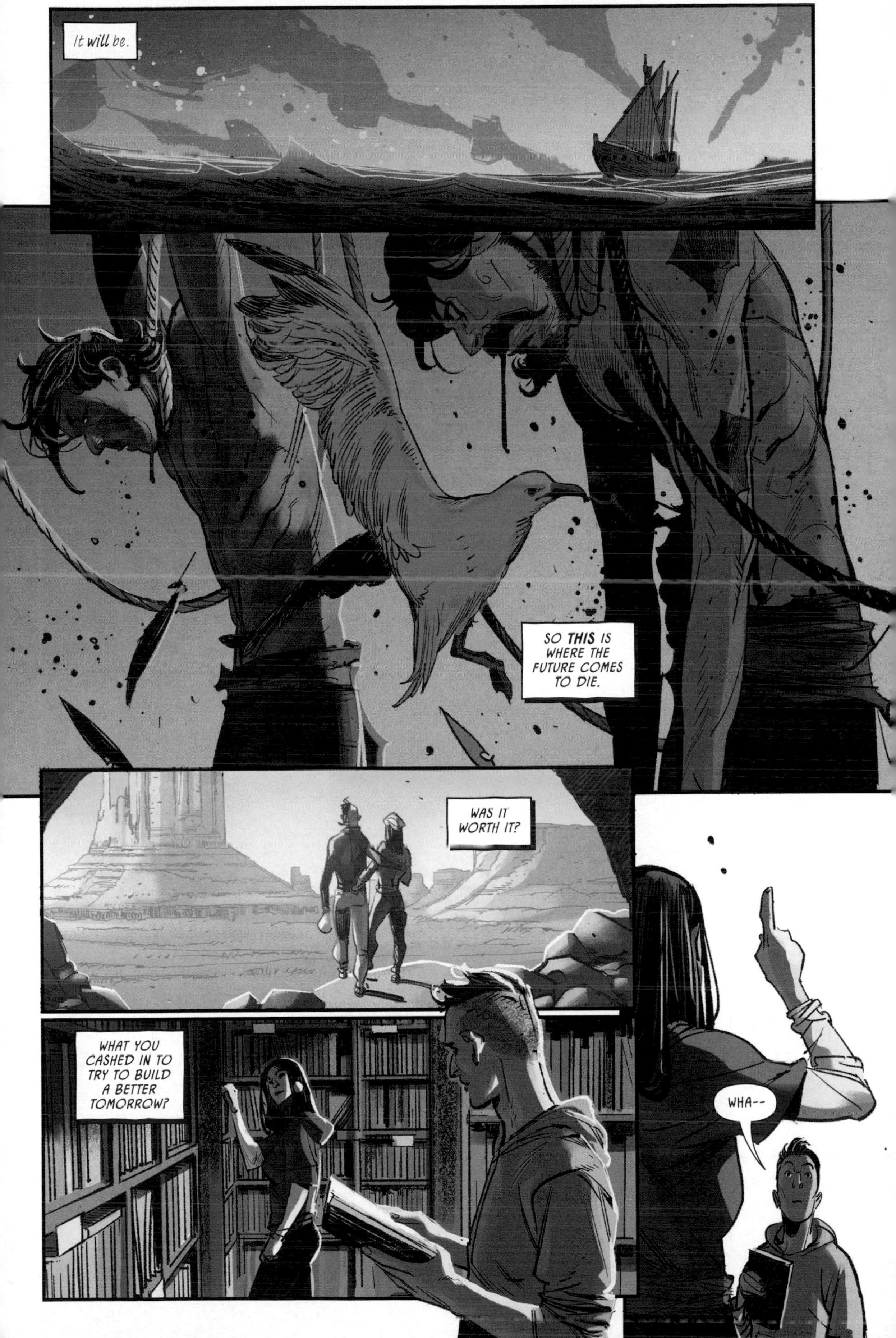
It will be.
SO THIS IS WHERE THE FUTURE COMES TO DIE.
WAS IT WORTH IT?
WHAT YOU CASHED IN TO TRY TO BUILD A BETTER TOMORROW?
WHA--

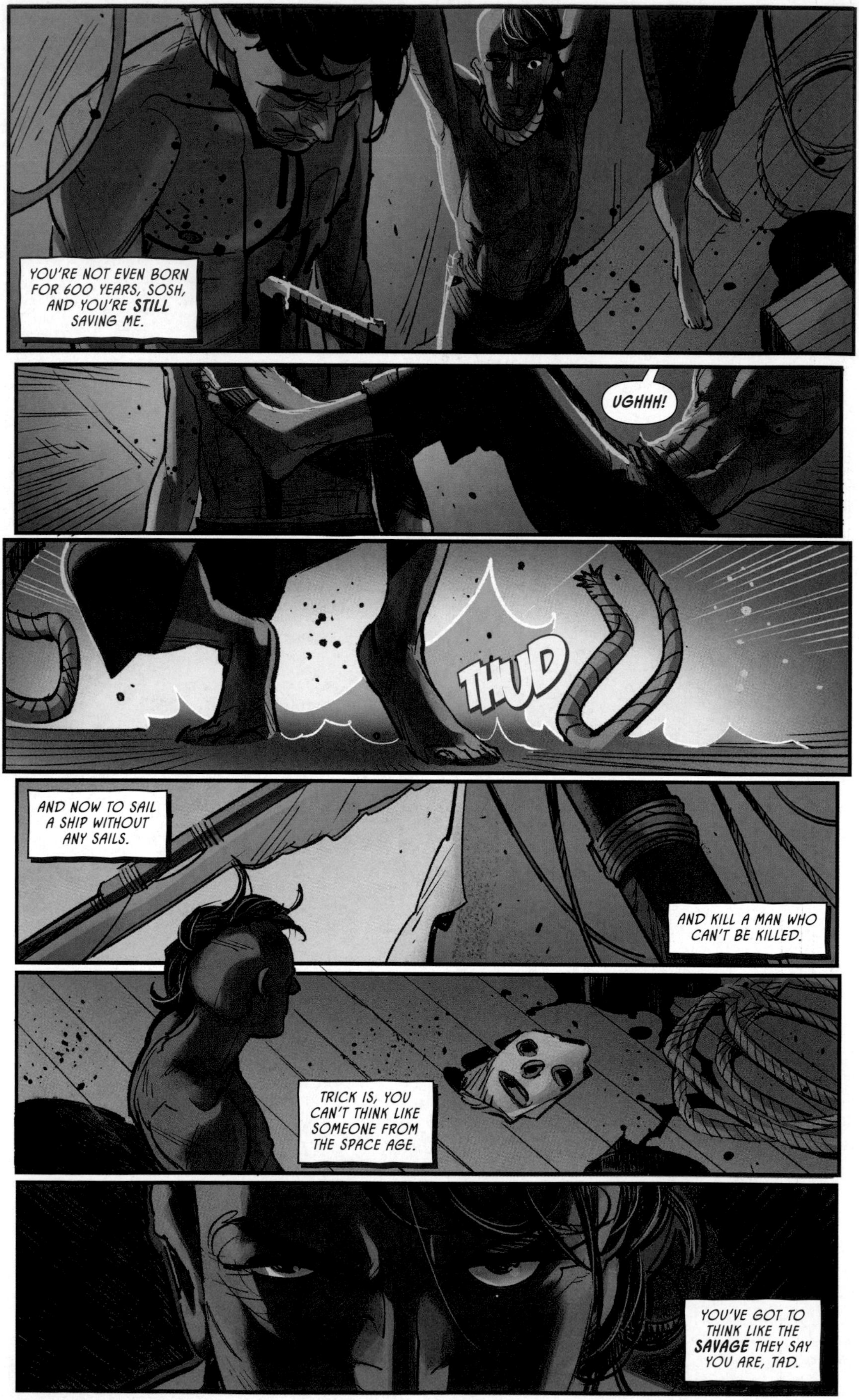
YOU'RE NOT EVEN BORN FOR 600 YEARS, SOSH, AND YOU'RE STILL SAVING ME.
UGHHH!
THUD
AND NOW TO SAIL A SHIP WITHOUT ANY SAILS.
AND KILL A MAN WHO CAN'T BE KILLED.
TRICK IS, YOU CAN'T THINK LIKE SOMEONE FROM THE SPACE AGE.
YOU'VE GOT TO THINK LIKE THE SAVAGE THEY SAY YOU ARE, TAD.

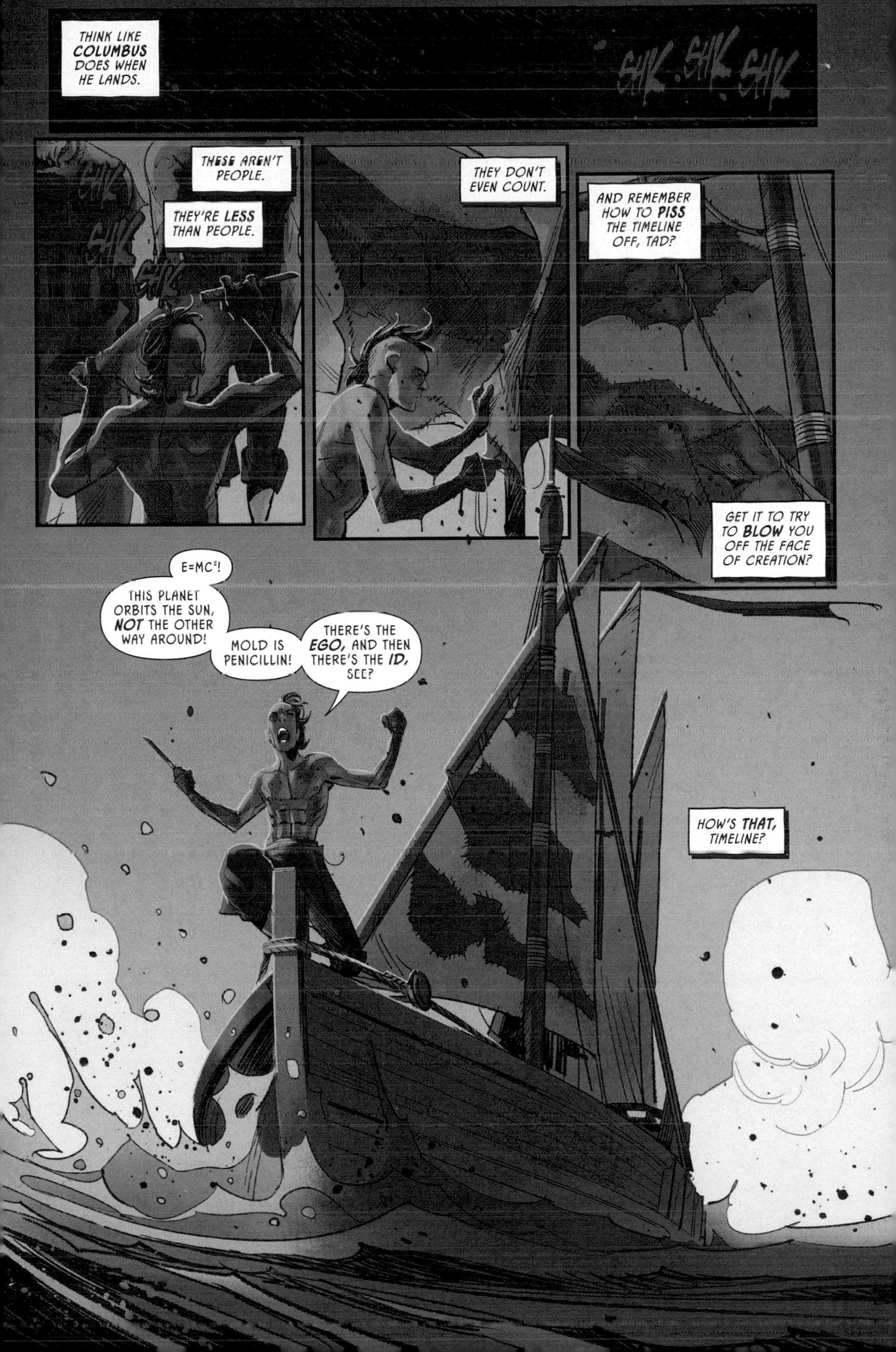
THINK LIKE COLUMBUS DOES WHEN HE LANDS.
SHK SHK SHK
THESE AREN'T PEOPLE.
THEY'RE LESS THAN PEOPLE.
SHK SHK SHK
THEY DON'T EVEN COUNT.
AND REMEMBER HOW TO PISS THE TIMELINE OFF, TAD?
GET IT TO TRY TO BLOW YOU OFF THE FACE OF CREATION?
E=MC²!
THIS PLANET ORBITS THE SUN, NOT THE OTHER WAY AROUND!
MOLD IS PENICILLIN!
THERE'S THE EGO, AND THEN THERE'S THE ID, SEE?
HOW'S THAT, TIMELINE?

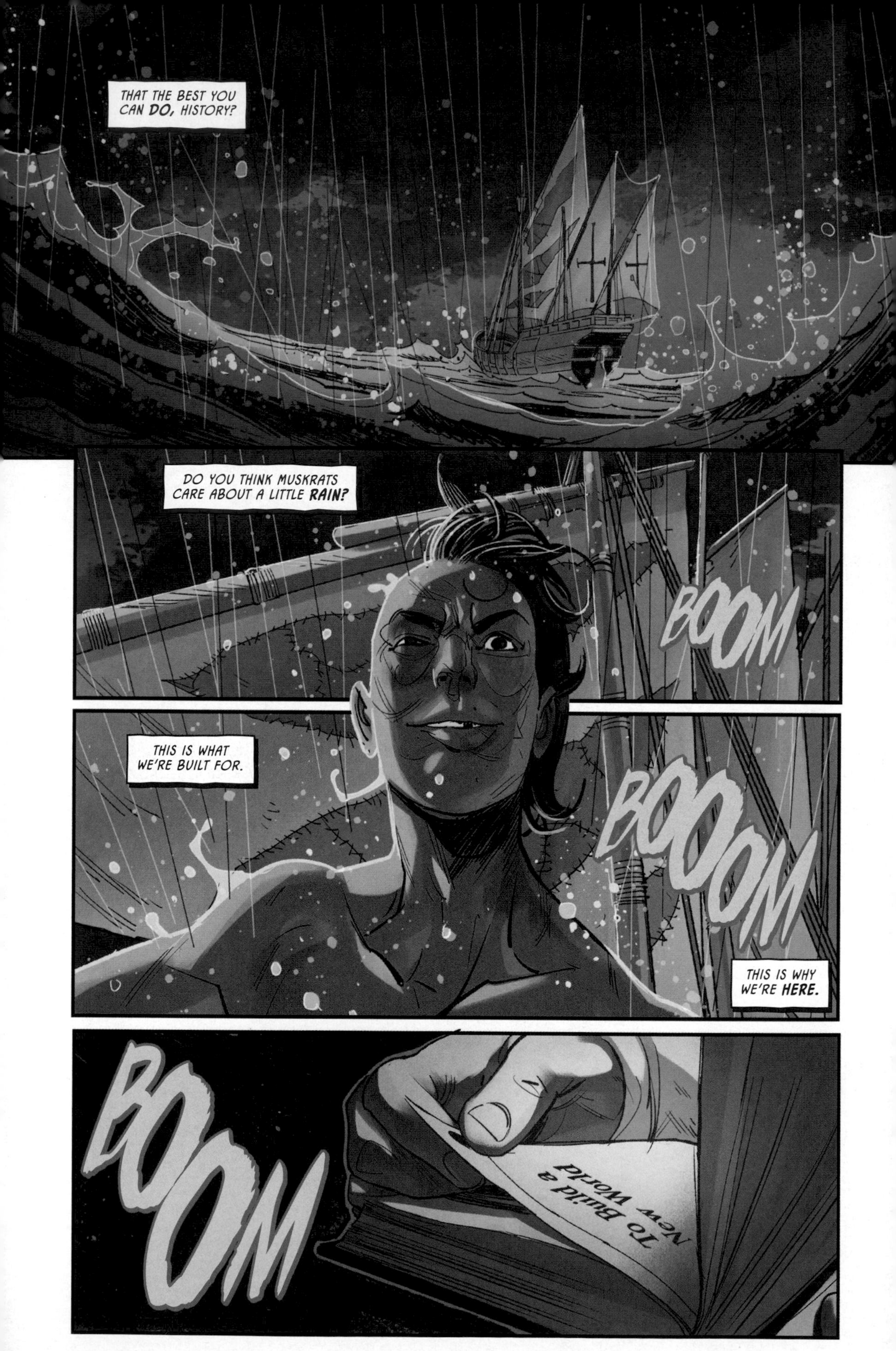
THAT THE BEST YOU CAN DO, HISTORY?
DO YOU THINK MUSKRATS CARE ABOUT A LITTLE RAIN?
BOOM
THIS IS WHAT WE'RE BUILT FOR.
BOOOOM
THIS IS WHY WE'RE HERE.
BOOM
To Build a New World

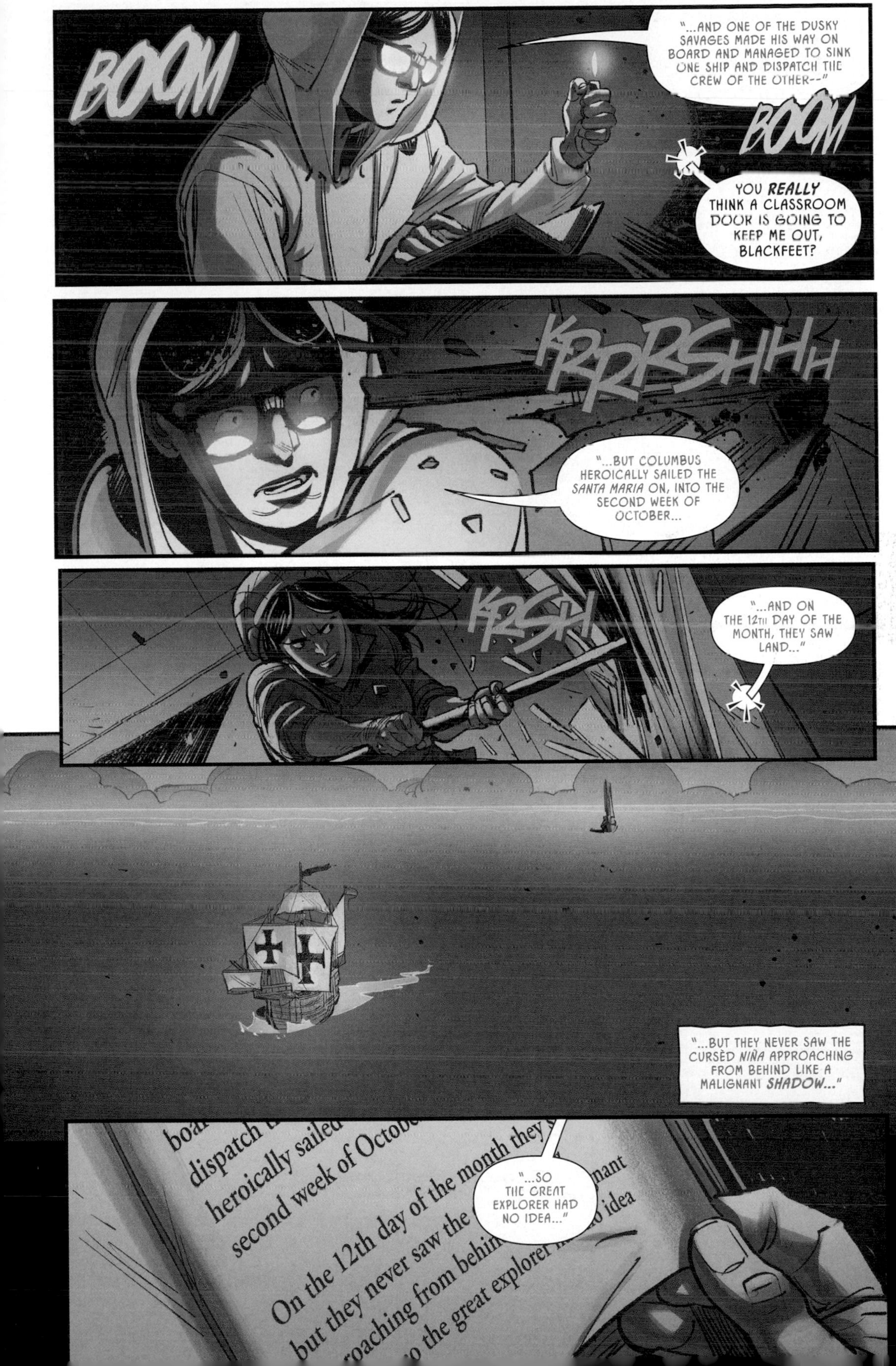

BOOM
"...AND ONE OF THE DUSKY SAVAGES MADE HIS WAY ON BOARD AND MANAGED TO SINK ONE SHIP AND DISPATCH THE CREW OF THE OTHER--"
BOOM
YOU REALLY THINK A CLASSROOM DOOR IS GOING TO KEEP ME OUT, BLACKFEET?
KRRRSHHH
"...BUT COLUMBUS HEROICALLY SAILED THE SANTA MARIA ON, INTO THE SECOND WEEK OF OCTOBER...
KRSH
"...AND ON THE 12TH DAY OF THE MONTH, THEY SAW LAND..."
"...BUT THEY NEVER SAW THE CURSED NIÑA APPROACHING FROM BEHIND LIKE A MALIGNANT SHADOW..."
"...SO THE GREAT EXPLORER HAD NO IDEA..."

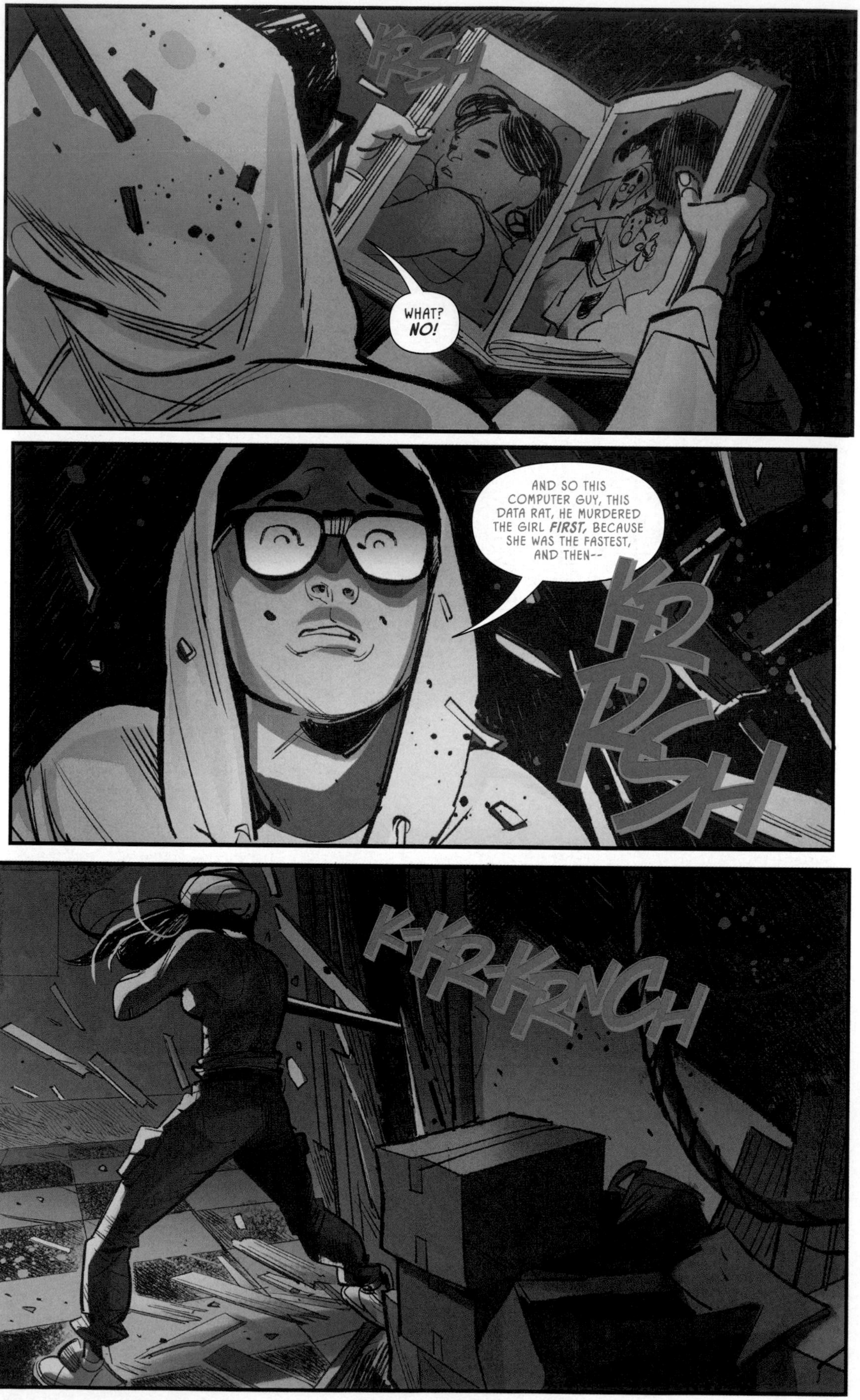
KRSH
WHAT? NO!
AND SO THIS COMPUTER GUY, THIS DATA RAT, HE MURDERED THE GIRL FIRST, BECAUSE SHE WAS THE FASTEST, AND THEN--
KR RSH
K-KR-KRNCH

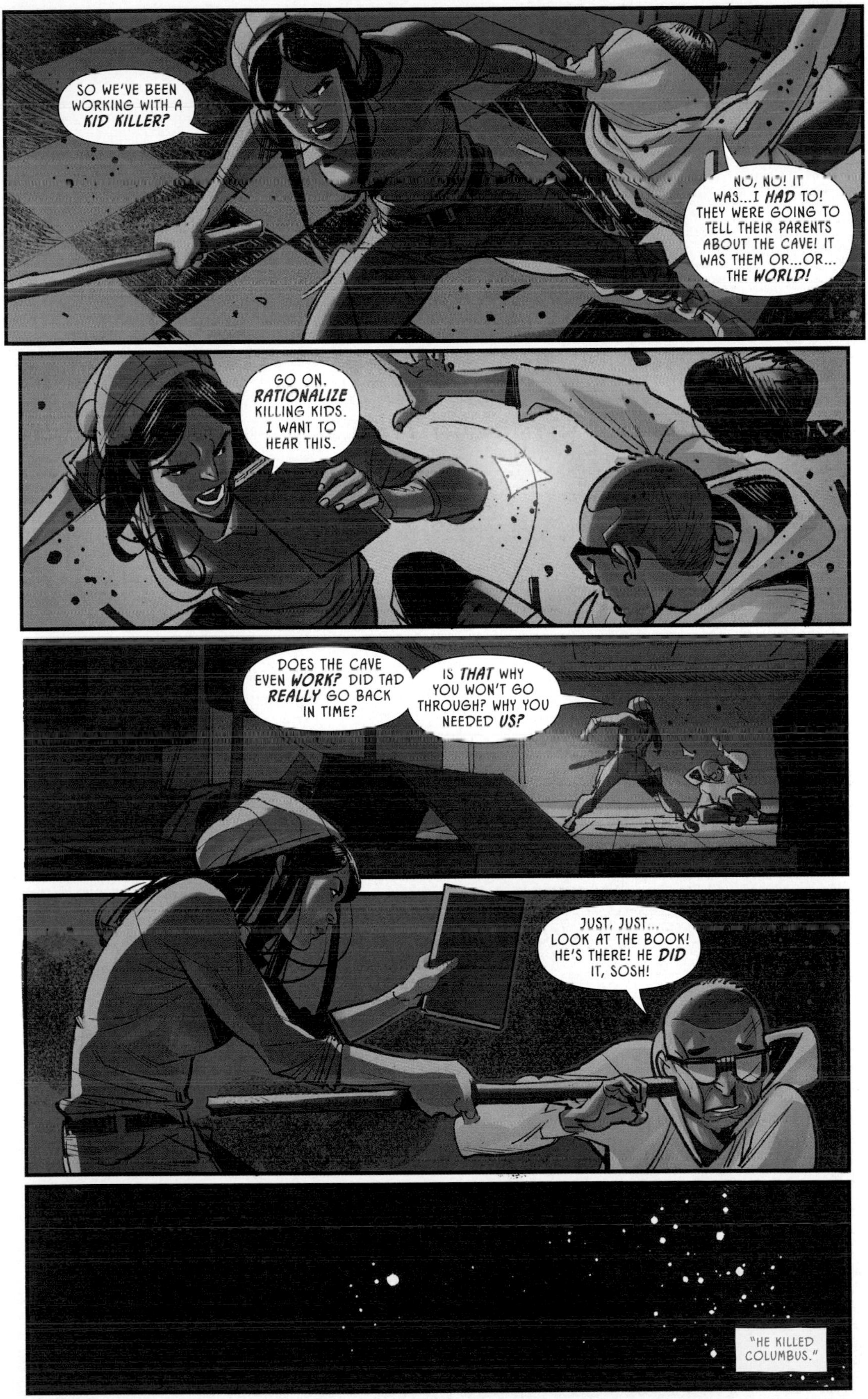
SO WE'VE BEEN WORKING WITH A KID KILLER?
NO, NO! IT WAS...I HAD TO! THEY WERE GOING TO TELL THEIR PARENTS ABOUT THE CAVE! IT WAS THEM OR...OR... THE WORLD!
GO ON. RATIONALIZE KILLING KIDS. I WANT TO HEAR THIS.
DOES THE CAVE EVEN WORK? DID TAD REALLY GO BACK IN TIME?
IS THAT WHY YOU WON'T GO THROUGH? WHY YOU NEEDED US?
JUST, JUST... LOOK AT THE BOOK! HE'S THERE! HE DID IT, SOSH!
"HE KILLED COLUMBUS."

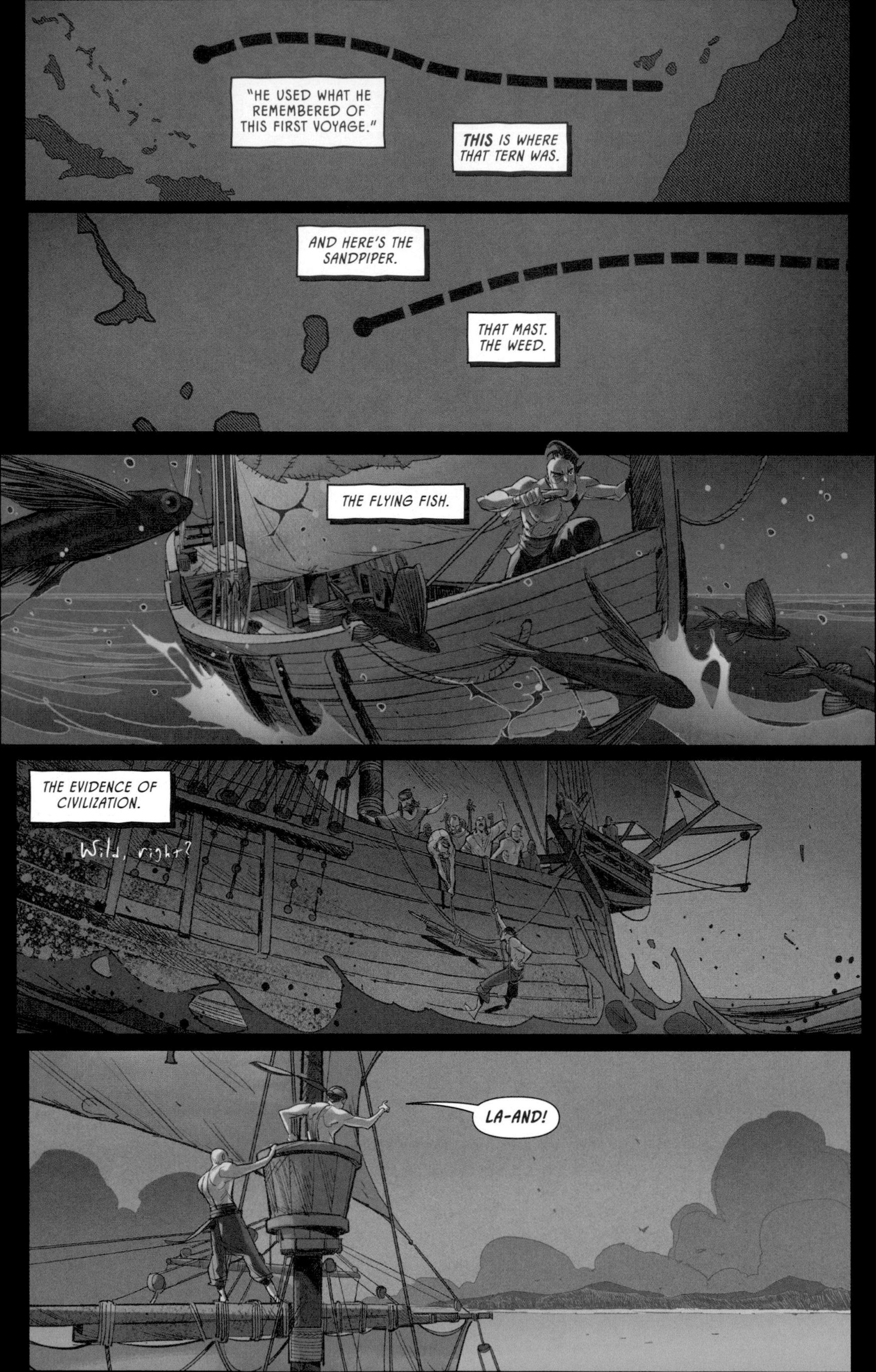
"HE USED WHAT HE REMEMBERED OF THIS FIRST VOYAGE."
THIS IS WHERE THAT TERN WAS.
AND HERE'S THE SANDPIPER.
THAT MAST. THE WEED.
THE FLYING FISH.
THE EVIDENCE OF CIVILIZATION.
Wild, right?
LA-AND!

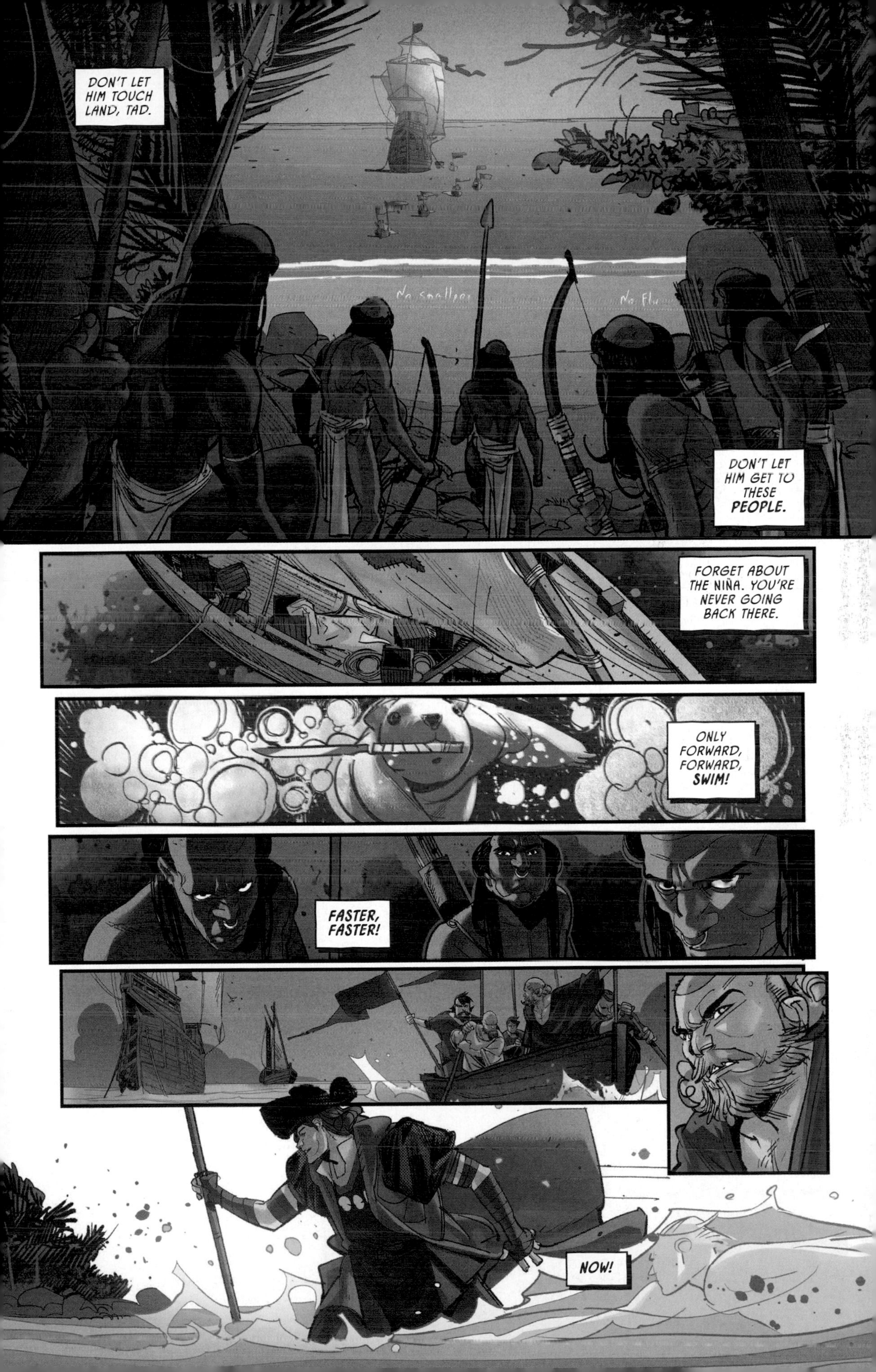
DON'T LET HIM TOUCH LAND, TAD.
DON'T LET HIM GET TO THESE PEOPLE.
FORGET ABOUT THE NIÑA. YOU'RE NEVER GOING BACK THERE.
ONLY FORWARD, FORWARD, SWIM!
FASTER, FASTER!
NOW!

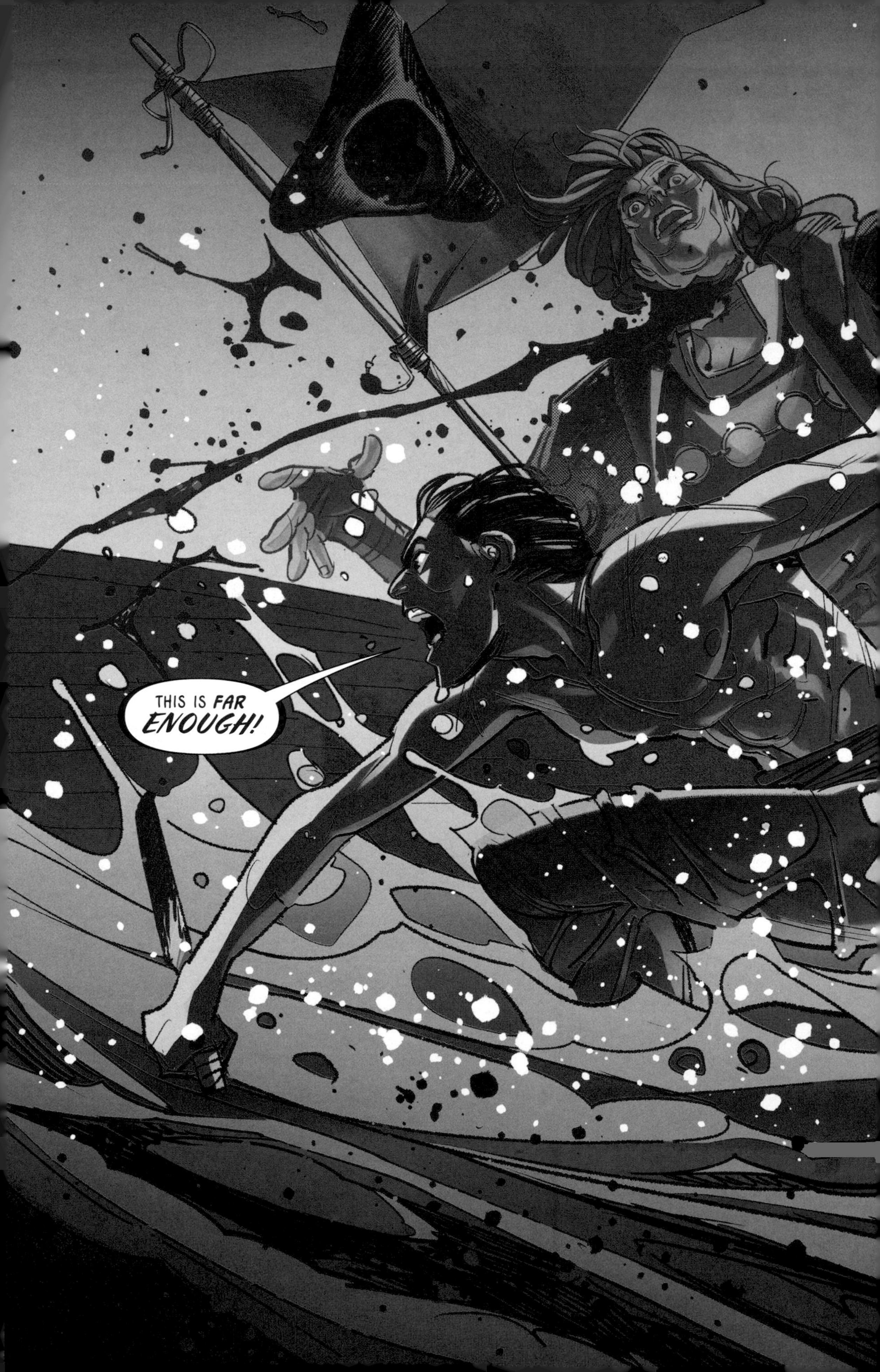
THIS IS FAR ENOUGH!

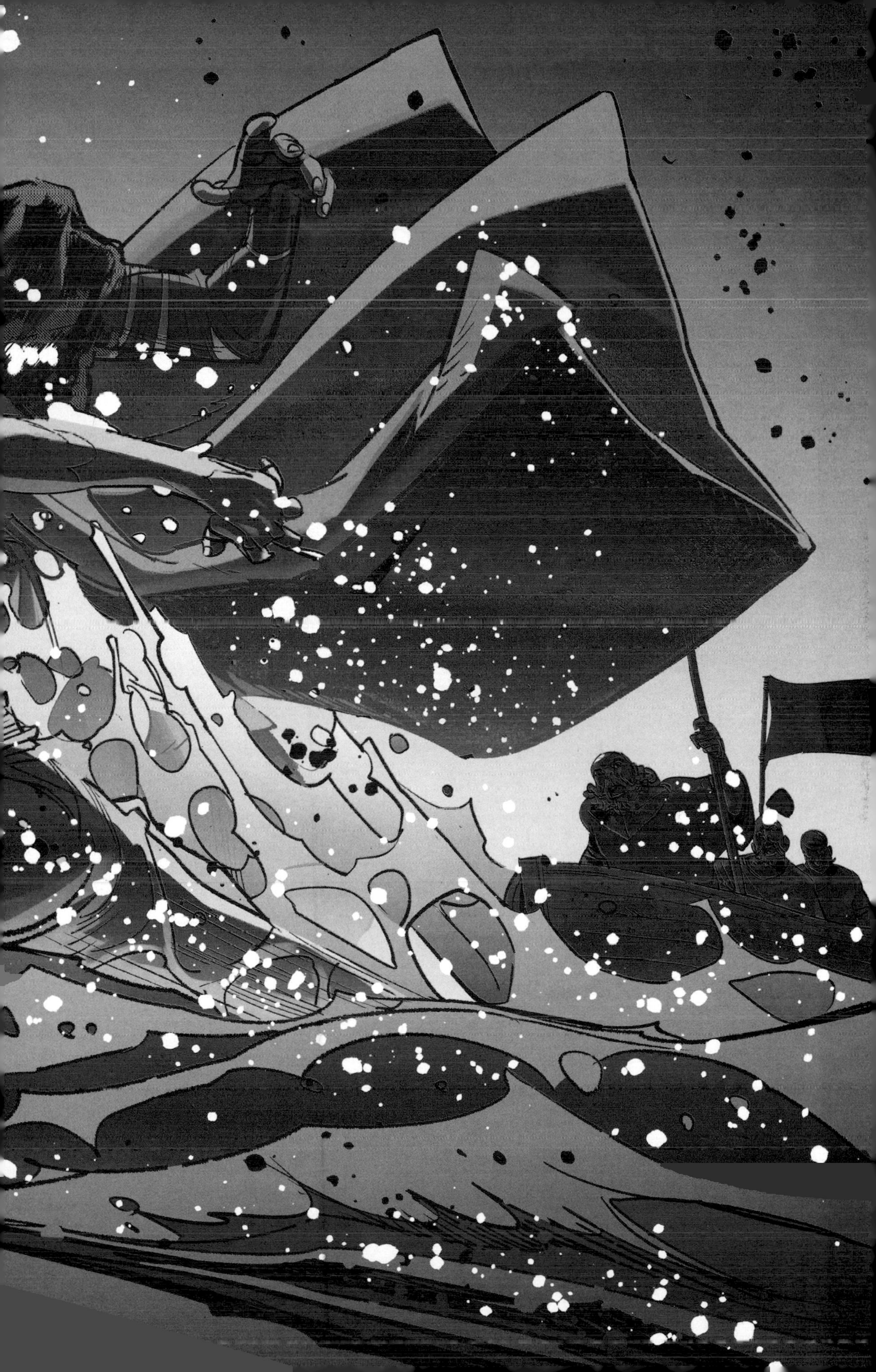

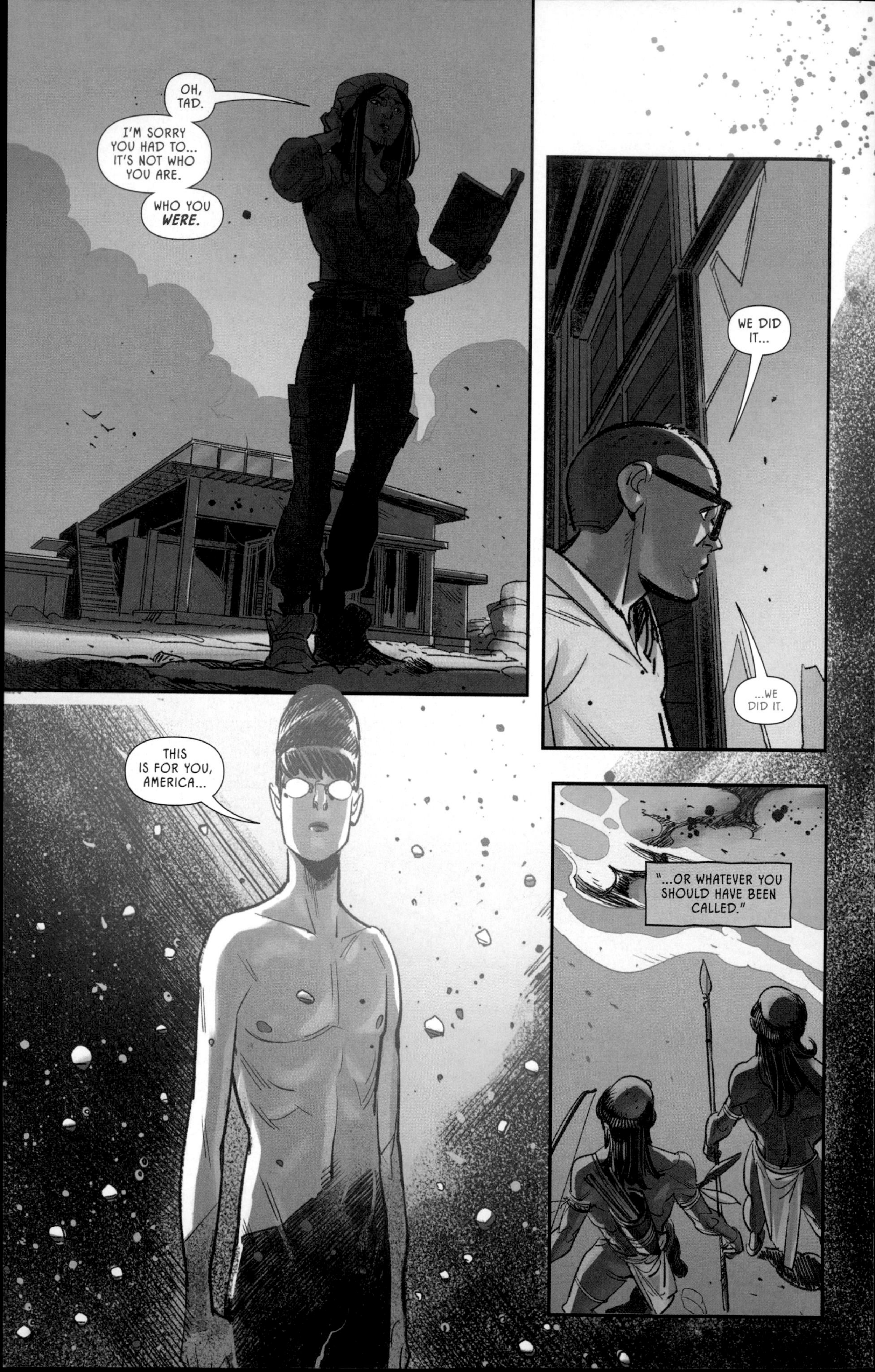
OH, TAD.
I'M SORRY YOU HAD TO... IT'S NOT WHO YOU ARE.
WHO YOU *WERE.*
WE DID IT...
...WE DID IT.
THIS IS FOR YOU, AMERICA...
"...OR WHATEVER YOU SHOULD HAVE BEEN CALLED."

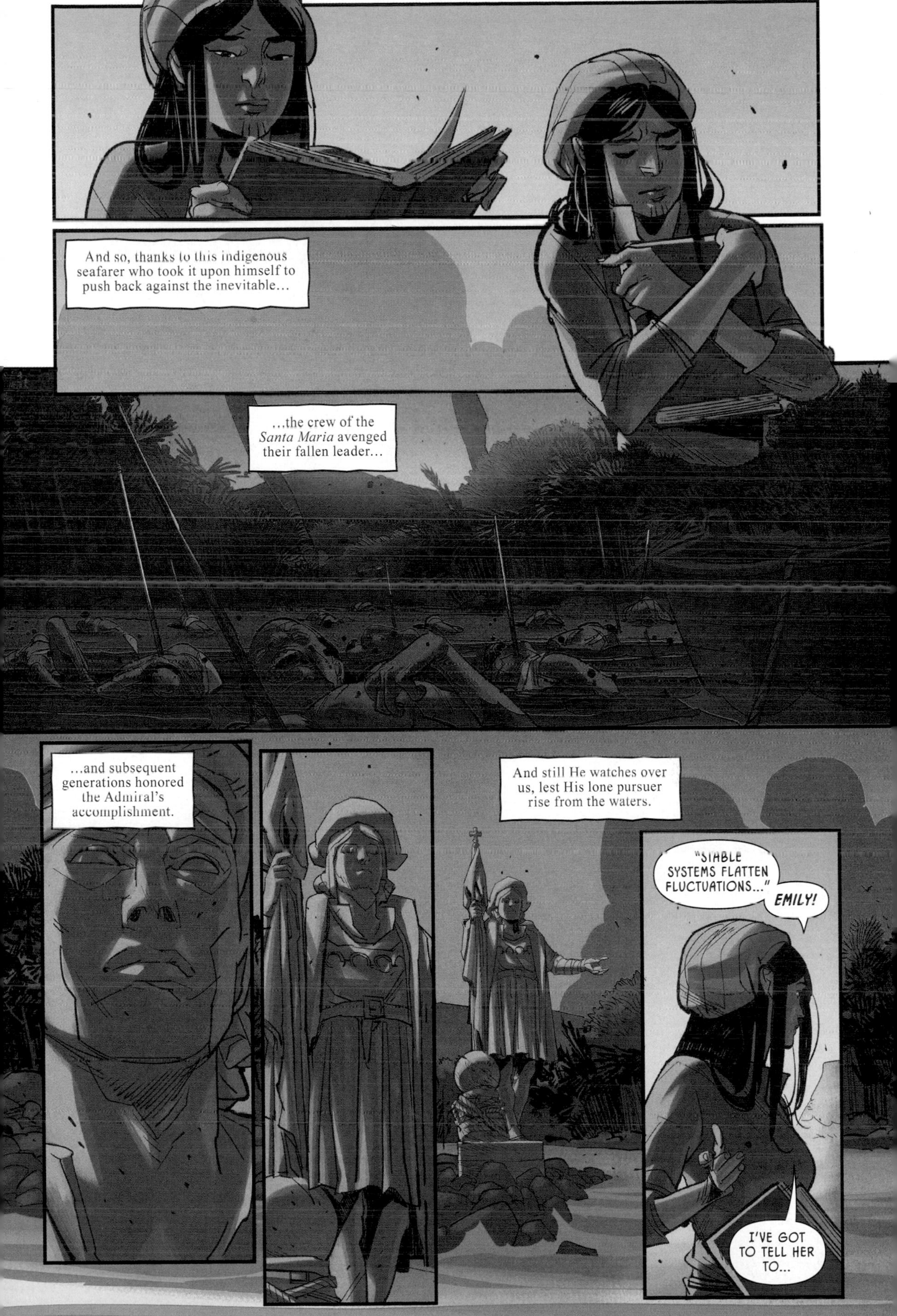
And so, thanks to this indigenous seafarer who took it upon himself to push back against the inevitable…
…the crew of the *Santa Maria* avenged their fallen leader…
…and subsequent generations honored the Admiral's accomplishment.
And still He watches over us, lest His lone pursuer rise from the waters.
"STABLE SYSTEMS FLATTEN FLUCTUATIONS…"
EMILY!
I'VE GOT TO TELL HER TO…

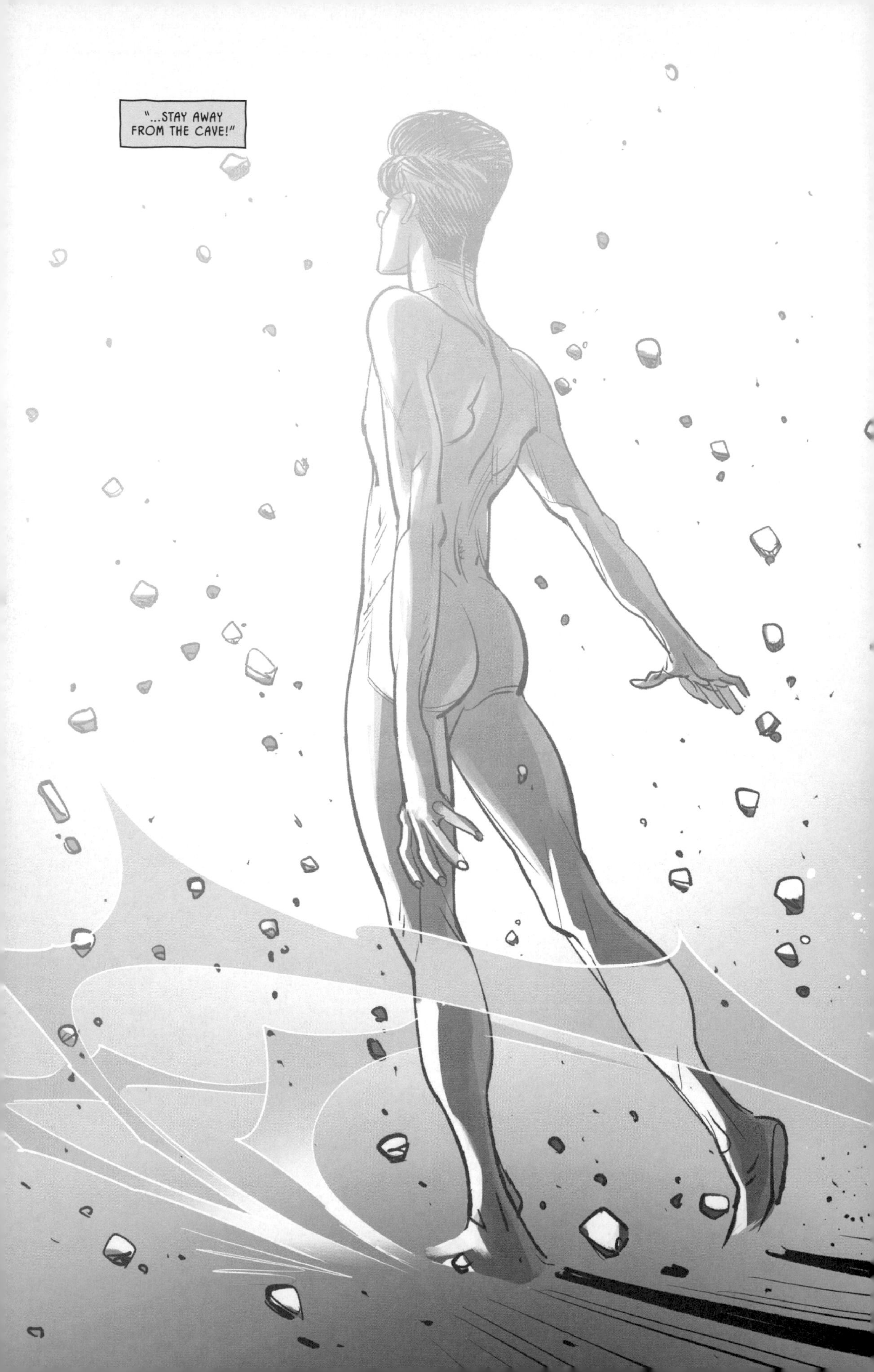
"...STAY AWAY FROM THE CAVE!"

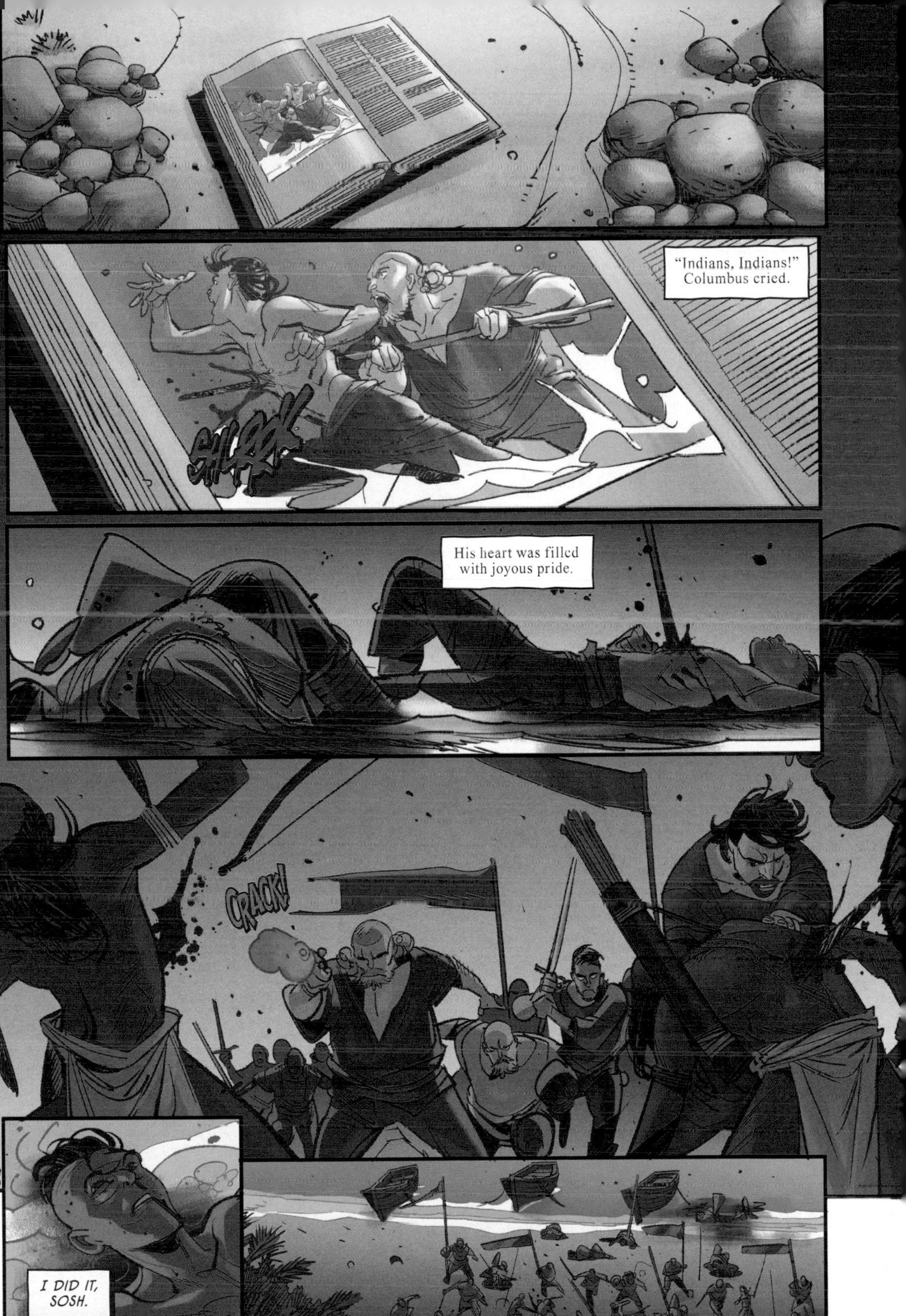
"Indians, Indians!" Columbus cried.
SHLOK
His heart was filled with joyous pride.
CRACK!
I DID IT, SOSH.

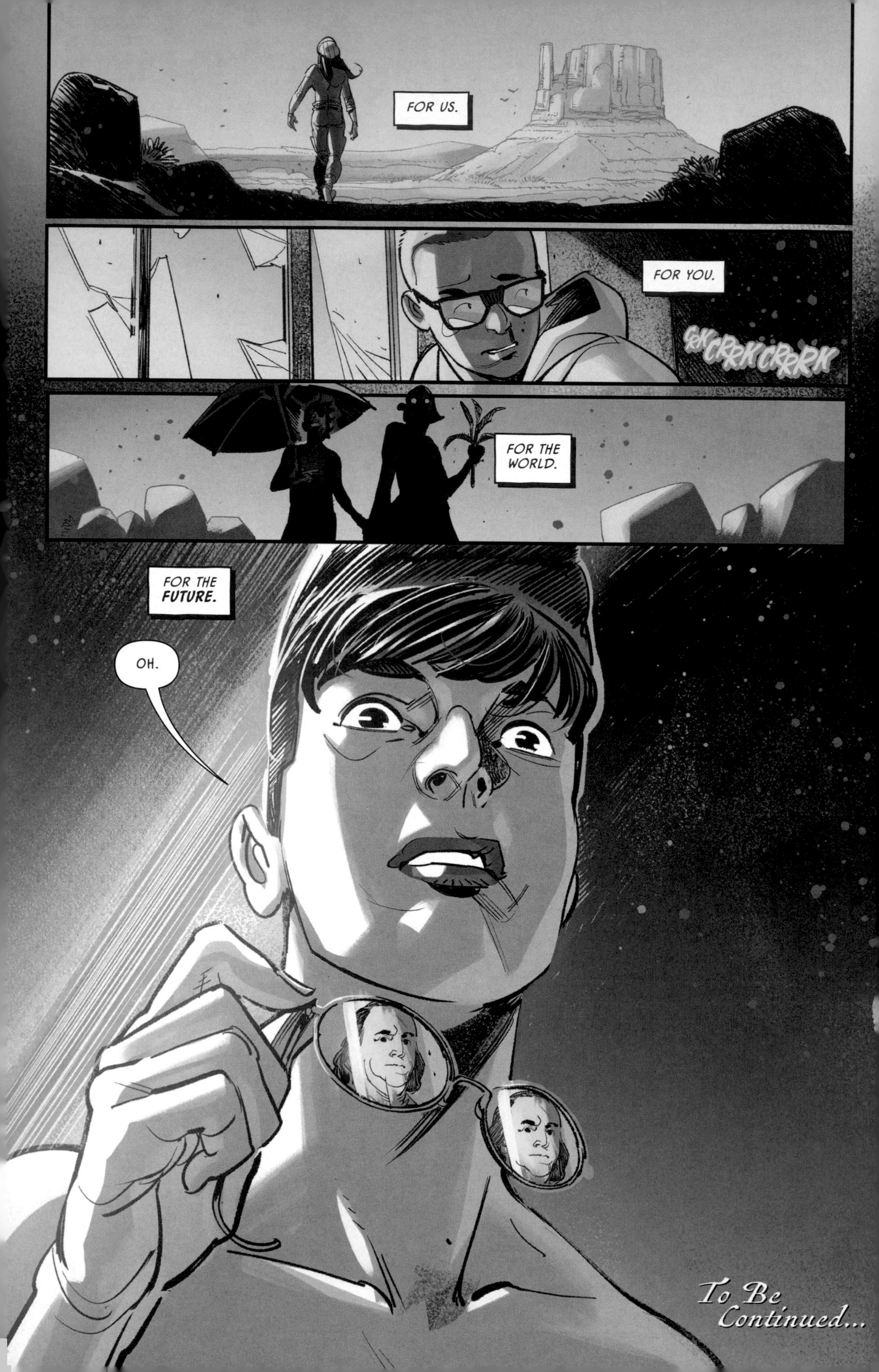
FOR US.
FOR YOU.
CRKCRRRKCRRRK
FOR THE WORLD.
FOR THE FUTURE.
OH.
To Be Continued...

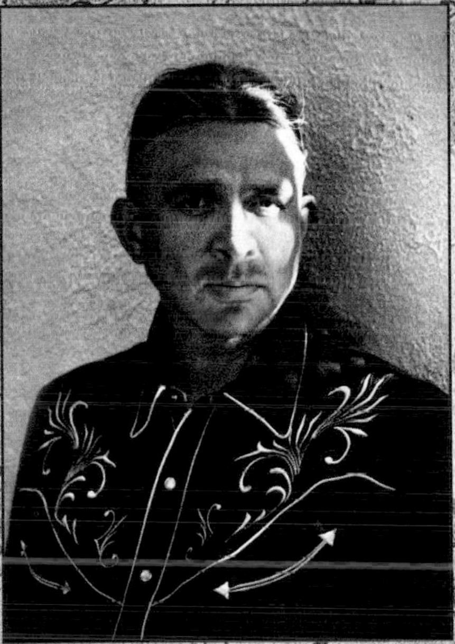

Stephen Graham Jones is the *New York Times* bestselling author of nearly 30 novels and collections (with some novellas and comics in there as well). Most recent are *The Only Good Indians, My Heart Is a Chainsaw, Don't Fear the Reaper,* and his IDW Original series *Earthdivers*. Stephen lives and teaches in Boulder, Colorado. He has a few broken-down old trucks, one PhD, and way too many boots.

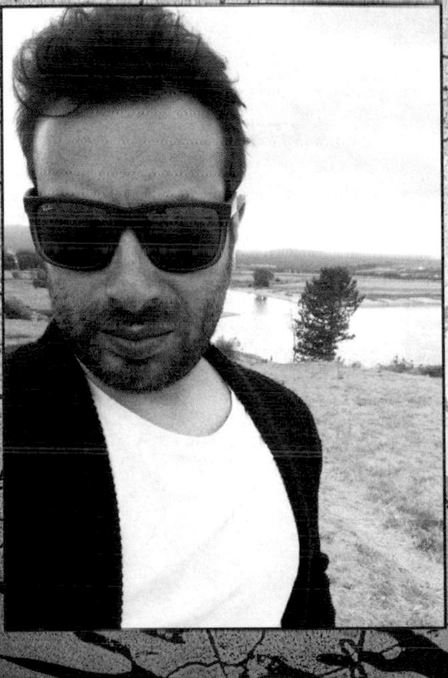

Davide Gianfelice was born in Milan, Italy, in 1977. He's a versatile artist who has worked for Vertigo on the acclaimed first run of *Northlanders* and *Greek Street*. He has also worked for DC Comics, Marvel, Dark Horse, Skybound, Image, and Boom! on several series. In his spare time, he enjoys traveling around the world with his dog.

EARLY CHARACTER DESIGNS
AND CONCEPT ART
BY DAVIDE GIANFELICE

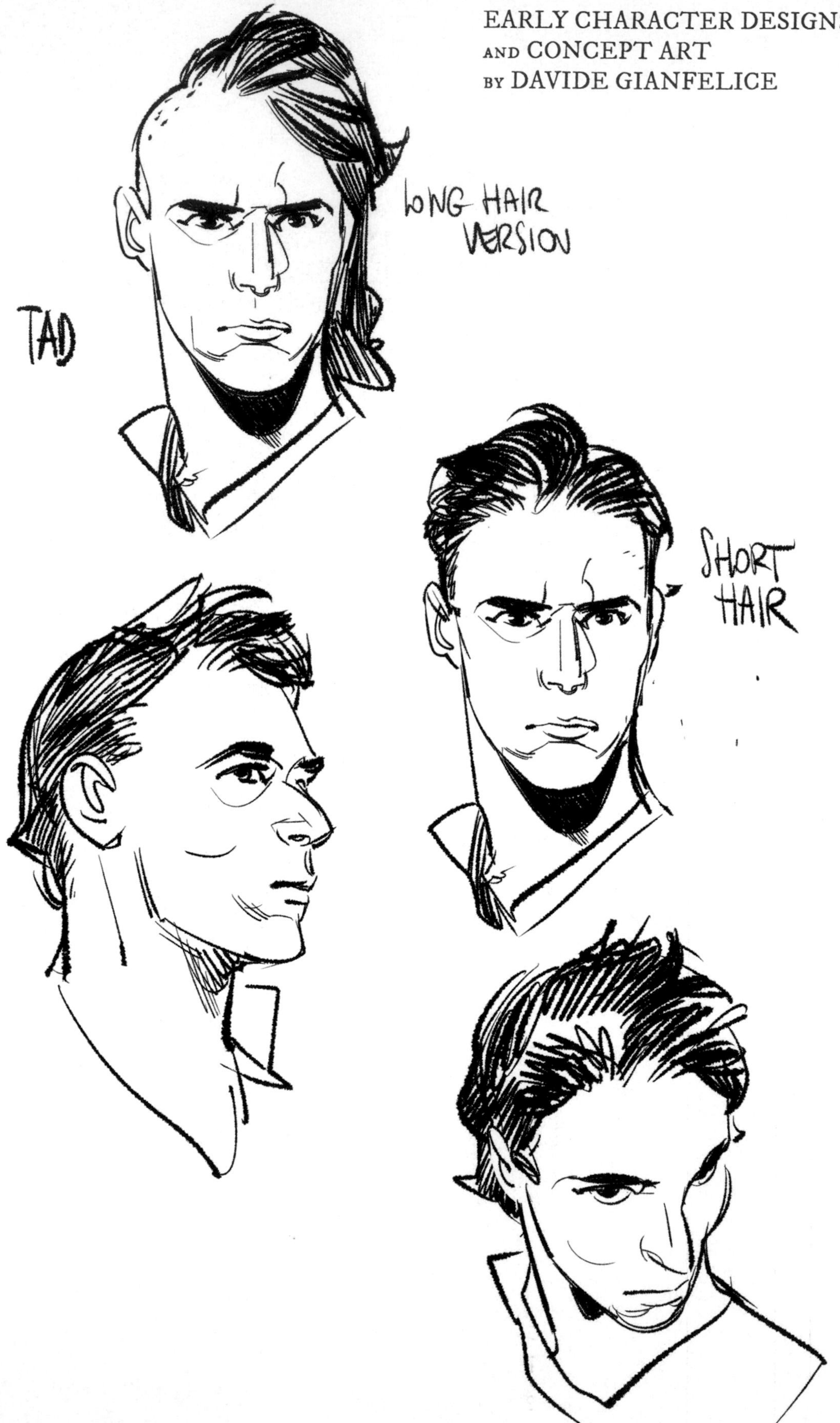
LONG HAIR VERSION
TAD
SHORT HAIR

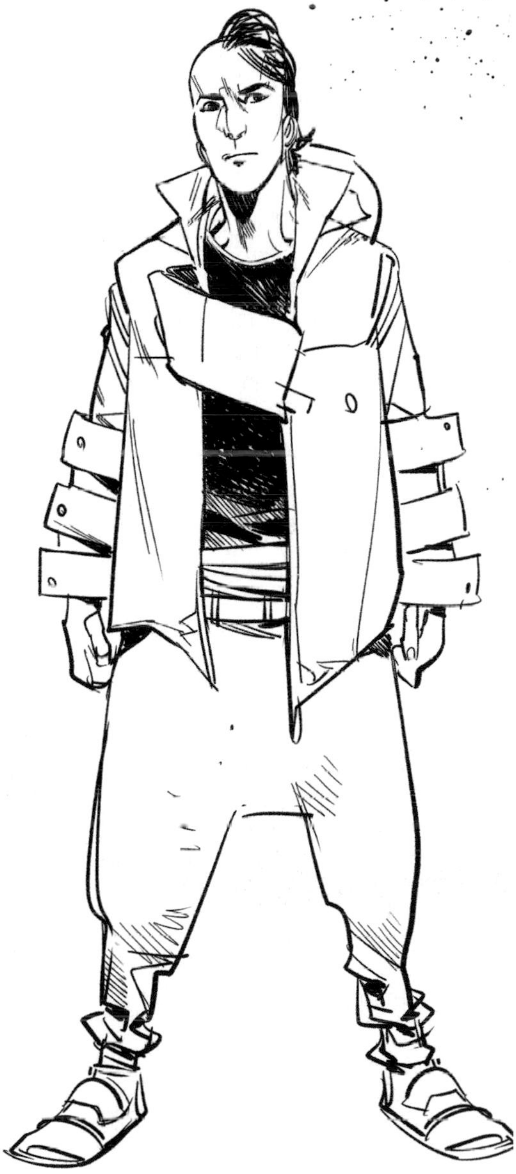
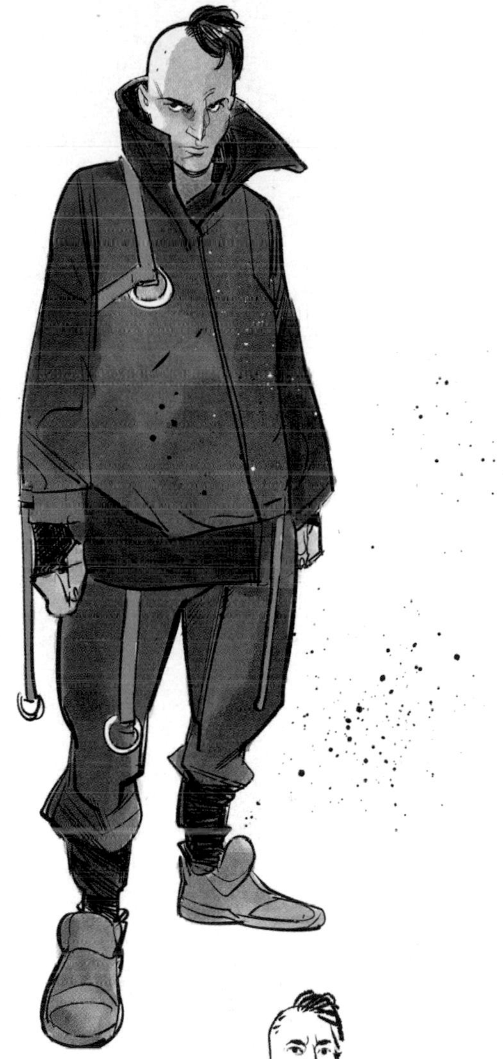
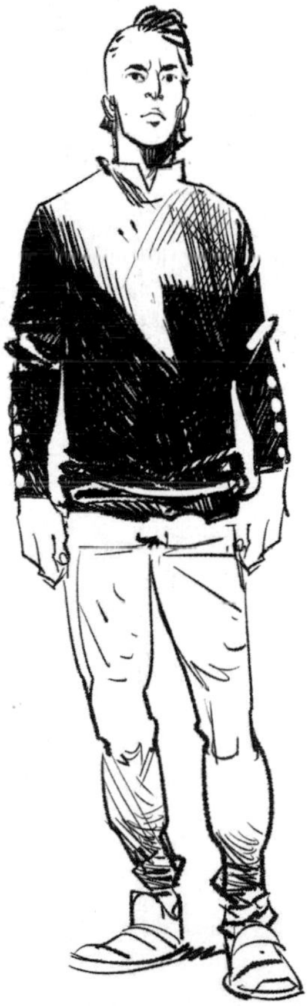

JOSH

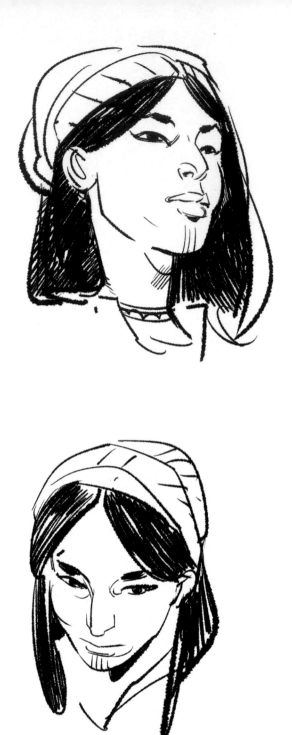

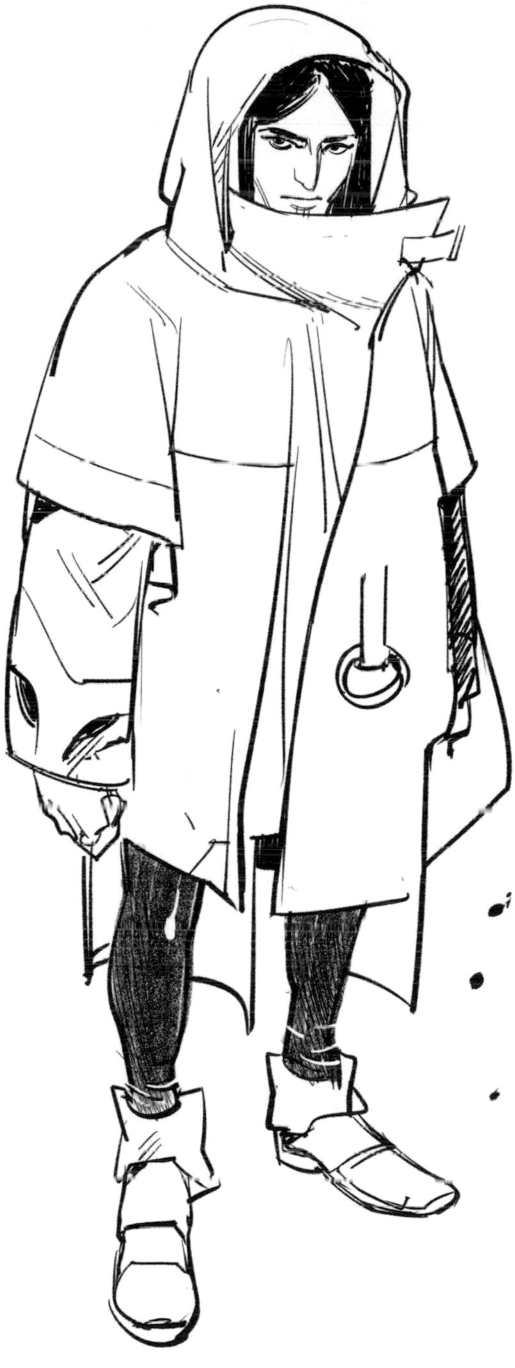

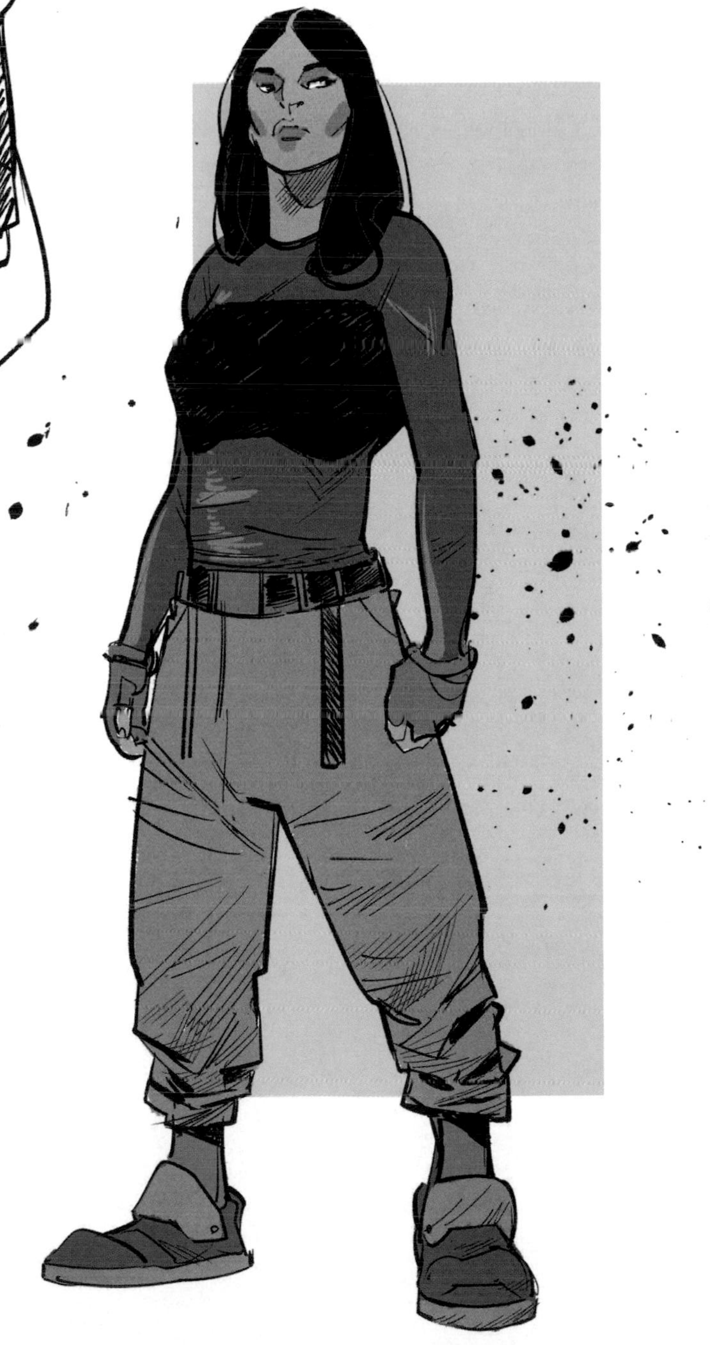

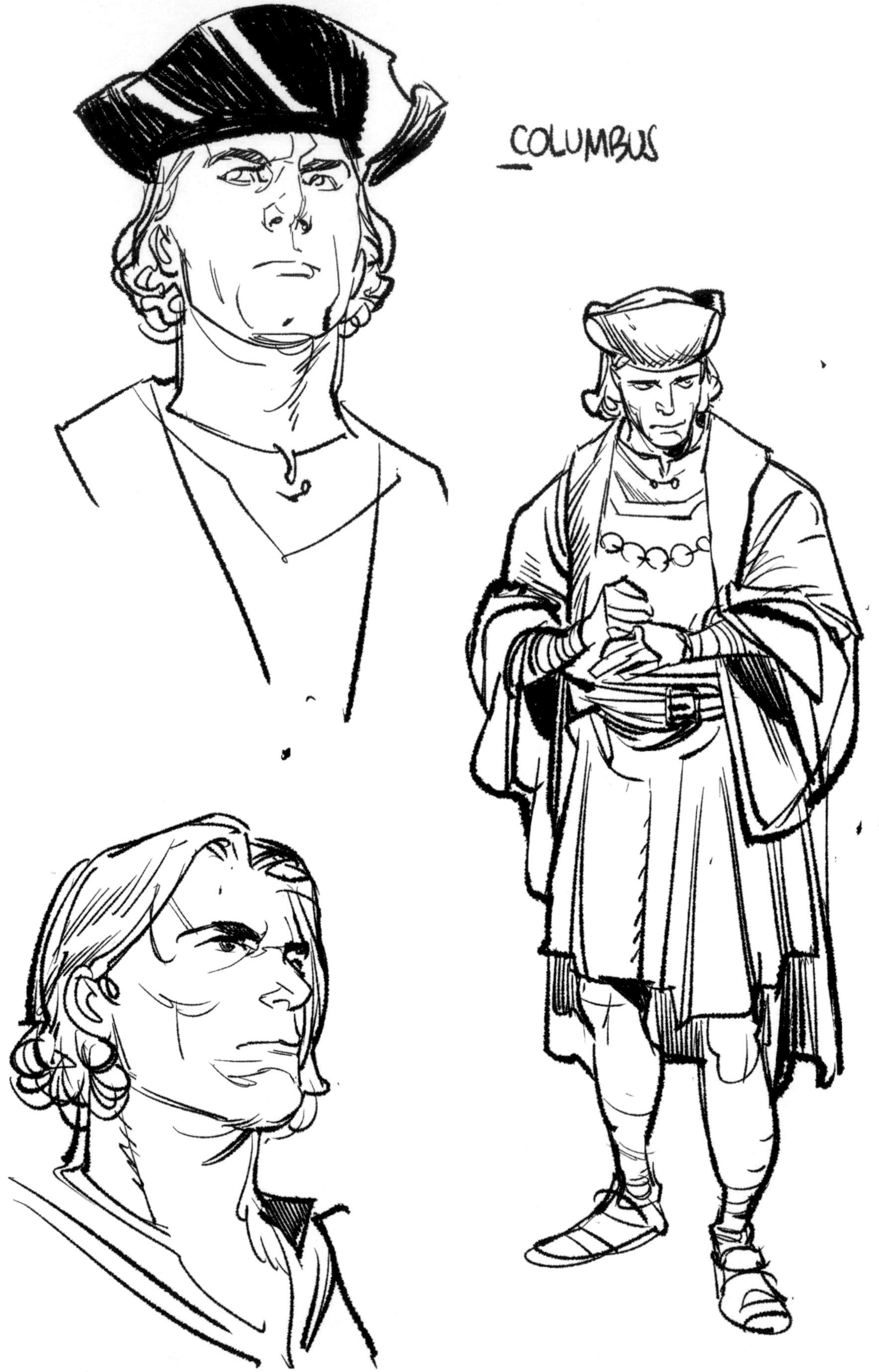
COLUMBUS

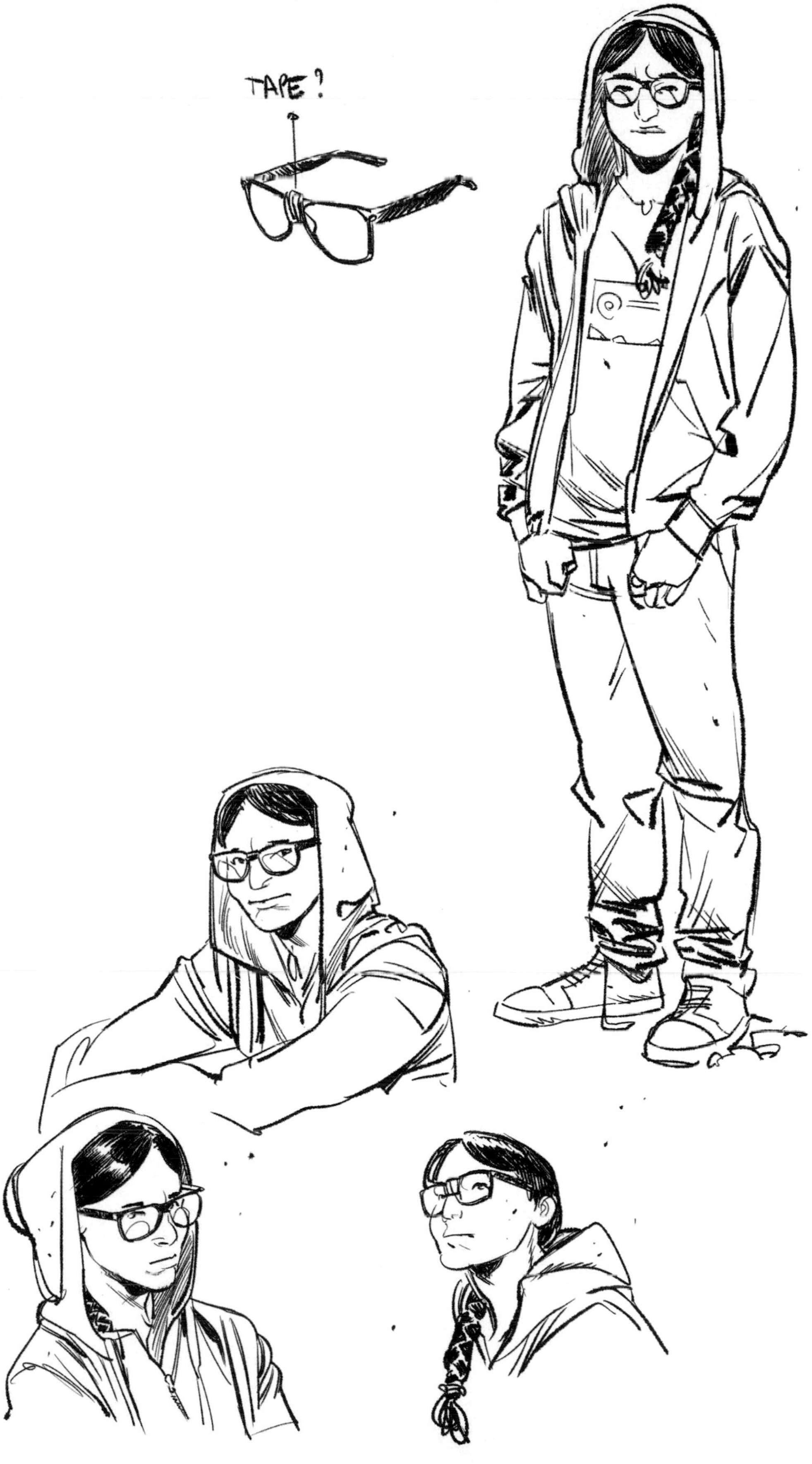
TAPE ?

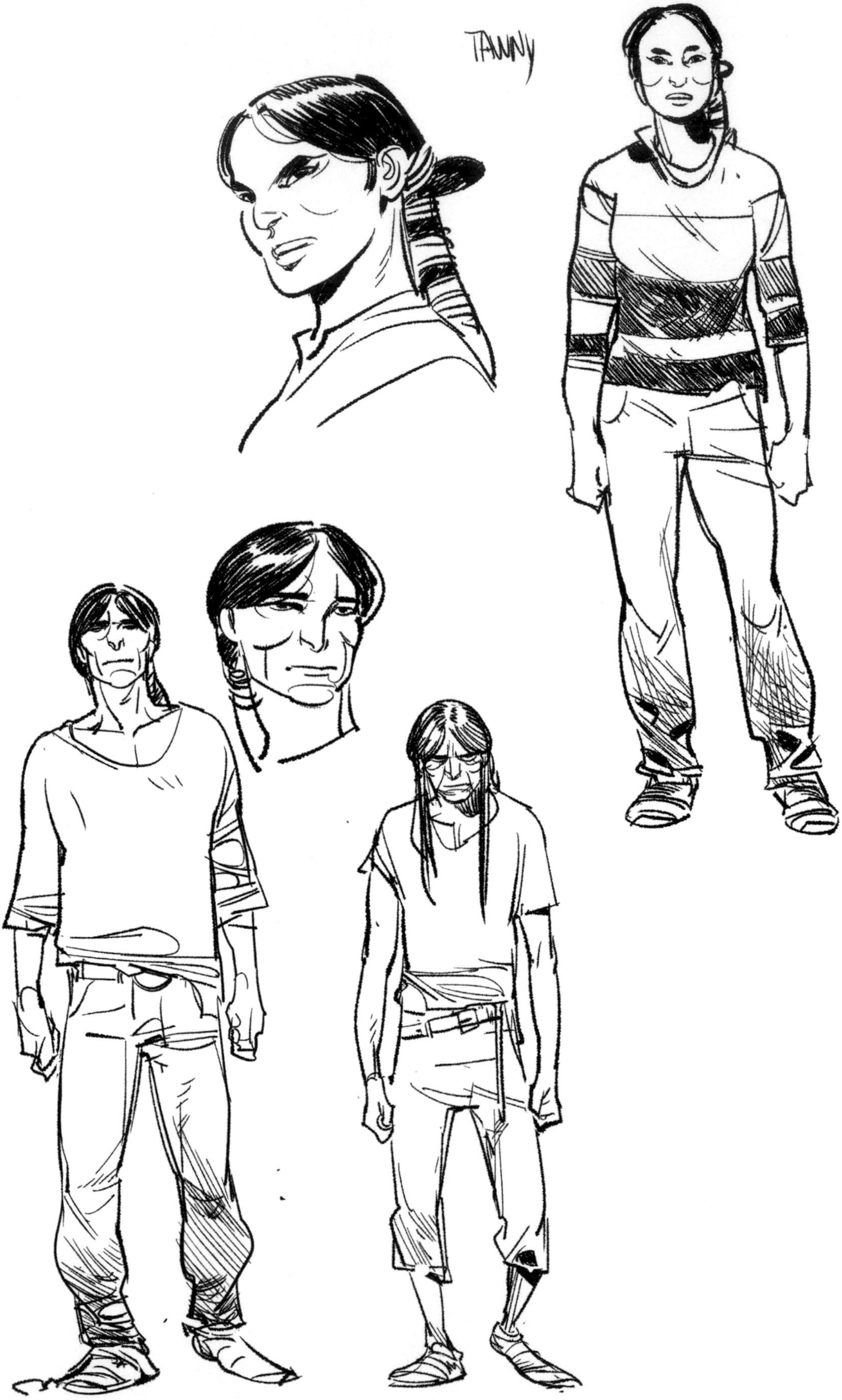
TAMMY

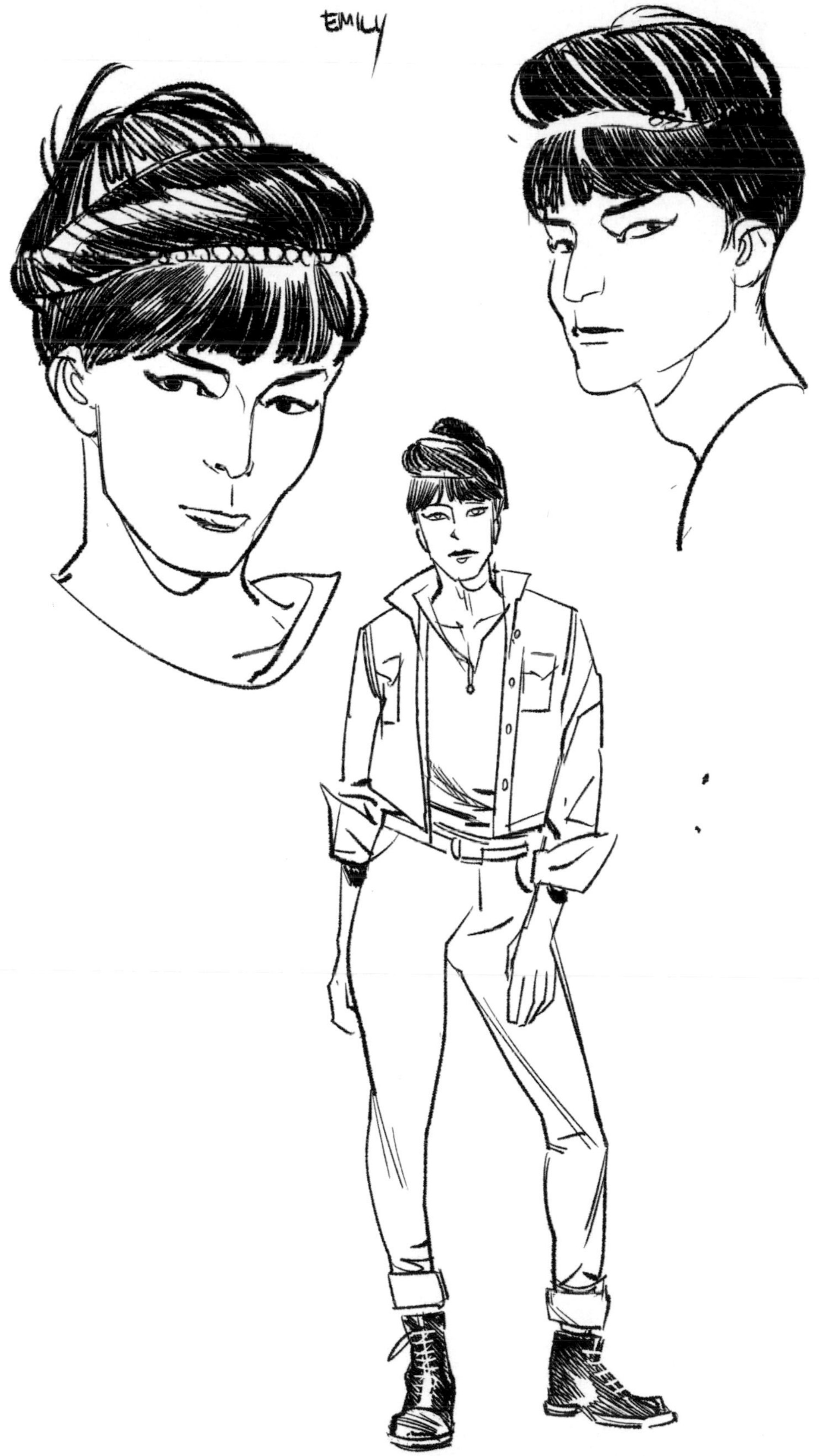
EMILY

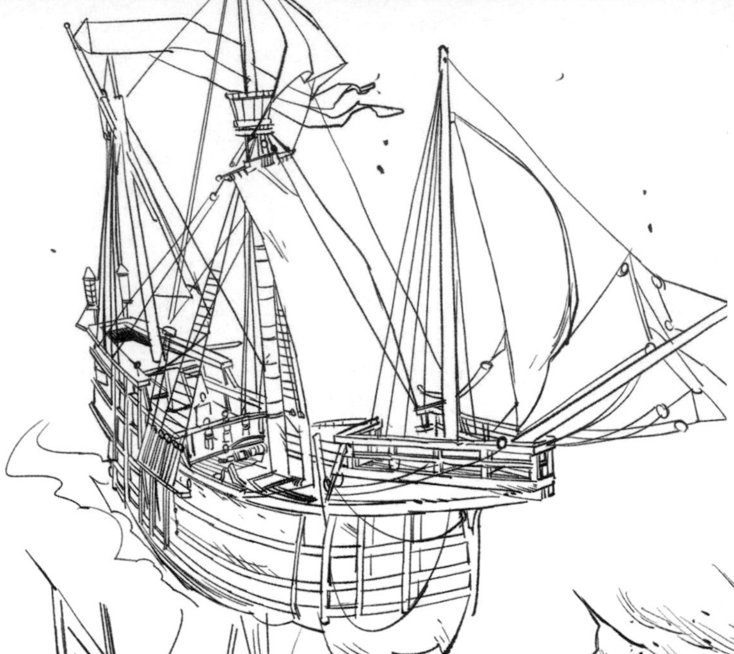

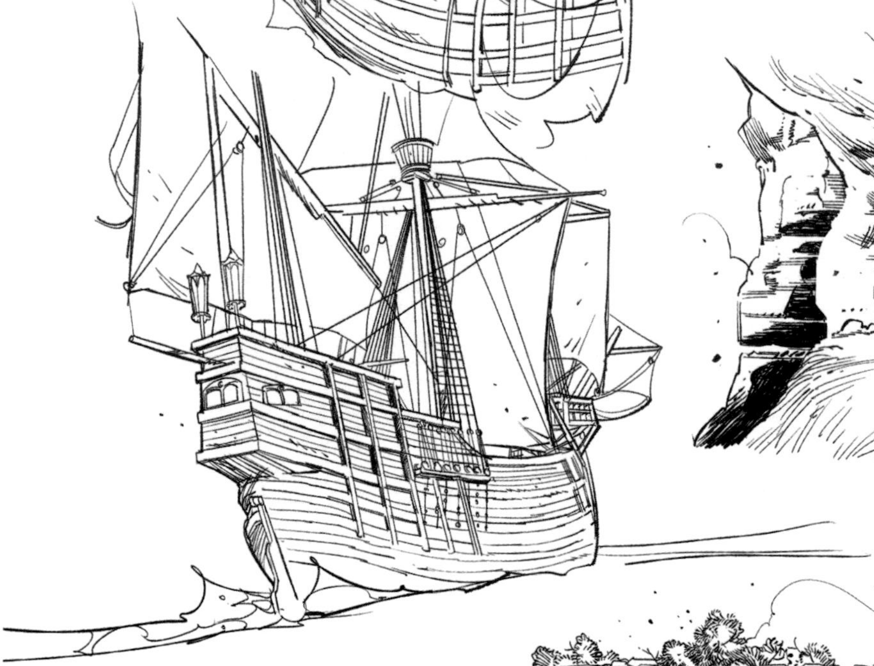

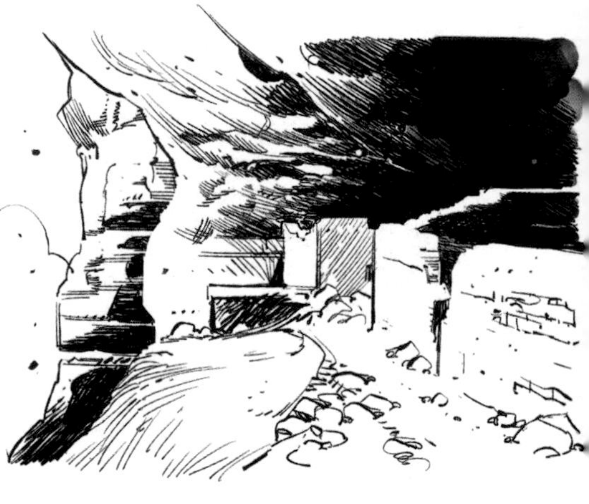

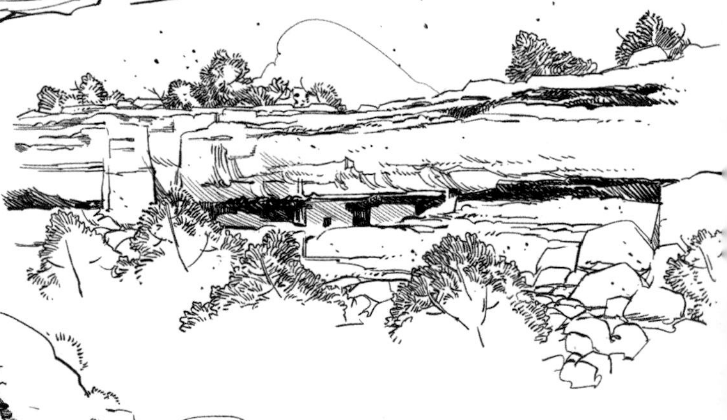

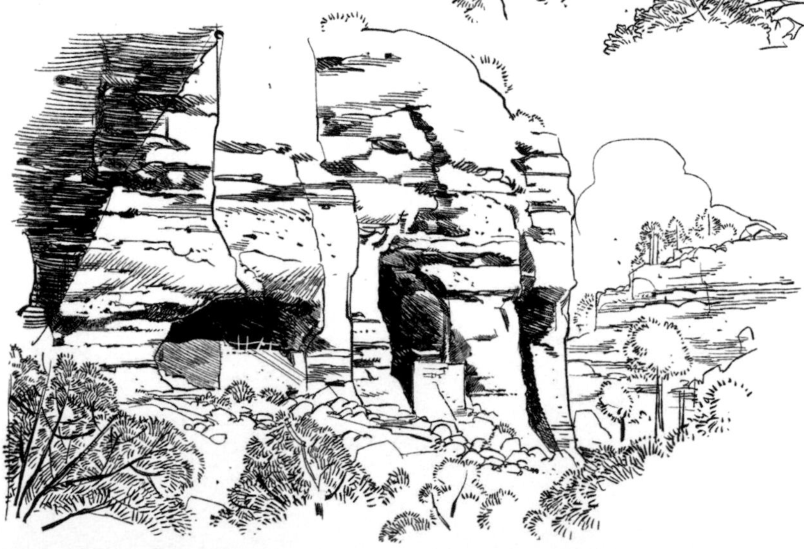

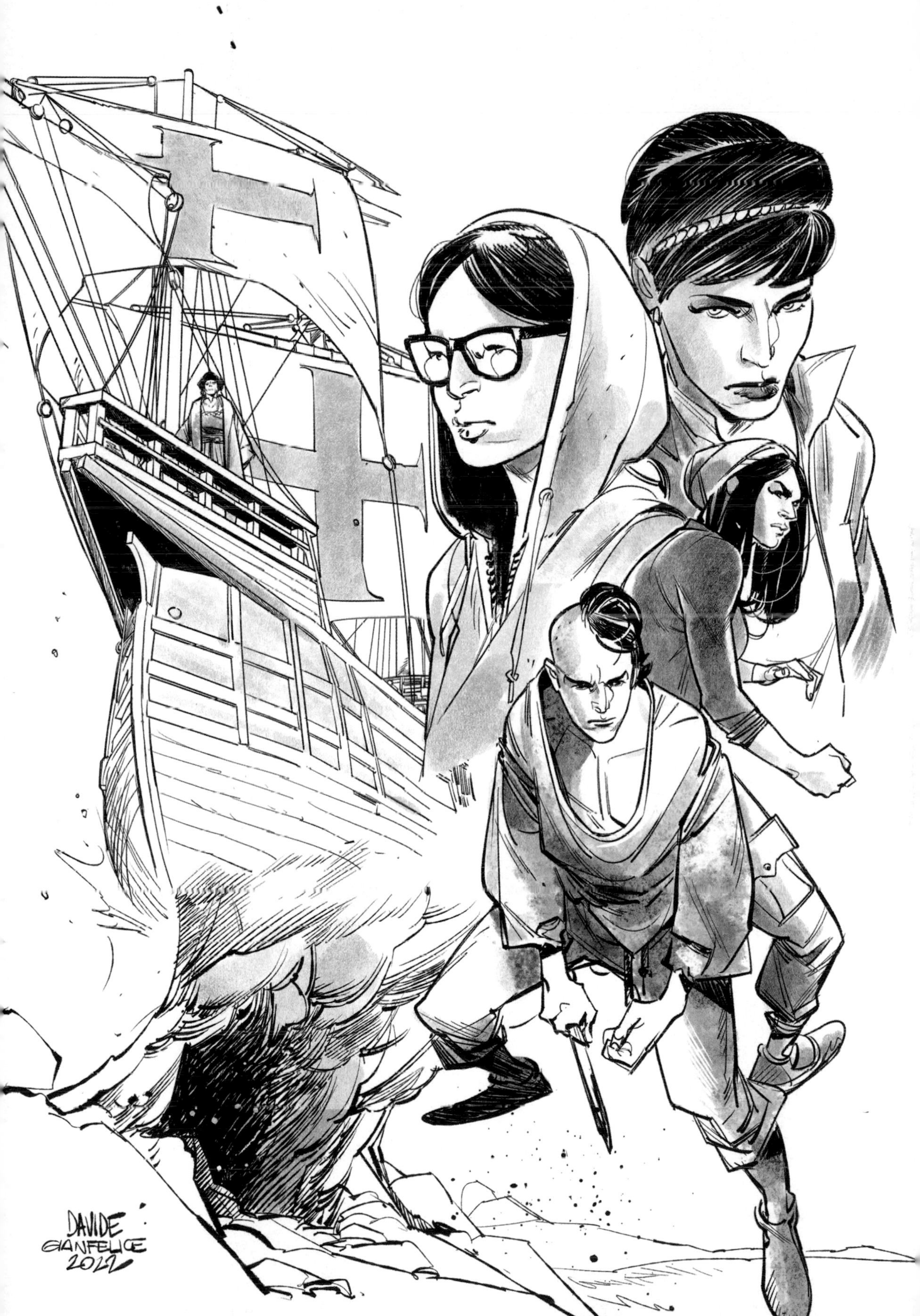
DAVIDE
GIANFELICE
2022

SCRIPT TO ART PROCESS

Earthdivers #6, pages 8-10

Page 8

Panel 1: The back of Emily's bare lower legs. She's standing at the edge of the cave, darkness in front of her. The coyote robe has fallen down around her feet (meaning, she's naked, she's prepped for time-travel).

1 EMILY NOTE CAPTION (maybe the script here can match Emily's handwriting?): And I'm sorry about your husband, Sosha.

#

Panel 2: The dune buggy, parked out in the desert. Nobody to drive it, because they're all gone/dead.

2 EMILY NOTE CAPTION: I'm sorry about a lot of stuff.

#

Panel 3: Close on the broken spectacles Emily's holding.

3 EMILY NOTE CAPTION: And -- I talked to someone from the world we changed.

#

Panel 4: Emily, facing the back of the cave, which is starting to shimmer.

4 EMILY NOTE CAPTION: It wasn't that different, Sosh. [no longer "Sosha"]

#

Panel 5: Emily's face. Her eyes. She's got the broken spectacles ON, now. Reflected in that glass is the shimmering blueness of the time-travel portal, flickering alive.

5 EMILY NOTE CAPTION: But it can be.

And I'm sorry about your husband, Sosha.
I'm sorry about a lot of stuff.
And... I talked to someone from the world we **changed**
It wasn't that different, Sosh.
But it can be.

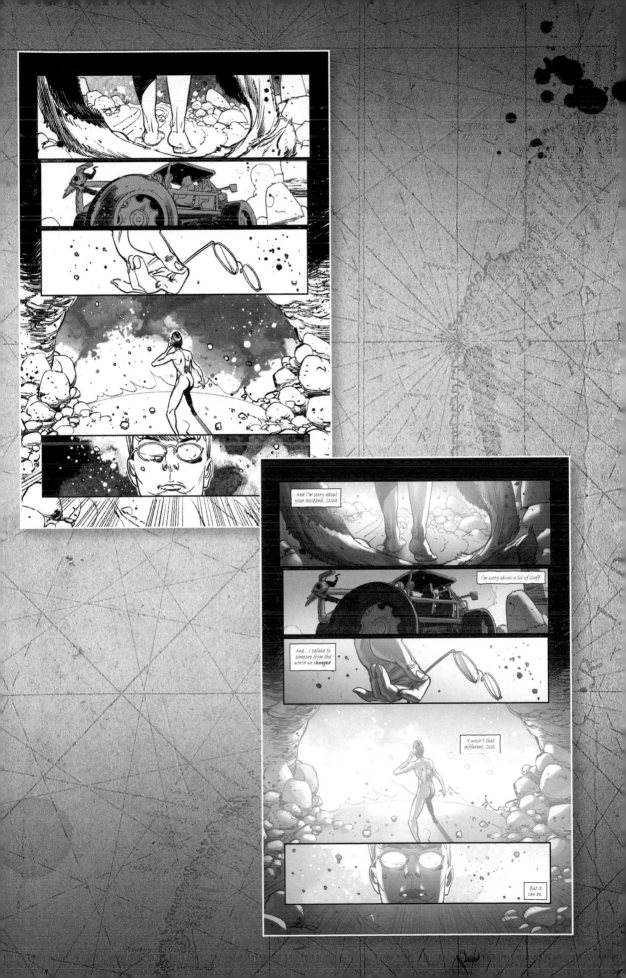

Page 9

Panel 1: The Niña, adrift, sail-less save that one sail.

1 EMILY NOTE CAPTION: It WILL be.

[Maggie, Davide: you can tell of course that I'm using this post-lap (as opposed to pre-lap) transition over and over in this issue. kind of the lowest level of transition, yes. nothing clever, nothing showy. reason: I'm trying to knit all three timelines into each other, make them a smear of narrative instead of dramatic installments meant to prolong. code: "we're not prolonging anymore, but ENDING."]

\#

Panel 2: Tad in bad shape, tied to the mast, arms out, affixed to the yardarm (which is to say: cruciform, yes). He's balancing on that upturned bucket and watching a seagull or boatswain or boobie or SOME bird scavenge grossly on a dead sailor (either one hanging up beside him, or one on-deck, whatever works best).

2 TAD INTERNAL CAPTION: So THIS is where the future comes to die.

\#

Panel 3: Flashback. Tad and Sosh by the wifi mesa in 2112. Maybe a repeat of or an alternate take on that panel from the end of issue 1, where their backs are to us and they're looking out/into the future? But, no Ship's Boy beside them this time. Another option: their hands in one another's.

3 TAD INTERNAL CAPTION: Was it worth it?

\#

Panel 4: Repeat of Tad looking up from that book in the 2112 library, and seeing Sosh.

4 TAD INTERNAL CAPTION: What you cashed in to try build a better tomorrow?

\#

Panel 5: Sosh, IN that library memory, is nodding or pointing up. Tad (in the memory as well) is looking around to what she means

5 TAD: Wha--?

[this is one of my more favorite transitions]

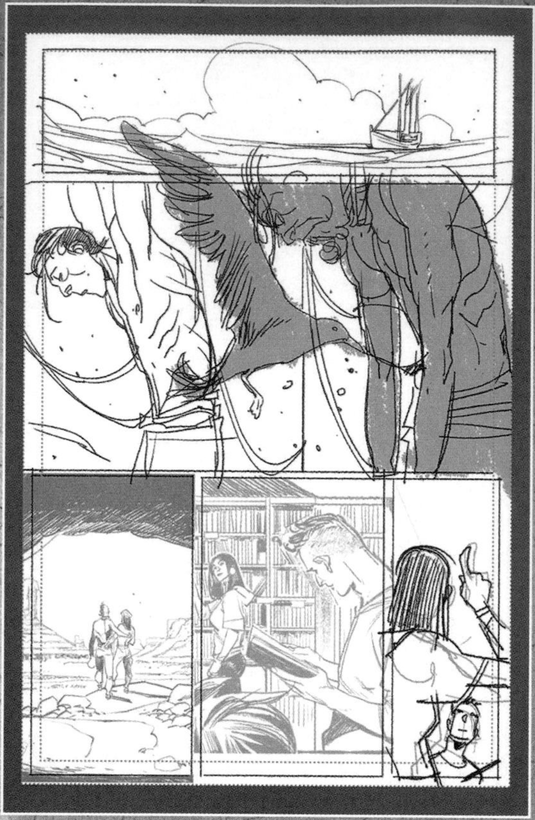

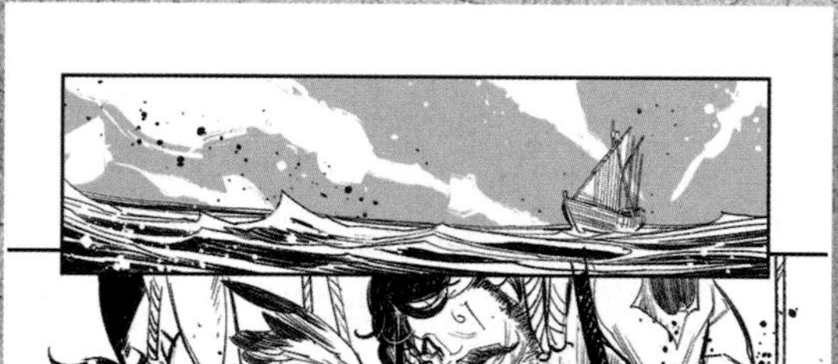

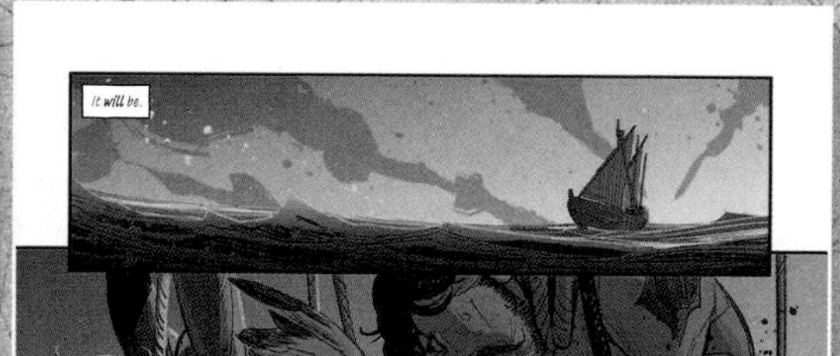
It will be.
SO THIS IS WHERE THE FUTURE COMES TO DIE.
WAS IT WORTH IT?
WHAT YOU CASHED IN TO TRY TO BUILD A BETTER TOMORROW?
WHA--

Page 10

Panel 1: What Sosh was indicating to Tad: the knife he threw at Columbus, buried in the hung-up sailor alongside Tad!

1 TAD INTERNAL CAPTION: You're not even born for 600 years, Sosh, and you're still saving me.

#

Panel 2: Tad's gymnastics to get that knife (feet? hands?). I was going to have him swing back and forth, but that takes too long, and we're already jammed for time. My guess? Feet. So, he can barely reach the knife with his toes, say.

2 TAD [his strain, the grossness]: Ughh.

#

Panel 3: Tad landing hard on deck. On his FEET. A decisive moment. The cut ropes falling around him.

3 TAD INTERNAL CAPTION: And now to sail a ship without any sails.

#

Panel 4: That mainsail, with those three tears in it, making it useless.

4 TAD INTERNAL CAPTION: And kill a man who can't be killed.

#

Panel 5: From the torn sail, Tad's now looking to Pinzon's face he skinned off, still where it landed on the deck on page 7.

5 TAD INTERNAL CAPTION: Trick is, you can't think like someone from the space age.

#

Panel 6: Black panel [really liking those for this issue]. But? put HIS eyes here, if you think that's cool.

6 TAD INTERNAL CAPTION: You've got to think like the savage they say you are, Tad.

YOU'RE NOT EVEN BORN FOR 600 YEARS, SOSH, AND YOU'RE STILL SAVING ME.
UGHHH!
THUD
AND NOW TO SAIL A SHIP WITHOUT ANY SAILS.
AND KILL A MAN WHO CAN'T BE KILLED.
TRICK IS, YOU CAN'T THINK LIKE SOMEONE FROM THE SPACE AGE.
YOU'VE GOT TO THINK LIKE THE SAVAGE THEY SAY YOU ARE, TAD.

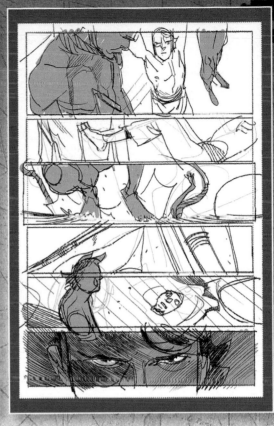

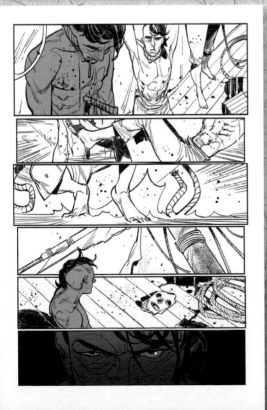

EARTHDIVERS VARIANT COVER PROGRAM
BY *Aaron Campbell*

EARTHDIVERS #1

EARTHDIVERS #2

EARTHDIVERS #3

EARTHDIVERS #4

EARTHDIVERS #5

EARTHDIVERS #6

EARTHDIVERS VARIANT
COVER GALLERY

EARTHDIVERS #1
ART BY *Maria Wolf*
COLORS BY *Mike Spicer*

EARTHDIVERS #2
ART BY *Angel Hernandez*
COLORS BY *DC Alonso*

EARTHDIVERS #3
ART BY *Jim Terry*

EARTHDIVERS #1
ART BY *Christian Ward*

EARTHDIVERS #2
ART BY *Werther Dell'Edera*
COLORS BY *Emilio Lecce*

EARTHDIVERS #3
ART BY *Ramon Villalobos*

EARTHDIVERS VARIANT COVER GALLERY

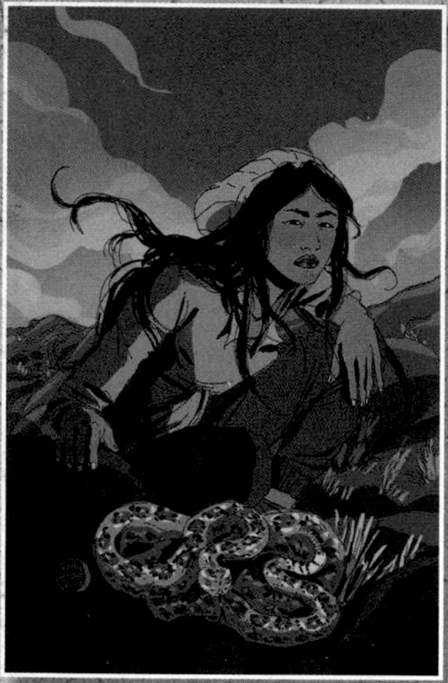

EARTHDIVERS #4

ART BY *Maria Llovet*

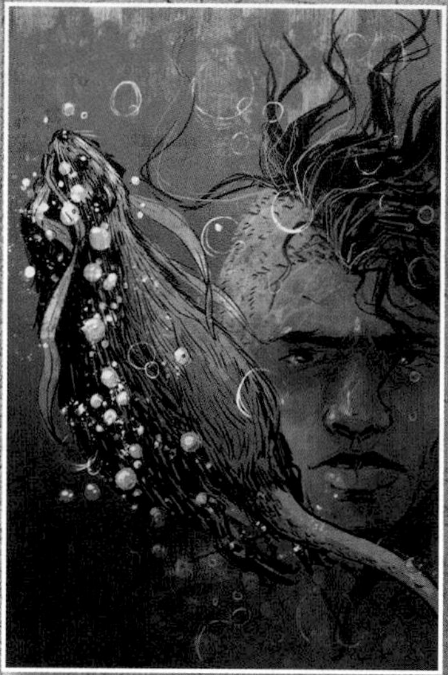

EARTHDIVERS #5

ART BY *Heather Vaughan*

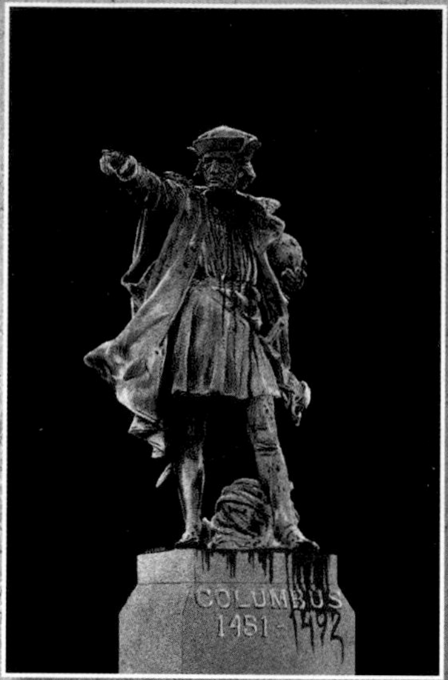
COLUMBUS
1451 1492

EARTHDIVERS #6

ART BY *J.J. Lendl*

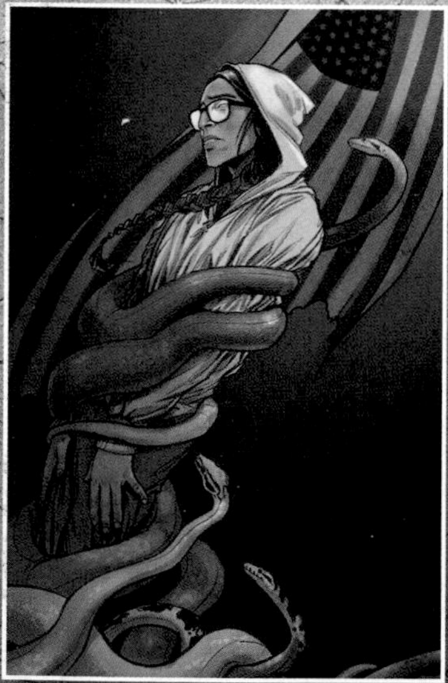

EARTHDIVERS #4

ART BY *Caitlin Yarsky*

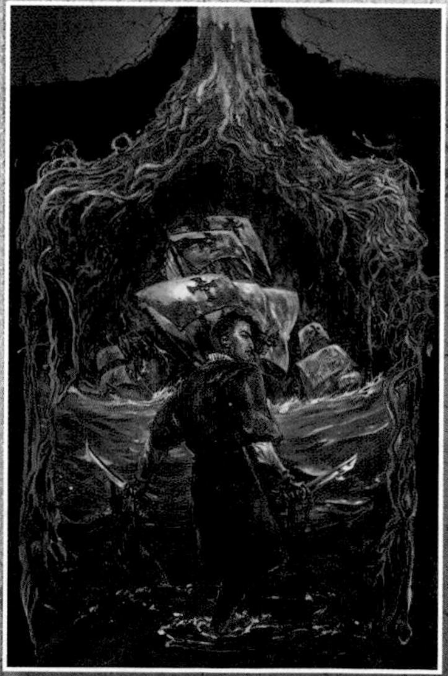

EARTHDIVERS #5

ART BY *Tiffany Turrill*

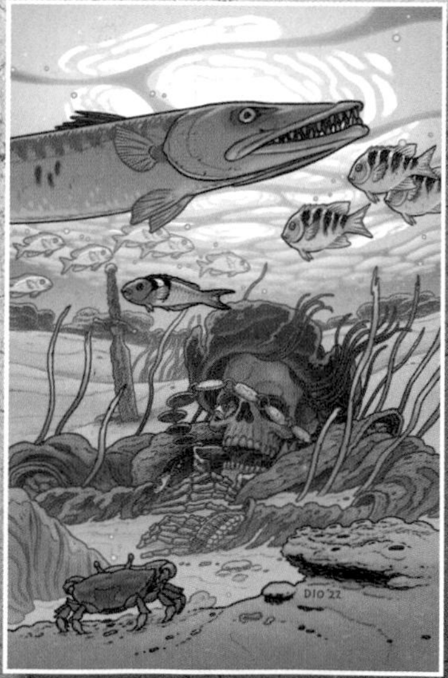

EARTHDIVERS #6

ART BY *Daniel Irizarri*